KT-459-857

BERNIE **ECCLESTONE**

KING OF SPORT

BERNIE **ECCLESTONE**

KING OF SPORT

TERRY LOVELL

JOHN BLAKE

Published by John Blake Publishing Ltd,
3 Bramber Court, 2 Bramber Road,
London W14 9PB, England

www.blake.co.uk

This edition first published in hardback in 2008

ISBN 978 1 84454 623 7

British Library Cataloguing-in-Publication Data:

A catalogue record for this book is available from the British Library.

Design by www.envydesign.co.uk

Printed in the UK by CPI William Clowes Beccles NR34 7TL

1 3 5 7 9 10 8 6 4 2

Papers used by John Blake Publishing are natural, recyclable products made from wood grown in sustainable forests. The manufacturing processes conform to the environmental regulations of the country of origin.

Pictures reproduced by kind permission of Sutton Images, PA Photos, REX Featues and Sporting Images. Every attempt has been made to contact the relevant copyright-holders, but some were unobtainable. We would be grateful if the appropriate people could contact us.

DEDICATION

This book is dedicated to my mum, a lifelong supporter and a lifelong fighter. She spent her life giving so much, seemingly getting little in return; yet she gained eternity. And to my dad, who did his best.

CONTENTS

PREFACE IX

1 'SENNA DEAD? NO, HE'S INJURED HIS HEAD' 3

2 HOW AUNTIE MAY CHANGED YOUNG BERNARD'S LIFE FOR EVER 15

3 THE RISE TO RICHES OF BRABHAM'S NEW BOSS 29

4 THE 'GARAGISTES' TAKE ON THE FIA 'GRANDIS' 53

5 CHAMPIONSHIP TITLE OR POLITICAL POWER? IT'S BERNIE'S DILEMMA 95

6 JEAN-MARIE BALESTRE: LE GRAND FROMAGE 113

7 THE KEY TO RICHES – TELEVISION RIGHTS 135

8 BRABHAM TAKEN FOR A SWISS ROLL 159

9 BERNIE GOES WEST – AND MEETS HIS MATCH 173

10	HOW CANADA LOST ITS NSA – AND BRANDS HATCH THE BRITISH GRAND PRIX	195
11	THE BEGINNING OF BERNIE'S TELEVISION RIGHTS STRANGLEHOLD	219
12	THE RISE OF PRESIDENT MAX, HOW THE FIA LOST MILLIONS, AND THE SHOWDOWN IN BRUSSELS	239
13	THE SINKING OF BERNIE'S $2.5 BILLION FLOTATION PLANS	267
14	BERNIE'S ANNUS HORRIBILIS	287
15	BRUSSELS DELIVERS ITS VERDICT – AND BERNIE MAKES ANOTHER BILLION	305
16	GOODBYE KAREL... HELLO LEO	321
17	THE CASH-FOR-ASH AFFAIR	335
18	MARRIAGE, MONEY AND BLACKMAIL	353
19	WHAT A FUNNY OLD GAME	369
20	THE ITALIAN CONNECTION	381
	NOTES	401
	GLOSSARY	405

PREFACE

A former team boss, who has known Bernie Ecclestone for many years, is talking about a controversial dispute involving a well-known motor sport figure:

'Bernie once said to me, "First you have to get on, then you get rich, and then you get honest. The trouble with – is that he's still trying to get rich."'

'We have not the liberty to choose whether we will serve or not; the only liberty we have is to choose the master we shall serve.' Anon

PART 1

1

'SENNA DEAD? NO, HE'S INJURED HIS HEAD'

The out-of-control Williams-Renault FW16 hit the concrete wall during the eighth lap of the San Marino Grand Prix at an estimated impact speed of 137mph. By the time the car had come to rest 1.8 seconds later, during the third round of the 1994 Formula One World Championship, the life of three times world champion Ayrton Senna was rapidly ebbing away. In less than two minutes, paramedics were at the scene cutting through his chin-strap to remove his helmet, from beneath which blood flowed freely, while at the same time intravenous infusions were intubated into his lifeless body.

Professor Sid Watkins, one of the world's leading neurosurgeons and Formula One's on-track surgeon for 16 years, rotated a plastic tube deep into Senna's trachea to establish an airway. As he lifted Senna's eyelids, the tell-tale signs of his pupils told Watkins that the world's most talented Formula One driver had suffered a massive brain injury, caused, an inquest later recorded, by the impact of the right-front wheel and the right-front suspension arm piercing his helmet at the edge of the visor opening. Watkins, a keen motor-racing fan since his teens, knew Senna could not survive such devastating injury.

The 34-year-old Brazilian was lifted carefully from the cockpit and laid on the ground, some ten metres from the fatal point of collision with the wall on the high-speed curve at the Tamburello corner of the Imola circuit, near Bologna, northern Italy. As they did so, says Watkins, Senna 'sighed, and though I am totally agnostic, I felt his soul departed at that moment.'[1] The driver was taken by helicopter on a 211-mile journey to Maggiore Hospital in the care of Dr Giovanni Gordini, the hospital's intensive care anaesthetist, who had been in charge of the medical centre at the circuit. All the while, Senna, although effectively dead, was kept alive artificially. A brain scan at the hospital, which revealed massive damage to both skull and brain, confirmed there was no hope. At 6 pm that day, Sunday 1 May 1994, Ayrton Senna da Silva was officially pronounced dead.

The news of his death was received in Brazil by a wave of national grief. Tears flowed openly for a man whose supreme racing skills had earned him legendary status. His body was flown to Paris, where a Boeing 747, the presidential aircraft of Brazil's leader, Itmar Franco, had been provided to complete its homeward journey to the capital city of São Paulo and Senna's birthplace. The government announced a three-day period of national mourning and the May Day mass in Rio de Janeiro was dedicated to his name. For 24 hours his body lay in the city's state legislature, where an estimated 8000 people per hour filed past to pay their final respects. On Thursday 5 May eight soldiers carried his coffin from the state legislature to a fire engine, which, escorted by a mounted guard, then bore it to Morumbi Cemetery. With the engine heading a procession of thousands of fans on motorcycles, bikes and foot, the short journey took an hour and 50 minutes.

Racing stars past and present, including Jackie Stewart, Gerhard Berger, Emerson and Christian Fittipaldi, Derek Warwick, Thierry Boutsen, Roberto Moreno, Rubens Barrichello and Alain Prost, once Senna's bitter rival, took turns as pallbearers, carrying the casket to its burial place. After a 21-gun salute, an air force fly-past traced a heart in brightly coloured smoke, topped with an 'S', in the sky. It was an occasion of immense sorrow for the people of Brazil, who genuinely shared the tragedy of Senna's death. But one person, someone who knew Senna well, was conspicuous by his absence.

He was Bernie Ecclestone, an elderly, diminutive man of unprepossessing appearance who, over the years, as his wealth and stature grew with each mega-buck deal and power battle won, had come to be variously described in the media as the Godfather, the dictator or, more apposite, the ringmaster of the Formula One circus. But, for all Ecclestone's power and stature, Senna's intensely private family, headed by wealthy businessman Milton da Silva, who doted upon the second of his three children, made it known that his attendance would be considered 'inconvenient'. The reason for their opposition to Ecclestone's presence was not made public, but it was believed to have been due to the way in which he had handled the news of Senna's death at the circuit. Members of the family, including his younger brother, Leonardo, were at the race and within minutes had been informed of the crash by senior officials.

At the suggestion of race press officer Martin Whitaker, they were taken to Ecclestone's palatial motor home, where, although it had yet to be confirmed, Ecclestone told Leonardo that Senna was dead. Leonardo was said to have become so distressed that Ecclestone, apparently in an attempt to calm him down, then told him that he had been misinformed, that his brother was not dead but had suffered head injuries. The damage was done, however, and it merely kindled a hope that would soon be dashed. An inquiry held a week later by the Fédération Internationale de l'Automobile (FIA), Formula One's governing body, did little to clear up the confusion.

Max Mosley, the president of the FIA and a long-standing political ally and friend of Ecclestone, corroborated Ecclestone's misunderstanding by stating that shortly after the accident he had received two phone calls at home from the Formula One boss – the first to tell him that Senna was dead, and the second to correct the first. Ecclestone, according to Mosley, said during the second call: 'I misheard Whitaker. He actually said he [Senna] has injured his head.'[2] It seems that Ecclestone thought Whitaker had said 'dead' instead of 'head'.

It is difficult to understand how he could have made such a mistake in the light of a statement read out by Whitaker some 45 minutes after the crash. Whitaker confirms that Ecclestone was present when he tersely announced that 'Senna had received serious head injuries and was being transported to Maggiore Hospital'. Ecclestone's subsequent confusion would seem all the more baffling because Whitaker recalls that Ecclestone then sought clarification from him of Senna's condition, when it was still not possible to say that the driver was dead. Whitaker called at Ecclestone's motor home, where he saw members of the Senna family 'totally distressed. I think the family were under the impression that Senna was dead, full stop. In fact, we did not know he was dead until some hours later.'

Sections of the Brazilian media offered their own interpretation of the events in Ecclestone's motor home. It was reported that Ecclestone had changed his mind about Senna's condition because he feared there was a real danger that his many dedicated admirers in the crowds would react in the same way that it was claimed that Leonardo, in particular, had, and that it would threaten the safe continuation of the race.

Eight years later, in recalling the events of that day, Ecclestone believed that his first information on Senna's condition came in a walkie-talkie message from Watkins. 'Sid must have said that to me [that Senna was dead]. He was on the spot. I think that is what happened. And afterwards I went to our little motor home and the Senna family hot-footed behind. I said what Sid had said. Then Martin said to me, "No, he's not dead, it's his head." Then I said to the brother [Leonardo], "Thank God he is not dead, but you know..."' Ecclestone did not, he said, tell Leonardo that his brother was still alive in order to calm him down. 'Obviously he wasn't overjoyed, his brother. Not over the moon with the whole thing. But there wasn't distress in a way that one would tell them something that wasn't true to make [him] undistressed. The one that was more distressed was his PR lady.'

Ecclestone says he didn't attend Senna's funeral – not because of any animosity towards him by the driver's family – but because of the hypocrisy he perceives in people who attend church without believing in God or, at least, as regular churchgoers, a principle he practised even when his parents died. 'I am not very religious so I don't want to go to church. That's the first thing – because I don't think people should use churches to get married and go to funerals. If you want to go to church, you should go to church, [and] not just when it suits you.'

He also believes that to attend a funeral out of respect for the deceased is a double standard. 'If somebody is dead, they are dead. It has nothing to do with respect. Half the time the people who go to the funerals don't respect the people when they are alive. Better to look after them when they are alive and don't worry when they are dead. As I don't believe in this afterlife, if, when I get up there, they start screaming at me because I didn't go to the funeral, then I'll apologise. But I'll have to wait until that happens.' And when the time comes for him to shake off his mortal coil, a corner of a field somewhere without a single mourner will do him nicely. 'Absolutely. If it's cheaper, I'll be happy.'

While he did not attend Senna's funeral, he did accompany his wife, Slavica, to São Paulo in his Learjet so that she could do so. 'She was very close to Ayrton, and she believes in all this business. She walked along [in the funeral procession] with the mayor.' Ecclestone killed time in a hotel watching the ceremony on television. But his absence was described by a former associate as 'one of the saddest things. He was very close to Senna and helped him in so many ways.' His low-key presence in the city was in marked contrast to another public event nine years earlier, when, amidst a pageant of back-slapping hype in the state legislature in Rio de Janeiro, the title of 'Honorary Citizen and Provider' was conferred upon him to mark the signing of an agreement for the city to stage the Brazilian Grand Prix for the next three years.

If Ecclestone was guilty of gross insensitivity, his comments three years later did nothing to lessen the offence. Attempting to rationalise the national expression of public grief that followed Senna's death, he said that if he had been killed like Roland Ratzenberger, a 32-year-old Austrian driver who had died the previous day during a practice run in a Simtek-Ford, and which hadn't been seen on television, 'it wouldn't have created such a terrific impact. It was the fact that for an hour people were saying: "What's happened to him [Senna]? Is he going to make it?" It was a public death. Like crucifying Jesus Christ on television.'[3]

The Italian authorities immediately announced an investigation into the cause of Senna's accident and impounded the wreckage of the car, seizing even the driver's helmet. A lengthy investigation was predicted by those who knew the ways of Italian bureaucracy, and with good reason: following the death of Jochen Rindt, who died during a practice session at Monza in 1970, his car remained locked away in the possession of the police for twenty years. Fear of legal action caused considerable concern among the Formula One teams. A successful prosecution would, they believed, leave them vulnerable to similar action. Four months after Senna's death, Max Mosley issued a warning at the Hungarian Grand Prix that the teams might be unwilling to race in Italy if the investigating authorities decided to prosecute. Closer to home, Flavio Briatore, boss of the Benetton team, announced that he would not race in his home country if members of the Williams team were to be held culpable. Ferrari bosses were also uneasy at the implications of criminal proceedings.

In December 1996, almost two years and eight months after the accident, prosecuting magistrate Maurizio Passarini finally announced that Frank Williams, founder and managing director of the Williams team, and five others – chief designer Adrian Newey, technical director Patrick Head and three senior track officials, Roland Bruynseraede, Federico Bendinelli and Giorgio Poggi – would face charges of manslaughter. It was alleged that the steering column of Senna's car had been cut, expanded to satisfy Senna's demand for more space in the cockpit, but had been poorly re-welded, which had caused the column to break. It was also alleged that the way the track had been maintained could have contributed to the accident.

But Frank Williams and his colleagues had no reason to fear prosecution. Such is the political power of Formula One and its importance to Italy in particular that the loss of the Italian Grand Prix – and there can be little doubt that Mosley, supported by Ecclestone, would have successfully recommended its cancellation if matters had come to such a head – would have provoked an uprising in the streets. Under Italian law, the authorities were obliged to investigate the fatal crash but in the end it could never have been more than an administrative exercise.

Eleven months after the announcement of the charges, which Williams and his co-defendants vigorously denied, Passarini, who had been zealous in his investigation, made a remarkable U-turn. Williams, he stated, should 'be let off for not having committed the offence' and Newey and Head should each receive a one-year suspended sentence because their 'error' had been 'microscopic'. Although the cause of the accident remained unresolved, the following month, on 16 December 1997, Judge Antonio Costanzo announced his verdict in a makeshift courtroom in Imola into which the world's media were crammed. Only the defendants themselves, already notified of the contents of Costanzo's report, were absent as he formally cleared all six men of the charges.

Earlier in Passarini's investigation, Ecclestone himself had been in danger of ending up in court, along with three of his employees. Ecclestone's company, FOCA TV, had been providing in-car television coverage for the Italian television company, RAI, through cameras mounted on 20 of the 26 cars. Videotape footage requested by Passarini showed that a camera had been running in Senna's car until nine-tenths of a second before the fatal collision. According to on-site director Alan Woollard, because the picture showed a clear track and was of limited interest, the picture was switched to another car. The next frame, shot from the car of Gerhard Berger's Ferrari 412T1, showed another empty section of the track. That, said producer Eddie Baker, had been a mistake. The picture should have been switched to the Tyrrell 002 car of Ukyo Katayama, which promised more dramatic coverage.

Passarini complained of a delay of more than two years in receiving the videotape, caused, said FOCA TV, by a misunderstanding. He rejected this explanation, choosing to interpret the delay, and the shot of an empty section of the track, as evidence that the tape had been tampered with to remove the final frames, which might have indicated that Senna was having problems with the steering. Woollard, Baker and camera-car technician Andrew James were in danger of being charged with perjury, said Passarini, while Ecclestone was being investigated 'for other possible charges, such as aiding and abetting'.[4] Ecclestone vehemently denied the accusations, and, on hearing Passarini express his doubts about the videotape to reporters outside the court, threatened legal action. Neither side pressed charges, criminal or civil. But, again, there was very little chance indeed of Ecclestone finding himself in court. He was far too powerful to be hauled before a court to face the humiliation of public prosecution.

At the time of Mosley's warning at the Hungarian Grand Prix, Ecclestone had been talking to one of his high-powered political friends, media magnate and Prime Minister of Italy Silvio Berlusconi, who was seeking reassurances about the future of Formula One in his country. Soon to be voted out of office and the subject of several judicial investigations into bribery, corruption and tax evasion, Berlusconi was, in May 2001, ranked as the world's fourteenth richest man with a personal fortune estimated at $12.8 billion. The politician, who would be re-elected Prime Minister, had a personal interest in retaining the good will of the Formula One teams in general and Ecclestone's in particular.

His company, MediaSet, owned three of Italy's independent television stations, Rete 4, Italia 1 and Canale 5, which had the exclusive contract to screen the Italian Grand Prix at Monza. Berlusconi was in a position to give Ecclestone every assurance of a satisfactory outcome.

Senna's death was seen as a serious body blow to Formula One. Because he was considered by many to be the greatest driver of all time – three years later a motor sports magazine's all-time-greats poll would put him well ahead of Juan Fangio and Jim Clark – it was feared that fans worldwide who lionised his driving genius would turn away from the sport and cause television viewing figures to plummet. The marketeer supreme, Ecclestone knew that Formula One required a big name to keep the all-important television fans glued to their seats. But who could replace Senna's moody, charismatic genius? There was Benetton's rapidly rising young German star, 25-year-old Michael Schumacher, who that year would win the first of his five World Championships, and Damon Hill, 34, the Williams team's number-one driver, who came second in the championship title race, but Ecclestone did not consider either of them at that time to be box-office.

Instead, he came up with a name that immediately lit up the dollar sign in his head: Nigel Mansell, who, after winning the 1992 World Championship, had had a serious dispute with team boss Frank Williams which led to him quitting Formula One for the IndyCar Racing Championship in America. At the heart of the issue was the contractual terms being offered to 38-year-old Mansell for the following season. He was also concerned about the forthcoming arrival of three-times world champion Alain Prost and his displacement as the team's number-one driver. Although Ecclestone publicly denied that he played any part in advising Williams – 'I'm not in the business of telling people how to spend their money'[5] – the team's boss did, in fact, seek Ecclestone's counsel on how best to handle the situation. Mansell was known as a tough negotiator who made all his own deals, and was judged to be at the peak of his driving form. The advice was short and sweet: 'Stick to your terms but give him a deadline. If he doesn't meet it, that's it.' Williams followed Ecclestone's advice. As the deadline drew near, Mansell backed down. He was ready to accept Williams's terms. But by now, with Ecclestone's support, Williams was ready to play hardball. He offered Mansell less than half of what he had initially put on the table – a cut from £7 million to £3 million. Mansell packed his bags and headed for Indianapolis, while Prost went on to win his fourth championship title in 1993. Mansell enjoyed his own success in winning the IndyCar championship title.

How much Ecclestone knew in advance of Williams's negotiating tactic to reduce his offer by more than half is uncertain, but he certainly approved:

'Nigel was offered a price and given a deadline by Williams. When the deadline passed, the price dropped. When you play poker, you ask yourself: "How strong is my hand? How much am I prepared to risk." If you have a mediocre hand, you'd better be careful.'[6] However, Ecclestone now found himself in something of a quandary: if he wanted to see Mansell take on Schumacher to the delight of fans and sponsors alike, he had to find a way to lure him back to Formula One, and resolve the problem of his contract with the Newman-Haas team.

Within two weeks of Senna's death, he was on the phone to Mansell in Indianapolis. At the same time, co-owner Carl Haas was sounded out to see whether he would sell Mansell's contract for the rest of the season. The two men had done business before. In November 1986 Ecclestone had bought Formula One Race Car Engineering Ltd, a company set up less than two years earlier to run Team Haas, but which was forced to withdraw from Formula One when Ford decided, after one season, to terminate a three-year contract supplying the team with its Cosworth-developed V6 turbo engine. Ecclestone bought the company, sold some of its assets and re-leased the factory and offices.

Haas was not pleased to hear from Ecclestone. He was preparing for the Indy 500 and wanted Mansell totally focused. At the same time, Mansell was privately dissatisfied with the way the Newman-Haas car had been performing that season and the call from Ecclestone inviting him back into Formula One was not altogether unwelcome. Ecclestone discussed his approach to Mansell with Frank Williams, who was not keen to have him back. Prost had retired at the end of the 1993 season and Williams favoured keeping Hill as his number-one driver, with the promising young Scot David Coulthard as number two.

But Ecclestone continued to see Hill as a poor substitute for Mansell, beloved by Italy's devoted *tifosi* as 'Il Leone' because of his gutsy and spirited determination, when it came to television billing. Mansell, he believed, was the obvious choice. So did Renault, who supplied the 3.5-litre turbo engine for the brilliant FW14B car in which Mansell had won the World Championship. With Ecclestone making the approach, and with Renault picking up a generous part of the bill, Williams agreed to a four-race deal worth £2 million. With the same subtlety, he also persuaded Haas to release Mansell, said to have agreed 'a nominal sum', according to Williams, for the French Grand Prix, the first of the four races, while still under contract. It proved a disappointing return. Schumacher and Hill came first and second, while Mansell was forced to retire in the forty-fifth lap with gearbox trouble.

His second race at the European Grand Prix at Jerez also failed to live up to expectations, when he spun off the Spanish circuit during the forty-seventh lap. But if Mansell's return had thus far done little to animate spectators and television audiences, his performances in the last two races of the season – in Japan and Australia – were considered to be the most exciting of the entire 1994 season. Hill won at Suzuka, with Schumacher and Mansell coming second and fourth. Mansell took the honours at Adelaide after Hill and Schumacher collided during the thirty-fifth lap. Ecclestone wanted to see Mansell's contract with the team extended, but this time Williams refused to oblige. He wanted to stay with Hill and Coulthard.

Undaunted, Ecclestone began trumpeting Mansell's importance to Formula One on the sports pages, while, at the same time, persuading McLaren boss Ron Dennis to sign him for the season. McLaren agreed a $5-million contract, mostly funded by Marlboro, who were swayed by the publicity Mansell would attract. But it was to be the beginning of Mansell's swansong. He missed the first two races of the 1995 season – in Brazil and Argentina – while the McLaren MP4-10 was modified to accommodate his size, before finishing tenth in the San Marino Grand Prix and retiring after 18 laps in the Spanish Grand Prix, complaining of the car's poor handling. It brought to an end both his brief time with McLaren and his illustrious 15-year Formula One career. To Ecclestone, though, Mansell's departure had by now become a matter of little interest. There was now emerging increasingly bitter rivalry between Schumacher and Hill for the World Championship title. It led to some breathless, if not, at times, irresponsible, clashes between the two drivers, as illustrated that season by their collision in the forty-fifth lap of the British Grand Prix, which would provoke a flow of bitter accusations from both parties. But it created what Ecclestone wanted – dramatic television to keep the spectators, the sponsors, and, above all, the television audiences happy.

No one could doubt that he had worked relentlessly for 20 years to exploit Formula One's enormous television potential. Whatever was good for television, which provided unequalled global brand exposure for eight months of the year, was good for Formula One. It was Ecclestone's Brabham team that introduced the drama – and the dangers – of pit-stop refuelling at the Austrian Grand Prix at the Österreichring in 1982, which saw 13 crew members with a pressure hose blasting fuel into the tank at the half-distance point. It enabled cars to run faster with lighter fuel loads and softer tyres. Time lost in the pit would be quickly regained on the track. In addition to the drama of the human element, it also had the bonus of pleasing the sponsors: it gave their logos valuable television exposure. The following season other teams joined in. But then a near-disaster occurred at the Brazilian Grand Prix when fuel spilt from Keke Rosberg's Williams car exploded into flames. It led the Fédération Internationale du Sport Automobile (FISA), the body which at that time controlled motor sport on behalf of the FIA, to ban pit-stop refuelling on safety grounds.

But Ecclestone believed that the risk was well worth the television 'entertainment' value. By 1993, with his authority within and without the FIA considerably increased in the intervening years, he was keen to see its reintroduction, all the more so to subdue mounting criticism that Formula One was becoming boringly predictable. The teams seemed to be split – at a meeting at Hockenheim they voted in favour, only to change their minds, apart from Ferrari, two months later at the Portuguese Grand Prix – but, predictably, Ecclestone, the prime mover, won the day, with Mosley's support, to reintroduce pit-stop refuelling the following season.

It was not long, though, before another serious incident occurred. During the fourteenth lap of the German Grand Prix, Dutchman Jos Verstappen pulled into the Benetton pit. Petrol spilt on to the hot engine caused the car to be instantly engulfed in a fireball. Verstappen was uninjured but seven crew members were taken to hospital with burns of varying severity. The incident created all the television 'entertainment' that Ecclestone could have wished for, as well as a fresh call by some teams for pit-stop refuelling to be once again banned. Ecclestone remained phlegmatically defiant: 'The accident does not worry me any more than an accident happening on the circuit. We have not had any problems with it this season. It does not make me rethink refuelling. You saw how quickly the fire was put out.'[7]

An inquiry into the incident established that a filter had been removed from its refuelling apparatus to increase the fuel flow rate by about 12.5 per cent to give a one-second saving in an eight-second pit stop. But Benetton team boss Flavio Briatore claimed it had nothing to do with the cause of the fire. An investigation by fire-safety experts commissioned by Benetton put the blame on a faulty part of the fuelling valve. Over the next two years there were a further two pit-stop fires – involving Jordan and Ligier and both caused by fuel spillage – until technical improvements to the refuelling apparatus, which pumped fuel into the tank at a rate of 3.3 gallons per second, eliminated the hazard. By now, though, pit-stop refuelling had become a regular feature welcomed by spectators, television broadcasters and sponsors. Ecclestone's entrepreneurial instinct had been vindicated.

He keenly supported another controversial innovation, proposed by Max Mosley and the then president of the FISA, for the benefit of television coverage – the introduction of a safety car, or pace car, as it is known in IndyCar racing, from which the idea was imported. Its purpose is to slow cars down in the event of an accident while marshals clear the track. Ostensibly introduced as a safety move, its purpose, in fact, was to avoid lengthy restarts, which, it was feared, encouraged bored viewers to switch to another channel. It was a move that was greeted with some opposition by Mosley's more conservative colleagues, who objected to the principle of copying an

American tactic. Others, including Ayrton Senna, objected for safety reasons.

Senna was among the drivers who were concerned that the slowness of the safety car could cause tyre pressure to drop dramatically and crucially affect the car's handling. Before the start of a race, electric-blanket tyre-warmers – illegal in IndyCar racing but for reasons of cost rather than safety – are fitted to wheels to pre-heat tyres to a certain temperature. The temperature is increased and maintained by friction during the race, but if it drops, so does the air pressure, which can make a Formula One car virtually undrivable. Senna was said to have been sufficiently concerned that he expressed his misgivings at the drivers' briefing before his fateful race, but in vain.

Until recent years Ecclestone was little known outside of the sports pages, and even then he kept a low profile, happy to quietly work away on his next multi-million-dollar deal. When he did make the news it was invariably because of off-the-cuff remarks that reinforced an image he seemed to go out of his way to cultivate, of a hard-headed character with a heart of stone to match. He didn't appear to care what people thought of what he said or did.

Likening Senna's 'public death' to the crucifixion of Jesus Christ had its insensitive equal in his comment on the death in a flying accident of 32-year-old Brazilian Carlos Pace, who was second driver for the Brabham team owned by that time by Ecclestone. Of his reaction to Pace's death, he said: 'If I felt anything, it was that he shouldn't have been fooling around with light aircraft. He took enough risks as it was, without having to fly as well.'[8] And seven months before Senna's fatal accident, he had been quoted by motor-racing correspondents Bob McKenzie and Oliver Holt, in the *Daily Express* and *The Times* respectively, as saying that drivers' deaths were a form of 'natural culling'. In the furore that followed, he denied making the comment, insisting that he did not even know what the word meant. McKenzie and Holt declined to comment on Ecclestone's denial.

Yet Ecclestone would not deny what would seem to many to be a cold, calculated attitude: Sure, they risk their lives, he would concede, and that's why they are paid tens of millions of dollars a year. Besides, as a result of improved safety regulations, in the fourteen years prior to Senna's death there had been only two fatal accidents. Formula One isn't a technical confrontation run for the benefit of the teams, he would argue, or staged for spectators prepared to take out a small mortgage to pay for a Grand Prix ticket. It is, based on figures supplied by Ecclestone's company, Formula One Management Ltd, the world's biggest televised sport, viewed in 2000 by a staggering total of 53 billion people in 195 countries, compared with 33.4 billion television viewers in 196 countries who watched the 1998 World Cup in France, and 19.6 billion viewers in 200 countries who watched the Atlanta Olympics in 1996, the last time cumulative figures were used by the International Olympic Committee to calculate viewing figures. But basing the total number of viewers on cumulative figures can be deceptive.

For example, the cumulative total claimed by Formula One Management includes not only the audience for the races themselves, including qualifying, free-practice and warm-up sessions, but sports programmes, which might briefly feature footage of a Formula One race, and news broadcasts. It is the news broadcast figures that hugely inflate the figures claimed by Formula One Management. According to a leading UK sports marketing survey company, it is a format that is 'somewhat misleading. If, say, the news is broadcast that Michael Schumacher has won a particular Grand Prix, then the viewing audience figure of that news programme is included.' Once news broadcasts are stripped out, the figures tell a somewhat different story. Monitoring of programmes dedicated to Formula One has put the global audience figure at a much reduced 4.5 billion. In a sport of smoke and mirrors, news broadcasts were first included in 1993 to dramatically boost dedicated viewing figures that had actually fallen by 12.5 per cent. Said Ecclestone: 'I don't know anything about this, because the only figures we put out are the ones given to us by broadcasters. We take whatever figures broadcasters give us.'

The promotion of Formula One, by fair means or foul, has consumed almost 30 years of Bernie Ecclestone's life. He has survived supremely in a world of lies and deception, unscrupulous power politics and corruption, perpetrated by men with egos the size of Africa, to become one of the richest men in the world. This indeed is Bernie's game.

2

HOW AUNTIE MAY CHANGED YOUNG BERNARD'S LIFE FOR EVER

St Peter South Elmham is a rural backwater of little more than a row of houses and a church, the kind of place you pass through on your way to somewhere else. It is located three miles from Bungay, an ancient and charmingly soporific town in east Suffolk, and more easily located on an Ordnance Survey map. It was here, on Tuesday 28 October 1930, that the name of Bernard Charles Ecclestone was added to the hamlet's roll of noble sons. The event took place at Hawk House, a converted public house of that name situated next door to the early twelfth-century St Peter's Church, and the home of his grandmother, Rose Westley, who may well have played the role of midwife.

Ecclestone's mother, Bertha, then 23, and his father, Sidney, 27, had married at St Peter's Church three years earlier and set up home in the nearby village of Wissett, which comprised a few tied cottages, a church, a shop, a garage and a school. But with her husband, a fisherman, often away at sea from September to early December with a herring fleet that fished out of the coastal town of Lowestoft some 20 miles away, Bertha spent much of her time during the winter months at her mother's home. In this rustic environment, where fishing and farming were the main industries, young Ecclestone spent his early childhood, either in St Peter South Elmham or in Wissett. His temperament, it seems, reflected the isolation of his surroundings; he was known as a child who preferred his own company. He also began to display signs of a trait that in later years would become a dominant feature of his business style.

His cousin, Pauline, the daughter of his mother's brother, Godfrey, vividly remembers the tantrums of a fractious child who 'was always wanting his own way'. There was, she recalls, the occasion of a village celebration to mark the Silver Jubilee of King George IV and Queen Mary on 6 May 1935, when the two five-year-olds were invited to pose for a photograph. She was dressed as a nurse in a blue and white crêpe-paper uniform and he as a wounded soldier with bandages round his head and leg. 'He was supposed to hold my hand for a photograph, but he just wouldn't do it,' says Pauline. 'There was such a fuss.'

Around this time, his mother's younger sister, May, had qualified as a nurse and shortly began work at Westhill Hospital in Dartford, Kent, on the outskirts of London, where she met and married a local fishmonger, Arthur Birmingham. They moved to a house in King Edward's Avenue, Dartford, a decision of little significance other than for the bearing it would have on young Bernard's life. For May, the youngest of four children, was the favourite of her mother, Rose Westley, who, deeply upset by the thought of her daughter living so far away, decided to sell her home in St Peter South Elmham – the father of her children was no longer on the scene – and move to Dartford. It was a decision that in turn upset Bertha, the second youngest, who was no less grieved by the thought of her mother moving so far away.

It led, in 1935, to the Ecclestones moving from Wissett to a three-bedroomed semi-detached house in Priory Close, Dartford, around the corner from Bertha's mother's new home, where they remained for at least the next three years. This was the family's address when Bertha gave birth to a daughter, Marian, in September 1938, but soon after they moved again, to Marcet Road in Dartford, settling down in a working-class environment of 40,000 people whose economy was based on engineering, pharmaceutical and papermill industries. Dartford, considered a buffer zone between London and the more genteel county of Kent, was abundant in greenfield sites and seized by post-war planners for widespread development of estates to rehouse the residents of bomb-blitzed London. It was here that Bertha got a part-time job and Sidney became an electric crane driver with a local engineering company. Culturally, it was a far cry indeed from the rural idyll of Suffolk; but for Auntie May falling in love with Uncle Arthur the fishmonger, how differently Ecclestone's life might have otherwise unfolded.

It was in this street-sharp urban environment that Bernard, an undersized kid with a sharp brain and a precocious eye for a quick penny, honed his nascent business skills. One of his earliest enterprises, at the age of 11 or thereabouts, saw him stopping off at a local baker's shop to buy buns at a penny halfpenny each, which he would then re-sell in the school playground for twopence each. When his mother asked him if he ever ate one himself, says his sister, Marian, he replied: 'No, that's my profit.' Known as 'Titch' because of his size, he protected that profit with the assistance of bigger schoolboys, who ensured that he was not taken advantage of by his customers. He also claimed in later years that he had 'a little gang' working for him to prevent him being bullied.

Young Bernard's profit margins were further increased by subsidiary activities – two newspaper rounds and, during his school holidays, picking vegetables in local farms. A significant source of revenue came from the sale of fountain pens, which he would buy wholesale in Cutler Street, in London's East End, for sale in nearby Petticoat Lane, a well-known street market, where he would stand holding out his wares to attract the attention of passing shoppers. Whoever he inherited his early entrepreneurial skills from, it was not his private and humble parents, whom he describes as being 'very caring people who wanted to see me get on'.

His desire to do so was driven by a firm resolution to provide for his own needs at a time, during the days of food rationing in the forties, when the British economy was trying to recover from the crippling cost of the Second World War. Acquiring what he wanted by his own initiative and ingenuity became a way of life. Rationed food and sweets were certainly not beyond his reach. 'We had a cupboard that was full with boxes of Black Magic chocolates and sugar and all the other things you couldn't get.' Some 60 years later he explained: 'I never wanted to bother my family to buy me something. I wanted to earn my own money. I knew they didn't have it anyway. When I wanted things I hustled and bustled until I got them. I'm an independent bastard.'

His business success in the school playground and in Petticoat Lane was not matched by his efforts in the classroom. At the age of 15, he left West Central Secondary School, Dartford, with little academic distinction. Media coverage of his education repeatedly credit him with achieving a BSc in chemical engineering at Woolwich University, south London. It is given greater credibility by Ecclestone's entry in *Who's Who*, which lists the degree among biographical detail. But it is a fanciful claim. School records show that he attended what was then known as Woolwich Polytechnic, during his final year at West Central Secondary, for no more than one day a week to take part in a job-training scheme (although he is adamant that he attended the Polytechnic five days a week for two years). He left school in December 1946 to work as a junior in the laboratory of the regional gas board where he had high hopes of becoming a chemist.

The one certain area of Ecclestone's early life was the passion that would prove the driving force of his life – a love of quick-buck wheeler-dealing. By his mid-teens his business activities were taking on a serious turn – he was now dealing in second-hand motorbikes, an enterprise that his mother's brother, Godfrey – Uncle 'Goff', who apparently saw in his nephew the son he never had – helped to kick-start with an occasional modest financial donation. One of his customers was Jack Surtees, a top motorcycle sidecar racer, and the father of John, who in 1956 would win the first of his seven world motorcycle championships, then become a Formula One world champion in 1964 and the boss of his own Formula One team from 1970 to 1978. Surtees recalls standing in the kitchen of Ecclestone's home in Marcet Road as his father, a motorcycle dealer, agreed to buy a 250cc Excelsior from the boy businessman. The passage of time made it impossible for Surtees to fix the year, 'but I was in short trousers and Bernie hadn't been long out of his'.

The young Ecclestone's enjoyment of motorbikes ensured that he would not remain for long in the unfulfilling employment of the local gas board. Within a year he had approached a motorcycle retailer, Les Cocker, a modest man of limited ambitions and twenty years his senior, who ran Harcourt Motor Cycles, in Broadway, Bexleyheath, a small shopping centre situated a few miles from his home in Marcet Road. Suitably impressed by Ecclestone's enthusiasm and knowledge of motorbikes, Cocker was persuaded to employ him as a junior salesman, a decision that earned him a unique footnote in Formula One history as the man who set Bernie Ecclestone off on his career path, although one that he did not pursue for long at Harcourt.

He was ambitious for bigger things, namely his own motorcycle business. He saw its realisation in an astute proposal that would require the agreement of the owner of a car showroom called Compton & Fuller situated on the other side of Broadway. Ecclestone, now aged about 18, walked confidently into the showroom to attempt to persuade the owner, Frederick Compton, to let him have, in return for a reasonable rent, part of his forecourt for the sale of second-hand motorbikes. Compton, in his early thirties and no mug punter, was hugely unimpressed, telling the slight figure standing before him – 'he was like a child' – to go away. To him, motorbikes were filthy, dirty machines that had no place anywhere near his showroom. Undaunted, Ecclestone continued to call. Each time, he increased the proposed rent until Compton finally capitulated to an offer he couldn't refuse: half of Ecclestone's profits in return for a part of the forecourt, plus a desk inside. Ecclestone had his foot on the first rung of the ladder.

During the ensuing months the business of Compton & Fuller underwent a dramatic change. In austere post-war Britain, when a second-hand motorbike could be bought for £15, and when a teenage culture of rock 'n' roll, Teddy Boys and James Dean movies embraced motorcycles as a symbol of rebellion, Compton could do little more than look on as Ecclestone's sales of motorbikes soared, while the sale of his cars remained more or less static. 'When people came into the showroom, they were coming to see him, not me,' said Compton. 'It soon became obvious that he could make more money selling motorbikes than I could selling cars.' Within a year Compton & Fuller's last car went out of the showroom. By now Ecclestone had become such a dominant force in the business that he was in a position to negotiate a partnership. Shortly after his twenty-first birthday, in December 1951, Compton & Fuller became Compton & Ecclestone. One can imagine an enraptured Ecclestone standing on the other side of the street, gazing in delight at the sight of his name on the new sign over the shopfront.

With ready access to machines ranging from the latest Velocette using an explosive methanol-based fuel to a five-stud double-knocker 350 Norton JAP engine fitted to a Triumph frame, which he raced on the grass track at Brands Hatch and at its first tarmacadamed practice session in 1950, Ecclestone was able to freely indulge himself in his hobby of motorcycle racing. Once he had been no more than a face in the crowd. Now he could afford to compete. In his immaculate leathers he became a frequent competitor at Brands Hatch, during which time he developed a friendship with a south London car dealer called Jimmy Oliver, who, before dying of prostate cancer at the age of 89 in January 2000, spoke of the 'kid' who approached him at Brands Hatch in 1948 looking for a particular American car.

Oliver, then aged 38 and the successful manager of a Tankard & Smith car showroom in Peckham, south London, and who raced a 250cc Velocette himself at Brands Hatch, said: 'This kid, who was about 18, says to me, "I understand you're in the car business. I've got a customer who wants an American car. Have you got anything?" The following week he turns up at my showroom in Peckham to have a look at a Hudson "straight eight". "That'll do," he says. He took it away on a sale-or-return basis. We did that in those days. I knew then that he was going to turn out to be a right whizz-kid.' Compton was convinced that Ecclestone's size was a major factor in his early business successes. 'I am sure it gave him quite an advantage because you couldn't believe this kid could be so smart. Of course, people soon discovered otherwise.'

Ecclestone's skills on the motorcycle track, though, lacked the necessary fearlessness to ensure even modest success. It was, he decided, too dangerous. He claimed to have woken up in hospital once too often. Four wheels seemed a safer bet. It led to him racing at Brands Hatch and Silverstone in 500cc single-seater events – the cars consisted of little more than chain-driven double-knocker Norton engines – which later became Formula Three. Ecclestone had a brand-new Cooper, bought through the new-found partnership, with the cockpit designed for his slight build, as were his driver's overalls by Lewis's of London. The immaculate condition of both car and driver came to hallmark his pre-race appearance – early signs of an extreme compulsion for order and cleanliness that came to pervade every area of his life. At the same time, it generated, then and later, some innovative thinking: he arrived at Brands Hatch with a racing tender, the first of its kind, to transport his car and equipment, with the company name of Compton & Ecclestone emblazoned along its sides to promote business. 'Everything about Bernard,' said Compton, 'had to be that way – organised and professional. Going into racing was, in fact, a way of getting our name known. It worked. Everyone in the south of England knew us.'

The highlight of his motor-racing career probably took place in 1950 when he drove alongside a promising young driver called Stirling Moss in a support race to the first-ever World Championship Grand Prix at Silverstone in 1950. Moss vaguely recalls Ecclestone 'being around', but that he 'wasn't that active'. Although Ecclestone continued to race irregularly up until 1956, any aspirations he might have had to pursue a career in motor racing effectively came to an end at Brands Hatch in 1953, when he collided with his friend and fellow car-dealer Bill Whitehouse. Ecclestone was said to have gone flying over the heads of spectators. Whitehouse scrambled out of his car to wind him up: 'You better pretend you're dead, Bernie, you've killed one of the spectators.' When help reached him, he refused to be touched until the medics arrived, but he sustained nothing more serious than severe bruising to his ego. Whitehouse, a more talented driver, took part in the British Grand Prix in 1954, but three years later, at the age of 48, died when his car, a Cooper works car, burst into flames after an accident at a Formula Two event in Reims, France.

Ten months after Ecclestone celebrated his partnership with Frederick Compton, he entered into another: he married Ivy Bamford, a brunette three years his senior and the daughter of a retired carpenter's assistant, who worked as a telephonist at the local GPO exchange and whom he had known since their early teens. Ecclestone and Compton had become such good friends that Compton and his wife, Jean, acted as witnesses to the marriage at Dartford Registry Office on 5 September 1952, while Ecclestone accepted an invitation to be godfather to their daughter, Jennifer. With business going from strength to strength, the newly married couple were able to buy the Comptons' old house, a substantial 1930s-style four-bedroomed semi-detached in Pickford Close, Bexleyheath, a few minutes' drive from Compton & Ecclestone, and for which Ecclestone paid £10,000. Two years later they moved further up the social scale when they purchased an imposing four-bedroomed detached house in Danson Road, Bexleyheath. It was while at Danson Road that the Ecclestones had their only child – Deborah Ann, born at Bexley Maternity Hospital on 9 September 1955.

By now Compton was little more than a figurehead in a partnership that had come to be totally dominated by the overwhelming young Ecclestone, who could be seen in the showroom, neatly turned out in suit and tie, standing next to rows of motorbikes whose front wheels were positioned at precisely the same angle, complete with oil drip trays and covers over the number plates. Compton found himself in awe of Ecclestone's methods of dealing with both suppliers and customers. 'He'd come back with two lorry-loads of motorcycles after seeing them all priced up and saying to the seller, "I'll give you £2700 for the lot." He'd do that in seconds. It was instantaneous. His brain was like a calculator.' He was equally quick in responding to a customer's request for a demonstration ride. There was no need, he would tell them. The motorbikes were covered by his personal guarantee, and that was good enough. Another former associate confirmed Ecclestone's 'high reputation for being an instant wheeler-dealer, someone who would make decisions very quickly. People would not quite realise the deal they'd done until they had done it. He was known for being extremely astute and very quick.'

The future looked bright indeed for Compton & Ecclestone, but the frantic pace at which his young partner operated took its toll on Compton's health. He developed a stomach ulcer which left him seriously ill. 'I couldn't live with the speed of Ecclestone and his methods of business. I wasn't doing any business at all in the end. It wasn't his fault, but I had become a useless object,' said Compton. He became so ill that he lost all interest in the business. He willingly accepted an offer from his partner to buy him out, although he was unable to recall the details. 'I think I must have sold him at least half the stock.' Despite his illness, Compton was shrewd enough to retain the freehold of the property, charging his tenant a rent of £1500 a year. There was, he said, no legal documentation of the sale. 'It was quite incredible what one did in those faraway days.' It was not, he conceded years later, the best deal he could have struck, 'but I was very unwell at the time, so I was only too pleased to get out. But I don't want to knock Bernard because it was my fault. I accepted these terms.'

Compton moved successfully into property investment and art dealing, while Ecclestone, by November 1955, was the sole owner of Compton & Ecclestone, a situation better suited to a temperament that insisted on being in control of every area of business. His success continued apace, so much so that by the following year he and his family moved to Barn Cottage in Parkwood Road, Bexley, an impressive five-bedroomed house. The Ecclestones' time at Barn Cottage was notable to his sister for two incidents. The first demonstrated his obsession for extreme orderliness. Marian said: 'He had a well-stocked bar, and he walked in one day and saw where the cleaner had disturbed one of the miniatures – the label wasn't quite facing the front. He walked over and straightened it. There were dozens there and yet he spotted that one.' The other incident demonstrated his business opportunism. When a friend discovered, on leaving Ecclestone's house, that one of his car tyres was flat, he saw the chance for a quick sale. 'Instead of helping him to replace the tyre,' said Marian, 'Bernard sold him his own car.'

By the mid-fifties Ecclestone was ready to move up a couple of gears, to dealing in cars as well as motorcycles. In August 1956 he acquired a business called Hill's Garage situated in Crook Log, Bexleyheath, about quarter of a mile from Compton & Ecclestone. Nineteen months later he acquired another car company, James Spencer Ltd, and its owner, Jimmy Spencer, a middle-aged motor dealer who enjoyed a smoke and a drink and would die of a heart attack nine years later, became a director. Hill's Garage became James Spencer (Bexleyheath) Ltd, although Spencer would not enjoy for long the prestige of the company name. In August 1959 he departed suddenly in uncertain but apparently acrimonious circumstances, according to both Spencer's widow and daughter.

At her home in south London, 85-year-old Mrs Ethel Spencer said she believed her husband 'wasn't very pleased with something that had taken place, but I wouldn't know what, because we never discussed [his business] at home'. Spencer opened his own company, called Chris Steel Cars, in Bromley, Kent, with his son-in-law, Roger Wilson. In 1971 the business folded and Ecclestone, said Wilson's widow, Sheila, was interested in buying it. But her husband, who, she added, knew of the cause of the partnership split between her father and Ecclestone, was not interested in selling the business to Ecclestone. 'Roger said, "Over my dead body."' Mrs Wilson did not know the reason for her husband's attitude towards Ecclestone. 'There always seemed to be some underlying thing we didn't know about.' On Spencer's departure, Ecclestone appointed his father to be manager of the showroom and a director of the company, a position Sidney held with a number of his son's other enterprises.

Towards the end of the fifties, with the British motorcycle industry hitting a serious slump, Ecclestone decided to dispose of Compton & Ecclestone. He had by now, incidentally, also acquired his former employer's business, Harcourt Motor Cycles, a much smaller premises, from where he sold sidecar motorbikes. The buyer was 37-year-old businessman John Croker, who, among other interests, owned a hire-purchase finance company, a company importing washing machines from Italy, and car showrooms in Chadwell Heath, Essex. East London-born Croker met Ecclestone through two fellow car dealers, Victor White and Harold O'Connor, both of whom were close friends of Ecclestone's with a penchant for vicuña overcoats, cigars and silk monogrammed shirts.

O'Connor and Ecclestone used to travel together to different locations in the UK, such as the then Midland Hotel in Manchester, to meet groups of dealers among whom vehicles would be bought and sold during night-long trading sessions. At these gatherings it was not uncommon for the two men to earn profit on non-existent cars. O'Connor, for example, would introduce a car for a certain price, which would be sold from dealer to dealer. It was crucial that, at the end of business, it was bought back by O'Connor or Ecclestone at a price less than they had sold it for in the first place. If it left them for, say, £600, and was bought back for £400, a nice profit of £200 could be pocketed. If not, they could end up out of pocket. It was similar, said Ecclestone, to the Stock Exchange dealing known as 'selling short': selling shares about to dive, buying them back when they hit rock bottom, and then selling them for a handsome profit once they have recovered. 'I tell you, there's nothing new in life.'

Croker bought Ecclestone's second-hand motorcycle business in September 1959. 'He struck me as a being a shrewd and charming man,' said Croker, 'but he had this funny thing about cleanliness. He was always washing his hands, straightening his tie and making sure there wasn't a speck of dust about. I thought there was something wrong with the man.' Croker's ownership of Compton & Ecclestone was brief – and disastrous.

Gross mismanagement by a trusted employee, he said, led to serious financial problems which required a considerable bank loan to shore up the business. But it wasn't enough to prevent the collapse of not only Compton & Ecclestone but also Croker's other companies. Just two months after signing the deal with Ecclestone, he was forced to accept an offer for the business from O'Connor and White. The demise of his various companies led to the loss of his luxury home, several properties and his brand-new Rolls-Royce. Twenty-eight years later Croker, whose business fortunes never recovered, ended up living in a two-bedroom council flat in Canning Town, east London.

Ecclestone's fortunes, though, continued in their ascendancy, despite a fire that razed to the ground the premises of James Spencer (Bexleyheath) Ltd in the mid-sixties. The efficient way in which Ecclestone was able to recover from the calamity astonished those who saw the fire damage. One of the witnesses to the aftermath was motor dealer Bobby Rowe, who quit the motor trade in the early seventies to earn substantial wealth through property investment, but who at that time leased from Ecclestone the former Harcourt Motor Cycles premises. As he was passing by at 10 o'clock at night, he saw firemen damping down the smouldering debris of the showroom and burnt-out cars within it. Yet what he saw the following morning on his way to his business left him highly impressed. He said: 'By eight o'clock that morning – this is no exaggeration – those cars were all gone, the showroom was all swept out, there was a Portakabin on the front, complete with telephones, and he was back in business, with cars on the forecourt.'

From the ashes emerged a new showroom and offices so impressive in design and décor – the walls displayed murals of cars painted by Ecclestone himself and sufficiently skilled to prompt admiring comments – that fellow car dealer Jimmy Oliver used to take colleagues to see the 'fabulous' showroom. When another former associate remarked how clean and smart the showroom looked, Ecclestone replied: 'Yeah, the trouble is, people come in and spoil it.' During a heavy winter snowfall his concern that customers would make a mess of the showroom floor prompted him to phone the local council to demand that the snow outside his premises be removed. Unhappy with the indifferent response, he arranged for it to be shovelled into the roadway to obstruct passing traffic. It had the desired result: council workmen soon arrived to clear it. A garage at the rear of the premises, used to service cars before being displayed in the showroom, was also noted for its immaculate condition, with white tiles covering the floor and walls. 'Nobody in the trade had ever seen anything like that before,' said Frederick Compton. 'He was the first to think of it.'

Ecclestone's social life, then as now, had no pretensions. He enjoyed playing the guessing game spoof in the pubs and a serious flutter on the gaming tables – 'he was a great gambler,' said a former friend – at the Beaverwood, then a top nightclub in Chiselhurst, Kent, where the likes of Tom Jones would pull in the crowds. During the day, when he bothered to have lunch, it would frequently be at a working men's cafe about half a mile down the road from the James Spencer showroom, to which he and Bobby Rowe would race, there and back, on their motorbikes. But his main social activity was regular visits to Brands Hatch, where he was introduced by 'Pops' Lewis-Evans, a well-known and much-liked figure in the motor-racing world, to his son, Stuart, who was establishing a reputation as a racer ready to challenge the best.

Stuart made his debut in a Grand Prix car at an Easter meeting at Goodwood in 1957 – the year his father retired following a serious crash – after winning more continental events in the 500cc Cooper class than any other driver. He drove the latest Connaught at the invitation of its designer, Rodney Clarke, to beat the likes of Stirling Moss and Tony Brooks. A month later he was in the Connaught again, making his Grand Prix debut at Monaco, where he came a very creditable fourth. His performance led to Tony Vandervell signing him up for his Vanwall team, alongside Brooks and Moss, who described his new colleague as 'very, very fast'. A few months later, in only his fourth outing in a Grand Prix car, he lapped the Reims circuit at 129mph, only a fifth of a second slower than world champion Juan Fangio, in a Maserati.

Ecclestone, six months younger than 27-year-old Stuart Lewis-Evans, developed a friendship with him, and regularly attended his races. He saw in

Lewis-Evans perhaps what he secretly desired – the skills to be a world-class racer. He attempted to advance his friend's potential when Connaught Engineering, founded by Rodney Clarke and Mike Oliver in 1948, encountered serious financial difficulties after its principal backer, Kenneth McAlpine, a director of a well-known British building company, withdrew his support. Oliver and Clarke, whose cars had swept the board at Formula Two events attended principally by privateers, were also hit by a restructuring of the formulae, which pitched Connaught against works teams in Formula One. By the beginning of 1957 – two years earlier Tony Brooks had a stunning triumph in a Connaught at the Syracuse Grand Prix in Sicily, the first Englishman to win an overseas Grand Prix since Henry Segrave won The Grand Prix, as the French Grand Prix was known in those days, in June 1923 – the writing was clearly on the wall.

According to more recent newspaper reports, Ecclestone went out and bought the entire Connaught team. As with his imaginary BSc, his *Who's Who* listing claims ownership of the team. But, again, not quite true. He bought two cars – the B3, described as the 'toothpaste tube' model, and the B7 – that came under the hammer of auctioneers Goddard, Davison and Smith in September 1957. Six Connaughts were sold for between £1600 and £2100. Two, the C8 and B6, were withdrawn after failing to reach the reserve price. 'The company was certainly not bought by Bernie Ecclestone in any way at all,' said Oliver. 'He was simply one of a number of purchasers at the auction.'

Stuart Lewis-Evans and another young talented driver, Roy Salvadori, raced the cars in the New Zealand Grand Prix at Ardmore in January 1958. But Ecclestone's motive for entering them had less to do with any expectation of success – Salvadori, plagued by an engine misfire, finished a poor fifth, and Lewis-Evans was eliminated by loss of oil pressure, all of which was too much for the one mechanic hired by Ecclestone to cope with – than with the opportunity to sell them on to an Australian or New Zealand market where such cars were keenly sought after. The 'start' money negotiated by Ecclestone with the organisers made a substantial contribution to their transportation costs.

Lewis-Evans had been instructed by Ecclestone to handle their sale. Not the sharpest of businessmen, he was on the verge of exchanging the two cars for a stamp collection when Salvadori urged him to first get Ecclestone's approval. The response was short and clear. The cars were shipped backed to England. One or two other drivers raced them but without notable success, including Ecclestone himself, who attempted to qualifying for the Monaco Grand Prix in 1958, a performance that did little to enhance his reputation as a driver. Although he was one of the 14 out of 30 entries who failed to qualify, his effort was described in the record books as 'not a serious attempt'.[1]

At one stage Ecclestone had hoped to build a Formula One team around Lewis-Evans and the Connaughts. But, happy at Vanwall, where he had established his reputation, Lewis-Evans declined the invitation. With his plans still-born on the drawing board, Ecclestone settled for a role as the racer's unofficial agent, principally advising him on his business affairs. It was an arrangement that, tragically, did not last long. At the age of 28, the driver described by world champion Mike Hawthorn as 'one of the best up-and-coming British drivers' died after his car crashed and burst into flames in the Moroccan Grand Prix in Casablanca on 19 October 1958. He was flown to Queen Victoria Hospital, East Grinstead, Sussex, where he died from his burns six days later. Within a matter of weeks Tony Vandervell, said to have been guilt-stricken over Lewis-Evans's death, suffered a heart attack. He recovered but was unable to recapture his enthusiasm for the sport. The Vanwall team lost its competitive edge and gradually faded from Formula One after the French Grand Prix in 1960, six years after its debut at the British Grand Prix.

Ecclestone also disappeared, temporarily, from the Formula One scene, only to emerge, as newspapers later claimed, to race in a team set up by seven-times world champion motorcyclist Phil Read. Glamorous stuff, but not true. He did sponsor a couple of motorcyclists, one of them being Bobby Rowe, whom he supplied with a 500cc Norton for the Isle of Man TT in 1959, where Rowe received a newcomer's award. It was the only year that Rowe made any money out of racing, thanks to Ecclestone organising a sponsorship deal with Shell. He notched up the odd win, and an occasional second and third, but little more. Ecclestone missed one win, at Brands Hatch, when it started to rain. With everyone else in greasy leathers, he arrived immaculately dressed in a suit and highly polished shoes. As the rain threatened his sartorial elegance, he became tired of tiptoeing round the puddles to protect his shoes, and made an early exit.

Back in the office, Ecclestone, over the next decade, began to expand his business activities to include hire-purchase finance and property. The hire-purchase company was called Arvin Securities and formed in March 1961. It was based at the premises of James Spencer (Bexleyheath) Ltd, which was given the address of Arvin House to promote a more substantial image. Ecclestone was now able to offer his customers an extra service – a credit facility to buy his cars. It was a lucrative one. Dealers able to finance their own hire-purchase agreements made more money through the interest on the loan than on the sale of the car. In 1968 Ecclestone set up a similar company at the same address offering the same services under the name of Arvin Credit Facilities. His property interests began with a company called Pentbridge

Properties Ltd and, later, Pentbridge Services. He had also acquired a sizeable plot of land in Manor Road, Erith, Kent, where he had three single-storey buildings constructed for leasing to small companies. It was there, in 1969, that he opened a car auctions company, Mid-Week Car Auctions, and where, in the very early days, it was not unknown for Ecclestone himself to pick up the auctioneer's gavel.

Shortly after the mid-sixties he began moving around the Formula One circuits again. Through his friendship with privateer John Cooper, he met in 1967 a young Austrian called Jochen Rindt, who had joined Bruce McLaren in the Cooper team two years earlier following an impressive showing in Formula Two. In 1968, with the Cooper cars considered to be uncompetitive, Rindt signed for the Brabham team as number two to Jack Brabham. Over the ensuing months a firm friendship developed between the two – Rindt was the first to call Ecclestone 'Bernie' rather than 'Bernard' – on and off the track. It extended to the gaming tables of Acapulco during the 1968 Mexican Grand Prix, which Rindt, in a Brabham-Repco, failed to finish through ignition failure. It was a friendship, though, founded on a mutual admiration rather than social interests: if Ecclestone was a fervent admirer of Rindt's skills and the business potential they offered, Rindt was no less impressed by Ecclestone's shrewdness as a negotiator. Such was his faith in Ecclestone's astuteness that Rindt was happy for him to represent his interests when in late 1968 the Lotus team boss, Colin Chapman, who had just signed a controversial £100,000 sponsorship deal with Imperial Tobacco, approached him with an offer to join the Lotus team to become joint number-one driver with Graham Hill following the death that April of the brilliant double world champion Jim Clark at a Formula Two event in Hockenheim, Germany.

On Ecclestone's recommendation, Rindt agreed to leave Brabham, which was going through a bad spell. Widely considered the most daring and aggressively skilful driver of his day, Rindt came fourth, behind Bruce McLaren, Jacky Ickx and Jackie Stewart in the 1969 World Championship. Towards the end of that year Ecclestone, no doubt sensing the time was right to put their business association on a more formal footing, proposed, in the days when it was not unusual for top drivers to race virtually every weekend in different formulae, that they went into partnership to set up a Formula Two team. At the same time he would become Rindt's manager. The Austrian agreed, and in January 1970 Jochen Rindt Racing was formed. Clearly, Ecclestone was ever determined to establish his presence in motor racing. But, as with Lewis-Evans, it was a partnership that would end tragically.

Eight months later 28-year-old Rindt died during the Saturday practice session at the Italian Grand Prix at Monza, when his Lotus 72 veered sharp left, as he was under-braking, into the Parabolica, diving under the Armco crash barriers and bouncing back on to the track. He refused to wear crutch straps on his harness, and his throat was cut by the seat-belt buckle after he was thrust deep into his cockpit. In addition he suffered severe chest injuries. Ecclestone was the first person to reach Rindt, who was barely still alive and died, at least officially, in hospital. The trackside medical facilities were so haphazard that he was taken to the wrong hospital in a Volkswagen ambulance after the driver lost his way. 'With the medical facilities we have today, he would have had a better chance of surviving,' said Ecclestone. After winning five Grands Prix with three more races to go, Rindt had done enough to become the first driver to win the World Championship title posthumously. Of his decision to move to Lotus, Ecclestone said: 'I recommended he took the offer [from Colin Chapman] because I wanted him to be world champion. But, sure, there were a couple of things I wasn't happy about, safety being one of them. Chapman tended to push things to the limit.' He added: 'But if the [track] safety regulations we have today had been in place then, he would have survived.'

More prophetically than Rindt could possibly have imagined, he had said of his manager: 'You should keep an eye on little people like ... Bernie Ecclestone because he has big ambitions and the drive to achieve them.'[2] Shortly before his death, Rindt had, in fact, already and unknowingly played an instrumental role in laying the ground for Ecclestone to achieve his ambitions, not least the ownership of his own Formula One team, which would herald the beginning of a remarkable career and culminate in his iron grip on Formula One.

3

THE RISE TO RICHES OF BRABHAM'S NEW BOSS

Ron Tauranac had had enough. The tall, rangy Australian, known as a tough, prickly but deeply caring man, believed the time had come to get out of Formula One. Like many of his day, he had graduated the hard way, in times when design and technology were largely a suck-it-and-see science and the financial rewards were slim indeed. He had been a leading name in car design for most of the sixties, soon after setting up in business with fellow Australian Jack Brabham, whom he had known back home in Sydney in the late forties. In those days Brabham was driving Midgets and hill-climbing, and, with necessity truly proving to be the mother of invention, they machined car parts they couldn't buy, with Tauranac constructing Formula Three cars around 500cc motorbike engines.

Their friendship was interrupted by Brabham's decision – prompted by a suggestion from Dean Delamont, the competition manager of Britain's Royal Automobile Club (RAC), at a New Zealand Grand Prix – to move to England to test his skills in the European arena. He arrived in 1954, but, racing in non-competitive cars, made little impact. He took part in 16 Grands Prix – finishing nine – before he won his first Grand Prix at Monaco in 1959 in the radical rear-engine Cooper T51, opening a season which he concluded by becoming world champion at the age of 33. On the strength of his success, Brabham, keen to set up his own team and car production company, sent a return air ticket to Tauranac with an invitation to try the water for six months. Tauranac, who was actually born in Gillingham, Kent, but whose parents emigrated to Australia when he was three, believed such a move had to be all or nothing – and used the money to buy one-way tickets on a ship for his wife, Norma, and their three-year-old daughter, Jann, while he flew to Los Angeles to be with Brabham, who was racing in a sports-car event at Riverside, before flying to England ahead of his family's arrival in March 1960, the year when Brabham won his second World Championship.

It marked the beginning of a tough baptism for Tauranac. By day he was working on converting cars for Jack Brabham Motors and by night in his bedroom in a flat above a shop in Tolworth, Surrey, designing his first racing car – the MRD Formula Junior – for Motor Racing Developments Ltd, a company formed by Tauranac and Brabham in 1961 and based in rented garage space a few miles away in Esher. It became established, after moving briefly to Repco's new premises in nearby Surbiton, in a factory next to the River Wey at New Haw, near Weybridge. It was here that Tauranac, as technical director, produced the first Climax-powered Formula One car for the Brabham team debut in 1962.

Financed by the sale of Formula Three and Formula Two Libre production cars and Esso and Goodyear sponsorship deals, the combination of Tauranac's design and technical expertise and Brabham's driving skills soon established the Brabham team as a crowd-pulling contender, not least in classic battles with Colin Chapman's Lotus Ford team. In 1966, at the age of 40, Brabham won his third World Championship in the first Repco V8-powered car – and became the only driver to win the title in a car bearing his own name.

The following season he came second in the World Championship title race to co-team driver, New Zealander Denny Hulme, who then left Brabham for McLaren. But 'Black' Jack felt time was running out. There was little more he wanted to prove or needed to achieve. He confided in Tauranac that he wanted to retire, which led to his partner acquiring his share in Motor Racing Developments Ltd in 1969. At the end of the 1970 season, Brabham, aged 44, made public his decision, bringing to a close an illustrious fifteen-year career spanning 126 Grands Prix, 14 wins and three World Championships. He returned to Australia to run a farming operation he had bought the previous year and to set up a Ford agency in Sydney with Tauranac's younger brother, Austin.

Back in New Haw, it was business as usual for Tauranac. But he found Brabham's absence unsettling. He very much missed his countryman's support and friendship. The end of their partnership meant more than the end of a business relationship. The two men had created a formidable team and through many highs and lows had developed a close friendship. Brabham's departure hit Tauranac harder than he could have imagined. It caused him to reflect on his own future in Formula One, which came to be influenced by other changes.

Following Brabham's departure, chief mechanic Ron Dennis and his number two, Neil Trundell, decided to leave to set up their own Formula Two team, the unsuccessful and short-lived Rondel Racing; Goodyear, following a senior management reshuffle, were about to drop the Brabham team for newcomers McLaren, who had moved into Formula One in 1966 following the team's success in IndyCar and CanAm racing in America; and lead driver Graham Hill, who hadn't fully recovered from breaking both legs in an horrific accident in the US Grand Prix at Watkins Glen in 1969, was past his prime. Running the whole show was proving a massive burden for Tauranac to carry alone.

Tauranac had one other ball to juggle: finding the all-important sponsorship money, which had been his former partner's expertise. As the ship's chief engineer, more at home with a spanner and an oil rag, it wasn't his natural style to sweet-talk the corporate suits. Diminishing financial fortunes had, in fact, cost the Brabham team the services of Jochen Rindt. When Colin Chapman approached Rindt in 1968 to join the Lotus team, Tauranac had been unable to put a counter-offer on the table to keep him. Rindt's departure was all the more difficult for Tauranac because of a friendship so strong – they even shared hotel rooms at overseas Grands Prix – that the Austrian had been prepared to stay with Brabham for half the money on offer from Chapman. But Tauranac couldn't match even that. It was a combination of these factors that persuaded him to agree to a suggestion from Rindt, who, although unaware of the pressures on his friend, told him that he knew of someone who might be interested in buying the company. His name was Bernie Ecclestone, of whom Tauranac knew little.

Their first meeting took place on board a private yacht during the Monaco Grand Prix in May 1970. Ecclestone came straight to the point: he proposed a partnership in return for which he would provide the management nous and finance that the company sorely needed. Rindt would return as lead driver to get Brabham back on the podium. The proposal had its attractions for Tauranac, not least the prospect of Rindt returning to Brabham, but he cared little for the idea of a partnership. He was far from certain that, after working with Jack Brabham for so long, he could settle easily into a similar business association with someone else. For this reason he made a counter-proposal: he would sell the company to Ecclestone and, if it all went well, he would be happy to buy back in. Ecclestone was not keen; Tauranac stood firm. The discussions proceeded no further.

However, Ecclestone's sights were set on acquiring the Brabham team, although his plans would no longer include Jochen Rindt. Less than four months after the aborted meeting, he had his tragic accident at Monza. During the autumn of 1970 Ecclestone began fresh discussions with Tauranac for the purchase of Motor Racing Developments Ltd. This time Ecclestone agreed to buy the company, with Tauranac remaining as joint managing director. The deal was finalised that October. Ecclestone had been so confident Tauranac would sell that, while still in negotiations, he phoned the factory at night to ask a number of questions about the Brabham team. The call was answered by Nick Goozée, responsible for building the Formula One cars, who was working late. Perplexed by the specific nature of the questions, Goozée asked why he wanted the information. Identifying himself as Bernie Ecclestone, the caller added: 'I've bought the company.' Tauranac reassured Goozée the following morning that he hadn't, which, at that stage at least, was true.

But the manner in which the sale of Motor Racing Developments Ltd was concluded did not go according to plan. At least, not to Tauranac's plan, the consequences of which left him considerably out of pocket. Tauranac claims it had been verbally agreed that the purchase price would be based on his valuation of the company's assets. The figure came to £130,000, and this, accompanied with an itemised list of the assets, was duly submitted to Ecclestone. Tauranac claims that he heard nothing more from Ecclestone and had therefore assumed that his valuation had been accepted. However, shortly before the deal was due to be concluded, he received a night-time phone call from Ecclestone with an offer of £100,000 (worth in 2002 about £860,000).

Said Tauranac: 'We had a verbal agreement that he was going to buy it for the assets value of the company. I did an honest stock-take and valuation of it all and passed it on to him. I had gone ahead on that basis and more or less committed myself to selling the company, and at the eleventh hour he made an offer of £100,000. I should have said, "We have this agreement" and bartered a little bit. But I was a little bit naïve and, due to my lack of business experience, I thought it was "take it or leave it". So I thought about it for five minutes and said OK. I should have had a solicitor or an adviser, or someone to talk things over with, but I didn't.' With a substantial part of the money earmarked for a trust set up for the benefit of his two daughters, then aged nine and 15, Tauranac remains today remarkably phlegmatic: 'People in business, that's the way they work. It was down to me.' All the same, Tauranac would have given a wry smile to a motor sport magazine report which some years later claimed that Ecclestone had paid 'something in the region' of £500,000 for the company.[1]

Ecclestone gives a different account of events, which he remembered 'very, very well'. He added: 'There was an agreement involving the stock, which he didn't know [the value of]. He said, "I've no idea what the stock is worth."

And I think I said to somebody, "Can you value the stock?", and when they said whatever it was ... when I met Ron, I said, "Ron, this is the value of the stock", and he... I remember standing in the corridor outside the solicitor's office [where the sale documents were signed] ... and he said, "That means, then, it's only a hundred [thousand pounds]..." I said, "Well, whatever it means is whatever it means. If you don't think that's true, then do it properly." That was it. I remember it so clearly.' There was no hint of a take-it-or-leave-it offer, Ecclestone said. 'At the time I bought that company I wasn't even sure whether I wanted it or not. Nobody told him to go ahead. Nobody told him to do anything. Actually, he said to me, "I need to think about this again, because I am not sure whether I want to sell." I said, "It's up to you entirely."' Tauranac, he added, then agreed the deal.

To Ecclestone, the acquisition was surely a bumper bargain. In addition to stock and engineering equipment, the assets included five DFV engines with an estimated value of £5000 each, and two Formula One cars worth an estimated £10,000 each, totalling almost half the price he had paid for the company. It also included a lucrative sponsorship deal for the following year with YPF, a state-owned Argentinian fuel company, which Tauranac had arranged with new driver Carlos Reutemann through the Automóvil Club Argentino.

From day one Ecclestone's attitude towards Tauranac was one of indifference. On his arrival as the new owner, without first stopping off as a matter of courtesy at Tauranac's office, he went straight to the workshop to talk to the mechanics about what they thought of the company, including the new joint managing director. It was the start of a fraught relationship between the two men, made worse when, without notice or consultation, Ecclestone instructed the company accountant, Brian Sheppard, to stop paying Tauranac's salary. The problem was resolved by Tauranac writing out his own salary on a company cheque each month after being advised of the net figure by Sheppard, who, incidentally, later became accountant to several of Ecclestone's companies. Said Tauranac: 'I don't know why he did it. It's the way he works. He never spoke directly [to me]. He did everything unilaterally.'

But Tauranac's problems were only just beginning. He returned from a Christmas holiday to find that Ecclestone had appointed someone else as joint managing director. 'I went for my usual skiing holiday at Christmas – I would go for two weeks every Christmas because that way I only missed about four days' work – and when I came back someone else was ensconced and running it, and there was virtually nothing for me to do.' While Ecclestone was apparently trying to drive him out, Tauranac nevertheless continued to attempt to fulfil his responsibilities by working at home on various project drawings – but it was not long before that was brought to an end.

In March 1972 he received a letter from Ecclestone requesting the return of the drawings and adding that it was time to 'finalise' their relationship. 'So I took the drawings back, got a signature for them, and that was it.' Once again Ecclestone's account differs from Tauranac's. The projects Tauranac was working on, he claims, were for Mo Nunn's Ensign team. 'All I know is that he was paid by us, employed by us, and went to work for Mo Nunn. And I said, "I think you had better stay with Mo Nunn." That's how he left us.'

Tauranac, described as the first professional racing-car designer, cleared his desk and walked away from the Brabham works – and a million memories of a unique but dying era in Formula One. 'But I had no regrets,' he said. 'The way things were going I was happy to get out.' To this day Tauranac remains unclear about Ecclestone's motives. 'The production of the custom-built cars (for which he was responsible) was never an issue. There were never any discussions about it, or anything else. He never discussed how or why. He just did these things. I can only imagine it was his way of sidelining me so he could be in complete control.'

Ecclestone was now established as a wealthy and successful man. By 1968, at the age of 38, he had moved into a large mansion-style house, comprising seven bedrooms and three bathrooms, in Farnborough Park, Kent, bought for £40,000 from a property developer who owned a fair-sized chunk of Mayfair. The new owner had one large room turned into a library, filled with books bought by the yard to line the walls, some of which were used to create a concealed door. The 26 acres of woodland, which Ecclestone bought with money borrowed from a Guernsey-based offshore tax haven, became his private park, with a two-acre lake brimming with perch and golden orfe, which, standing by the lakeside with a large scoop and a sack of fish food he bought wholesale, he enjoyed feeding. He invited privileged friends to fish the lake, although he was so fond of the fish – 'they were enormous,' said a former associate, 'and I think he saw them as his pets' – that he insisted they were returned to the water uninjured. This he ensured by supplying rod and line with hooks whose barbs had been removed. Along with the rods, about six in number and racked neatly against the wall of a wooden lakeside hut, seats and keep-nets were also provided.

Sharing this opulent lifestyle with Ecclestone was his girlfriend, Dora Tuana Tan, a beautiful Singaporean, whom he appointed director to several of his companies. They had met several years earlier at, it was believed, the gaming tables, and began living together in a more modest but nonetheless imposing house in Chiselhurst Road, Chiselhurst. His marriage to Ivy, described as a plain, aloof but well-groomed woman, had long come to an end. 'Ivy was a very nice girl,' said a friend who used to socialise with the couple, 'but never for Bernie. Not from the word go. Mind, you, who would be right for Bernie?'

Ecclestone even owned a B.125 twin-engine Beagle Bulldog, bought through his company partnership with Jochen Rindt, in which they travelled to European Grands Prix. He bought several of the aircraft, in fact, for a knock-down price after the manufacturers, taken over three years earlier by the Labour government from the British Motor Corporation, went into receivership in 1969 for the lack of £6 million for necessary development and expansion. They were put up for auction and sold overseas, except, that is, for one Ecclestone sold to March Engineering, owners of the March racing team, through Max Mosley, one of the four founders of the company. It proved an unfortunate purchase at £10,000 (worth about £95,800 in 2002), particularly as it came without an airworthiness certificate.

Said Mosley: 'It was a lovely aeroplane, but never flew. I should have said to Bernie, "I'll buy it when it's got a certificate of airworthiness."' It didn't get a certificate, apparently because the cost of carrying out certain necessary work turned out to be prohibitive. Ecclestone's comment suggested that Mosley should have looked on the bright side: 'At least it didn't cost much to run.' The plane was sold for £7000, recalled Mosley, to 'this poor chap, an American, who flew off to America'. Did he arrive safely? 'Well, he never paid the second instalment so there's a suspicion that perhaps he didn't.'

Ecclestone made another killing that same year when an Italian car company, Iso SpA, of Bresso, Milan, which produced the Iso marque from 1962 to 1975, hit financial difficulties. He bought a number of the two-seater Iso Grifo cars with Chevrolet engines – a former close associate said as many as 14 for £3000 each – plus some parts and spares, which he sold on through an Irish car trader. Said the former associate: 'He was able to write a cheque out for 50 grand or whatever ... made one phone call to a chap, who was an Irish trader, right, and in less than two or three weeks, he had sold the lot for a bit of a commission.' Ecclestone, he added, was always able to get 'the best deal' because he had the money available to pay cash.

Three years earlier, in 1972, he moved quickly to buy the German team Eiffeland Formula 1 and its equipment as 'as a pure business exercise' after the team's sponsors, caravan manufacturers Eiffeland, were taken over. Apparently Ecclestone was keen to acquire two '12-series' Cosworth engines especially obtained for the team by Ford Germany in January and May of that year and described as 'particularly good ones'. There was, in fact, no such series. They were standard DFV 3-litre V8 engines supplied by Cosworth to all teams but were so described to persuade Ecclestone that they were something 'special'. It was in this quick-buck world that he excelled. To extract an extra percentage point or two in a deal was a challenge he passionately embraced, to an extent that strains belief.

A classic example is demonstrated by events at a car auction in Southampton where, in the early sixties, car dealer Chris Marshall, a touring-car racer who went on to manage the Formula Three career of James Hunt, regularly took cars for sale. He had discovered that he could buy cars at an auction in Tunbridge Wells, Kent, more cheaply than elsewhere and the next day have them driven to Southampton, where they would go under the hammer for perhaps ten per cent more.

He would regularly buy four or five cars a day in this way for a quick resale. In the days when a Morris Oxford cost about £400, a profit of £40 on each car added up to a quick and attractive turnover. And it was in Southampton that Marshall arrived one day with an Austin A40 for sale. He took up his customary position behind the rostrum, from where he could see the auctioneer's foot tap the floor, a signal that told him that a genuine bid had been made. Up until then the auctioneer would often take bids 'off the wall' until a car reached its reserve price. Interest in the A40, with a reserve price of little over £400, continued until it reached a final figure of £450. Marshall was delighted.

The buyer, he claims, had been a small, immaculately dressed man, whom he recognised as Ecclestone, accompanied by two well-built associates. A few minutes later a tannoy announcement from the engineer's office requested Marshall's presence. He was informed that there had been a complaint from the buyer: the engine 'sounded rough' and he wanted £25 knocked off. It was a plea that fell on deaf ears. Ecclestone was compelled to pay up. Ecclestone dismissed Marshall's account as 'pure crap. We would never go to Southampton to buy bloody cars. And I certainly wouldn't have been there.'

The two men, according to Marshall, had met, in fact, about a year earlier. This time, he claims, it involved a two-seater Tripacer Piper plane that Marshall's car business, then based in Hove, East Sussex, had advertised for sale in *Flight* magazine for £3750. Among the interested calls was one from Ecclestone. He said that if Marshall, a qualified pilot, was prepared to fly the plane to the former wartime RAF base at Biggin Hill – which, incidentally, Ecclestone would later acquire – he would be there to meet him with a banker's draft for £3500. The deal was agreed.

A few days later Marshall flew to Biggin Hill from Shoreham-by-Sea, Sussex, and, as he taxied to park, a car drew up, from which a gofer emerged to apologise that Ecclestone had been delayed by business and couldn't be there in person. It was suggested that Marshall left the keys and logbook in the plane to be driven to Ecclestone's office at his plush car showrooms, James Spencer Ltd, in Bexleyheath. Once there, Marshall was kept waiting for about

30 minutes before being shown into Ecclestone's office, where he was told that the plane had been checked over and was OK.

Ecclestone then put a proposal to Marshall: would he take some cars in part exchange? No, Marshall replied firmly, the price of £3500 had been agreed. Ignoring Marshall's reply, Ecclestone continued: 'Come with me, I've got some cars to show you.' Marshall followed Ecclestone to a row of lock-up garages at the rear of the showroom where he was invited to cast an eye over several sports cars, including a 3500 Maserati. Marshall liked the look of none of them. 'One side of the Maserati looked as if it had been damaged and repaired.' He remained unswayed by Ecclestone's offer and continued to insist that he be paid the agreed sum.

Back in his office, Ecclestone, clearly annoyed, threw a banker's draft on to his desk, followed by a sales contract for Marshall to sign. The deal done, Marshall asked Ecclestone for a lift to the local railway station for his return journey to Sussex. To his astonishment, Ecclestone refused. He then asked if he could use a phone to call a taxi. Ecclestone issued the same response. When Marshall asked the reason for his refusal, Ecclestone replied testily: 'Because you've been bloody awkward.' Marshall was left to make his way to the station without Ecclestone's assistance.

If Marshall had been treated to an almost comical display of Ecclestone's churlishness, he was soon to appreciate the shrewd efficiency of his business style. The next day, when he informed the management at Shoreham airport that he would no longer require a hangar for the Piper, an air-control staff member casually commented that he hadn't remained long at Biggin Hill, adding that the plane had taken off 15 minutes after landing. Marshall then realised why Ecclestone hadn't met him as arranged. While he was being driven from Biggin Hill, another car was arriving with a potential buyer. And he was kept waiting in Ecclestone's office until it was reported back to Ecclestone that its sale had been agreed. If there had been a hitch, Ecclestone would have doubtless told Marshall that he was no longer interested in its purchase. As it was, Ecclestone had sold on the plane, doubtless at a handsome profit, before he had even bought it. 'It was a neat, shrewd deal,' said Marshall. 'At the end of which I was stuck in a public phone box trying to get back home.' Ecclestone was also quick to denounce the story of this alleged deal, but added: 'That's another thing I don't remember anything about [but] it's no good me saying anything because I don't remember Chris Marshall.'

Although by the end of the sixties, Ecclestone, then in his fortieth year, was well into the millionaire class, it was a status not easily confirmed by the annual returns of his various companies at that time. Newspaper and magazine articles charting Ecclestone's rise to riches suggest it was made possible through considerable wealth generated by his successful business ventures and their subsequent disposal. For example, it has been consistently reported that he built up Compton & Ecclestone into the third-largest operation of its kind in the country, which made him a wealthy man, before its sale to John Croker in September 1959, and which, just two months later, Croker, through sudden financial misfortune, was forced to sell to the two car dealers, White and O'Connor, who had introduced him to Ecclestone.

But, apart from Harcourt Motor Cycles, Compton & Ecclestone was the only motorcycle business that Ecclestone owned, and then one of modest profits. Albert Shucksmith, president of the Motor Cycle Retail Association, who had been in the motorcycle retail business for 40 years, said the biggest distributors of motorcycles in the late fifties and sixties were Kings of Oxford, Pride and Clarke, Claude Rye and Comerford. The biggest dealers in second-hand motorbikes were thought to be Grays, based in Tewkesbury, Gloucestershire, with 18 branches. Compton & Ecclestone? 'No, I've never heard of them,' said Shucksmith.

Under its new owners, White and O'Connor, Compton & Ecclestone was to prove no more successful, but its demise led to Ecclestone indulging in sharp practice to deprive the Inland Revenue of almost £10,000. The circumstances were created by the company's trading slump, which caused the owners to put up its property and assets as collateral in order to secure overdraft facilities from Lloyds Bank, which, by January 1960, had reached £25,000. That month Ecclestone, fully aware of the value of the property and its assets, paid off the overdraft in return for the debenture. Less than three months later he appointed a Receiver to close the company down. The Receiver proceeded to freeze the company's assets and to collect money owing to the company totalling £6134. He also discovered that Compton & Ecclestone owed the Inland Revenue, who were preferential creditors, the sum of £9700. At this point Ecclestone embarked on a rather unorthodox strategy in breach of company law.

On 1 June 1961 he discharged the Receiver and instructed him to return all monies and assets to the company. In doing so, he also gave the Receiver a statement indemnifying him against all liabilities. The next day, White and O'Connor, the two sole directors of Compton & Ecclestone, agreed to assign to Ecclestone, in return for the £25,000 now owed to him, the leasehold of the property, their possession of motorcycles and scooters, and the £6134 owing to the company. Ecclestone subsequently disposed of the property and its assets for an unknown sum but for certainly more than £25,000. The Inland Revenue did not receive its due of £9700. The business of Compton & Ecclestone came to an end just one month later. Two of the company's creditors, St Margaret's Trust Ltd and BSA Motor Cycles Ltd, petitioned for the company to be wound up, which took place on 24 July. By which time, of course, the cupboard was bare.

Ecclestone was finally brought to book ten years later when, in December 1971, in the Chancery Division of the High Court, the Inland Revenue sued him and the Receiver for the recovery of the £9700, with interest and costs. Justice Goff, who found against Ecclestone and the Receiver, described the 'machinery' of Ecclestone's dealings with the Receiver and the two directors as 'altogether extraordinary'. Ecclestone declined to appear in court to give an account of his actions. Commented Mr Justice Goff: '...the documents themselves and the admissions made out of court cry out for an explanation ... and [Mr Ecclestone] does not condescend to give one.' Ecclestone strongly refutes the charge of business trickery. It had not been his plan. Had he acted on the advice of tax lawyers? 'Not tax lawyers. Just an accountant, probably.'

It has also been claimed in newspaper articles that some of Ecclestone's early wealth had come from what was described as his 'highly prestigious'[2] car auction company, Mid-Week Auctions, and its sale for a substantial sum to British Car Auctions, the biggest company of its kind in the country, and which in August 1983, with Toyota, went to the rescue of a near-insolvent Lotus with a £6.69-million finance package after Colin Chapman's company was badly hit by the collapse of the fraudulent De Lorean gull-winged sports car project. In fact, this 'highly prestigious' company, which Ecclestone set up in May 1969 on a plot of land he bought in Manor Road, Erith, Kent, was in business for little more than a year, ceasing to trade in June 1970. Nor was it purchased by British Car Auctions.

Looking for an auction site south of the River Thames, the company rented the premises from Ecclestone for a period of about three months before establishing an auction at Brands Hatch. Its then chairman, David Wickins, said: 'We ended up in a legal argument about the state of the premises because they kept falling down. They were tumble-down buildings and one of them fell down in a storm.' There was some doubt in Wickins's mind as to whether Ecclestone had obtained regulatory permission for auctions to be held on the property 'but I wouldn't swear to that. But we certainly didn't buy his company.' His criticism of the structural soundness of the buildings was deemed by Ecclestone to be 'all bollocks. That was the best car auction Wickins ever had, and you can tell him I said so.'

Another tenant whose premises were unable to withstand too much stormy weather was Belmont Mechanical Instruments Ltd, a light-engineering company which Ecclestone's company and the owner of the Brabham team, Motor Racing Developments, began using in 1971 to machine its Formula One and production-car wheels. A sudden afternoon gale brought down a 14-inch thick wall, which sent the desk and chair of a director of the company, Alan Smith, plummeting through the floor. Fortunately, he was not sitting in it at the time, but when he complained to Ecclestone of the damage caused, his landlord, he said, jokingly replied: 'So what's wrong? You're still alive.' Miraculously, no one was hurt. Smith, concerned that talking about the incident might upset Ecclestone, added that the next day his landlord had builders at work repairing the damage 'and he replaced damaged office furniture and equipment'. Ecclestone said of the incident: 'Yeah, but that's the way it goes. We had gales the other day, and didn't walls come down and roofs come off houses?'

His wealth was further increased, according to newspaper claims, by the 'disposal of his businesses, which made him very wealthy indeed'.[3] Ecclestone, in fact, didn't dispose of any of his businesses any more than he ran his businesses down in 1973 in protest at the introduction of VAT, as claimed in a book on successful entrepreneurs.[4] One broadsheet newspaper article stated that at some point he disposed completely, in a single deal, of his garage business but was unable to remember whether it took place in the mid-sixties or mid-seventies, a curious lapse, as the newspaper pointed out, for someone so precise about figures when they come with dollar or percentage signs attached. It might have been due to the fact that he did not dispose of it at all. The extent of his garage business was James Spencer (Bexleyheath) Ltd, which throughout its history recorded a small turnover and losses and, by February 1978, had ceased to trade.

The only company that appeared to reflect the level of profits able to support the lavish lifestyle to which Ecclestone had become accustomed was his hire-purchase company, Arvin Securities, formed in 1961 and based at the James Spencer car showroom premises in Bexleyheath. By 1969 – the earliest records available for the company – it had cash in the bank of £192,000, but even then it appears to have been a cash injection by Ecclestone himself from an unidentified source. The money was withdrawn 12 months later. This was around the time when Ecclestone first began talking to Ron Tauranac about his interest in the Brabham team and the money may have been used for the purchase of Motor Racing Developments Ltd for £100,000 (worth in 2002 about £860,000).

One of Ecclestone's employees at the time – 'the man's a bleedin' genius' – was Ron Smith, described by former associates as a 'minder' but by Smith himself as Ecclestone's 'right-hand man'. Aged 73 when interviewed, a failing memory prevented him from recalling precise details of his work but his duties included repossessing cars purchased with loans from Ecclestone's finance company and 'taking cash' to different people.

There remains Ecclestone's property interests, the most probable source of much of his early wealth. On the evidence of trading figures, it does not appear to have been generated, though, through Pentbridge Properties or Pentbridge Services, which were set up in July 1971 and July 1989 respectively. Pentbridge Properties seemed to do little more than handle Ecclestone's personal properties, the biggest of which deals took place a month after it was formed. Pentbridge Properties went to an offshore tax haven, Rochelle Ltd, based in Guernsey, to borrow £95,000 for the purchase of 26 acres of woodland at the rear of Ecclestone's home in Farnborough Park, a part of which had been the subject of an unsuccessful planning application to the local council for housing development. It was an unusual source of funding. Rochelle Ltd's UK address was given as 25 Harley Street, London, the same as Pentbridge Properties, as well as that of its auditors. By 1980, when Rochelle Ltd went into voluntary liquidation, the loan had still to be repaid.

In 1984 the land was sold by Pentbridge Properties to Centaur Property, a company based in Woolwich, south London, and set up two years earlier by furniture retailer Alan Fernback, a neighbour of Ecclestone's. Pentbridge loaned Centaur Property half of the purchase price of £200,000. Surprisingly, Fernback denied knowing Ecclestone, or having had any dealings with Pentbridge Properties. Yet, in 1978, a property company called Linemoor Ltd was formed with Fernback and Ecclestone as joint directors. Its only trading activity was the loan of £24,900 to Pentbridge Properties in January 1980, which was repaid that July, before Linemoor Ltd was dissolved in 1984. Fernback declined to respond to questions about the company.

The source of Ecclestone's early wealth, in fact, came through shrewd property speculation, which began when he was barely out of his teens and at a time when London, still recovering from the wartime Blitz and when planning regulations were far less stringent, offered rich pickings for property speculators. It was a natural hunting ground for someone of his shrewdness, energy and hunger for money. One of his first deals, he recalls, took place around 1950 – he would have been about 20 – when he bought some industrial premises in Greenwich, south London, the only detail he was able to remember. More memorable, probably because of his passion for motorcycle racing at that time, was his attempt to buy Brands Hatch a year earlier. He had agreed with Joe Francis, a former TT motorcyclist, successful motorcycle dealer with several premises in Kent and principal shareholder in the company which owned the circuit, to buy it for £46,000 (worth about £897,000 in 2002), but the deal fell through at the last minute. All the same, that a 19-year-old was in a position to raise such considerable capital offers a measure of his substance and commercial precocity.

According to Ecclestone's former partner, Frederick Compton, typical of his risk-taking opportunism was an approach in the early fifties to buy the premises of the Strood Motor Company, based in Strood, Kent, and the biggest retail distributors of the British Motor Corporation, the leading UK car manufacturer of its day. Although he didn't have the capital to complete, he was able to raise the money for a deposit to secure first option, which he then sold on at a considerable profit to University Motors, a now defunct company specialising in sports cars, who completed the purchase. 'It was a major property on a plum location,' said Compton, in admiration of Ecclestone's shrewdness, 'but it took a lot of nerve to pull it off.' His nose for a good profit was just as sharp in the acquisition of Jennings, an old-fashioned draper's shop with a huge frontage in Bexleyheath High Street, which he split up into units to make another considerable killing.

Fellow car dealer Jimmy Oliver, from whom Ecclestone bought a number of cars, believed that his young colleague had accumulated considerable wealth by the time he was 24. It was based on a comment made over lunch at the exclusive Poole Yacht Club in Dorset in 1954, after Oliver had quietly pointed out some distinguished fellow diners, including Sir Bernard and Lady Docker, and a couple of millionaire businessmen. Ecclestone, distinctly unimpressed, said Oliver, replied: 'I suppose if you've only got a hundred grand, you'd be regarded as a pauper here.' Whatever the precise state of his wealth at this time, it did not apparently meet with the all-round approval of his family. 'He was thought of as a bit of a "wide boy",' said a relative. 'Money meant a lot to him. Different members of the family said he was a sharp cookie.'

Ecclestone declined to confirm that his early property activities, none of which went through company books – 'It would be me personally doing those deals. I didn't know about companies probably then' – created the foundation of the early wealth, which allowed him to buy the Brabham team. In a style familiar when he chooses not to answer an unwelcome question, he brushed it away with a joke. 'No, I probably stole it. It was probably the Great Train Robbery.' This was a mocking reference to a consistently recycled newspaper rumour that he was involved in the Great Train Robbery, which took place in England in August 1963, when a London-to-Glasgow mail train was robbed of £2.6 million.

It had been planned, it was claimed, by 'an underworld mastermind', which, in more fertile imaginations, implicated Ecclestone – all on the evidence of a brief meeting he had with Roy 'The Weasel' James, a one-time Formula Three driver and the gang member who drove the getaway car. From Parkhurst Prison on the Isle of Wight he wrote a letter dated 6 September 1970 to former world champion Graham Hill, then with Brabham, expressing a desire to return to racing. Hill arranged for James to meet Ecclestone shortly after his release three years later – only to be told that, after 12 years in prison, he had little chance of succeeding. On learning that James was a qualified silversmith, and to help him on his way, Ecclestone commissioned him to make a trophy. It was an act of charity that fired the rumour mill to create a sinister link. Ecclestone's attitude, then and now, was one of total indifference. If people want to think he's Al Capone, so what? What does he care what people think?

Many years later there was another former 'prisoner' Ecclestone was able to help, although a gesture of compassion on this occasion was hardly necessary. In the early nineties it was a regular habit of Ecclestone's to spend an hour or two on a Saturday morning with close friends in a café in London's Mayfair. On this particular occasion Max Mosley joined the number and ordered a cup of coffee. Some five minutes later a waitress returned to the table with a plate weighed down with eggs, sausages, bacon, tomatoes and beans. Mosley explained that he had ordered only a coffee. The waitress said, well, he could have the breakfast anyway. No, said Mosley, he really didn't want it. Yes, said the waitress, he really should. And, not to worry, he wouldn't have to pay for it. Further protestations that he really didn't want it were answered by the waitress smiling amiably and walking away.

It may well have been that by now Ecclestone and his friends were having some difficulty in keeping a straight face. Shortly before Mosley's arrival the café proprietor had been told by Ecclestone that he and his friends would shortly be joined by someone who had just come out of prison. He was down on his luck and without a penny. 'Make sure,' said Ecclestone, 'that he is given a really good breakfast, with all the trimmings.' And there was one other thing – because he was a very proud man, he would probably refuse it. 'Just ignore what he says and make sure he has it, no matter what he says.' Despite the waitress's best efforts, the proud 'old lag' left the breakfast untouched.

The person Tauranac had found sitting at his desk on returning from his Christmas skiing holiday was the dapper figure of Colin Seeley, British motorcycle sidecar champion in 1962 and 1963, and third in the World Championship in 1964 and 1966. Nine months before retiring in June 1967 he set up Colin Seeley Racing Developments, which, with a 27-strong workforce by 1970, specialised in the production of custom-built 350cc and 500cc racing machines and Seeley's version of the single-cylinder Matchless G50 engine, which won the British championship in 1968 and 1969 and was runner-up in 1970 and 1971.

In those days Ecclestone and Seeley, whose factory was based at Belvedere, Kent, not far from Ecclestone's car showrooms in Bexleyheath, had known of each other's business activities for several years, but knew little else about each other. The beginning of their professional relationship came out of a meeting around the end of 1970 when Seeley, in the market for a car, called at the James Spencer showroom and bought a Ford Capri ('As it happens, it was a bloody good car'). A casual acquaintanceship developed which led to Ecclestone, after hearing that tobacco manufacturer, John Player & Co, was keen to move into sponsorship of motorcycle racing, offering his services to Seeley. He suggested that he acted on Seeley's behalf in approaching the tobacco company to negotiate a sponsorship deal. With nothing to lose, Seeley agreed. It turned out that the company was looking, in fact, for a 750cc machine and the sponsorship went to Norton. Seeley, though, was not too disappointed. Given the percentage of the deal Ecclestone had intended to take for himself, he was left wondering whether there would be enough money left to cover his costs. It was Seeley's first insight into Ecclestone's entrepreneurial opportunism. And, to his great regret, it wouldn't be the last.

While Ecclestone was still in the early stages of his negotiations with Tauranac, Seeley received a phone call requesting a meeting. Ecclestone told him of his discussions with Tauranac, of his intention to purchase Motor Racing Developments, and how he believed that Seeley's company and Motor Racing Developments could operate more efficiently and profitably if their skills, machining and equipment were brought together under one roof for both car and motorcycle production. As Seeley clearly understood it, Ecclestone was proposing a merger of the two companies, which, given the financial circumstances Seeley was in at that time, commanded his immediate interest. With frame-design skills which had attracted the business of major foreign racing teams, he was also producing an expensive road motorbike called the Condor – the first model to cost £1000 – for export only, but its future, not to mention the business itself, was being threatened by severe cashflow problems.

As he continued to listen to Ecclestone's ambitious plans, which included a joint managing directorship brass plate over his door, and a purpose-built factory to accommodate the two companies on the land he owned in Manor Road, Erith – where Ecclestone had run Mid-Week Auctions – Seeley became increasingly enthusiastic. The clincher was Ecclestone's proposal to inject the necessary capital into Colin Seeley Racing Developments to resolve its cashflow crisis. Thirty-five-year-old Seeley, an open and affable character, readily agreed, and left the meeting believing that, with Ecclestone's business acumen and financial backing, he was placing the future of a business he had spent six years building in capable and trustworthy hands.

Two weeks after Ecclestone had bought Motor Racing Developments, Seeley became a director of the company and Ecclestone a director of Colin Seeley Racing Developments. On his first day at the Brabham works, Ecclestone, without a word to the redundant Tauranac, took Seeley to the workshop, where, standing on a wooden box, he tersely announced the presence of their new joint managing director and stepped down. Seeley, totally unprepared, was ordered to stand on the box and deliver a few words.

Following Tauranac's departure a few months later, Seeley became responsible for Formula Two, Formula Three and Formula B production cars. Ecclestone used media interest in the amalgamation of the two companies to declare his intention to launch a 'major assault' on Formula One and motorcycle racing. 'Although we are a car-racing stable, we are certainly not neglecting our interests in two-wheel sports,' he said.[5] A priority would be the production of a four-cylinder motorcycle to compete against the best in the World Championship. He added: 'I intend to make a major assault on both the two- and four-wheel arenas next year.' Motor Racing Developments also intended, it was announced, to sponsor bike racers and give financial support to promising private entrants.

Seeley began to regularly work an 18-hour day to oversee both car and motorcycle production, including the transition from tubular space-frame chassis to monocoque construction. His working day began at 6.30 a.m. with a call to his factory in Belvedere, before frequently meeting Ecclestone at his offices in Bexleyheath, from where he would drive across south London to the Brabham works at Byfleet, Surrey, invariably leaving at about 9 p.m. Such was the pressure of meeting production deadlines that it was not unusual for Seeley, a self-taught welder, to find himself working until 2 a.m. in his frame shop at Belvedere, welding a racing-car instrument dash hoop so that it could be coated later that morning to meet a delivery time. Along with the punishing work pressure, which included a short-lived cost-cutting venture of servicing Brabham's Cosworth DFV 3-litre engines, Seeley found himself under ever greater financial strain.

For, as the weeks turned to months, it became increasingly clear that Ecclestone's grand plans of bringing the two companies together under the same roof were not going to materialise. The factory on the site at Erith had been built – Pat Mahoney, a top racer friend of Seeley's, dug the footings for the foundations to save costs – but by then, it seems, Ecclestone had lost interest in production cars, a highly profitable section under Ron Tauranac, because of poor profit margins. Instead, he decided to concentrate his resources on Formula One. It was a decision that sounded the death knell for the much-vaunted merger of Motor Racing Developments and Colin Seeley Racing Developments, and, with it, Seeley's hopes of the necessary capital Ecclestone had promised to pump into his motorcycle production. According to the accounts of Motor Racing Developments, a one-off payment of £4252 was made to Colin Seeley Racing Developments in 1972 – a 'very limited' amount of the agreed funding, said Seeley.

Seeley, who had held great expectations of Ecclestone's plans, was stunned. By now he was in even deeper financial trouble. He had not only been financing his own salary as joint managing director of Motor Racing

Developments Ltd, but, he claims, suffered a serious financial blow when the company failed to pay a considerable sum of money owing for work carried out by Colin Seeley Racing Developments Ltd. In early May 1973, about 17 months after he agreed to the proposed merger that promised so much, Seeley's company, now in dire trouble, was forced into liquidation. It was a bitter blow for someone whose personal reputation was no less respected than the quality of his bikes. The closure of his factory happened at a time when the legendary Barry Sheene, who in 1973 won the British 500 Championship and European 750 Championship on Seeley-Suzukis, was testing the first Seeley monocoque motorcycle with a newly imported Suzuki TR50011 and Seeley's own custom-built magnesium-alloy wheels. The closure of the factory meant the bike's potential was never realised.

Seeley suffered not only the collapse of his company but also the indignity of seeing some expensive machinery, which was auctioned off on the instructions of a Receiver appointed to wind up the company, ending up on the premises of Motor Racing Developments. Defeated and depressed, the placid Seeley made no complaint to Ecclestone about their unfulfilled agreement which had cost him so dearly, financially and professionally. In fact, he continued to do 'jobs' for Ecclestone to bring in some income. But now that he was no longer important to Ecclestone's plans, Seeley noticed a dramatic change in their relationship to the point of offensive indifference. It was typically expressed, he said, by a comment made after he and two mechanics worked on the engine of a BT37 – a revised version of the one-off 1971 'lobster claw' design by Tauranac for Graham Hill – for the 1973 Belgian Grand Prix at Zolder.

The car was for Andreas de Adamich, a young Italian driver, who had brought in some sponsorship money to finance five races. Ecclestone, though, didn't want it to interfere with the preparation of his two lead cars, so he brought Seeley in to get the car ready in time. Oil-pressure problems meant two engine changes on which Seeley worked through the night to emerge from the garage in the early morning sunlight 'covered in oil and absolutely knackered'. At that moment, the immaculately dressed Ecclestone was passing by, and, noting Seeley's dishevelled state, ordered: 'Get yourself cleaned up!' Seeley, still, at least technically, joint managing director, said nothing. His consolation was that de Adamich came in fourth, the Brabham team's best position.

A few months later, after nearly two years with Brabham, during which time he had had been responsible for the production of a total of 105 Formula Two, Formula Three and Formula B production cars, Seeley finally quit. Surprisingly in the circumstances, his decision was prompted not by anything that he had endured, but by Ecclestone's reaction when he asked a favour on behalf of a friend, former Swiss hill-climbing motorcycle champion Ernst Weiss, who was to be hired to drive the Brabham race truck to European events. On arriving in England Weiss's tractor unit broke down. He phoned Seeley requesting the use of one to move his trailer. When Seeley put the request to Ecclestone, he refused. 'That was the last straw,' said Seeley. 'Ernst was a good mate and he needed a bit of help. That really upset me.' The deep disappointment that Seeley felt on his friend's behalf was in keeping with an obliging and good-natured personality that could never be compatible with Ecclestone's.

Reflecting on their business partnership, Seeley, now a wiser 67-year-old, believed he allowed his enthusiasm to cloud his judgement: 'I get into projects and I get enthusiastic. It's always been one of my faults – or advantages, I don't know. When I look back at the hours I worked I must have been totally bonkers. But I was so fit and young and enthusiastic, and it was a tremendous opportunity at the time, with plans for a new factory and all that. I had been running my own business and I knew how to deal with people. I am very good at getting things done. He needed someone like me to get people motivated. It was a hell of a challenge. When Bernie asked me take it on, I didn't falter at all. My attitude was: right, let's go. He knew the [financial] situation I was in, and looking back, because I was so committed to making things work, I was just thinking, "Well, tomorrow Bernie's going to do what he said he was going to do." Then we finally reached a point when he didn't, of course, and then it was all too late.'

Seeley placed so much trust in Ecclestone's commitment to the merger that he agreed to Ecclestone's solicitor drawing up the agreement between them – and even then he failed to insist on receiving a copy. He finally received a copy, he said, following a dispute over a National Insurance stamps bill of £1200 in respect of former employees. Ecclestone was attempting to pass the entire bill over to Seeley, who, without a copy of the agreement, had no proof of Ecclestone's liability as a partner in their joint business activities. For several months, said Seeley, he was told that no such agreement existed, until a copy was inadvertently faxed by a junior to the office of Seeley's solicitor. Ecclestone, said Seeley, then agreed to pay his half of the bill.

Ecclestone's reputation as an ill-tempered taskmaster, he added, caused 'a lot of people to be frightened of him, but I think I was intrigued by him. I was intrigued by how he operated ... it was unbelievable ... you never knew what was going to happen next. You were in awe of him.'

Ecclestone denied that he had owed Seeley or his company any money. 'Anything he was owed he would always have been paid for.' But he admitted it was 'probably true' that the money he was to put into Seeley's business didn't take place. 'Probably that was what the intention was, but when I realised it wasn't going to work like that, I closed it down. He was more full of enthusiasm for the bikes, being a racer ... and he built the motorbike [the first monocoque] at Brabham, actually. It was his baby. I wasn't so enthusiastic about the whole thing. He was going to productionise them but it didn't happen.

'Eventually he went into liquidation. I think he got a bit bitter in the end. Expecting something to happen and it didn't. But it was nothing to do with me that it [Seeley's company] folded. It was already in trouble before. That's why he came to us. He didn't come to me because he had a thriving business. I gave him a job, basically. People like to think of these things differently. But we built the bloody bikes and everything for him. Things that never had been done, with magnesium wheels and things. So it wouldn't be a bad idea to have a rethink about what he's said.'

Once Ecclestone had completed his acquisition of Motor Racing Developments, he began assembling a new team of mechanics. With the headhunting assistance of Herbie Blash, a mechanic at Lotus who began as an apprentice with wealthy private entrant Rob Walker, of the Johnnie Walker whisky company, he brought together four or five mechanics from various teams for a meeting at a hotel in central London. The new boss of Brabham introduced himself and spoke of his ambitious plans. Bob Dance, a young mechanic with Lotus, who agreed to join Brabham as a senior mechanic, was impressed by what he heard: 'He came over as a very sharp fellow.'

Some months later Ecclestone sacked four of the five-man design team. A much earlier, self-imposed casualty was Blash, who had been appointed team manager. Unable to get on with Tauranac, and to the alarm of the mechanics he had recruited, he had quit by lunchtime on his first day. The only survivor of the much-reduced design team was Gordon Murray, a long-haired, 24-year-old South African who had joined Brabham just a couple of years earlier as a draughtsman.

Ecclestone then turned his organisational talents to restructuring the haphazard layout of the works, which offended his acute sense of orderliness. First on his list was the large open-plan production-car workshop, which also accommodated the machine, fabrication, fibre-glass and assembly areas, and the spares store. The sight of men working on different activities in the same area was more than he could stand. It was put right by the unannounced arrival one morning of a bricklayer, a cement mixer, several bags of cement and enough breeze blocks to transform the area into units. Once doors had been fitted, every poster and non-essential decoration that had adorned the grime-stained walls for years was removed. Along with the woodwork, the walls and ceiling were all painted white. A white surface, said Ecclestone, was easier to keep clean.

To ensure the mechanics clearly understood the discipline of the new order, he marched into the workshop one evening to announce that that night all toolboxes would be emptied, painted dark blue and kept at precise areas of the bench, which he would mark out. 'Anybody got a problem with that?' he asked sharply of his silent audience, before marching out. He also disliked the habit of mechanics casually leaning on a hatch counter in the motor vehicle spares store while waiting for a part. He forced a change of posture by having the hatch lowered to a level that made it impossible to lean on.

However, the sight of the haphazard movement of human traffic constantly criss-crossing between the company offices, the production-car workshop and, on the other side of a narrow gravel roadway, the Formula One workshop, called for more radical action. Ecclestone issued instructions for the two doors at the front of the production-car workshop to be bricked up and replaced by one door at the rear. A high wire-mesh fence was then constructed along the frontage of the workshop and just beyond the adjacent company offices, around which employees would have to walk in order to cross the roadway. It succeeded in creating an orderly single-line flow between all three buildings.

Ecclestone's keen preference for the colour white manifested itself in the most obvious canvas of all – the Brabham cars, which were immediately repainted from racing green to virgin white. When he clinched his first major sponsorship deal with Martini Rossi in 1975, after the success of Carlos Reutemann's three Grand Prix wins the previous season, his pleasure was diminished by the sight of the Brabham cars in the company's eye-catching but garish red livery stripes. The team's race transporter, an articulated lorry formerly used by Trusthouse Forte as a training vehicle and the first of its kind in Formula One, was also painted white. Its conversion was carried out by mechanics Bob Dance and Gary Anderson, who went on to become chief designer at Jordan. A third trailer even had its own plush hospitality unit, another first. It was also the scene of an angry outburst by Ecclestone when he spotted a trumpet and injector on the sink in the eating compartment, which, moments later, he hurled out of the trailer.

But for all Ecclestone's aggressive and obsessive style of management, with all the tension it caused, there were some who could understand the need for changes in working practices. Nick Goozée, who left Brabham in 1974 to join Penske Cars in Poole, Dorset, where he later became managing director, said: 'We found some of the changes, which were introduced quickly, a little over the top, but, in fact, we were not an efficient company. We were very basic in some of our methods, which had been fine in the sixties and seventies, but once Bernie bought Brabham change was both inevitable and necessary.'

The two-car Brabham team, run in those days on a budget of £100,000 a year, was no more than seven strong and the Formula One workshop was virtually open all hours. Herbie Blash, who rejoined Brabham as team manager for the start of the 1973 season, said: 'You had to be a workaholic or crazy. You had to dedicate your life to the team. But you would give your right arm to work for a Formula One team, so basically you were working for very little and you were working night and day.' Blash, though, became one of Ecclestone's keenest fans, applauding not only his business acumen but also what he described as his 'compassion'.

'Bernie's a very caring person. Only the people who have been looked after by Bernie realise that he is a very caring person. An example is Jochen Rindt. When Jochen was killed, Colin Chapman [the Lotus team boss] just left Italy immediately, and it was left to Bernie to sort everything out.' And when, he pointed out, Frank Williams had his car accident in 1986 on his way to Nice Airport after a Nigel Mansell testing session at the Paul Ricard circuit, which would leave him a paraplegic, it was 'Bernie who arranged the flight home. If anybody ever suffered in any way, he always ensured they had the very best treatment available.' Ecclestone is also blessed, added Blash, with a lightning-fast brain. 'He has this natural ability to calculate complex sets of numbers and percentages in amazingly quick times. At a business meeting he would leave people for dead.'

But, in the Brabham factory, while men like Blash and Goozée could understand the need to adopt new working practices, there was general alarm caused by Ecclestone's mood swings. The good days for staff and mechanics were those that he spent at the premises of his car showroom in Bexleyheath, from where he controlled his various business interests. Senior mechanic Bob Dance said: 'You could never be sure whether he'd be in a good mood or a bad mood, when he could be pretty unpleasant.' Apparently, mud splashes on his car as he drove along the unmade gravel road leading up to the works, or the sight of an office door left open, would be enough to ignite his hair-trigger temper. 'I once saw him throw a phone across the room because it rang during a meeting,' said Dance.

Colin Seeley was also stunned by Ecclestone's sudden outbursts. Displeased for some reason with bodywork being fitted to a prototype of the BT38, Brabham's first production-car monocoque, Ecclestone expressed his anger in an extremely direct manner. 'He stamped all over the bodywork, breaking it up,' said Seeley. On a later occasion Ecclestone arrived in the production workshop to find a cleaner using a pay telephone. The call came to a sudden end when Ecclestone ripped the phone off the wall. 'It was frightening to see him in that state,' said Seeley.

Another new boy to enter the Brabham crucible was Keith Greene, aged 33, a former Formula One driver whose modest five-year career between 1958 and 1962 was funded by his father's company, Gilby Engineering. He was appointed team manager responsible for looking after the cars of Graham Hill, Carlos Reutemann and Wilson Fittipaldi. Greene, a Formula One competitions manager who had enjoyed considerable touring car championship success with Alan Mann Racing, was approached for the job by Ecclestone soon after he bought Motor Racing Developments. But he too would soon feel the lash of his dictatorial boss's tongue.

At a meeting with Ecclestone and the drivers, one of whom was complaining that his car was not getting as much attention as he felt it should, Greene, who had been under a lot of pressure from a heavy workload of long days and weekends, uncharacteristically flared up. Ecclestone turned on him and snapped: 'Shut up – or piss off.' It was a humiliatingly public rebuff to Greene, but, in need of the job, he decided to shut up.

But for all Ecclestone's bellicosity, Greene became a firm admirer. 'Yes, he was extremely hard, but also extremely clever. He is extraordinary, make no mistake about that. In the business world, he is a genius. A part of that asset, which is obviously God-given, is a fantastic retentive brain. He remembers every detail. He'll remember if a mechanic stole a nut and bolt 20 years ago, so you had to be sharp to keep up with him. He could call you up at any time during the night – he used to have about four hours' sleep a night – and whatever it was you had to have the answers. He wasn't interested in excuses.'

Greene even came to admire Ecclestone's no-nonsense style of decision-making. Recalling the Argentine Grand Prix in 1972, when there was some friction between Graham Hill and the Argentinian Carlos Reutemann over their engines, Ecclestone summoned Greene and asked for the list of engine numbers. 'Bernie said: "Right, I'm not having any more arguments with these drivers. What we are going to do now is decide their engines for the year, OK?" So he got the drivers to alternately call out heads or tails while he flipped a coin and that decided who would have which engines for the year. Once the "draw" had finished, he said: "I don't want to hear any more about engines", and he was gone.' And, confirmed Bob Dance, there were no further complaints.

However, the level of pressure – 'you felt all the time that you were totally his' – through working more than 100 hours a week caused Greene to quit after just 12 months, following a request for a salary increase. Responsible for transport, running the Formula One workshop, engineering one or more of the cars, liaising between Murray, the drivers and the chief mechanic, taking care of job sheets for the cars, and even the team's limited public-relations efforts, Greene asked Ecclestone for an extra £10 a week. He had, he said, difficulty in even eliciting a response. 'I spent several weeks walking down the drive by the side of his Merc asking for that tenner, which wasn't even a packet of fags to Bernie, and he kept saying, "Yeah, yeah, I'll think about it." But he spent a bit too long thinking about it and I was out of there.'

As the owner of the Brabham team, Ecclestone took up his seat within the Formula One Constructors' Association (F1CA), an organisation set up to represent the interests of the team owners, a disparate and querulous bunch of maverick characters, among whom he would have felt immediately at home. It was the base on which King Bernie would set his throne, and from which would flow Croesian riches that even he couldn't have imagined.

4

THE 'GARAGISTES' TAKE ON THE FIA 'GRANDIS'

Until 1957, when Vanwall, with Stirling Moss and Tony Brooks sharing the car, became the first British team to win a championship round by winning the British Grand Prix at Aintree, Formula One had been the almost exclusive domain of the continental manufacturers, such as Ferrari, Maserati, Alfa Romeo and Mercedes-Benz, whose road-car production financed their race programmes. During the late forties and fifties they dominated the formula introduced in 1946 by the Commission Sportive Internationale (CSI), a body set up to represent the motor sport interests of the Fédération Internationale de l'Automobile (FIA), formerly the Association Internationale des Automobile Clubs Reconnus, which had been responsible for reviving Grand Prix racing at the Bois de Boulogne circuit, Paris, on 9 September 1945.

Formula One proved so successful that the FIA followed the lead of the Fédération Internationale Motocycliste, which in 1949 had launched the first motorcycle World Championship – and on 13 May 1950 the first round of the Formula One World Championship series took place with the British Grand Prix at Silverstone, a former military bomber base in Northamptonshire, where 21 cars lined up on the grid. In perfect weather and in the presence of King George VI and Queen Elizabeth, the late Queen Mother, 100,000 spectators watched 43-year-old Italian Nino Farina enter the archives as the winner of the first Formula One World Championship. Driving an Alfa Romeo 158, he completed the 70 laps in 2 hours 13 minutes and 23.6 seconds. Briton Leslie Johnson found his own place in the archives – as the first driver to retire in a Grand Prix, when the supercharger on his E-type ERA packed up during the second lap. Despite the World Championship title, it was very much a European affair, with Britain, Monaco, Switzerland, Belgium and France hosting the rounds. The organisers included a US Grand Prix, which was, in fact, the Indy 500 race at Indianapolis, in a token attempt to 'globalise' the series, until it was dropped from the calendar in 1960.

These were the legend-making days of five-times world champion Juan Fangio, Alberto Ascari and Farina, who ended the 1950 season by becoming the first Formula One world champion; of the gentlemanly blazer-and-flannels brigade to whom the talk of money was unseemly; of the likes of amateur driver Eric Thompson, a Lloyds marine insurance broker, who drove in a ski jacket and trousers tucked into his socks, and was paid £82 2s 2d, which included bonuses from Esso and Dunlop, for coming fifth in a Connaught in the 1955 British Grand Prix; of the grass paddocks at Goodwood, where, for five shillings, the public could stand next to their demigods and machines; of 'privateers' of inherited or self-made wealth who, in lower formulae, financed drivers in 20-lap races at Goodwood, Silverstone, Snetterton, Crystal Palace and Charterhall; and of the majestic Stirling Moss, whose gross earnings, as the world's highest-paid driver in 1961, totalled £32,700. But such innocent, halycon days were even then numbered by the rapid progress of events that would take place over the next decade or two.

By the end of the fifties, the supremacy of the manufacturers, whose successes had bred a complacency which would leave them fatally vulnerable, was no longer taken for granted. But the real challenge came not from Vanwall, who in 1958 won the inaugural Constructors' Championship, or the other British competitors at that time, British Racing Motors (BRM) and Connaught Engineering, relatively wealthy entrants who followed the manufacturers' standard front-engine design. It came from the garage in Surbiton, Surrey, of father and son Charles and John Cooper, who constructed Formula Three cars around chain-drive 500cc engines and off-the-shelf components from gearboxes to suspension parts, which, in austere, post-war Britain, gave the less well-off an entry into car racing.

The first Formula One Cooper car, the T20, made its debut in the 1952 Swiss Grand Prix with a 2-litre Bristol engine, but it wasn't until the Argentine Grand Prix in 1958 that the Coopers' single-seater bob-tailed Formula Three car, with a twin-cam Climax engine situated at the rear, made its stunning debut. Driven by Stirling Moss and built for the aristocratic Rob Walker – he gave his occupation as 'gentleman' on his passport – it was probably viewed by the manufacturers with amused curiosity. If so, they would not be amused for long.

With less frontal area and the driver much lower in the cockpit, the nimbler car proved lighter and faster than the more powerful 2.5-litre Ferraris and Maseratis as Moss left them in his slipstream to take the chequered flag. It was the beginning of a revolutionary development in the design and construction of Formula One cars.

The 1958 season was significant for two other reasons. Firstly, it heralded the arrival, at the Monaco Grand Prix, of Colin Chapman's Team Lotus. It was Chapman's creative genius that developed and refined the rear-engine Cooper concept, introduced the monocoque chassis, experimented with aerodynamic wings and, perhaps most far-reaching of all, defied the establishment to embrace major commercial sponsorship. Secondly, it confirmed the arrival of a new wave of driving talent led by the British. Mike Hawthorn became the first British world champion, with Stirling Moss, Tony Brooks, Roy Salvadori and Peter Collins occupying the next four slots in the 1958 World Championship series. Britain was supplying the men as well as the machines. About to add their weight to the ranks of the constructors were the likes of Jack Brabham, who left Cooper to set up his own team with Ron Tauranac in 1962, New Zealander Bruce McLaren, who also quit Cooper to form his own team in 1966 and, in 1967, former Formula Three mechanic and driver Frank Williams, who would receive a knighthood in 1999 for his services to motor sport. All, in their own unique ways, would soon grace the Formula One stage.

At the 1967 Dutch Grand Prix, another historic day in new technology took place, when the design skills of Chapman's Team Lotus and Keith Duckworth's Ford Cosworth DFV 3-litre V8 engine produced the Lotus 49 driven by Jim Clark, who, until his tragic death, was considered the greatest driver of the sixties. He crossed the finishing line 23.8 seconds ahead of Jack Brabham in the Repco V8-powered Brabham BT19. The Cosworth, on its first outing, would soon establish itself as the most radical engine since the Coventry Climax, eliminating all opposition until the emergence of turbocharged engines brought about the Cosworth V8's final victory – the last of an astonishing 155 wins – in 1983. The sixties had begun with 1.5-litre engines developing 160bhp and standard narrow tyres, and ended with the Cosworth V8 developing close to 440bhp and new tyre technology producing increasingly wider tyres.

In addition to Chapman's pioneering contributions, the decade also saw the introduction of transistorised ignition and fuel injection. To the haughty and imperial Enzo Ferrari, known as 'Il Commendatore', the constructors were mere parvenus playing around with car kits, whom he had mockingly described as 'garagistes'. All the same, while Ferrari and the continental manufacturers had been the driving force of the past, the 'garagistes', whose number in 1970 was further increased by the arrival of new kids on the grid – the Tyrrell Racing Organisation, Team Surtees and March Engineering – were the driving force of the future. And, unlike Ferrari, and the other manufacturers, they had to cope with constant financial pressures in the days when sponsorship meant little more than free oil and tyres, and then only for the more successful.

A substantial part of the constructors' income came from the production of custom-built cars for the specialist commercial market, plus 'start' money paid by the Grands Prix organisers or promoters, but even this would depend on their judgement of a team's public appeal. For the likes of Ferrari and Lotus, whose epic clashes attracted audiences in their tens of thousands, it was never an issue: organisers were happy to pay them a large part of their 'start' money budget, leaving the crumbs for the smaller teams. Only the likes of Rob Walker, who had the crowd-pulling skills of Stirling Moss, were able to negotiate more than a few hundred pounds. The organisers held the whip hand, particularly at prestigious Grands Prix such as the Italian or Monaco, the biggest event in the racing calendar, and which, they well knew, a team couldn't afford to miss if it wanted to make its name. It was a desperate state of affairs for teams way down the grid – and a grossly unfair one. In the fifties, perhaps eight to ten cars were regular competitors. Now, in the early seventies, there were as many as 25, most of them living off overdrafts and the Micawberesque hopes of tomorrow.

The presence of the 'garagistes' greatly increased the number of spectators, which, in turn, substantially increased the organisers' profits. But the constructors saw little of it. On occasion they saw none at all. It was not unknown, for example, for an organiser to claim that the race hadn't attracted the anticipated number of spectators, smartly adding that it was therefore not possible to pay the agreed 'start' money. Even a team such as Lotus was not immune from this ploy. At the end of one Italian Grand Prix two heavies physically removed team manager Andrew Ferguson from the organiser's office after he had been refused payment of the agreed fee. Such dubious ethics, though, were not always one-sided: some teams entered a no-hope second or even third car purely for the 'start' money, knowing full well that they would do well to complete a lap.

It was these uncertain days that gave birth to what over the next two decades would become the most powerful force in Formula One – the Formula One Constructors' Association (F1CA). It was modelled on the Formula 2 Association, which was formed in late 1963 to represent the interests of English constructors Lotus, Brabham and Cooper, who had agreed to compete the following year in the Grands Prix de France, a series of Formula Two races organised by the French motor-sports body, the Fédération Française du Sport Automobile (FFSA), to take place at Pau, Reims, Rouen, Clermont-Ferrand and Albi. It worked sufficiently well to prompt the constructors to form a similar association for Formula One, which, for reasons related to personalities, did not include in those days Louis Stanley's BRM or Enzo Ferrari's team, the former being considered too domineering and the latter too disdainful. Its administration was carried out by Ferguson, who, at Colin Chapman's invitation, agreed to look after its affairs in return for an annual fee of £15 per team. Two years later, in 1966, it was being run from Ferguson's home, a cottage adjoining Chapman's splendid Carleton Manor, at East Carleton, Norwich.

In these more placid days the F1CA did little more than oversee the co-ordination of transportation costs, particularly to transcontinental Grands Prix. It was a benign, low-key and loosely grouped organisation of no serious political intent, but events across the English Channel were soon to change its disposition. The catalyst was a long-simmering domestic power battle between the FFSA and the French motoring organization, the Automobile Club de France (ACF), which prevented British drivers from competing in France and French drivers from competing outside of France. Without formal association with the Fédération Internationale de l'Automobile (FIA), the F1CA could only look on impotently from the sidelines. It led to a meeting at a London hotel on 4 December 1967 between the F1CA, the British Grand Prix Drivers Association (BGPDA), represented by Swedish driver Joakim Bonnier, and the Commission Sportive Internationale (CSI), which governed motor sport on behalf of the FIA.

Its purpose was to strengthen the links between the CSI and constructors and drivers, but primarily with the F1CA, which wanted a voice within the FIA's decision-making bureaucracy. The best it got was an agreement that regular meetings would take place between the CSI and the F1CA to discuss matters affecting the constructors and drivers. Nevertheless, the constructors had taken their first step in the political arena, albeit one that remained dominated by the self-important aristos of the French and German motor clubs. It was a stage made for the brash, aggressive and ego-pricking style of Ecclestone, who, in 1972, as the self-made millionaire boss of the Brabham team, arrived on the grid in time for the first serious clash with organisers keen to keep the 'kit-car' constructors in their place.

The issue was the number of cars on the grid and the clash was with the powerful Automobile Club de Monaco (ACM), the organisers of the Monaco Grand Prix and the Monte Carlo Rally. The club insisted there should be no more than 16 starters on the grid, although the previous year the number had been increased to 18 after forceful representation by the teams. The following season, at the Spanish Grand Prix, Ecclestone and Max Mosley, a principal of the March team who would become Ecclestone's closest ally in the turbulent years to come, had a meeting in a Madrid hotel to persuade the newly appointed president of the club – a young, bright lawyer called Michel Boeri – to agree a limit of 26. It ended with Boeri acknowledging that there was no rational reason for the number to be limited to 16 and that the Monaco Grand Prix, just two weeks away, would run with 26 cars.

However, the teams arrived in Monaco to discover that senior officials of the ACM would agree to 22 cars but not as many as 26. It was a political salvo, fully supported, it was suspected, by the FIA, intended to let the constructors know that it was the organisers who called the shots. A hurried meeting of the teams decided that it would be 26 cars or none, and the message was relayed to senior club officials by the French-speaking Mosley. The unity was such that even the French team, Matra, stood solid with the constructors. But the ACM hardened the stand-off by deciding to impound the constructors'cars. The gates to an underground garage, where the teams' cars had been parked, were locked, and guarded by several police officers to ensure that they remained so.

As the spectators began to fill the streets and the time for the practice sessions neared, the constructors responded by refusing to take part. Eventually, Boeri arrived to reassure them that if they went ahead with the sessions, the number would be sorted out. No deal, said Ecclestone. The number first, then the practice sessions. Boeri argued that it was necessary for the FIA representative to sign the document endorsing 26 cars and that he couldn't be found. No signature, no cars, said Ecclestone. Within half an hour the paper had been signed and the cars were on their way to the first practice session – but not before Ecclestone, in the cockpit of a Brabham being pushed by mechanics, managed to drive over the foot of a policeman. The race, won by Frenchman Jean-Pierre Beltoise in a BRM, started with 25 cars on the grid.

The constructors, with Ecclestone at the centre of the ring, had begun to flex their muscles.

The first F1CA meeting Ecclestone attended was held in a double bedroom at the Excelsior hotel – its budget couldn't run to a suite in those days – near London's Heathrow Airport, a location mutually convenient to the constructors and continental teams. His attitude appeared to be one of extraordinary deference towards his colleagues from McLaren, Lotus, Ferrari, BRM, Tyrrell, Surtees, Williams, Matra and March. Frenchman Gérard 'Jabby' Crombac, a motor sport magazine editor and a technical adviser to Matra, who attended the meeting as its representative, recalled that Ecclestone kept a low profile, claiming that he was simply happy to listen 'because you are all so much more experienced than me', a statement of astonishing humility for someone who believed he was inferior to no man. No less surreal is the imagery created by Crombac's claim that Ecclestone's sole contribution to the proceedings was a willingness to pour the tea. Crombac's opinion in later years was that this was merely an example of Ecclestone's sardonic wit.

They were soon to see an example of his entrepreneurial flair, which, even though Ecclestone himself couldn't have been aware of it at the time, would prove to be his first step in exploiting the commercial potential of Formula One. There are at least two accounts of the way in which it came about. According to Brabham team manager Keith Greene, it was born of the constructors' frustration at the way Andrew Ferguson had been negotiating the costs of the overseas transportation arrangements. For personal reasons, he was also pressing hard for the F1CA office to be transferred to Switzerland, a less than popular proposal as the overwhelming majority of the teams were based in England.

Ecclestone recognised the opportunity to usurp Ferguson – and seized it at an F1CA meeting held during the 1972 South African Grand Prix at Kyalami. When the agenda came to any other business, Ecclestone, said Greene, walked round the table and placed a sealed envelope before each team boss. 'Bernie told them to take five and read what was inside.' What they read immediately attracted their interest. Ecclestone had calculated how much he could save each team on overseas transportation costs, especially long-haul trips – 'I think it was £4500 per car on every long-haul trip' – through a package deal he had negotiated with a freight transport company, and which of course included a profit for himself.

The teams, most of whom were living hand to mouth, accepted his proposal without hesitation. It was agreed that, by way of payment for his services, he would receive two per cent of the prize fund – in the early seventies it was in the region of no more than £40,000 – that he would negotiate on their behalf with the organisers. The commission, suggested by Max Mosley, was attractive to the teams on the grounds that as they didn't know what they were going to get, they wouldn't miss it. Besides, there was no money in the F1CA's coffers to remunerate him in any other way. Its only income was a subscription fee that was rarely paid on time, putting the organisation's finances in a general state of uncertainty. The commission – later increased to four and then eight per cent – would come to represent a substantial sum as Ecclestone the shrewd negotiator proceeded to persuade the organisers to agree contractual terms ever more favourable to the teams. By the time the constructors had left the Kyalami Ranch hotel, which, incidentally, Ecclestone would reportedly buy in 1978 for an undisclosed sum, he had the constructors' full support, said Greene.

The second account came from John Surtees, who survived in Formula One for eight years, until 1978, before a costly legal battle with a main sponsor forced him to close down his team. Ecclestone, said Surtees, believed that he could do better than Ferguson in negotiating more profitable 'start' and prize-purse deals with the organisers. At an F1CA meeting, 'Bernard stood up and said, "One moment, this is going nowhere. I will better your lot. I will guarantee a better deal [with the organisers]." He actually quoted a figure he would go for, out of which he would take a certain percentage. That was it. From that moment, Bernie represented the constructors.'

Whatever the accurate record, Ferguson's role as the F1CA's secretary came to an end. He was sacked and replaced by Ecclestone's nomination, a former RAF officer and manager of the Red Arrows flying team, Peter Macintosh – nicknamed 'Overcoat' by Ecclestone – who, although without any experience of motor racing, was employed for his administrative ability. Ecclestone then set about putting into operation his package-deal proposal, with London-based freight transport company Cazaly Mills & Co, from whom he received a lucrative percentage of the F1CA business. He went on to buy the company and then dispose of it, claiming the company had too many internal problems. He took with him one of the company's key personnel, Alan Woollard, who would play an executive role in the setting up of FOCA World Travel, through which Ecclestone organised chartered air travel and hotel accommodation, a highly lucrative new market which it monopolised without threat. Ecclestone's method of pricing other costs, though, left at least one team manager somewhat bewildered.

During the late seventies McLaren's team manager, Alistair Caldwell, notified the rest of the teams that he was organising a week's test session at Kyalami. The cost of hiring the track for the week was £1000, plus £200 per day for the marshals. As was his usual practice, he informed the teams of the booking and invited them to take part to spread the costs. But Teddy Mayer, who owned McLaren with Tyler Alexander, and the other team bosses were, said Caldwell, persuaded by Ecclestone to go along with the package deal that he was pulling together.

During the week at Kyalami, a senior member of the Brabham team informed Caldwell of McLaren's share of the bill. The cost per car was $6000. 'When I asked him what it was for, he said it was for the hire of the track and the marshals. I told him to piss off. I knew how much it had cost, because I had rented the circuit, and it cost £1000 for the whole week, plus £200 a day for the marshals. We refused to pay what Ecclestone was asking, because we had already paid the bill. I told them [the other team managers] but they wouldn't listen. They still paid up. They never asked [Ecclestone]. That was Bernie.' With at least 20 cars at the test session, it meant, based on Caldwell's figures, a potential profit of $120,000. Ecclestone scathingly rejected Caldwell's claims. 'Why would I ask [for the money] if he had already paid the bill? A potential profit of $120,000? That is all shit. Without any possible shadow of doubt.'

The constructors were delighted that Ecclestone had the time and enthusiasm to represent their interests. Peter Warr, manager of Team Lotus, commented: 'If someone had asked me to go and negotiate with 12 or 14 different race organisers and run Team Lotus, I would have said forget it. And that was the same for everybody else.' But Ecclestone was a businessman first and a racer second. Cutting deals was no burden to him, more the very elixir of life.

He hadn't been long in his new role when the F1CA managed to obtain a copy of an FIA balance sheet, which showed their calendar fees – in those days it would have been in the order of £2000 to £3000 – but, far more alarmingly, just how much the organisers were making out of individual deals with the teams, each of whom had been told during negotiations that it was in their best interests to keep the details confidential. The constructors were incensed by the level of profits enjoyed by the FIA and the organisers compared to their rewards. Said a former team boss: 'When everyone saw what everyone was getting, how much the organisers were getting and how much the FIA was taking, the teams turned round and said: "Hang on a second, who is this being run for?" When ... it was discovered that a very small part went to them, they said: "Oi, oi!"' Newcomers such as John Surtees were particularly angry, claiming that they were being forced to meet much of their costs out of other business activities. Even Ecclestone complained that he was financing Brabham out of his own pocket to the tune of £80,000 per year.

During mid-1972 Ecclestone began a series of meetings with organisers to negotiate a massive increase in the prize purse, which since the mid-sixties had stood at about £5400 a race (paid in Swiss francs, which was considered to be the most stable currency at the time). He not only wanted it increased to £88,000 a race but also for the F1CA to be responsible for its distribution. Similarly, he wanted the F1CA to have control of the 'start' money to ensure more equitable distribution. Much alarmed, the organisers turned for rescue to the FIA's Commission Sportive Internationale (CSI), which led that November to the formation of an organisation called Grand Prix International (GPI) and the emergence of a negotiating triumvirate headed by Dutchman Henri Treu. It was the brief of Treu and his two colleagues – Martin Pfundner and Herman Schmitz – to negotiate on behalf of the organisers in the heroic hope of persuading Ecclestone to agree to more acceptable fees.

Commentators at the time believed, in fact, that the combined authority of the organisers, under Treu's leadership, would prove too great for the indolent 'garagistes'. A key figure, it was forecast, would be Enzo Ferrari, who allegedly had always been indifferent about joining the F1CA. Once he sided with the organisers, the constructors' new-found militancy would soon crumble. The organisers also believed they had in Treu the right man to take on Ecclestone. He was something of a maverick character himself, whose tendency to make decisions without going through the bureaucratic channels had led to his dismissal from the CSI six months earlier.

Others were inclined to another view, predicting that what the organisers saw as a strength would prove a serious weakness. An executive of a major sponsor described Treu as being 'too radical, too confrontational. His attitude was "we'll teach these constructors a lesson." With someone like Ecclestone that attitude simply won't work.' Sure enough, Ecclestone found Treu's autocratic style so grating that it was not long before he was refusing to negotiate with him and his colleagues, who, incidentally, had a practice of passing notes to one another. Rather carelessly, they would be thrown in a wastepaper basket at the end of each meeting, only to be retrieved later by Ecclestone. Unwisely, the Dutchman attempted to circumvent Ecclestone by approaching the constructors individually with offers based on their crowd-pulling appeal. With the constructors now very much aware of their strength in unity, it was a ploy doomed to fail. Treu then attempted a no less desperate tactic. He tried to broaden the arena of conflict by getting the CSI to introduce a new rule that would allow Formula Two and Formula 5000 cars to race in Formula One.

The Royal Automobile Club (RAC), the organisers of the British Grand Prix – then known as the John Player Grand Prix – agreed, at the CSI's behest, to announce the introduction of the new rule. It was hoped that, coming from such an influential body in their own country, it would have a measure of authority that would cause the constructors to rethink their position. Accordingly, the RAC issued a statement declaring that a clause had been inserted in the supplementary regulations to the 1973 Grand Prix: the purse would be £55,000, unless 'another sum' was agreed the next day. To pressure the constructors into accepting the purse, the clause added that, in order to be entitled to any financial benefit, entry forms also had to be received by the next day. The race, it was declared, would be open to all 'single-seat racing cars complying with the coachwork and safety requirements prescribed for Formula One as may be agreed by the CSI to allow Formula Two and Formula 5000 cars to race if the Formula One quota of entrants fell short'.[1] The F1CA's response was indifferently defiant. If it happened, said Ecclestone, the race couldn't be called a round of the World Championship series, so the constructors wouldn't want to take part anyway. He then hit back with a warning from the constructors that unless organisers agreed to the F1CA's financial terms, the CSI should not agree to sanction Grand Prix races.

Around the same time, Treu stepped up the propaganda campaign by enlisting the support of Graham Hill, world champion in 1962 and 1968, who, considered to be way past his best, was in his last season at Brabham. At the annual dinner and dance of Silverstone's British Racing Drivers' Club the previous November, Treu suggested to Hill that he should race under his own name. It seemed an unlikely prospect. Who would agree to bankroll such a team? Nevertheless, by the following March, Hill had secured a three-year £100,000 contract with tobacco manufacturers W. D. & H. O. Wills. The previous month it was announced that he had become the first entrant to agree terms with GPI, and that he had been retained as a roving ambassador to promote its aims. It was believed that, in return for Hill's public support, Treu had used CSI influence to help bring off the highly lucrative deal with Wills.

Ecclestone was so angered by the alliance that it was believed he had tried to sabotage Hill's plans by offering provisional F1CA membership to AVS if the company refused to sell Hill a car. It was an attractive offer: membership of the F1CA and entitlement to its collective transportation benefits was normally not considered until a team had been racing for a season to ensure it had the necessary financial backing and commitment. But AVS declined the offer, and Hill made his debut as team boss and driver in an Embassy-backed AVS Shadow in the Spanish Grand Prix in April, which he failed to finish due to a problem with the brakes. It set the scene for much of the rest of the season, with his Tony Southgate-designed car suffering a series of minor faults and more seriously, chassis failure. He switched to a Lola for the 1974 season, which, with just two points, he ended by finishing eighteenth in the World Championship title race. Hill, one of the front-rank racers of the sixties and whose five wins at the Monaco Grand Prix with BRM and Lotus ensured his place in Formula One history, died on 29 November 1975, when a light aircraft he was piloting crashed in fog.

By now, the confrontation between the F1CA and Grand Prix International had become sufficiently hostile to cause Philip Morris Europe, the manufacturers of Marlboro cigarettes, and Formula One's biggest sponsor, to publicly express its concerns. At a lavish function in Geneva in January 1973 to announce the teams and drivers to run under the Marlboro banner, rugby-loving Englishman Ronnie Thomson, the company's president of Europe, Middle East and Africa, said that motor racing 'must take a long hard look at itself. It must become more professional and start to behave with the responsibility that its size and public interest dictate. It must work for the ultimate interest of the spectator, teams and drivers. Ultimately, their interests are the same as our own.'[2] This comment was interpreted as a criticism of both the semi-professional attitude of the FIA hierarchy and the threatening approach of the F1CA, which, through Ecclestone's aggressive efforts, was beginning to gain the upper hand. One by one the organisers made individual agreements with the F1CA, and the 17-race calendar for the 1973 season was secured on Ecclestone's terms. Such was the establishment snobbery at the RAC that it refused to concede defeat to Ecclestone personally. Mosley, more their cup of tea, received a phone call from one of the senior negotiating figures informing him that, while the committee was quite prepared to agree to the F1CA's terms and to do so with him, it was not willing to do so with Ecclestone, someone they continued to view as a loud and disagreeable second-hand-car dealer.

GPI, and the Treu triumvirate, faded from the Formula One scene as the average purse agreed with the organisers increased to about £68,000, although it rose as high as £110,000 in South Africa, Brazil and Argentina due to long-haul costs. Its distribution, now transferred to the F1CA, had been based on 20 per cent being awarded on the qualifying results and 80 per cent according to race results, with the winning driver getting the major share. However, the F1CA replaced it with an arcane system designed to ensure fairer distribution, the details of which the constructors refused to reveal for many years, although, given its complexity, one wonders why they bothered.

Thirty-five per cent of the prize money was paid out on the previous season, and was divided into two sums – 17.5 per cent being divided equally among the top ten teams in the two previous half-seasons. In the first half-season it was based on the results of the previous season, and, in the second half of the season, it was based on the last half of the previous season and the first half of the present season. A further 17.5 per cent was also divided among the top ten teams, but in proportion to the number of points scored in the two half-seasons. Twenty per cent was paid out on the grid places of the first 20 cars, decreasing from two per cent for pole position down to 0.4 per cent for the last position. The remaining 45 per cent was distributed according to current race results, and it was paid out on the position of cars at quarter, half, three-quarters and full distance. One twelfth was paid out at quarter-distance, another twelfth at half, another twelfth at three-quarter and the remaining three-quarters of the 45 per cent on the end results. It was structured to reward previous performance and grid positions, and to compensate cars leading the race but failing to finish.

The F1CA's victory in its clash with the organisers and, consequently, the CSI, marked an important stage in the evolution of its political status. What had once been a necessity for the constructors – 'start' money and the size of the prize purse – had now become a qualification for the organisers. But while it signalled a shift in power in favour of the constructors, a consequence was to prove detrimental to the well-being of the independent teams, those privately funded or outside the protection of the F1CA, which had already been accused of operating a 'closed shop' policy.

In 1974, beginning with Monaco, the organisers, after consulting with the F1CA, decided to reduce the number of entries, a decision whose consequence fell exclusively on the independents. The organisers claimed that it was taking place in the interests of safety, while others believed it had more to do with organisers wanting to claw back some of the increased prize money by reducing the 'start' payments bill. That was certainly a benefit for the organisers but the principal beneficiary was the F1CA. The presence of fewer independents gave greater importance and power to the 'travelling circus' package, which strengthened Ecclestone's hand in negotiations.

In return for the improved purse, he had guaranteed that the F1CA teams would supply a minimum of 18 cars per race, or forfeit half the prize money. If an independent team chose not to turn up for a race – as could well occur through sudden cashflow problems – it was their choice, he argued. If an F1CA team didn't, it would suffer a severe cash penalty. The guarantee of a team's appearance also had consequences for F1CA members themselves, for it brought to an end the practice of a team that was way down the points table failing to show up at end-of-the-season races, or even a crowd-pulling team like Ferrari temporarily dropping out mid-season, as it had been inclined to do. Another rule to ensure a more professional approach provided for the disqualification of a driver who failed to finish the season because of his overwhelming points lead, as Niki Lauda had in 1977 when he won his second world title.

To keep teams competitive Ecclestone ensured that the considerable benefits of the F1CA's travel package could not be taken for granted simply through membership. A team's costs would not be covered until its performance had accumulated sufficient points to put it in the ranks of the top ten teams. Continuing enjoyment of the benefits was then based on performance results over two six-monthly periods: if the times of a team's cars began to slip it was in danger of being replaced by a team whose times were improving. The independents, who had to qualify before they could take part in qualifying sessions with the F1CA teams, claimed such rules favoured the established teams to their exclusion, but their protests, once again, were in vain.

There were rare occasions when the efficiency of the package could rebound if a team hit financial trouble. For example, in order to maintain a full cast Ecclestone acquired, although, it was believed, in the name of the constructors' association, the assets of Mo Nunn's down-the-grid Ensign team after it ran up debts totalling £100,000, forcing his company into voluntary liquidation. The team staggered on until the end of the 1982 season, when Nunn, who moved into IndyCar racing, signed over his half of the company to Teddy Yip, of Theodore Racing, which itself went under by the end of the 1984 season. Ecclestone rejected Nunn's claim that he had bought Ensign's assets, but not that he had financially helped the team out. He said: 'Absolute rubbish. What would I do with them [the assets]? It's more than possible I gave him money, or lent him money, but I never bought anything off him.' At different times both Ken Tyrrell and Frank Williams were rescued by Ecclestone's wallet to ensure that the constructors could fulfil their contractual obligations. Said Peter Warr: 'Ken was forever, after the Jimmy Clark era, not organising his affairs properly and running short of cash, and so Bernie would help him out. He was also helpful to Williams.'

Before the advent of television, a team's principal source of income to cover running costs and drivers' retainers – this was sometimes self-funding – came through sponsorship, supplemented by qualifying and finishing money from the organisers, which, by 1977, could total as much as $350,000 a race, depending on the size of the circuit. But, in practice, the balancing of the books, handled by team bosses whose eyes generally glazed over at the sight of a profit-and-loss account, was often an uncertain and neglected affair. Such were the pressures of survival in those early days that it was a precarious existence for most of the constructors, who tended to pay last year's bills with next year's sponsorship money. To reduce costs, the number of practice sessions also underwent a fundamental change. Rather than being held for three hours over a three-day period – a total of nine hours – to fix pole positions, the sessions were staged over two days, thereby considerably reducing operational costs, including teams' hotel and travel bills. Two general practice sessions were later introduced to run full tanks in preparation for the race and test tyre options, followed by two one-hour qualifying sessions to hype up television interest. It was part of a series of changes that resulted in the current regulations, which limit the number of laps, exclude practice cars and even specify the number of tyres that can be used.

The F1CA also tackled the long-neglected issue of track safety. The standard of fire-fighting expertise and equipment at tracks – invariably no more sophisticated than untrained stewards armed with standard fire extinguishers – was woefully inadequate and, over the years, had doubtless cost the lives of drivers. Medical facilities and emergency services had been no less sub-standard – at the 1978 Swedish Grand Prix the medical centre was a caravan, and at Hockenheim a single-decker bus. Backed by the Grand Prix Drivers' Association, and, for once, the FIA, the F1CA pushed for, and achieved, radical improvements, including the appointment of Professor Sid Watkins, a member of the RAC's motor-racing medical panel who had been at Ayrton Senna's side when the driver was fatally injured. He accepted Ecclestone's invitation in 1978 to become the teams' on-track doctor. Pressure was later put on the organisers to provide the latest on-site hospitalisation facilities and helicopters to provide transport to the nearest specialist hospital.

Proper parking zones were also introduced for the first time, so that teams' transporters and support vehicles could be positioned near their pits, an elementary facility neglected by organisers who had shown little regard or interest in the professional needs of the teams. It wasn't long before the pit areas themselves were transformed. Where once they had been no more than a roughly cemented or tarmacadam standing, with mechanics at some tracks working under a canvas canopy attached to the side of the transporter parked by the side of the pit, now spacious, purpose-built garages supplied with water and electricity gradually began to appear as an integral part of standard facilities.

With the F1CA's increasing self-determining authority, Ecclestone's influence exerted itself in all and every area of Formula One, even to the more mundane administrative procedures, including the responsibility for issuing passes to the paddock, which, until then, had been haphazardly and inefficiently carried out by the organisers. The distribution point would vary from race to race, to the extent of taking place at an off-track office, where, once located, a team might find that it hadn't been allocated the required number of passes. Or teams would be refused admission to a circuit because they didn't have the required passes, which were being issued from the organiser's office – inside the circuit. The system was so inefficient that at one Monaco Grand Prix the teams staged an impromptu 'strike' after paddock officials refused to give entry tickets to the tyre companies.

'It was infuriating,' said a former team boss, 'because you had all these poofter fellows walking up and down the paddock in Johnnie Walker gear, 150 glamorous models with their tits hanging out, and 450 relatives of the local police, while the teams couldn't get in.' The teams became so exasperated by the petty officialdom of the organisers' system that the constructors took it upon themselves to introduce a new and more efficient one: the annual issue of paddock passes to all team members and registered personnel which authorised access to all circuits. The passes were first issued at the Italian Grand Prix at Monza in 1974, despite reservations from some of the constructors themselves, who believed it wouldn't work without the organisers' agreement. It took about an hour to persuade officials of their unilaterally declared validity. Soon the authority of the constructors' pass was accepted without question, although the more powerful circuits put up more spirited opposition before capitulating. Even then, until the late eighties, Monaco held out with its own passes but ceded their distribution to the constructors.

Another popular move with the teams was the banning of free-wheeling VIPs, PR flunkies and 'pit popsies' from the pit lanes. They were considered an obstruction to the work of the teams as well as a safety hazard. The constructors, or at least Ecclestone, also assumed greater control through the issuing of paddock passes to motor-racing journalists, once he had approved their accreditation. Similarly, he became responsible for approving the accreditation of local journalists whose names were submitted by organisers.

He was also responsible, through the Paddock Club, for Formula One becoming as much a corporate social event as a sporting one, although this development was initiated and successfully developed by others, who had been the first to see its commercial benefits: an exclusive social area for the entertaining of favoured clients provided a natural setting for marketing executives keen to wring every dollar out of their sponsorship budgets. As early as 1973, Philip Morris was laying on, in the paddock at Formula One races, a huge camion complete with kitchens, freezers and cool stores, opening to a massive awning described as 'a canvas Cafe Royal'. Contracted to assist in the promotion was GBM Editorial Associates, which was set up that year by public-relations specialists Barrie Gill, Anna O'Brien and Andy Marriott with seed capital of £2000 provided by Michael Tee, the then managing editor of *Motorsport* and *Motoring News*, founded and owned by his father, Wesley.

GBM Editorial Associates later changed its named to Championship Sporting Specialists, which, following a dispute caused by his father's refusal to move into PR, Tee subsequently joined as vice-chairman in 1977. The company went from strength to strength, covering every area of motor sport promotions, from press releases to corporate hospitality. At a Silverstone Grand Prix, there were as many as 15 hospitality tents which were positioned, at the sponsors' insistence, as close as possible to their respective teams. It presented a disorderly sight, though, that Ecclestone couldn't tolerate and which he was keen to reorganise. With this in mind, he approached Tee with a proposal that they should work together. But it was conditional, said Tee, on his dumping a partner whom Ecclestone disliked, something that he declined to do. His decision was followed by the gradual demise of Championship Sporting Specialists' corporate hospitality business – the two events were unconnected, said Tee – and the emergence of a new, more powerful enterprise.

The force behind its founding was Ecclestone, who agreed with senior executives of Eurovision, the trading arm of the Geneva-based European Broadcasting Union (EBU) – a professional association of public-service broadcasters formed in Torquay, England, in 1950 to negotiate on behalf of its members the acquisition of television rights – that advertising hoardings and banners were becoming too unsightly, thanks principally to the practice of promoters agreeing to their display between the cameras and the action to maximise revenue potential. Monza was cited as one of the worst examples. Ecclestone, with his eye for meticulous organisational detail, immediately concurred with the suggestion that track signage should come under the control of a company able to impose a more visually agreeable formation.

He looked around for a suitable candidate to head such a company, and his thoughts settled upon a figure known to him through his public-relations work with Marlboro. He was Patrick 'Paddy' McNally, an occasional rally driver and former freelance motor sport journalist, who had been hired by Marlboro as a PR adviser in mid-1972. By 1974 he had his own desk at Marlboro's new European headquarters in Lausanne, Switzerland, and was primarily involved in various follow-up tasks of the Marlboro sports programme, such as Grand Prix activities, a rally series and high-speed boat racing, as well as promoting television coverage of the events for the American and European market. He was a close friend of former Swiss racing driver Baron Toulo de Graffenfried, the winner of the Silverstone Grand Prix in 1947, who was hired by Marlboro as a consultant to open the doors to the 'club' of retired aristocratic drivers of pre-war vintage who were then dominating the organisation of Grands Prix. Suave and well connected, McNally knew his way round the best restaurants as well as the exclusive Swiss ski village of Verbier, a favourite haunt of the idle sons and daughters of the British upper classes. Years later he was described in the British tabloid press as a former lover of Sarah Ferguson, with whom he frequented Verbier's social scene before 'passing her on', in the summer of 1985, to Prince Andrew. Following their marriage a year later, she became the Duchess of York.

The invitation from Ecclestone to set up a company to resolve the EBU's concerns came at a fortuitous time for McNally. Married to a woman from a wealthy British family who died a tragically early death in the late seventies, he had been told that his independent contractor status with the Marlboro team was not being renewed. McNally was ready for the challenge. Said a former colleague: 'One thing for sure, he was a pretty bright lad, knew his way around and had learned a lot at Marlboro.' Ecclestone agreed. 'He had the contacts to do it. I said, "If you can do it, do it." That's how the business started.' But from the beginning McNally was under no illusion as to the extent of Ecclestone's backstage influence and the importance of his goodwill. He was aware of how difficult life could be made by Ecclestone, and in many different ways, right down to obtaining vital passes for access to the circuits for personnel and vehicles.

The deal agreed with McNally was simple: he would buy the signage rights from Ecclestone and whatever he made over that figure was his profit. It led to the setting up in December 1983 of AllSport Management SA. It was registered in Geneva, where, for tax reasons, it established its base, to buy the signage rights of all Formula One circuits – a condition that Ecclestone would include in his contracts with promoters – which would then be sold on at highly lucrative rates to advertisers. Ecclestone denies that he bankrolled the company's early capital costs, although others believe that he did. Said Tee: 'I once jokingly asked Bernie where he [McNally] had got the money from, and he looked at me in a way that suggested I should have known better. McNally was the just the front man.'

McNally's appointment was one that Tee did not envy. 'It would have been me he'd have been shouting at rather than McNally,' he said. 'I remember him once going berserk and shouting at McNally because a sign was in the wrong place. Anyone who worked for him he treated abominably.' McNally would have already been aware of Ecclestone's pugnacious style. A former business associate recalled seeing McNally at the Brabham team works as he and Ecclestone, driving a Mercedes, were about to drive away. 'Paddy's talking to him as the window's going up and Bernie's driving off, leaving Paddy just standing there, talking to himself.'

The arrival of AllSport Management led to the founding of the Paddock Club – an idea suggested to McNally by Ecclestone, who had seen the success of a similar money-spinner introduced by Mark McCormack, the American sports management agency boss, at Wimbledon – into whose exclusive, highly priced designated area corporate hospitality tents were moved to resolve Ecclestone's displeasure at their haphazard siting. The company's early trading figures, though, proved so disappointing that it was not long before McNally was ready to quit. 'After the second year, he said he didn't think it was going to work,' said Ecclestone. His advice was to 'give it a little bit longer, because you've spent all that money in promoting it ... it would be silly to walk away now'. Business growth proved Ecclestone right. In his words, McNally 'has done very well for himself'.

With the company based in Geneva, it is not possible to gain access to company accounts to discover the current profits of AllSport Management, but it is possible to fix an approximate figure for the turnover of the Paddock Club. In 1999 – McNally declined to give information on more recent costs – a three-day weekend for one in the Paddock Club cost between $1500 to $2000, for which, in the words of a public-relations consultant, up to 3000 punters receive 'very nice food and drink, a grandstand view of the circuit and a goodies bag to take away, which probably costs about £10'. Calculated on a full house at, say, $1750 over 17 Grands Prix, the estimated revenue totals $89 million per year, which, no doubt, is a poor indicator of its final profits figure. The company also receives a share in the substantial rental fees of all off-track retail merchandise trailers, and in the constant quest to squeeze every penny out of Formula One, a £1-million-a-year deal with London-based Haymarket Publishing Ltd for the rights to publish motor sport programmes in its magazines *Autosport* and *Autocar*.

For someone who has consistently claimed to have no financial interest in the company – 'I never have been [involved] at all, any more than I am involved in any of the other race teams. I try to help where possible, where it helps us' – Ecclestone has over the years continued to exercise a remarkable degree of control. The principal director of a company which handled AllSport Management's Formula One interests in the UK claimed that when McNally decided to extend the company's activities to include motor sport at Brands Hatch and Donington Park, he was told by Ecclestone to concentrate exclusively on Formula One. McNally promptly obliged.

The UK company's relationship with AllSport Management, which lasted for four years, finally came to an end, incidentally, after constant last-minute changes of decision and demands for lower prices made it impossible to achieve a viable profit margin. There was also a major problem over the payment of VAT (Value Added Tax), which led to Customs and Excise inspectors combing through the UK company's books in an unsuccessful effort to uncover any irregularities in AllSport Management's operation. The payment of VAT, which the UK company had incurred and paid on behalf of AllSport Management, was described by the principal director, as 'a big problem'. It caused McNally to bring in-house the promotion of the company's Formula One interests in the UK. They wanted it 'very, very close to their hearts, and that was it'.

Today McNally, the one-time flesh-pressing gofer and PR flunkey, is one of the richest men in motor sport, with extensive property interests in Switzerland and Britain, including a £5-million estate in Wiltshire. And, like many in Formula One, he owes it all to the favour and patronage of Ecclestone.

During these formative years Ecclestone worked exceedingly hard to expand the Formula One calendar. By the mid-seventies he had restored Argentina to the calendar after a 12-year absence, and had completed successful negotiations with politicians, industrialists and businessmen for Grands Prix in Sweden, Brazil, Belgium, Japan and Long Beach, USA. Ecclestone claims never to have been in awe of the people with whom he negotiated. Nor, it seems, did he allow himself to be intimidated. In negotiating the return of the Argentine Grand Prix in 1972 officers representing the country's military junta flew to London for a meeting with Ecclestone, Mosley and Andrew Ferguson at a London hotel.

Accompanying the officers were members of the Argentinian Embassy, who arrived with an old-fashioned tape-recorder with two large spools through which the tape ran. It was assumed a recording of the meeting was required back in Argentina for intelligence reasons, although its purpose wasn't made clear. But Ecclestone didn't care for their pompous and high-handed military attitude – or for a recording of the meeting. During an early stage of the meeting, while Mosley held the audience, he feigned to stretch his legs. Casually passing a table on which some feet away the tape recorder was positioned, he deftly placed a piece of paper in one of the spools before returning to his seat. It was some time before anyone noticed the tape piling up on the floor.

The negotiations surrounding the Brazilian and Swedish Grands Prix were more indicative of his opportunistic and commercial flair. With the growing national acclaim of Brazilian driver Emerson Fittipaldi, he persuaded Rede Globo, the country's national television network, to sponsor a non-championship race at Brazil's Interlagos circuit in 1972. (It proved a tremendous success, although at one stage it seemed in great doubt after a last-minute delay in the payment of the teams' fees. Mosley was dispatched to Rio de Janeiro to collect the money in cash and then phone Ecclestone at the Excelsior Hotel at Heathrow Airport, where the teams were literally waiting to load their cars. Mosley informed Ecclestone and the teams – they wanted to hear his personal reassurance, such was the distrust within the F1CA – that, yes, everything was fine. But Rede Globo hadn't actually paid the money. Mosley was told that because of the country's economic problems, the only way the company could get the money in cash would be on the black market at a prohibitive rate. In any event, it would be illegal to take the money out of the country. However, Mosley was informed, they could get legal permission to transfer the sum to the F1CA's bank account risk-free although not immediately. Mosley, as he picked up the phone to London, decided to take a chance.)

That year Fittipaldi won the first of his two World Championship titles, which boosted considerably Ecclestone's efforts to persuade senior members of the Brazilian government that the country really ought to have its own Grand Prix. The talks led to a sponsorship deal financed by Rede Globo and the appearance in 1973 of the Brazilian Grand Prix as a regular round of the Formula One World Championship series. In Sweden, Ecclestone again went to the top. He secured sponsorship for the first Grand Prix at Anderstorp, also in 1973, by enlisting the support of Prince Bertil, who was instrumental in persuading the Japanese electronics firm Hitachi, who had major interests in Sweden, to agree to foot the sponsorship bill. Elsewhere, as in Nivelles, Belgium, which from 1973 to 1975 staged a Grand Prix on alternate years with Zolder – a diplomatic compromise to the French- and Flemish-speaking regions – Ecclestone set himself up as the promoter, the first of a number of similar arrangements that would gradually increase his power and personal riches.

His role as promoter, he insists, was a time of considerable personal risk for him, although he enlisted, according to a senior F1CA member at that time, the aid of the constructors to minimise it. He persuaded them to agree to cap their share of the money to improve the circuits' chances of success.

A week or two after Ronnie Thomson had made his critical comments on Formula One in Geneva in January 1973, on the other side of the world three men were relaxing on a beach in Guaruja, Brazil, playing racquet ball. They were Ken Tyrrell, the boss of the Tyrrell team; Lotus lead driver Emerson Fittipaldi, the 26-year-old Brazilian who had won the World Championship the previous year; and Patrick Duffeler, a 29-year-old Brussels-born American, who had moved from the New York head office of Philip Morris in March 1970 to become a director of the company's European, Middle East and African promotions at its headquarters in Lausanne, Switzerland. But it was inspiration, not perspiration, that they were looking for. The informal gathering had been assembled to discuss the concept of a 'super' team to defeat Colin Chapman's Team Lotus, which had completed the double by also winning the Constructors' Championship title.

Each man had a compelling interest in the conversation. Tyrrell's team had won the constructors' title in 1971 and had come second to Lotus in 1972, but he was uncertain of the renewal of his contract with his major sponsor, Elf, the French state oil company. The kind of serious money that Marlboro was pumping into Formula One could turn Tyrrell into that 'super' team, with Fittipaldi as lead driver. The proud Brazilian, for his part, was ready to leave Lotus – he was angry that Chapman had signed Ronnie Peterson from March as co-lead driver for the 1973 season. That evening, without Tyrrell, Duffeler and Fittipaldi continued looking at the options, which, in the final analysis, didn't include Tyrrell. The two teams they considered to have the greatest potential were Bernie Ecclestone's Brabham team and Teddy Mayer's McLaren.

Over the months ahead Duffeler spent virtually every working hour exploring and examining the problems and practicalities of creating a 'super' team. He believed it would be the only way of ensuring the success of the challenging brief he had been given by Thomson: to build the winning Formula One team that the Philip Morris management in New York wanted. It was a quest that had begun, in fact, two years earlier, when Thomson decided that Formula One offered a unique opportunity to introduce the Marlboro brand throughout Europe without having to decide on any particular advertising image, such as the macho cowboy promotion which worked well in America. He also believed that through an international sport such as Formula One his company could in one move circumvent complex tobacco advertising restrictions which varied from country to country. The team which had attracted Thomson's attention at that time was Louis Stanley's BRM, the only British factory-backed team producing its own engine. Unlike the 'garagistes', the company that Stanley grandiosely described as the 'Ferrari of England' had the corporate substance and image that Thomson believed offered the best return on the Philip Morris sponsorship dollar.

Stanley, who had been heavily funded by his wealthy industrialist brother-in-law, Sir Alfred Owen, whose family owned BRM, had a sponsorship deal – one of the first – with Yardley, the perfumery division of British American Tobacco, worth £50,000 over two years. But it was a relationship that was failing to come up to Stanley's financial expectations. Yardley, he complained, was unwilling to stump up the cash he considered necessary to fund engine development. Known as a 'charming and pompous dilettante' – or 'Big Lou' and 'Lord Trumpington' behind his back – who travelled everywhere in a chauffeur-driven Rover with a permanent suite at the Dorchester, Stanley, on hearing of Philip Morris's intention to promote its Marlboro brand through Formula One, was ready to dump Yardley.

He laid the ground in October 1971, after attending the funeral in Switzerland of Jo Siffert, a 35-year-old Swiss driver who had been killed in an end-of-season Victory Race at Brands Hatch, when his BRM P160 hit a bend at Hawthorn's Corner, causing the car to burst into flames and his death from smoke inhalation. Ironically, his rides with BRM were funded by Porsche, who agreed to foot the bill as long as he remained with them as their number-one works driver. The moment the service, in Siffert's home town of Fribourg, was over, Stanley, accompanied by his wife, Jean, drove off in his Mercedes 600 on a 70-kilometre journey to the headquarters of Marlboro in Lausanne, a ten-storey glass tower overlooking Lake Geneva, to present Ronnie Thomson and Albert Bellot, vice-president of marketing, with his vision of the benefits of a sponsorship deal between Marlboro and BRM.

It was a grand proposal, covering not only Formula One sponsorship, but also plans to build and market a Marlboro BRM sports car, golf carts and a series of accessories from watches to sportswear. A two-year contract between the two companies was signed the following month by Stanley and Thomson at the Dorchester Hotel in London. To BRM it was worth in excess of £100,000, plus bonuses for championship event wins and funds for other projects. At a time when the annual budget of running a Formula One team was between £100,000 and 150,000, it was a good deal more than Stanley had been getting from Yardley. It was also decided that Marlboro BRM, which came to be hyped as the Marlboro World Championship Team, would not be fielding just two or three cars in each race, but five – the drivers who were signed up were Jean-Pierre Beltoise of France, Peter Gethin of England, Helmut Marko of Austria, Alex Soler Roig of Spain, Gijs van Lennep of Holland, and Howden Ganley of New Zealand. Thomson was satisfied that the foundation was in place to considerably heighten the profile of Marlboro throughout Europe. Duffeler was assigned the task of making it all work.

Most of the constructors, no admirers of Stanley, had also beaten a path to Marlboro, including Ken Tyrrell, who flew to Switzerland for a secret meeting with Thomson and Duffeler – it proved no more successful than the informal Brazilian beach meeting with Fittipaldi and Duffeler two years later – followed by Frank Williams, whose team was in danger of going under from severe cashflow problems. Williams, described as 'charmingly persistent', was sufficiently charming and persistent to persuade Duffeler to involve Marlboro in a two-year deal with the Milan-based manufacturer Iso, who produced a limited edition of the Iso Lele for Frank Williams Racing Cars with the Marlboro World Championship Racing logo on the sides. But, elsewhere, Duffeler was having serious problems with BRM.

Despite Marlboro's generous funding, Stanley was constantly on the phone asking for more money to fund engine development costs to improve horsepower – the BRM engine was barely delivering 425bhp against the Cosworth V8's 470bhp and Ferrari's claim to exceed 500bhp. There were other worrying problems that were a crucial part of the whole. BRM's team manager Tim Parnell, the son of pioneer Formula One racing driver Reg Parnell, was honest enough to admit to Duffeler that BRM, due to cashflow problems, was consistently short of spare parts, sufficient sets of tyres for the five cars, and, not least, mechanics. Performance on the track confirmed what was becoming blindingly obvious – the BRM cars simply weren't competitive.

By mid-1972 the team of drivers was also unravelling, for reasons ranging from injury and lack of personal funding to conflict with the BRM management. Marlboro BRM finished the season seventh, with only Matra and Brabham doing worse. Jean-Pierre Beltoise, the team's most talented driver, finished eleventh in the drivers' championship. True, the team had won the highly prestigious Monaco Grand Prix but that was due to Beltoise's driving skills in appalling weather rather than the performance of the car. Across the Atlantic, Philip Morris management was critically monitoring the increased funding of a highly visible team that was not winning races. At the 1973 Dutch Grand Prix in July, Duffeler broke the news to Stanley that the two-year contract would not be renewed.

By now Duffeler was working on the radically different strategy that he had put to Thomson and Bellot towards the end of 1972 – the creation of a 'super' team, the concept that, in between playing racquet ball, he had been kicking around with Tyrrell and Fittipaldi on a Brazilian beach at the beginning of that year. This time, Duffeler avowed, Marlboro would become more closely involved with day-to-day management, even to the selection of the drivers. Duffeler received Thomson's backing and was given a free hand, plus a substantially increased budget. He would need it. When the decision was taken in late 1971 by Thomson for Philip Morris to move into Formula One, a preliminary annual budget of $115–150,000 was allocated. Within months it was increased by Bellot to $1 million, by June 1972 to $1.5 million, and to $3 million after Duffeler received approval for his 'super' team concept.

The driver selected to lead the team was, predictably, Emerson Fittipaldi – on a basic contract worth $250,000, which compared to no more than $10,000 paid to some of the Marlboro BRM drivers a little more than a year earlier. To help offset the level of escalating costs, Fittipaldi introduced Duffeler to John Goossens, a senior member of Texaco Belgium's marketing team, who went on to become director of Texaco racing worldwide before eventually becoming chief executive officer of Belgacom, the Belgian telephone company. There now remained the question of the team itself: whether it would be Brabham or McLaren, which Duffeler was by now convinced were the teams with the greatest potential. With the 1974 season not far away, a round of furious discussions opened simultaneously with Ecclestone and McLaren's Teddy Mayer. The central issue was who would provide the better engineering and team of mechanics.

Brabham's Gordon Murray was considered to be the most impressive, yet

Mayer was considered a solid manager, who had overcome polio at an early age to become a master skier, a man with a will of iron and a clear, sharp focus. His team manager, Alistair Caldwell, was also rated highly, particularly by Fittipaldi. Mayer, excited by the prospect of having Fittipaldi as his lead driver, was ready to leap naked through a hoop of fire for the contract. But there was a considerable obstacle in his way. His team was tied to Yardley, a subsidiary of British American Tobacco, which would not agree to release Fittipaldi from his contract to join a team to be sponsored by a rival company. Despite Mayer's best efforts, the company refused to co-operate. It was reinforced by a threat of legal action from British American Tobacco. Mayer was in a bind.

In the meantime, Ecclestone was pressing Duffeler to make a decision in favour of Brabham. With Mayer seemingly out of the race, Duffeler decided on a preliminary agreement with Ecclestone, which, bankrolled by Marlboro and Texaco, would come to be worth well over £100,000 a year (worth £750,000 in 2002). The news was announced to Ecclestone during the early afternoon of Saturday 1 September 1973, at a two-level villa in Lonay, situated in a picturesque valley ten kilometres west of Lausanne, where the Fittipaldi brothers – Emerson and Wilson – resided with their families in between races.

Ecclestone naturally appeared delighted with the news and a few minutes later, says Duffeler, invited him to take some fresh air on the balcony. What followed, he claims, left him stunned. 'Bernie asked me if he could take care of me, that is, with a financial gift.' Left momentarily speechless, Duffeler declined Ecclestone's offer, before, a moment or two later, they rejoined Emerson Fittipaldi and his wife, Maria-Helena. Presently, the two men left for Duffeler's home, a ten-minute drive away, where they had a celebratory glass of champagne. The day's business was concluded with Duffeler driving Ecclestone to Geneva Airport, a 35-minute journey, for his return flight to England. But, that evening, there was a sudden turn of events.

Duffeler received a phone call from Teddy Mayer to find out whether the contract had been closed. He was relieved to hear that it hadn't. Mayer, making it clear that he would close down McLaren rather than lose the opportunity of a contract with Marlboro, Texaco and Fittipaldi, said he believed he had found a way round the problem with Yardley. He confided in Duffeler that he proposed offering Yardley an alternative to an expensive legal dispute – he would split up the team, with McLaren's joint managing director, Phil Kerr, looking after a car driven by Mike Hailwood under Yardley colours, while he managed the Marlboro-Texaco team, with Denny Hulme, his lead driver, sharing the number-one slot with Fittipaldi. Duffeler was delighted. He agreed to stall further discussions with Ecclestone until Mayer had had time to talk with Yardley. British American Tobacco, aware that they had been outmanoeuvred, blinked and accepted. If nothing else it gave Yardley a face-saving exit from a sponsorship programme which, with its constantly escalating costs, they could no longer afford.

Over the next ten days lawyers for McLaren, Marlboro and Texaco worked on the contractual drafts in total secrecy. In the meantime, Ecclestone was becoming anxious, phoning almost daily for the draft contract he was confidently expecting. Finally, with the contracts between McLaren, Marlboro and Texaco signed, the news had to be broken to Ecclestone. A meeting was set up in London. Duffeler, who claims he wanted to ensure that Ecclestone was not tempted to repeat his offer, took one of his managers with him. Ecclestone, adds Duffeler, was furious when told the contract was going to McLaren. The brief meeting ended acrimoniously, without the courtesy of handshakes.

Ecclestone said he was unable to remember offering a 'gift' to Duffeler, or even inviting him out on to the balcony. 'You know, if you put me against a wall and put a machine gun to my head, and you said, "Are you absolutely 100 per cent sure you never said that?", I would have to be honest with you and say, "I couldn't", because I don't remember that much. But I may have said, "Let's take care of you for the efforts you made." It is the sort of thing that happens all the time in these situations. Normally, people say first, "I want a percentage." Y'know, they're part of business arrangements. People actually come up and ask for "commissions". Unfortunately, that's the way the world goes round.'

The partnership between Marlboro and McLaren turned out to be one of the most durable in Formula One. It finished the 1974 season with Fittipaldi winning the World Championship title and Marlboro McLaren team taking the Constructors' Championship title, marking the beginning of a sponsorship that would last for 22 years.

Duffeler, still only 32 years old, was learning fast about the politics and practices of Formula One – the offer from Ecclestone, he was told by the boss of another leading team, was certainly not unusual in sponsorship deals – and he was soon to witness Ecclestone's knack of squeezing extra money out of sponsors, as he would demonstrate in negotiating the constructors' transportation costs for Japan's first Grand Prix. The proposal for a Japanese Grand Prix came from the Asia-Pacific management of Philip Morris following the success of the 1974 season. It was believed that such a high-profile event would help boost the company's marginal presence and cigarette sales, which, in a country where cigarette sales were controlled by a state monopoly, were in decline.

On 19 April 1974 Duffeler left for Tokyo with Emerson Fittipaldi, one of the drivers most vocal on track safety, to meet officials of the Japanese Automobile Federation and assess two potential venues – Mount Fuji Speedway and the Suzuka racetrack, a visit which attracted coverage in *Sports Nippon*, the biggest-selling sports newspaper in Japan. More importantly, it attracted the personal interest of the publishing company's chairman, Mr Chikao Kano, an elderly gentleman who, during a visit to Europe in 1929, saw the first Monaco Grand Prix. He was so enthralled by the spectacle that he promised to do all he could to one day organise a Grand Prix in Japan. At a press conference in Tokyo the positive response by Marlboro to a Japanese Grand Prix was enough to cause Kano to send his son, Sentaro Kano, who was studying at the Sorbonne in Paris, to Lausanne to discuss with Duffeler how the two companies might work together to organise the event.

A fundamental step, of course, was the co-operation of the constructors, or, more precisely, Ecclestone. His response to Duffeler's approach was apparently far from enthusiastic, a tactic, it was suspected, to hike up the constructors' fees. Duffeler, anyway, had some powerful allies on his side – the cheque-signing sponsors. The likes of Martini, Elf, Texaco and Renault, through Duffeler's initiative, were very much in favour of brand exposure in a largely unexplored major industrial market. A Japanese Grand Prix also had the support of the president of the Commission Sportive Internationale (CSI), Prince Paul Metternich, a tall, sophisticated, multi-lingual German aristocrat, who, once having established that there would be no opposition within the FIA to its incorporation in the Formula One calendar, authorised representatives of the CSI's Safety Commission to ratify that Mount Fuji, the track favoured by Duffeler and Fittipaldi, met with FIA specifications.

In the meantime, discussions between Marlboro and *Sports Nippon* had ended with the newspaper agreeing to organise and sponsor the race. One of the paper's senior executives, Yoshinori Arai, was appointed project co-ordinator, and a Japanese consultant with international experience in motor sport, Shunichi Hirai, was appointed to assist. The Japanese began to bone up on the logistical complexities of organising a Grand Prix, as well as the relationship between organisers with the constructors and drivers. *Sports Nippon* representatives attended the 1975 German Grand Prix and, by the Italian Grand Prix at Monza the following month, were feeling more comfortable with the organising and management of a Formula One event.

But, behind the scenes, there was political opposition, locally and internationally, to a Japanese Grand Prix. The constructors, who wanted a maximum of 14 Grands Prix, were unhappy that 18 Grands Prix had been scheduled for the 1976 season – it would finally be reduced to 16 – while organisers in smaller European countries, feeling threatened by the expanding global dimension, were in a state of high anxiety over the future of their marginal races. The Philippines, through its president, Ferdinand Marcos, and Saudi Arabia, awash with oil dollars, had also expressed ambitions to enjoy the international prestige of a Formula One Grand Prix – senior CSI officials and Duffeler accepted an invitation from the Saudi royal family to visit their country

– all of which was enough to cause certain European organisers to voice strong objections to the FIA about the inclusion of the Japanese in the Formula One calendar. Their protests were in vain. A Japanese Grand Prix had the blessing of a greater force – Ecclestone and the constructors were now happy to compete.

By the early winter of 1975 negotiations between Ecclestone and *Sports Nippon* to decide the 'start' and prize money had been successfully concluded, including the funding of the transportation costs of personnel, cars and equipment. In January 1976 the FIA announced at a press conference in Tokyo that the Grand Prix would take place at Mount Fuji on 24 October. It was received in Japan as a momentous event, politically and culturally. Such was its esteem to Emperor Hirohito that planning began for a grand reception in Tokyo, to be hosted by his brother, Prince Takamatsu, for the FIA, the CSI, teams and international press. Everything, it seemed, was running smoothly for a highly successful Grand Prix. That is, until Ecclestone decided to wring some more money out of the Japanese.

With the Japanese Grand Prix just four months away, he approached Arai and Hirai, as they were enjoying a glass of wine in the Marlboro hospitality tent in the paddock at the French Grand Prix, to inform them that he thought the Grand Prix couldn't be held after all. Visibly shocked, they stood in dumbfounded silence as Ecclestone went on to explain that the costs agreed to cover transportation wouldn't be enough. If the Grand Prix was to go ahead, more money would be required. The two men were strongly advised by Duffeler not to agree to a tactic that was seen to be a feature of Ecclestone's negotiating style. If they stood firm, they were reassured, Ecclestone would be forced to back down. He wouldn't dare risk the controversy the constructors' withdrawal would provoke.

The stunned Japanese, particularly Hirai, did not want to take the risk. There was too much 'face' at stake. Ecclestone was informed that they would have to speak to Tokyo. A series of hurried meetings were held over the next few weeks. By the Italian Grand Prix at Monza, on 12 September, the Japanese capitulated and agreed to a substantial but unknown increase in transportation costs. Ecclestone then expressed his disapproval of facilities and arrangements at Mount Fuji, which saw costs for *Sports Nippon* escalate almost by the day. Ecclestone did not deny that the transportation costs may have been increased. 'That may be true, I suppose. I don't remember, but maybe we agreed to do something and there were more cars. I've no idea. But nobody upped the price. If we did a deal we did a deal.' He did concede that there were increased costs due to the need to improve the circuit's facilities. 'Yes, the place was shit. I used to do the circuit inspections in those days. I remember going over three or four times and I said, "Look at this"..."Oh, no, no, we are going to change that"...and you went back and everything was exactly the same.'

No doubt to the great relief of the newspaper's management, the Japanese Grand Prix took place with no further dispute or demand. The last race of the season, it attracted massive media coverage, including the stirring interest of television, as the race that would decide the World Championship title battle between James Hunt in a McLaren – a frantic replacement for Emerson Fittipaldi, who had decided to join the Brazilian team, Copersucar – and Ferrari's Niki Lauda. It turned out to be less than a white-knuckled nail-biter, when after two laps Lauda was forced to withdraw through bad weather, leaving Hunt to take third place and the World Championship title by one point. But it was a considerable marketing success for Duffeler. With Fittipaldi's triumph in 1974, it was the second drivers' championship title for Marlboro McLaren in three years.

A few weeks later Duffeler left Marlboro to start his own marketing consultancy shortly after Ronnie Thomson, who had been a bulwark against criticism in New York of the European operation's marketing style and its autonomy, had moved on to a senior executive position at cosmetics manufacturer Revlon. With the departure, too, of Fittipaldi, Duffeler, having achieved the corporate objective of creating a World Championship 'super' team, decided it was time for a fresh challenge. It would not be long in coming – in representing the interests of the beleaguered organisers in their negotiations with Ecclestone, a confrontation that would see them once again toe to toe, and come close to bringing about the fatal splitting of Formula One.

By the mid-seventies Ecclestone had begun to look for a new financial package with the organisers to cover, for the first time, a three-year period. He was looking for a massive increase of 60 per cent, from what was now an average of £92,000, to £150,000 for a European race. The intercontinental organisers – in North America, South America, South Africa and Japan – faced even more swingeing increases, as high as $350,000 (worth then about £194,000). Ecclestone's demands triggered public protests from North America. Bob Hanna, executive director of the Canadian Automobile Sports Club (CASC), the organisers of the Canadian Grand Prix, believed the F1CA represented a serious threat to the future of Formula One. He said: 'The future of Grand Prix rests in the fact that this little group has to be broken up.' Tracy Bird, executive director of the Automobile Competition Committee for the United States (ACCUS), agreed: 'Something has to happen because the control of motor sport has passed out of the hands of the FIA to the Formula One owners and drivers – some 25 people.'[3]

Their comments were made in support of two Canadian businessmen, Harvey Hudes and Bernie Kamin, the owners of the Mosport circuit, the Toronto home of the Canadian Grand Prix. The 1975 race was scheduled to take place on 21 September, until, that is, Hudes and Kamin refused to agree to the teams' latest terms as presented by Ecclestone. They claimed that the increase in the teams' fees had left them too little time to renegotiate with the race sponsors. The F1CA argued that as a contract for the new three-year period had yet to be signed, the constructors were free to increase their asking price. Hudes and Kamin were given a deadline of midnight on Friday 1 August to accept the deal. The deadline came and went without reply. At that time the teams were at the Nurburgring getting ready for the German Grand Prix. A press release was issued stating that the teams would not be going to Canada.

This time Hudes and Kamin responded quickly – they agreed to pay. A meeting of the teams was called in Graham Hill's motor home – he was the only one with a motor home big enough to accommodate the teams' principals – and the general consensus, although with Ecclestone in opposition, was in favour of going. A belated Max Mosley arrived to support Ecclestone's view: if the teams didn't stand by the deadline, it could fatally undermine the F1CA's credibility in negotiations. It would embolden others to take on the teams. The team bosses gradually came to share their opinion. The meeting ended with a decision not to go to Canada.

Hudes and Kamin appealed to the CSI to intervene, but without success. Its members doubtless believed they were on a hiding to nothing in taking on Ecclestone and the constructors. The Canadian Grand Prix was duly cancelled, leaving Hudes and Kamin to their only recourse – a lawsuit against the F1CA seeking $8 million in damages. Less than ten months later it was withdrawn and the Canadian Grand Prix was back on track for the 1976 season after Labatt's Brewery came to the rescue as sponsors with the necessary financial backing. It was a decisive episode for the teams. It sent out the desired signal: if anyone wanted to play hardball, they were happy to provide the arena.

Ecclestone argued that fees demanded of the organisers in North America, South America, Africa and Japan were justified by the costs of the long-haul trips, which, he claimed, were five or six times greater than those incurred in attending the European Grands Prix. In fact, he complained, travelling so far was 'bad news' for the F1CA, 'because we ferry cars and engines back and forth, we fly people home, mechanics get tired and headaches get worse'. It was 'a bargain at the price' for the organisers.[4] The long-haul trips had been possible, he trumpeted, due to the generous travel concessions the F1CA was able to offer the racing teams. True, but those concessions, he omitted to add, had been possible because the organisers themselves had been forced to pick up the bills.

It was all part of the package deal: if they wanted a Grand Prix, they would have to pay the freight, travel and hotel costs. No travel costs, no Grand Prix. These costs were considerable. For example, the estimated bill in 1977 for transporting one car plus spares, air tickets for seven people and hotel accommodation was £18,600. The travel concessions, incidentally, were only made available to the top ten teams and for two reasons: first, there was only so much money that even Ecclestone could squeeze out of the organisers, and, second, it helped to maintain a high level of competitiveness between the teams to stay in the top ten.

Years later, Ecclestone put some dazzling spin on the reason behind his financial demands in those days. It seems it had nothing to do with getting a better deal for the teams, or even for his financial betterment. Rather, it was for the good of the organisers themselves. Such demands forced them to become more efficient or go out of business. 'In the old days the FOCA's [as the F1CA became] role was to kick these lazy amateur organisers into the 1970s and 1980s and 1990s. We kicked them into becoming professionals and running their races efficiently to make money so they could pay.'[5] He added that the prize money wasn't important to the teams because it represented a small percentage of annual budgets. While sponsorship was the teams' principal source of income, it was somewhat disingenuous of Ecclestone to have dismissed the prize money as not being important, given the huge increases that he had successfully demanded and the grave conflicts they caused.

But if Ecclestone's latest financial demands were causing serious concerns to the organisers, the FIA was also becoming increasingly alarmed at the authority Ecclestone, on behalf of the F1CA, was taking upon himself. The constructors were now seeking a greater say in the rules and regulations governing Formula One, including the number and type of Grand Prix support races, what type of cars should supplement a grid if there should be a shortage of Formula One cars, the method of qualification for the twenty-sixth car on the grid, either from lap times 'or by whatever other means the Association [the F1CA] shall decide', and the facilities and amenities that should be available to F1CA members and common to all circuits.[6] The gentlemen's club that was the FIA seemed powerless to check the constructors' aspirations.

The all too apparent inability of the CSI's president, Prince Paul Metternich, to do so on its behalf led to him being kicked upstairs to the presidency of the FIA itself. In this new rough-house environment he was considered to be too full of old-world courtesy and civility to counter the upstart Englishman, whose popularity around some of the European circuits was clearly reflected in the message of a banner carried by a group of spectators at Monza: 'Away with the English Mafia!' For his successor the FIA went outside its functionary ranks, to find someone who would not feel cowed or intimidated by Ecclestone's reputation. Certainly there were few candidates indeed within the ranks of the FIA delegates, senior motoring-club officials described as semi- or fully retired amateur bureaucrats more interested in the social jollies and political prestige of Formula One than the hardheaded administration of its management.

In the late autumn of 1975, the FIA appointed Brussels-born Pierre Ugueux, aged 62, who had been joint general director of Belgium's Public Energy Services Works, which controlled the country's gas and electricity industry. He had been involved to a minor extent with the affairs of the Royal Automobile Club de Belgique, but knew little about motor racing, That, as far as the FIA was concerned, was a prerequisite of little importance; of more interest was his reputation as 'a tough little manager', with, it was hoped, the political wit and mettle to outflank the constructors.

From the FIA battlement, Ugueux began encouragingly enough: shortly after taking office, he proclaimed that the 1976 World Championship wouldn't take place until the financial terms had been agreed between the FIA, the organisers and the F1CA. Aware that Ecclestone had concluded terms with at least two organisers, Ugueux declared such contracts to be invalid on the grounds that they had not been sanctioned by the respective national sporting authorities, invariably a country's national motoring organisation appointed by the FIA to ensure races were run in accordance with its rules and regulations. The two races were the British Grand Prix at Brands Hatch, which had, in fact, already been approved by the national sporting authority, the Royal Automobile Club, and the USA West Grand Prix at Long Beach, which was to debut in 1976. Ecclestone had agreed to reduce the risk for promoter Chris Pook by cutting the F1CA's fee in exchange for a share of the gate receipts. (A further issue between the CSI and Ecclestone involved the Royal Automobile Club de Belgique, which wanted the Belgian Grand Prix to take place at Nivelles, a preference overruled by Ecclestone in favour of Zolder, and which would win the day.)

In November 1975 Ugueux requested a meeting with Ecclestone in Brussels to discuss the growing concerns of the mainly European organisers. Accompanied by Max Mosley, Ecclestone agreed. Also present was a Frenchman called Jean-Marie Balestre, who, as president of the Fédération Française du Sport Automobile (FFSA), the governing body of French motor sport, was an influential member of the CSI. He was someone who would soon loom large in the affairs of the constructors, but of whom, at that time, little was known.

The meeting had been called by Ugueux in the hope of bringing some uniformity to the European race fees being demanded by Ecclestone, and it began with one of Ugueux's colleagues making a presentation of the organisers' views. At this point Ecclestone expressed his indifference by getting up and making great play of straightening a number of pictures on the walls. As an unsettling tactic, it worked perfectly. Ecclestone countered objections to his conduct by reassuring Ugueux and company that he was listening to every word. Balestre became so furious that he snapped a pencil he had been rolling between his fingers. It gave Ecclestone and Mosley an insight into his explosive temper, a quality they would come to know well.

Once the case for the organisers had been stated, Ecclestone put the teams' case – for a European race fee that was finally agreed, after long and laboured bargaining, at $275,000 in a deal that was known as the Brussels Agreement. Ecclestone had actually agreed to accept $270,000, but, at the point of closing the deal, he suddenly upped the figure by a further $5000. Whatever Balestre might have thought, Ugueux was too weary to fight the organisers' corner any longer. He agreed without further comment. It was the kind of negotiating tactic that deeply impressed Mosley, who, as they left the meeting, calculated that, over 16 races a season, that last-minute ploy had earned the teams a further $80,000. In triumphant tone, the FIA announced that the 1976 Formula One World Championship was back on, implying that the CSI had won the day.

During 1976 Ugueux, seemingly encouraged by his 'success', began lobbying organisers to unite once again, in the style of Grand Prix International, but this time with the CSI as their negotiating body. It provoked a sharp response from Britain's Royal Automobile Club, which believed that the CSI had no role to play in negotiations between the F1CA and the organisers. Its influential chairman, Sir Clive Bossom, president of the RAC's Motor Sports Association and a vice-president of the FIA, fired off a sharp communiqué to Ugueux advising him as 'forcefully as possible' that financial negotiations between the F1CA and the organisers were no business of the CSI. A consortium of organisers would be to create an 'illegal cartel', which, he insisted, would leave him no option but to report the matter to FIA's executive council.[7]

The legal ammunition for Sir Clive's missive was handed to him by Mosley, who had discovered that the organisers' consortium fell foul of Articles 85 and 86 of the Treaty of Rome, the very European Union legislation that would be used so effectively against the FIA and Ecclestone some 20 years later. Sir Clive, a former Conservative MP with a distinguished military and parliamentary career, who became parliamentary private secretary to Margaret Thatcher, added that any hope some organisers might have that the CSI would be able to solve their problems was 'just wishful thinking'. His public admonishment of Ugueux and support of the F1CA may have cost him his hope of becoming president of the FIA. Appointed chairman of the RAC after being approached by Lord Mountbatten, under whom he served in the Far East, because, in his words, he was 'clean', Bossom came to be considered to be too politically partial towards the constructors, to be appointed to the prestigious post. Ironically, he had approved the appointment of Ugueux, a neutral unknown and therefore seemingly acceptable to all, as a less controversial appointment than a Frenchman or a German, thereby discouraging a Franco-German union against which the RAC had often found itself in opposition.

His warning was one to which Ugueux gave little heed; and he did so with all the authority of someone who had the full support of Metternich, the newly appointed president of the FIA, and his powerful ally, Baron Fritz Huschke von Hanstein, Porsche's public-relations manager and sports secretary of the Automobilclub von Deutschland, Germany's second-biggest motoring organisation. (A colonel in the SS, he was photographed in 1940, after having won the Mille Miglia in a BMW 328, proudly wearing its insignia on his overalls.) The CSI believed it had lined up the right man to lead its negotiating initiative.

He was Patrick Duffeler, who, during his six years as a director of Philip Morris's promotions in Europe, the Middle East and Africa, had come, of course, to know personally the teams, drivers, organisers and FIA officials at the highest level. Approached by von Hanstein at the 1976 Italian Grand Prix at Monza, he was keen, at the age of 36, to renew dealings with Ecclestone. He shared the FIA's view that the constructors' tactics, spearheaded by Ecclestone, had tipped the balance of power dangerously in their favour. He believed that 'centralised negotiation' between the F1CA and the organisers was 'a logical development' as 'sponsors want to deal with recognised neutral authorities recognised not only within the sport but by national governments'. Such was his appetite for the task that lay ahead that he agreed to do it initially without remuneration.

At a meeting attended by most of the organisers, Ugueux announced that Duffeler had been appointed to represent their negotiating interests, and, in a hard-line move to bring about a greater unity than had been evident with Grand Prix International under Henri Treu, warned that if they failed to stand behind Duffeler their licences to stage Grands Prix might be revoked. To avoid a repeat of the Grand Prix International debacle, Michel Boeri, president of the Automobile Club de Monaco, the organisers of the Monaco Grand Prix and the Monte Carlo Rally, who were among the keenest to reverse the constructors' political and financial advances, proposed that the organisers should pledge their support by each putting up a $100,000 bond, which would be forfeited if an organiser broke rank and negotiated individually with Ecclestone.

The proposal was unanimously agreed, and thus was born what became known as the Hundred Thousand Dollar Club. Alongside Boeri at the hard core of the CSI's offensive, was von Hanstein, Jean-Marie Balestre, president of the Fédération Française du Sport Automobile, the legendary Juan Fangio, and former driver Juan Manuel Bordeu, head of the Automóvil Club Argentino's sporting commission, and delegates from Austria, Italy and Spain.

There was a touch of irony to Duffeler's appointment. The power that Ecclestone and the F1CA now enjoyed, and which he was about to stand against, was due in no small measure to Marlboro, which, during the six years of Duffeler's central involvement, had forked out many millions of dollars to broaden the global appeal of Formula One. Most of the vast and constantly increasing expenditure had gone to the constructors, which had strengthened Ecclestone's hand in his hard-line negotiations with organisers and promoters.

Across the English Channel, Ecclestone and the constructors were in defiant – and confident – mood. Without reference to the CSI, the F1CA organised the 1976 Dutch Grand Prix to its own rules. Ecclestone was delighted by the result – the pit lane was closed 20 minutes before the race, he reported, and all the cars were on the grid well in time – 'it was perfect'. It was, of course, meant – and perceived – as a direct challenge to the CSI. The constructors' rebellious stand was underlined by the announcement that the F1CA intended to publish its own Grand Prix rule book for the 1977 season once it had consulted with the teams' designers to clarify technical regulations. As for the One Hundred Thousand Dollar Club, Ecclestone's response was as contemptuous as that expressed towards Grand Prix International. He simply refused to negotiate with Duffeler.

The relationship between the two sides plumbed a new level of hostility after Duffeler announced, with the CSI's unanimous support following a meeting in Geneva, the formation of a Monaco-based not-for-profit company called World Championship Racing (WCR), to whom organisers wishing to stage Grands Prix on the basis of a structured three-year contract would be expected to delegate their negotiating authority. One of its first moves, with the support of Fangio, was to persuade the Automóvil Club Argentino to tear up the contract it had signed with the F1CA for the Argentine Grand Prix, the first championship race of the 1977 season, and just two months away. The club effectively did so by failing to respond to Ecclestone's request for the necessary financial guarantees to cover the F1CA's aircraft charter and travel arrangements. Ecclestone, on a vote of the teams, promptly announced the cancellation of the Argentine Grand Prix.

The emergence of WCR split Formula One's 17 organisers almost down the middle. The traditionalists, alarmed by what was seen as the excessive political ambition and greed of Ecclestone and the constructors, sided with Duffeler, posted their $100,000 bonds and contractually agreed to let WCR be their sole representative in negotiating the financial arrangements. They were: Argentina, Spain, Monaco, France, Germany, Austria, Holland and Italy. Others, more influenced by the power of Ecclestone, to whom some of them owed their existence and others their survival, than loyalty to the political battle of their European counterparts, either allied themselves with the F1CA or remained on the sidelines. They were: Brazil, South Africa, USA West (Long Beach), Japan, Belgium, Sweden, Britain, USA East (Watkins Glen) and Canada. In a stalemate situation, when only confusion reigned supreme, who would end up backing whom at the death was not at all clear. For example, in the same week, the organisers of the Belgian Grand Prix at Zolder had signed a contract first with

WCR and then with the F1CA. At a private meeting Ecclestone and Duffeler surprised each other by both producing copies of their 'exclusive' contracts.

With the passing of each week the battle became increasingly more acrimonious and entrenched. Even peace-making attempts by Fangio to bring the two sides together fell on deaf ears. Ecclestone's terse reply was that 'no useful purpose could be served by such a meeting'. Formula One was grievously – and some thought irreparably – divided. Such was the extent of the chaos that no one could be sure when the first round of the 1977 World Championship series would actually start, how many races there would be, which circuits would take part, or how much money would be available in prize funds. Once again the long-suffering sponsors were becoming seriously alarmed at the battle being waged through newspaper sports pages, a conflict that could do nothing but harm the one thing that mattered to them – their corporate image. One or two major sponsors, exasperated by the instability once again threatening their massive investments, began to warn of their withdrawal.

An example of the negative publicity that caused the sponsors to blanch was headline stories in which Ecclestone was accused of using 'muscle' to persuade the more vulnerable organisers to sign contracts on his terms. According to Duffeler, one of the reasons why WCR had been formed was to protect the organisers from Ecclestone's tactics. The Japanese Grand Prix, with a last-minute demand for more money to cover transportation costs, was, he claimed, an example of a regular practice that saw fee increases as high as 20 per cent. 'He'd call the guy about four days before the Grand Prix, saying they [the teams] couldn't go unless the kitty was increased.' Ecclestone, he alleged, tended to pick on 'some of the lesser clubs ... who were more influenced by [his] very aggressive tactics ... they were more susceptible to fear than the more powerful clubs'.

Another tactic, he alleged, was for Ecclestone to claim that the drivers were unhappy about a circuit's safety conditions, but that they could be persuaded to race if the fee was increased. Duffeler recalled one event when the drivers had raised safety concerns with Ecclestone in his trailer. His response was to tell the drivers that they were paid to race and that their opinions on the issue were not relevant. 'This had taken place at a Grand Prix where Ecclestone had been very comfortable with the total contractual arrangements.' He became convinced that track safety was not one of Ecclestone's central concerns but rather a lever to prise more money out of the organisers. Another tactic, he claimed, was to offer favours to people negotiating on behalf of organisers in return for their support in agreeing to his financial terms. 'He would use any potential selling tactic ... to get his way ... [and] I don't know there were too many limits.' But, on the other hand, some of the organisers, he conceded, were not always scrupulously honest. When negotiating financial terms with Ecclestone, they would often underestimate their revenue and overestimate their costs. 'While many acted like gentlemen, they did not always reflect gentlemanly virtues.'

Accusations of unscrupulousness in his dealings with organisers were roundly rejected by Ecclestone. He refuted media claims that the F1CA had acted like the Mafia. 'I know that in the past the constructors' association has been likened to the Mafia and people have even called me the Godfather, but that's just not true. I wish I was a Godfather. They have millions of pounds, don't they? And travel about in jets instead of railway trains like me. Believe me, if I were a Godfather, I would not be getting involved in wrangles over racing cars roaring round a circuit.' If anybody could be accused of acting like the Mafia, he insisted, it was Duffeler and Ugueux. 'Well, I'm not frightened of a fight if that is what they want. I shan't put up my hands and let them kick me. I'm not a little girl and I believe in fighting for what is right.'

As for allegations that he had acted unscrupulously in his dealings with organisers, he dismissed them by saying: 'What, my friend, does unscrupulous mean? I don't understand the word.' He seized the opportunity to portray himself as a much misunderstood man, someone who did what he did purely for the love of the sport. 'I have taken nothing out of motor racing. My expenses are not even paid by the constructors' association, and just to show how much I love the sport I ran my own racing team for three years without a sponsor,'[8] a claim that unfortunately didn't coincide with the facts. It also contradicted somewhat the comment he made on acquiring the Brabham team five years earlier. He was, he said, 'a businessman and this move is first and foremost a business venture with the objective of selling the finest racing cars available'.[9]

The confrontation between the F1CA and WCR had become so acrimonious that in early December 1976 the UK-based Guild of Motoring Writers organised a press conference at the RAC's Clubhouse in Pall Mall, London, to which both sides were invited for the purpose of clarifying the future of a season that was now less than four weeks away. Ugueux agreed to attend, but failed to turn up at the last minute, claiming 'unexpected business' in Belgium. In the circumstances it was considered an implausible excuse and seen as an affront to both the F1CA and WCR. Duffeler believed that Ugueux the politician was beginning to back-pedal. 'He had become concerned about the visible strength being gained by WCR, and accusations by Ecclestone that he was prejudicially favouring the organisers over the constructors.' From the head office of the FIA in Paris, said Duffeler, his 'more reserved position' angered the organisers who had backed the creation of WCR in the belief that it had the full support of the CSI.

From the outset the mood of the press conference was so hostile that Ecclestone and Duffeler refused to sit at the same table. By Ecclestone's side sat Max Mosley, who was occasionally seen to whisper into his ear. Unhappily placed in the middle of exchanges of personal abuse between Ecclestone and Duffeler was the diplomatic Sir Clive Bossom, who found himself representing an opinion of one, when he denied that Formula One was in 'a big, bloody mess, because we are not',[10] adding that he believed an FIA-approved World Championship series would take place. The meeting ended nearly three hours later as it had begun – in uncertainty and disunity – although Sir Clive issued reassurances that the CSI would be reviewing certain rules and regulations to prevent misinterpretation, another area of contention that had caused clashes between the two sides.

It was in the circumstances of this most pessimistic state of affairs, with both sides seemingly refusing to step away from the cliff edge, that a week later the FIA called an emergency meeting in Paris at the offices of the Automobile Club de France in what was seen as a last-ditch attempt to avert a far-reaching disaster. Contrary to all expectations, a breakthrough was achieved, with, to the astonishment of most, Ecclestone backing down. According to Duffeler, the constructors agreed to attend the Argentine Grand Prix on WCR's terms. Ecclestone, said Duffeler, also agreed to the payments – the 'start' and prize money – put on the table on behalf of the organisers the WCR represented, which was based on a varying scale of payments fixed, among other factors, by the size of gate, revenue and travel distance involved.

That evening a jubilant Fangio, Bordeu and Duffeler made various calls to Buenos Aires to confirm that the Argentine Grand Prix was back on. The teams began a frantic rush to get cars, engines and equipment air-freighted to Buenos Aires in time for the Grand Prix on 9 January. The logistics were made no easier by the track being under strict military police control after a right-wing military junta coup some ten months earlier. It was feared that opposition forces might use the event to launch an attack to grab world headlines. But the race took place without hitch, with Ugueux, von Hanstein and Duffeler there to represent the CSI and WCR.

It was in Buenos Aires, incidentally, that Ecclestone enjoyed the rewards of a couple of successful wagers. The first occurred during the 1974 Argentine Grand Prix after a number of drivers, idling away time at their hotel swimming pool, challenged each other to see who could swim the farthest under water. Jochen Mass, a German driver with the Surtees team, managed a superhuman four lengths. Ecclestone, who had been observing the proceedings, ambled over to the side of the pool to announce that he could do better. He could swim five lengths underwater. And if anyone wanted him to prove it, they could each lay $100 in his hand. As Ecclestone was hardly known for his swimming prowess, there were no shortage of takers. 'Right,' said Ecclestone, 'let's get it straight: five lengths under water, right?' That's right, was the chorused reply. 'OK,' ordered Ecclestone, 'somebody get me a snorkel!' In a similar hotel setting at a

Grand Prix several years later, Colin Chapman, spotting the immaculately dressed Ecclestone approaching the swimming pool, wagered Mario Andretti, one of his drivers, that he wouldn't push Ecclestone into the pool for $1000. Andretti accepted the wager, approached Ecclestone and told him of Chapman's challenge. Ecclestone replied: 'OK – for half the money.' He stood there while Andretti pushed him into the pool.

Two weeks later, at the Brazilian Grand Prix at São Paulo, Ugueux, von Hanstein and Duffeler were joined by Metternich and Bossom. All were cautiously confident that WCR had achieved its purpose. Ugueux offered Duffeler his congratulations. He added, said Duffeler: 'Now that this is all done, it is the CSI's job to finalise the European agreements; this will give us multi-year contracts for all the European clubs. That is what we always wanted. Leave it me.'

Duffeler, though, returned to Europe with nagging doubts. Still 'shocked' by the duplicity of the circuit owners at Zolder in signing an 'exclusive' contract with both the F1CA and WCR, he wondered how long the terms agreed with Ecclestone would remain intact. He was also disturbed by 'numerous petty jealousies inside clubs, between clubs, between organisers. I had lot of respect for the likes of Metternich and von Hanstein and the organisers who had put up the $100,000 bond [but] there was certainly a great deal more professionalism and business-like thinking on the other side.'

After the teams returned to Europe, Ugueux attempted to conclude what had been considered a formality: getting Ecclestone to put his signature on a contract, based on the terms agreed with WCR, to cover the European organisers. By March, though, serious disagreements had arisen between the CSI and the F1CA. Ecclestone was no longer willing to put its name to the contract. According to Duffeler, Ugueux 'dropped the ball'. It allowed Ecclestone to 're-enter the fray' and successfully include fresh terms to the three-year contracts which made them more favourable to the F1CA. 'Ecclestone outmanoeuvred him,' said Duffeler. Ecclestone did a U-turn knowing that, with the season underway and peace seemingly restored, the last thing his adversaries in Paris would want was another bloody confrontation to threaten the entire calendar. It effectively meant the end of WCR, which was laid quietly to rest alongside Grand Prix International.

Duffeler, who had hoped that World Championship Racing would become a permanent arrangement to broker future deals between the organisers and the F1CA, said: 'When I look back, I can see that WCR was doomed from the start. I was not really seeing reality when I accepted the position of bringing together a coalition of organisers that would create the "right balance" for the sport. I actually succeeded briefly but by the time the Argentine Grand Prix had taken place, I already had my nose full of the political intrigues and discord that were pervasive in the background of the CSI, the clubs and the track owners. Bernie, on the other hand, was smarter than the majority of the organisers. He was a very high-pressure salesman and a very good tactician, who out-performed, out-negotiated and out-smarted a great number of the people he dealt with. He was driven by money and power, his two principal motives.'

Duffeler had come to realise that the great strength of the constructors was their unity. Unlike the organisers, who met most infrequently and didn't even share the same language, the teams moved as a single force, and were able to plan and decide their tactics with a flexibility and spontaneity that their adversaries were unable to counter. The fragmentation of the organisers, geographically and culturally, also enabled the constructors to exploit a relationship weighted heavily in their favour – if an organiser decided to sacrifice his Grand Prix rather than meet Ecclestone's demands, another circuit, albeit just about passing muster, could be found. To the teams it was just another race. To an organiser it meant the loss of a major part of his revenue.

The only real threat to the constructors in these battle-worn days was posed by Enzo Ferrari. If the Duffelers and Treus had been able to persuade him to break ranks with the constructors, the appeal of the Ferrari team would have ensured a breakaway Grand Prix, with, doubtless, others to follow. Fully aware of his advantageous position, he would move camp in the direction of the constructors or the FIA, depending on which best suited his commercial or political interests or mood at any particular time. By inching this way or that way, like the fulcrum of a balance, he was able to wield a power out of all proportion to the fact that he represented but one team.

So it seemed that peace had been restored to Formula One. But it would prove, as tension increased between the constructors and the FIA establishment, to be a most fragile one.

While Ecclestone was seen as the thrusting, decision-making leader of the constructors, he needed nevertheless to carry with him their goodwill, which could never be considered a given. It could hardly have been otherwise when endeavouring to represent the common cause of such volatile characters as Frank Williams, Ken ('when the flag drops, the bullshit stops') Tyrrell, John Surtees and Colin 'Chunky' Chapman, whose team in these early days, when he was said to have considered himself too grand to attend the meetings, was represented by team manager Peter Warr. Another distinguished absentee, for very much the same reason, was Enzo Ferrari, who was represented by team boss Luca di Montezemolo. These were men, principals or team bosses, who were no less aggressive, egotistical and competitive than Ecclestone. They also shared a mutual mistrust of one another, careful to give nothing away at their meetings, particularly if a technical issue was on the agenda. Although a constructor might well have a solution in mind, he would be careful not to give too much away. And whenever Ecclestone rattled off a proposed deal, those round the table would hastily scribble their calculations on paper well screened from curious eyes. Some would do their best, too, to sneakily read Ecclestone's notes on the yellow stickers in front of him, but always unsuccessfully due to the illegibility of his writing. At the end of the meeting these would join dozens of other similar yellow stickers in his briefcase.

Even after Ecclestone's arrival, and with support from Mosley, who soon became established as Ecclestone's co-negotiator with the FIA establishment, meetings could become so unruly, with a red-faced Tyrrell trying to shout the loudest, that Warr would be appointed chairman in an effort to bring some order out of the chaos. According to Warr, it was Ecclestone's practice to let discussions rage as points of view coalesced into different cliques, until he announced that he believed he had the solution. 'The reaction would be: why the hell didn't we think of that…?' These meetings of men enjoined by common interest and mutual suspicion were skilfully handled by Ecclestone, added Warr. 'He had a very, very tough job, trying to keep many balls in the air in the interests of everyone in the business. He was always very, very fair and very, very correct. You wouldn't get anyone to say in Formula One that Bernie ever did an underhand thing in his life.'

One of the balls Ecclestone had to keep in the air for the constructors was the support of Ferrari. The wily Enzo Ferrari knew the value of his name to Ecclestone in the constructors' negotiations with the organisers and used it to obtain certain concessions. When, for instance, Ferrari insisted on flying from Milan, rather than Heathrow as part of the collective travel arrangements, and, moreover, that they should be allowed to take more than the agreed number of personnel, Ecclestone had to find a way of covering the considerable additional cost, which he would achieve by either charging the organisers more, or levelling out benefits to the teams. 'Ferrari were always the odd people out,' said a senior team member. 'They were always getting the pants beaten off them by these "garagistes" in England, but they were an essential part of the package. So concessions had to be made to keep them on board.'

Ecclestone had also, said Warr, acquired a reputation as the man in Formula One who 'fixed things', the one person who could bring to bear whatever was necessary to get things done. Warr had personal experience of this ability. While he was running the Wolf team, which was funded by multi-millionaire Canadian businessman Walter Wolf, from 1977 to 1979, he hit a problem in his first season with Jody Scheckter, who was leading the World Championship. Because he was from apartheid South Africa, Scheckter was refused a visa to travel to Japan to compete in the Grand Prix at Mount Fuji. A desperate Warr called Ecclestone to explain his predicament. A short while later Ecclestone had solved the problem, even though it meant Scheckter entering Japan irregularly – on a journalist's visa. Added Warr: 'I bet you there is not a team in F1 that at some stage hasn't phoned Bernie up and said, listen, we've got a bit of bother with this and he's said, leave it with me, I'll sort it.'

The political pressure on South Africa at this time, when the death of human rights activist Steve Biko at the hands of security police in September 1977 caused an international furore, was intense. The United Nations was urging a global anti-apartheid embargo on trade and arms. Sporting authorities were also urged to isolate the country, all of whom agreed. But, to Ecclestone, it was business as usual. While the political storm raged, he quietly proceeded to hold negotiations with controversial businessman Louis Luyt, who had fronted a secret government bid to acquire South African Associated Newspapers and subvert its liberal newspapers. He was also involved with the pro-government *Citizen* newspaper, sponsors of the Grand Prix.

South Africa's international political embarrassment strengthened Ecclestone's negotiating hand. Aware that the government was keen to do all it could to maintain international sporting links, he took full advantage of the situation to extract every penny, to a degree that threatened the 1978 Grand Prix. The total cost came to more than £350,000, a very considerable sum in those days, which included £187,000 prize fund money, £85,000 for the charter of two cargo planes, £40,000 for the teams' travelling expenses and £10,000 for promotional expenses. Luyt, who had guaranteed £100,000 sponsorship of an event whose ticket sales were not expected to exceed £215,000, was so alarmed by Ecclestone's demands that, unable to find a co-sponsor, he threatened to withdraw. The day was saved when an engineering company agreed a one-off deal to cover the balance. The South African Grand Prix was sponsored through Luyt for at least three years. During this time passport entry stamps were recorded on separate cards and destroyed on departure to avoid any political complications when entering other countries officially opposed to apartheid. 'There was simply too much money at stake to scratch Kyalami,' said the race manager of one of the leading teams at the time.

For the next eight years Ecclestone continued to ignore mounting international pressure on South Africa, until, finally, even he had no choice, although his decision was not due to any political consideration. But he went down fighting. The writing was writ large when Renault decided to pull out of the 1986 Grand Prix, and the metalworkers' union at Ferrari threatened that its members would not prepare the cars for the following Grands Prix at Brands Hatch and Adelaide if the team didn't follow suit. Amid fears that terrorists might use the Grand Prix for an anti-apartheid protest, the Brazilian government requested Nélson Piquet and Ayrton Senna not to take part. A similar request was made to Ferrari's Stefan Johansson by Svenska Bilsportforbundet, Sweden's national racing authority.

Until then, Ecclestone appeared to all the world to be unmoved by such threats and concerns. He had already signed a deal with Selwyn Nathan, promotions director of Southern Suns Hotels, by now the race sponsors. Publicly, he was supported by the FIA, although, privately, it was said to be keen to cancel the race. But it was feared that if it did, the constructors and the sponsors could sue the FIA for damages. The South African judicial system inadvertently added to the pressures on the teams by deciding to hang a black activist on a date that coincided with the penultimate South African Grand Prix. It was a ruling that provoked world protest, and, over lunch with senior government figures, Ecclestone and Mosley voiced strong disapproval of the execution as well as its timing. The government, they were told, could not interfere with the judicial process.

Apparently, ignoring the political pressures and flak that was coming from all sides, Ecclestone continued to insist the South African Grand Prix was on – until, that is, several international television networks, facing internal pressure from unions, announced they would not be broadcasting the race. It was only then, when the race was faced with the loss of all-important television coverage, that Ecclestone announced the Grand Prix would not take place. The power of television, it seemed, had succeeded where all other efforts had failed. But Ecclestone claims today that such public perception did him an injustice. He had been fully in favour of cancelling the race but feared that FOCA would have been sued by the promoters, Southern Suns Hotels. Indeed, he adds, in looking for a reason to cancel it, he went to Renault 'and, I think, Enzo Ferrari', which led to the withdrawal of Renault and the union threat at Ferrari. 'I needed a reason to cancel it. I certainly didn't want it to go ahead. I said to the promoters that we would make up for it, do something later.' It turned out, in fact, to be the last South African Grand Prix until 1992, which survived for another year before disappearing from the FIA calendar altogether.

5

CHAMPIONSHIP TITLE OR POLITICAL POWER? IT'S BERNIE'S DILEMMA

While Ecclestone was busy with the affairs of the F1CA and his sundry business ventures, the Brabham racing team was effectively under the control of the newly promoted chief designer, South African Gordon Murray, who had replaced Colin Seeley as a director of Motor Racing Developments, and Herbie Blash, now back as the Brabham team manager. The son of a Durban motor mechanic, and a mechanical engineering graduate who designed and built his own racing car at the age of 19, Murray wrote to Colin Chapman for a design job interview. He arrived in England in 1970 – 'it seemed to be the centre of the universe if you were interested in racing' – clutching Chapman's reply agreeing to see him, only to find that Lotus was going through a lean time. There was no work for Murray's eager skills. After spending six months looking in vain for a job in general car design, he was advised to try Brabham. From the moment he met Brabham's technical director, Ron Tauranac – 'the most practical and logical car designer I have ever met' – they got on well, and Murray joined the team as a draughtsman.

Murray, the only survivor of Ecclestone's cost-cutting purge of the design team soon after his acquisition of Motor Racing Developments, was flattered but puzzled by his appointment as chief designer. 'I have no idea to this day why he decided to keep me and get rid of everybody else. When somebody asked him about that, he said he made some joke about finding me under a dustsheet.' But the appointment posed a problem for Murray. With rumours abounding about the company's future, he had been ready to quit prior to Ecclestone's arrival. Uncertain of his prospects, he agreed, as a private job, to design a car for Le Mans. When Murray explained the situation to Ecclestone, his new boss agreed that he could moonlight as long as priority was given to the production of a new Formula One car. The Brabham cars, said Ecclestone, were 'all crap'. Over the next six months Murray had a punishing schedule: working single-handedly on a new Formula One car until 10 o'clock at night, and then until three or four in the morning on the Le Mans car.

The result was the BT42 for the 1973 season, the first of Murray's pyramidal monocoques, and, for Le Mans, a car which came fourth. The strain caused Murray to have his first physical collapse. But the experience failed to slow him down. If he and Ecclestone had anything in common, it was their need to be in personal control. For that reason, Murray, then an arrogant, self-confessed control freak, refused to take on any assistance. He drew every Brabham part himself, from the gearbox to the final graphics, for the simple reason that he believed that nobody could draw to his standards. Until the BT42, the 'crap' cars which the Brabham drivers – Graham Hill, Carlos Reutemann and Wilson Fittipaldi – had been racing were Tauranac's BT34 'lobster claw' and the BT37, which was nothing more spectacular than a revised version of the BT34.

It was in Murray's 'triangular' BT44, based on the BT42 and driven by Carlos Reutemann, that, at the South African Grand Prix in 1974, the Brabham team scored its first win under Ecclestone's ownership. It was also an occasion for Ecclestone to exercise his roguish sense of humour at the expense of John Goossens, then a senior executive of Texaco Belgium's marketing division, which, with Marlboro, had succeeded in luring the 1972 world champion Emerson Fittipaldi away from Lotus to join McLaren. Fittipaldi, who had come second in the 1973 series, had just won the Brazilian Grand Prix, the second race of the new season.

Ecclestone and Goossens had been playing gin rummy for two days, with Ecclestone coming out the loser to the tune of about $1000. 'It was enough to make him sick,' said Goossens. In a gesture of disgust, Ecclestone finally threw down his cards, before announcing: 'Here is a guy who understands nothing about motor racing. He's lucky enough to pick Fittipaldi, who will probably win the World Championship [he did], and he's just been lucky enough to win in Brazil. Now he's lucky enough to beat the hell out of me at gin rummy. I suppose if I put a Texaco sticker on my car, I will win the race.' Goossens laughed, and the two men parted company.

The next morning Goossens was stopped by two journalists who asked if it was true what Ecclestone had just told them. What did he say? asked Goossens.

'He said he lost so much money playing you at gin rummy that he couldn't afford to pay you and you forced him to put a Texaco sticker on the Brabham car.' Disbelieving what he'd been told, Goossens rushed to the Brabham pit to see a large Texaco sticker on the front of the car to be driven by Reutemann. He protested in vain to Ecclestone that he mustn't do it, that Texaco had a monopoly contract with McLaren. Why not? countered Ecclestone. It wasn't illegal. 'In any garage in the UK, you can pick up a Texaco sticker and put it your car,' he added, and refused to have the sticker removed. It was a race which, with one car after another breaking down, Reutemann, of course, won. News of the win, with photographs of the winning car, featured on a number of sports pages – and soon afterwards Goossens was summoned to the company's headquarters in America. The newspaper photographs seemed to confirm what they had heard. Was it true, his bosses wanted to know, that he had pressured Ecclestone into putting the Texaco sticker on Reutemann's car in lieu of a gin rummy debt that Ecclestone couldn't afford to meet? An abashed Goossens, with hand on heart, assured them that he hadn't, and explained that it had simply been Ecclestone's way of getting his own back.

The South African Grand Prix win was a first for the moody 32-year-old Reutemann, who ended the season by also winning the Austrian Grand Prix and the US Grand Prix at Watkins Glen. Formula One commentators began talking about the renaissance of Brabham, although predictions of the team's emergence as a World Championship force were somewhat premature.

Although Reutemann finished third in the 1975 World Championship and Brabham second in the Constructors' Championship, his relationship with Ecclestone deteriorated sharply after a dispute over his retainer. Ecclestone declined to pay the kind of money the Argentinian thought he was worth. Like Enzo Ferrari – 'I take a driver that no one wants to sign and in three races he can win a Grand Prix ... it is my car that wins'[1] – Ecclestone believed it was the car, not the driver, which won races. Reutemann signed with Ferrari – he had to pay Ecclestone $100,000 for breaking his contract – which briefly propelled Ulsterman John Watson, who had joined Brabham in 1973, to the number-one slot. But the Brabham team would soon tragically lose its second driver, the promising Brazilian Carlos Pace, who had arrived at Brabham the previous season sponsored by a Brazilian coffee company. On 18 March 1977, two weeks after the South African Grand Prix, in which he came thirteenth, he died in a flying accident.

Ecclestone, realising that Watson, who won five Grands Prix in 154 appearances during a 12-year career and whose best year would be a joint second in 1982, was unlikely to bring Brabham the World Championship title, began talking to Niki Lauda, the 1975 world champion, who had joined Ferrari in 1974 under newly appointed team boss, Luca di Montezemolo, to take the Scuderia to renewed success. In August 1977 the 28-year-old Austrian, on his way to winning his second championship title, flew to London the week before the Dutch Grand Prix at Zandvoort for a secret meeting with Ecclestone, who was keen to sign him for the following season. Ecclestone was also keen on a sponsorship deal that Lauda believed he could bring with him.

The company was Parmalat, the Italian dairy farm conglomerate, which at the time was seriously considering sponsoring the Brazilian driver Emerson Fittipaldi, in whose country it had recently opened a new factory. Lauda introduced Ecclestone to senior executives at Parmalat, which led to a series of meetings to discuss a proposal that, as part of a sponsorship agreement, would have Ecclestone overseeing a marketing operation in England to which he would commit his expertise. In return, Parmalat would pay $500,000 to cover a penalty payment for Lauda's defection from Ferrari, and also make up the deficit in the annual retainer that Ecclestone would be paying Lauda, which was considerably less than the £200,000 on offer from Ferrari. Parmalat agreed and began to wind down its sponsorship commitments elsewhere to meet the costs.

Lauda's defection from Ferrari caused uproar among Italy's *tifosi*. Not only had he rejected a personal invitation from the venerated Enzo Ferrari himself, but Lauda, in a media interview, was less than complimentary about the Ferrari team. Heroically in the circumstances, he turned up at a test session prior to the Italian Grand Prix at Monza the weekend after his outburst. He was greeted by a hail of potatoes and tomatoes thrown into the Ferrari pits by a large and angry crowd. Ecclestone, though, was a happy man. Within a short time Parmalat was paying most of Brabham's $10-million annual budget. How pleased Parmalat was has proved more difficult to gauge.

In July 1978 a company called Parmalat UK Ltd was formed and Ecclestone was appointed its sole director, with its registered offices at 14–16 Great Portland Street, London W1, the address given for many of the 17 Formula One-related companies which in later years he would set up. But, on the evidence of the company's annual accounts, it seems he did little indeed to advance Parmalat's marketing interests: it failed to trade and remains a dormant company to this day. A central figure in this partnership was public-relations consultant Gianni Scarica. He declined to discuss the UK operation. It was, he said through an interpreter, 'delicate and confidential'. Further questions were referred to the office of Parmalat's General Director, Domenico Barili, in Italy, who said: 'I can only tell you that this company was formed with the view of running a possible Parmalat business in the UK market. It is still a dormant company because we did not have the opportunity to use it, but the friendship which binds Mr Ecclestone and Parmalat is still very strong.'

Lauda remained with Brabham for less than two years in a relationship that disappointed all expectations. Although he finished fourth in the 1978 World Championship table, the following year he plummeted to fourteenth, and, long before the Italian Grand Prix, where he recorded his best result of the season by coming fourth, he was making it known at the circuits that he would be leaving Brabham at the end of the season. It was due, he said, to a loss of motivation – 'I don't want to drive in circles any more' – and his dissatisfaction with the Brabham cars, which he described as 'totally uncompetitive'.[2] Ecclestone responded by offering three-times world champion Jackie Stewart, 40, who had retired six years earlier, $2.5 million if he signed for Brabham for one season. Lauda described the offer, which Stewart declined to accept, as 'a joke', while others saw it as a ruse by Ecclestone to create a headline and wind up Lauda. If so, it worked on both counts.

Backed by Parmalat and Marlboro, Lauda changed his mind when Ecclestone offered him $2 million for the season. He was also influenced by Ecclestone's decision to move from the Alfa Romeo 12-cylinder engine to the Ford Cosworth DFV V8. Nevertheless, Lauda remained deeply unsettled. A few days after signing new terms for the following season, he suddenly got out of his car during the practice session at the Canadian Grand Prix in Montreal, the penultimate race of the season, to tell a stunned Ecclestone that he was quitting for good, explaining he could no longer race simply for the money. 'I told him I had had enough and wanted to do different things in my life ... that I couldn't drive any more ... that I didn't *want* to.'[3] Ecclestone, he reported, understood his decision perfectly and wished him well, an attitude that for the hard-nosed Ecclestone, given the money he was investing in the new Cosworth-powered car, bordered on the saintly.

Shortly after breaking the news to Ecclestone, Lauda, whose ailing business fortunes would compel him to return to Formula One three years later, in 1984, to win his third World Championship, bumped into Alistair Caldwell, former team manager of McLaren, as he walked through the lobby of his Montreal hotel. He told Caldwell about his decision and his reason. Caldwell was more than usually interested. He had just agreed to join Brabham as development engineer to give the team's performance greater consistency, a factor behind Lauda's earlier criticism.

Caldwell says he had no illusions about working for Ecclestone, whose abrasive management style was well known. 'I made it clear when I went to work for him that he would only shout at me once, which would be the day I left,' said the man who had his own reputation for wanting things done his way. It had led to his departure from McLaren, which he had joined as a junior mechanic in 1967 after arriving in England from New Zealand, and where, five years later, he became team manager. After guiding McLaren to World Championship titles in 1974 and 1976, and runners-up in 1975 and 1977, he had a serious difference of opinion with team co-founder Teddy Mayer after the team began to deteriorate in the 1978 season. Caldwell, who wanted the team to adopt a change of tactics, made the conflict a resigning issue, and lost the day.

He went to Brabham because of his admiration for Gordon Murray. He believed that with Murray's design skills and his experience the team could achieve what he believed they had always lacked – consistency. 'They always suffered from a philosophy of trying to win races instead of championships,' he said. 'Jack Brabham lost sight of that, and it didn't change when Bernie took over. Look at Keke Rosberg – he became world champion in 1982, and he won only one Grand Prix. Reliability has to predominate over winning races.' One of the Brabham team's major faults, added Caldwell, had been that their cars had lacked that reliability. 'I wanted to introduce some of the disciplines that had been an essential part of McLaren's success, such as records on basic things like engine failure or modifications, just quality control, really, which was all part of helping to keep the cars reliable.'

In 1980, Caldwell's first full year with Brabham, 28-year-old Brazilian Nélson Piquet, a Formula Three champion who had joined Brabham in 1978 to team up with Niki Lauda, came second to Williams's Alan Jones – the closest the Brabham team had come to producing a world champion since Ecclestone had taken over – but the relationship between Caldwell and Ecclestone was beginning to live up to its stormy expectations. 'There was constant tension,' said Caldwell. 'Bernie ran a very, very unhappy ship. He thrived on aggravation, he thrived on fear. The whole place was always worried about Bernie. If a mechanic was found somewhere he shouldn't have been, he'd be sacked. Tea-making equipment was banned because stopping for tea meant stopping work.' Caldwell claims his clashes with Ecclestone, at least inside the factory, were invariably caused by his response to his employer's frugal habits.

'The lighting in the factory was so bad that the mechanics, when working under a car, had to use hand torches, for which, by the way, they had to buy the batteries. Without consulting Bernie, I commissioned the installation of more powerful fluorescent strip lighting which was much lower to the ground and made the mechanics' work easier. When he saw what I had done, he went epileptic with rage because of the cost. He would also come into the drawing office, where I might be with Gordon, and he'd turn off the lights, which made it very difficult for the draughtsmen to see. I would immediately switch them back on again, which was the sort of thing that added to the friction. I think he couldn't cope with me because I was the only one there who wasn't frightened of him.'

But Caldwell's clashes with Ecclestone on the track were more serious. The first occurred at the 1979 Canadian Grand Prix shortly after his arrival, when it was decided not to change engines in the spare car prior to the race. During the race the engine blew while Piquet held a commanding lead. It led to a major row between the two men, which almost equalled the fracas at the Brazilian Grand Prix in 1981, when Caldwell went against Ecclestone's instructions and agreed with Piquet that he should stay with dry tyres. A sudden downpour as the track was drying in unpredictable weather saw Piquet, who started in pole position, finish twelfth. They parted company a couple of months later after a public row at the Monaco Grand Prix – 'I really can't remember what sparked it off' – when Piquet, again on pole position, finished ninth. 'Yes, Bernie sacked me, but I had no problem with that. He sacked me before I could quit. I said I would the day he shouted at me.'

Their parting was made all the more bitter by of a dispute over a bonus which Caldwell claimed was overdue. Ecclestone, he said, refused to pay him, alleging that he had probably already received his bonus by way of backhanders from one of three engine builders to whom Caldwell gave the Brabham business. Said Caldwell: 'I went to three different companies to play one off the other, to get the best engine and the best service. It seemed Bernie thought I was doing it to get a bribe from them. The thought had never entered my head. They didn't even used to give me a Christmas card, and I used to give them millions of pounds [in business].' That season Piquet went on to win the World Championship, due, insists Caldwell, to his efforts. Following a brief spell with the ATS team, he quit the world of motor sport for good to set up a successful storage rental business.

Gordon Murray, one of Formula One's most creative designers, was left smarting by Lauda's reference to Brabham's 'totally uncompetitive' cars. He had been referring to the BT48, introduced in 1979, his final season with Brabham, and powered by Alfa Romeo's 3-litre 12-cylinder engine, which hit a series of problems from the fuel system and gearbox to a water leak and brakes. It was proving a testing time for Murray, whose ingenious efforts the previous season, with the BT46 and BT46B, had also come a cropper, although with problems of design rather than engineering.

The BT46, which first appeared at the South African Grand Prix, incorporated a surface-cooling system intended to replace radiators and therefore radically reduce aerodynamic drag. Water and oil was cooled by passing through a double-skinned channel which formed the outer skin of the chassis – the same principle as the conventional radiator but spread over a much larger area. Unfortunately, the technology wasn't available to provide the degree of oil cooling the engine required. With minimal drag, it proved exceptionally fast but boiled like a kettle by the end of a lap. Critics claimed it would have worked – if the car had had the surface area of a London

Transport double-decker bus. Murray's tongue-in-cheek reply was that it did have that surface area – if the surface fin convulations were unravelled. The BT46 survived until the Spanish Grand Prix, to be replaced at the next race – the Swedish Grand Prix – by the more controversial BT46B, whose design caused a confrontation between Ecclestone and the other teams of such hostility that it threatened the unity of the F1CA (which, incidentally, that year – 1978– changed its name to the Formula One Constructors' Association (FOCA), when it was somewhat belatedly realised that 'F1CA' was similar to an Italian expletive).

The BT46B was Murray's answer to Colin Chapman's revolutionary 'ground effect' Lotus 78, whose underside was designed to form a venturi 'throat' while ceramic and polypropylene strips – or 'skirts' – were fitted along the sides of the car, brushing the track to 'force' air underneath and increase air pressure and downforce to give greater suction and thus cornering speeds. Launched in 1977, it was replaced the following season by the sleeker Lotus 79, in which Mario Andretti won the World Championship and Lotus the Constructors' Championship. It became the new technology that all the other teams strove to match. Unable to copy the Lotus 79 because the configuration of the wide Alfa Romeo 3-litre B12 engine used by Brabham prevented a venturi crucial to creating the same degree of downforce, Murray came up with a car similar in effect to the Chaparral 'sucker' car that Texan Jim Hall had pioneered in CanAm racing eight years earlier.

The fundamental difference was that Hall had used a secondary motor to create suction, while Murray used a fan at the rear of the car geared to engine speed, but it achieved the same result: a tremendous downforce and a much faster cornering speed. Such was the secrecy used to protect the BT46B from prying eyes, which Ecclestone and Murray were convinced was a world-beater, that in the pits at Anderstorp, where Niki Lauda notched up a brilliant victory, the fan was hidden from view with a dustbin lid-like cover. But the other teams – led by Colin Chapman, Ken Tyrrell, Frank Williams, John Surtees and Teddy Mayer – claimed that the fan, clearly intended to improve the car's aerodynamics, was movable, contrary to FIA rules. Not so, argued Ecclestone and Murray. In sucking air from beneath the car, which then passed through a rear water radiator mounted horizontally on top of the engine, the fan was a legitimate cooling aid and, as such, came within the FIA rules.

The teams remained unconvinced and demanded official clarification: was the fan a movable aerodynamic device or not? Ecclestone made his position clear. The teams would attempt to block the BT46B at their peril. He warned that he would go to law 'if we suffer any financial loss from anyone who tries to stop us [from racing the car]'.[4] The clash became all the more acrimonious when some drivers claimed that the fan was dangerous. It sucked stones and grit off the track and spat them out at cars behind, they claimed. But that allegation, said Murray, was inspired by Colin Chapman, who was said to have seen the Brabham car as a serious threat to the Lotus 78.

Said Murray: 'One of Chapman's drivers lobbied all the drivers. Some of them went along with him because their team bosses said they should, and others came to me and Bernie and said they were not going to say that because it was bullshit. The fan couldn't spit anything out at the back because the fan e-flux [exit speed] at maximum speed was only 55mph. Besides, the radial fan would have sent any stones flying sideways.' John Watson, supporting Murray's claims, said the drivers' objections 'perpetrated the lie. They were doing it to protect their competitive position.' At one stage Chapman, who reckoned development of the principle would see drivers wearing 'G-suits' to counter the gravity load, threatened to produce a twin-fan car – one for each venturi – but decided against it 'in the better interests of racing'.

The opposition mounted against Ecclestone became so intense that his role within the FOCA itself was threatened. Chapman and other leading team bosses made it clear that unless he withdrew the BT46B he could forget about representing the constructors. This, they knew, was Ecclestone's Achilles heel and were ready to exploit it. Ecclestone went to Murray to explain his predicament, adding that he was going to propose a compromise solution, which would allow the car to run for another three races for the championship points before being withdrawn to 'keep the constructors happy'. Murray was incensed, firmly convinced that his adapted-Chaparral design would win the Constructors' Championship. Ecclestone, he added, was of the same opinion, but stressed the importance of building up the FOCA to make it stronger. Murray, a car designer, not a politician, was not mollified; months of hard work, and the team's hopes of major honours, were about to go down the drain through political expediency.

At a meeting of the FOCA, Ecclestone duly agreed to shelve the BT46B. A statement subsequently issued by the FOCA said that while certain aspects of the fan might not have complied with FIA regulations, members foresaw 'further developments of the principle resulting in cornering speeds of such magnitude that existing circuit safety precautions may be rendered ineffective'. A new rule would be drafted by the FOCA in collaboration with the technical sub-committee of the Commission Sportive Internationale (CSI) to outlaw the relevant aspects of the design. Its introduction was to be delayed to allow it to compete in the next three Grands Prix. The CSI, however, stepped in to insist that if it was agreed that some aspects of the design might be illegal then it had to banned forthwith. The BT46B never raced again, while Lotus went on to take the Constructors' Championship and Mario Andretti, Chapman's lead driver, the World Championship. The decision to kill his design was all the more exasperating to Murray. He claimed that subsequent airflow measurement tests carried out by the CSI had proved that the primary purpose of the fan was as a cooling aid. 'I felt sick,' he added. But the Brabham team had some comfort at the next race, the French Grand Prix, when John Watson took pole position in a conventional car. Said Watson: 'That was one of the sweetest moments of my Grand Prix career. It was sticking two fingers up at all the other teams who had been upset at what Brabham had done.' Murray believed Ecclestone took the ban hard. 'I think it might have been worse for him than it was for me, because he loved getting the cars on pole position and bringing them in and putting the covers over them. He loved it.'

It was a brief but acrimonious episode that revealed the intensity of the competition that existed between the constructors and also how far they were prepared to go to nullify another team's edge, even to the detriment of the FOCA, whose cohesion of will and purpose under Ecclestone's leadership had, in the space of a few short years, made it the most powerful single force in Formula One. It also illustrated the importance to Ecclestone of his position as the constructors' deal-maker, even at the estimated cost of the £500,000 (about $1.625 million) it took to build the BT46B and a serious chance of winning the constructors' title. Much more important, because to the pragmatic Ecclestone tomorrow was always another day, and the financial rewards that he fully anticipated were dependent on the power invested in him by the constructors.

Ecclestone would not have been surprised by the opposition of Chapman and his fellow constructors. While the FOCA stood as one against the outside world, its members were prepared to pursue all means fair or foul to protect or promote their own interests. Then, as now, fortunes were spent on finding new ways of shaving hundredths of a second off the speed of a car as designers dreamt of discovering some new aerodynamic or engineering concept. Murray's BT46B wasn't a time for quiet professional admiration, but for official protest to keep it off the track, unless, that is, it could be easily copied. That was the guiding principle: if it was possible to copy, it was legal; if it wasn't, it wasn't legal.

In addition to the 'fan' car fracas, 1978 was notable for two further reasons. The first was in the formalisation of Ecclestone's leadership role within the FOCA, along with the arrival of Max Mosley in an influential role that would ultimately lead to his presidency of the FIA. The second was a company set up by Ecclestone that would deprive European governments of substantial sums of sales-tax revenue.

In the first instance, Ecclestone was given the title of President of Administration and Chief Executive of the FOCA, while at the same time the group's General Purposes Committee, which consisted of Ecclestone, Mosley and Teddy Mayer, a co-founder of McLaren, was dissolved and the duties of Peter Macintosh, as secretary, brought to an end. One of Ecclestone's first duties was to make an appointment of his own – that of Max Mosley, as the FOCA's legal adviser. He was keen to retain the services of Mosley, who, bored and looking for new challenges, had sold his interests in the March team a year earlier. (The team's assets were subsequently bought by German self-made millionaire Hans Gunther Schmidt for his ATS team.)

The urbane 37-year-old Max Mosley, silver-tongued in more than one language, had established his worth in helping to draft the contracts between the constructors and the organisers, as well as taking an advisory role in the negotiations themselves. He had also been at Ecclestone's side during the skirmishes with Treu, Ugueux and Duffeler. Mosley had known Ecclestone from his first days as the owner of the Brabham team and had come to admire his business acumen. 'Here was a guy who knew how many beans made five,' Mosley observed. Ecclestone, in return, respected Mosley's political and legal brain.

Certainly the two could not have been more dissimilar in manner or mien. Mosley was an épée to Ecclestone's cutlass, privileged upbringing to working-class survival, intellect and subtlety to visceral logic and ruthlessness, charm and good looks to bluntness and rough-hewn features; qualities that complemented each other. Mosley believed they got on well together because they were, as he put it many years later, 'both outsiders'. Ecclestone was an 'outsider' because the one-time second-hand-car dealer possessed the neither the social graces nor the professional qualities preferred by the FIA establishment; Mosley because of the legacy of his father's name, a burden which dissuaded him from pursuing a full-time career as a Conservative politician.

He was the son of Sir Oswald Mosley, the 1930s British Fascist leader, and socialite beauty Diana Mitford, who had the unique distinction of being on good terms with both Winston Churchill and Adolf Hitler. (Baron Fritz Huschke von Hanstein, the former SS colonel, first greeted Mosley with the words: 'It is good to meet the son of an old Nazi.') Mosley's political rallies, which sparked riots in the streets, led to their imprisonment in 1940 under Regulation 18b of the Emergency Powers Act, an internment law invoked 'in the interests of public safety or defence of the realm'. The domestic turmoil caused the young Mosley to spend much of his early life in France and Germany before entering Christ Church, Oxford, to study law and physics and, in 1961, become secretary of the Oxford Union Society. He graduated with a BA in Natural Sciences, but embarked upon a legal career, specialising in patent and trademark law, after serving a pupillage in the chambers of Quintin Hogg, then a QC and later Lord Chancellor, head of the British judicial system.

At the age of 21, he developed an interest in motor sport and his weekend social life was often spent at Silverstone, a welcome diversion from his law books. He took part in club racing before buying a Brabham and moving on to Formula Two, his first race, at the age of 28, taking place at Hockenheim in the Deutschland Trophy, alongside the ranks of Graham Hill, Jean-Pierre Beltoise and Jim Clark, an event which was marked by the death of Clark. In a two-heat race, Mosley finished a creditable tenth in a field of 18 cars. But, a year later, he had a lucky escape at Nurburgring, when the front wishbone of his Lotus dropped off and jammed the front-left wheel, causing the car to career off the track to leave him shaken but unhurt in an adjacent caravan park. It brought an end to a fancied career as a driver but not to his ambitions in motor sport. He took his legal expertise into management to become a director of March Engineering, set up in 1969 with Graham Coaker, who founded the company, Robin Herd and Alan Rees, each contributing £2500 to fund start-up capital of £10,000. Working out of a small rented workshop in Bicester, Oxfordshire, the following year the March racing team caused a minor sensation.

The season began at the South African Grand Prix with Jackie Stewart, signed that year by new arrival Ken Tyrrell, on pole position in a March 701, with one of March's drivers, New Zealander Chris Amon, next to pole. During that season there was as many as six 701s on the grid – two works; two for Tyrrell, who, in the meantime, was building his own car for its debut that season in the US Grand Prix at Watkins Glen; one for the STP Corporation; and one for Colin Crabbe Racing. They also built a car for Hubert Hahne for the German Grand Prix, but it failed to qualify, and, for the 1971 season, one for Rhodesian businessman John Love. That season was also noted for the arrival of a 22-year-old driver called Niki Lauda, who joined March in time for the Austrian Grand Prix after graduating through Formula Two, which had cost him £40,000 in paid-for rides. At the end of the 1972 season he moved on to the BRM team.

Despite its promising start, the March team, in common with most of its rivals, was living on a financial knife-edge. One respected Formula One journalist, apparently unable to elicit any information from Mosley or his colleagues about its sponsors, concluded in his magazine column that March stood for Much Advertised Racing Car Hoax. March was, in fact, an acronym for Mosley, Alan Rees, Coaker and Herd, but the company became so strapped for cash that Mosley's half-brother, the Hon Jonathan Guinness, a director of the brewery company and later to become Lord Moyne, arranged for a £20,000 loan to be made to March Engineering by an investment company called Woodglen Ltd, of which he and his wife, Suzanne, were sole directors.

During these days the closeness of Mosley's association with Ecclestone had been well noted within the Formula One brotherhood. It would be to Mosley that people would often take their grievances and entreaties, to be reassured that he would 'talk to Bernie about it'. It is most probable that Ecclestone's interest in Mosley had greater strategic depth than the FOCA's need of a legal counsel, as necessary as this no doubt was in the new role of authority the constructors were taking upon themselves. Rather, Ecclestone, always one to plan three moves ahead, saw in Mosley the necessary diplomatic and political skills that made him perfectly suited to the establishment of the FIA, an influential seating that could certainly do no harm to his ambitions.

Indeed, with his new role as the constructors' legal adviser barely in place, Mosley was ready in 1977, with Ecclestone's keen support, to accept the nomination of British and some Scandinavian manufacturers for membership of the FIA's Bureau Permanent International de Constructeurs d'Automobiles – the forerunner of the Manufacturers' Commission – an influential committee responsible for technical, sporting, rally and off-road sub-commissions, and which would have given Mosley access to the FIA establishment's corridors of power. His nomination was successfully opposed by the French, German and Italian manufacturers, who did not wish to share their table with an Englishman, and particularly one so close to Ecclestone. In the political circumstances, it was probably an attempt based more on hope than confidence. But nothing was lost. And Mosley's time would come.

As a postscript to these confrontational and splenetic days, the FOCA announced a further appointment around this time, which was made not without a touch of the mischievous humour that Ecclestone relished. A title was created to make Enzo Ferrari the FOCA's President of Sport, a purely honorific office giving him the responsibility of emphasising the sporting dimension of Formula One. The problem was, he had complained to Ecclestone at a meeting attended by Mosley and Marco Piccinini, he talked too much about business. It was not good for the Formula One image. 'Don't keep talking about money, talk about the sport,' he advised Ecclestone. 'After all, if you are going to run a brothel, you wouldn't put a big sign saying "Brothel". You would put a sign saying "Hotel" and run the brothel in the basement.' So it came to pass that the mighty boss of Ferrari was appointed by Ecclestone to promote the hotel.

The seething political turbulence of the second half of the seventies continued unabated, with Ecclestone emerging as the most powerful single voice in Formula One. Now an established team owner, he had become widely respected as a shrewd and skilful operator, even by those who had suffered at his hands. So when he announced in 1977 the launch of a new company – International Race Tire Services Ltd (IRTS) – to exclusively market and distribute Goodyear competition tyres to all formulae, excluding Formula One, in Europe, Asia and South America, its success was considered assured. And, briefly, it was. But its profits were in part achieved illegally.

The formation of IRTS followed discussions between Ecclestone and Leo Mehl, Goodyear's worldwide director of racing, who would know nothing of the manner in which his company's tyres were to be sold. The agreement was straightforward: Goodyear would supply the tyres and IRTS would market and sell them. A principal figure in the company was Jean-François Mosnier, who had been involved in racing since the mid-sixties. He had worked for Ligier, Cooper and Brabham, and in 1969 joined Firestone to oversee its Formula One activities. He became a director of Ecclestone's Motor Racing Developments (International) Ltd in December 1975, which was formed in February 1971 as a company specialising in marketing and promotions before changing its name to International Race Tire Services Ltd, of which he was appointed managing director. Recruited to organise the transport and fitting of the tyres was Keith Greene, the former Brabham team manager who had quit following a dispute with Ecclestone over pay.

Under Ecclestone's direction business boomed and the company, which began with a few pens at Heathrow, soon had to move to a 25,000-square-foot warehouse and offices at Uxbridge, Middlesex, where, incidentally, the FOCA's administration office was briefly based. With a set of tyres for a Formula Two car costing as much as £800, it proved a highly lucrative business. But with some teams, those who did not have an agreement with Goodyear, IRTS imposed a strict cash-only policy. It removed all evidence of a sale – and the legal obligation to pay VAT (Value Added Tax) in the country where the trade took place. It was a part of Greene's role to collect the cash and smuggle the money out of the country and safely into the UK. After 12 months, Greene, becoming aware that it might be illegal, became tired of being 'just a money collector' and resigned. 'Once it'd [the company] been set up, all I did was collect money for it. I told Bernie I couldn't go on just doing that,' said Greene, who later became team manager of Nissan's new UK-based World Championship sports car team.

Greene was replaced by Nick Parkes, a Formula Two tyre engineer for Goodyear, who later became competitions secretary of the British Racing Drivers' Club and a member of the organisers' committee of the British Grand Prix at Silverstone. He explained how the sale of the tyres was ingeniously concealed to dupe Customs officials at border checks: 'You go out with 500 sets of tyres, you come back with 500 sets of tyres, because what happened was ... the old tyres would come off [the cars] and you'd put them back on the truck. As long as your documentation showed that you went out with 500 tyres and came back with 500 tyres, nobody worried.' With VAT payable in the countries in which the tyres were sold, and for which IRTS should have been registered for trading purposes, 'the ... people who lost out were the VAT men in Germany, Belgium, France, Italy or wherever'. And, it seems, the Inland Revenue in England.

Like Greene, Parkes found himself responsible for the safe return to England of thousands of pounds of cash in various currencies. At the end of an event, 'you would have all this money, and you had to do something with it,' he said. 'The usual practice was to put it in a suitcase and just walk through Customs or drive back with it in the boot of a car.' In some countries, though, because of the number of Customs checks involved in the return to England, a different method was deployed to minimise the risk. 'You would have to go to a certain bank and deposit it and they'd give you a receipt and you'd get on the plane, fly back and ... by the following Thursday the money would appear in a bank in England. It would be transferred via Switzerland or wherever.'

International Race Tire Services Ltd enjoyed rapid growth and profits. In the first year its export business turnover totalled £148,720, with net profits of £19,954 – three years later the figures were £503,268 and £254,889 respectively. But the company did not prosper for long. By late 1980, when net profits peaked at £456,858, Goodyear, exasperated by yet another power battle which broke out at the Spanish Grand Prix, temporarily withdrew from Formula One due to the constant hostilities between the FOCA and the Fédération Internationale de l'Automobile (FISA), which by then had succeeded the Commission Sportive Internationale (CSI) as the FIA's motor sport governing authority. Within a few months Ecclestone and Mosnier were announcing a new partnership with Avon Tyres, who had dominated formula Ford racing in the seventies with a cross-ply tyre.

At its launch in January 1981, attended by team bosses Ken Tyrrell, Frank Williams, Peter Warr, Eric Broadley of Lola, and Morris Nunn of Ensign, who were curious to see what kind of tyres Ecclestone would be selling, along with specialised, ex-Firestone racing equipment, Mosnier made it clear the company was neither a promoter nor a sponsor – it was strictly a commercial operation. Mosnier declined to say how much their tyres would cost or name 'the two or three teams' who, he said, would be using Avon Tyres that season. They turned out to be down-the-grid teams ATS, Ensign and Theodore. But even at the launch of the new partnership things were not quite what they seemed. The radial tyre unveiled was not from Avon but Goodyear – the Goodyear name had been burnt off and the Avon name painted on. Goodyear had sold its moulds and equipment to Avon, which used them for its own programme.

International Race Tire Services could not repeat the success it had enjoyed with Goodyear. By April 1983, unable to compete with Michelin, Pirelli and Goodyear, who had now moved back into Formula One, it ceased trading, with losses of £34,242. Leo Mehl, after more than 30 years with Goodyear, retired in March 1996 to become executive director of the Indy Racing League from January 1997 until the end of 1999, still unaware of the activities of International Race Tire Services Ltd. In November 1992 Mosnier, who a month earlier had announced the launch of Bravo Formula 1, a team backed by the Spanish government, died in a hospital in Nice at the age of 46.

He was the one person, says Ecclestone, able to comment on the allegations made by Greene and Parkes. 'Jean ran that business for me. He did whatever had to be done. If there was money coming in or money going out, he did everything. He was 100 per cent in charge. He was a trustworthy guy. You should ask them if it was me they were bringing bundles of cash to. I never saw any cash from them. I think this is shit. If they paid it into a bank in Italy, no way the bank could transfer from there to here or anywhere else. The worst thing you could do is go to a bank in Italy and transfer to Switzerland. They would probably lock you up on the spot for mentioning Switzerland for a start. And if they [Greene and Parkes] did it, then we should inform the police in Italy, because they are criminals.'

By the time of the launch of International Race Tire Services, Ecclestone had sold his palatial pile in Farnborough Park, Kent, and, with his girlfriend Dora Tuana Tan, had moved into a sumptuous penthouse apartment, then said to be worth £500,000, in Alembic House on the Albert Embankment, whose 25-foot-high plate-glass windows commanded a panoramic view across the Thames to the House of Commons and the Tate Gallery. He had the apartment – he later sold it to author and politician Jeffrey Archer – refurbished to his expensive and exacting tastes. Hand-made Italian furniture, Modigliani paintings, his world-class collection of netsukes – Japanese finely carved miniature sculptures – created a setting described as 'an unsettling blend of the exotic and the austere' without any sign of 'the common debris of human occupation'.

Its eclectic and sanitised ambience accurately reflected the artistic and quirky in Ecclestone's forceful personality. As with all things in his life, it had to be precisely to his taste. He appeared to be particularly fastidious over the carpet, which he wanted in a particular shade of blue. He was supplied with a range of samples, from which he made a selection, and placed an order. Due to the difficulty in getting the carpet to the penthouse, a crane was hired to lift it, along with other crated items of furniture, and then guided through the balcony window. But, once it was delivered, he was far from pleased with his choice: it had to go. Having managed to sell it on, he phoned the Brabham works, inquired how many mechanics were there, and ordered six to be sent immediately to his penthouse. He instructed them to roll the carpet up and, with the area below cleared, throw it out of the window. 'I didn't need to hire a crane for that, although I suppose it could have ended up in the River Thames,' he said.

He was equally decisive in protecting the parking space exclusively reserved for his apartment. Driving a German-registered Mercedes 500SEL, he made a detour to his home while en route, with Murray and Caldwell, from Chessington, Surrey, to Silverstone for a test session. He arrived to find the driver of a brand-new Jaguar XJ6 pulling into his space. Ecclestone pointed out the mistake, to which the errant motorist replied that he wouldn't be a moment, before disappearing into the building. Ecclestone imposed his own solution. He put his foot on the accelerator of the Mercedes and rammed the rear of the Jaguar, causing it to spin round and collide side on with a wall.

Murray and Caldwell remained in the car while Ecclestone calmly went to his penthouse, collected a briefcase and returned to find a stunned driver examining his somewhat damged car. Said Caldwell: 'Bernie simply got into his car and we drove off. The Jaguar was basically a write-off. The rear wheel had been stoved in and badly damaged down the side where it had been rammed into the wall.' Ecclestone strongly disputed that the incident, confirmed by Murray, ever took place. 'I can't imagine why I would do a detour from Chessington to Silverstone via London, and I can't *ever* remember *ever* going to a test session at Silverstone. In fact, during the whole time I had Brabham, I think I went to about four test sessions in my life. So that's all *shit*.' All the same, it seems that his driving manners did leave a lot to be desired. In another incident, he was responsible for colliding with a car at a roundabout. Before getting out of his car to confront the innocent motorist, Ecclestone, according to his passenger, said: 'Don't forget – it was his fault.'

By 1977, with the 6000 square feet of offices and works at New Haw, near Weybridge, proving inadequate for the 40 employees now working on the Brabham cars, Ecclestone moved Motor Racing Developments Ltd a few miles to a 28,000-square-foot factory, with an adjoining office complex, on an industrial estate in Chessington, Surrey. The move was also precipitated by the need to accommodate a relatively new but already expanding venture that would be the foundation of Ecclestone's future riches. It was in the basement of the offices, known as 'the dungeons', that FOCA TV, the seed from which his digital television empire would grow, was launched.

But the move had hardly been completed before Ecclestone sent out the clear signal that if the premises of Motor Racing Developments had changed, the management ethos hadn't. He ordered the windows of a toilet block to be boarded up to plunge it into total darkness. He then had a time-switch fitted which was programmed to automatically turn off the lights after two minutes. 'It was to prevent us from sitting on the loo reading a newspaper in his time,' said a former employee. When Ecclestone learnt that the mechanics were able to delay the time-switch with ease, he began to make random visits first thing in the morning to check its setting.

The move to larger premises was a cause of joy to Gordon Murray. There was now space for something for which he yearned – a full-scale wind tunnel. 'Our wind tunnel,' he said, 'was wetting your finger and sticking it in the air. We didn't spend hardly any money on testing. You just built the car, it worked and you went racing.' But Murray soon found he had a battle on his hands. Ecclestone gave him short shrift when he learned that the estimated cost of its construction was $6 million. Murray persisted until Ecclestone finally relented – on condition that he supplied the labour and material through his business channels and Murray took on the work of its design, technical specifications and overall construction. Even on those conditions, it was an offer Murray couldn't refuse.

Similar economies enabled Brabham to be the first team to have its own carbon-fibre production facilities. Again on the grounds of costs, Ecclestone refused to put the work out to building contractors, but agreed to provide the labour and materials himself, while Murray oversaw the 'in-house' construction of small factory premises. He said: 'Bernie never said no to whatever I wanted to do ... except when it came to spending money.'

6

JEAN-MARIE BALESTRE: LE GRAND FROMAGE

The failure of the Commission Sportive Internationale (CSI), under the presidency of Pierre Ugueux, to check the advances of the FOCA bode ill for the Belgian. The regulatory body that had governed motor sport on behalf of the Fédération Internationale de l'Automobile (FIA) for almost two decades had, in the space of a few years, been seriously degraded by the self-proclaimed authority of Bernie Ecclestone and the constructors.

Lord Hesketh, who ran the Hesketh team from 1973 until 1975 until it was closed down by financial pressures, believed the constructors became so effective so rapidly because of a bureaucratic FIA's traditional attitudes. Said Hesketh: 'They [the constructors] weren't interested in the old hierarchy. The FIA wasn't so much stuck in a time warp as a mindset. Essentially, they saw the English as being vulgar. That was the problem they had. But what they didn't realise was that the English may have been vulgar, but actually it was the next generation. You could almost say that the F1CA took the running of Formula One by default. When they did it, they did a much better job.' Hesketh's own experience was an example of how the teams' fortunes improved under Ecclestone's militant negotiating skills. The Hesketh team 'start' money on its arrival in 1973 was negligible; two years later, when, during the second half of the season, it was second in the World Championship, it was £22,000 – in the days when a Rolls-Royce Silver Shadow cost £11,000.

With the constructors virtually riding roughshod over the FIA's authority, it had become patently clear that Ugueux was no match for Ecclestone. Prince Paul Metternich, the FIA's president, and his mandarins realised that a more aggressive and cunning strategist than he would be required if the constructors were to be brought to heel. Standing in the wings, eager for his entrance, was the tall, burly frame of Frenchman Jean-Marie Balestre, a man who saw himself as the FIA's saviour. In some respects he was not unlike Ecclestone: a self-made, egocentric and despotic figure described as fiery, erratic and intelligent. He also enjoyed being immaculately attired, occasionally appearing at Grands Prix in white suit and matching shoes.

Unlike Ecclestone, however, Balestre – born in 1921 in Saint-Rémy de Provence, near Marseilles, the son of a journalist who became secretary of the Socialist Party in Paris – came from more prosperous beginnings. During the war he fought with the French Resistance from 1 April 1942 until his arrest on 24 May 1944, which led to his appearance before a German military court and, he claimed in a biographical résumé which he supplied, a death sentence. However, he was 'tortured and deported' to a concentration camp, where, on 4 May 1945, he was freed by Allied troops.

In 1949, with the support of French media magnate, Robert Hersant, he founded a car magazine, *L'Auto Journal*, which marked the beginning of a highly successful publishing group and the making of his business fortune. A keen follower of motor sport, he helped to found in April 1952 the French motor sport organisation, the Fédération Française du Sport Automobile (FFSA), of which in 1968 he became secretary-general and then president for 23 years, until 1996. A logical step was his membership of the CSI, from where he observed at first hand the ineffectiveness of Ugueux's efforts to halt the arrogant English constructors. And it was there that others observed his peculiar habit of appearing to be dozing, only to suddenly come to life with an incisive question. The message was clear: beware the sleeping bear.

By the middle of 1978, with Ugueux shortly due to stand for re-election, Balestre let it be known that he was ready to put his name forward for the post. There were, in fact, few willing to do so. Commenting on Balestre's candidature, Fabrizio Serena, president of the Commissione Sportiva Automobilistica Italiana, Italy's motor sport authority, said later: 'Well, at the time, there was no really suitable alternative.'[1] Balestre did so with the blessing and support of the powerful Hersant, who was no less keen to see control of Formula One returned to the headquarters of the FIA in Place de la Concorde, Paris. Hersant, as xenophobic as Balestre, believed that his business associate was the one man able to achieve that objective.

The election became very much a one-horse race after Ugueux decided to stand down. Why he did so remains uncertain. According to a former senior

FIA official who was directly involved in the incident, Ugueux withdrew following pressure from Balestre over an incident at the Le Mans 24-Hour race in June 1978, less than four months before the election was due to take place. At the centre of it all was the design of a one-off car by Porsche, nicknamed 'Moby Dick' because of its size and shape. Concerned that it might infringe technical regulations, Porsche sought the guidance of two FIA technical representatives, who believed it conformed to the required specifications. However, French manufacturers protested to the FFSA's Technical Commission that it was illegal. A representative was instructed to raise the issue at the next meeting of the CSI's Technical Commission, shortly to be held in Madrid, where members declared the design of the 'Moby Dick' to be illegal. Porsche was informed accordingly, and that, it was thought, was the end of the 'Moby Dick' – until it arrived at Le Mans ready to compete.

The scrutineers at first refused it entry to the paddock, but were handed a letter by Porsche's racing manager, which, signed by Ugueux, authorised its inclusion in the race. The matter was hurriedly referred by phone to Balestre, as president of the FFSA, the organisers of the event. Because approval had been given by Ugueux as president of the CSI, Balestre said nothing other than to issue an instruction that the Porsche racing manager must hand the letter over to a senior official and that it was to be passed on to him. The 'Moby Dick' was then allowed to compete.

It seems that Ugueux agreed to write the letter of authorisation following a threat from Porsche that if the car was declared illegal, the company would withdraw from all sports-car racing for the rest of the season. As Porsche was a major entrant, this would have proved a serious blow, financially and prestigiously, to a motor sport at the height of its popularity. Ugueux was advised not to challenge the ultimatum, and, accordingly, permitted an illegal entry in direct violation of his own Technical Commission's ruling. Shortly before the election, Ugueux was made aware that his letter was in Balestre's possession, and that its contents, if made public, would prove highly embarrassing. 'Ugueux was an honest man, an important and much respected man in his country ... and he just made a mistake,' said the former senior FIA official. 'Balestre convinced him that he couldn't be elected with these mistakes behind him.'

However, Ugueux, today a sprightly 88-year-old with 12 grandchildren, gives another account, claiming that the 'Moby Dick' incident had no bearing on his decision not to stand. While confirming that he had authorised the car's illegal inclusion and that he had been warned that Balestre had a dossier on him, he denied that Balestre had used the incident to dissuade him from standing for re-election. He did so, he insisted, for family reasons. As a father of four children at university, he couldn't afford to remain in what he described as 'a position of poor remuneration'. He added that he was further influenced in his decision by Ecclestone, who had persuaded him that Formula One needed someone like Balestre to help continue the sport's transformation.

Balestre's vague comments do little to clear up the conflicting accounts. In a brief statement, he said no more than: 'Because of the influence and complicity of one of Mr Ugueux's Vice-Chairmen and his Technical Commission, Porsche flouted the rules and secured the homologation of an illegal car. Ecclestone was never involved in this matter [in that he had influenced Ugueux in his decision not to stand], and your entire story on this point is a fabrication.'

Ugueux's decision to withdraw led to a two-horse race between Balestre and Tom Binford, the popular president of America's national sporting authority, the Automobile Competition Committee for the United States (ACCUS). Binford was ranked an outsider runner, and a late one at that. It wasn't until August, a little more than two months before the election was due to be held, that he put his name forward, with the much-qualified support of colleagues who left unexpressed their doubts that the likeable Binford could win sufficient support within the membership of the European-based and politically dominated FIA. By then, Balestre, who, it is said, booked a Concorde flight to Brazil for a 40-minute airport meeting with leading officials of the Automóvel Club do Brasil, the country's national motor sport authority, to ensure their support, was more or less home and dry. And so it proved to be, although Binford did better than most had expected.

In October 1978 Balestre was duly elected president of the CSI – and at the same time, at his insistence, the name of the Commission Sportive Internationale was changed to the Fédération Internationale du Sport Automobile (FISA). The message was clear: the FIA had a new sports governing body under a new boss with a new broom ready to sweep away a slow-moving, committee-bound bureaucracy. He then set about implementing his election manifesto, which had promised a 'programme of action' to generate 'a worldwide spirit ... respect for the international regulations ... the reorganisation of the championships ... the complete revision and simplification of the regulations ... and the reduction of costs in motor sports'.[2]

He declared that there would be a reduction in the maximum number of cars from 26 to 24; a commitment from teams to take part in every round of the World Championship series; all drivers had to be Grade A licence holders to confirm Formula One-level driving skills, with each team nominating its season's drivers in advance; financial guarantees from teams who failed to score any points in the previous season that they would be able to meet their obligations; and teams who did not have contracts with race organisers – namely non-FOCA teams – had to deposit a £15,000 guarantee with the FISA.

Some contemporary commentators considered the proposed changes to be very much in accord with Ecclestone's aim to introduce a greater discipline. They also seem to give credibility to Ugueux's assertion that Ecclestone encouraged him not to stand for re-election as president of the CSI in favour of Balestre. But it is inconceivable that there had been any horse-trading between the two – Ecclestone's support in return for rule changes favourable to the FOCA. Ecclestone at that time was so unpopular within the FIA that his endorsement of Balestre's ambitions would have done nothing to have advanced them.

Nevertheless, Balestre's proposals did give hope of a more concordant relationship between the constructors and the establishment. Outside of French motor sport he was something of an unknown quantity. As one constructor put it: 'Nobody was quite sure [what to expect of him]'. In one of his early speeches he even displayed signs of modesty, admitting that he had not been 'a distinguished driver', that he could not 'build a Formula One car' and had 'never won a Grand Prix'. He had been no more, as he put it, than 'a passionate follower of motor racing for 30 years'. But any hopes of a new beginning were soon dashed.

Balestre had hardly settled into office before he seized the opportunity to demonstrate that his was the voice to be feared and respected. It took place at the opening race of the new season, the 1979 Argentine Grand Prix, his first as president of the FISA. Following a first-lap accident between John Watson, who had left Ecclestone's Brabham team for McLaren, and Ferrari's Jody Scheckter, Balestre, sartorially resplendent in white suit and matching shoes, took it upon himself to personally intervene. He summoned a meeting of stewards to arbitrarily declare that Watson had been at fault. The result of a stewards' inquiry, considered to be something of a foregone conclusion in the circumstances, imposed a punitive fine of £3000 on Watson, which was more than the team earned for coming third.

But Balestre was not done. He made it publicly known that he had actually considered disqualifying Watson from the race and even suspending him for a fixed period. Some observers, while critical of his style, nevertheless believed that his decision was correct. There had been five first-lap accidents in the six previous Grands Prix and the drivers, it was claimed, needed to be more disciplined, particularly at the first corner, the most dangerous stage of a Grand Prix. But, as would prove much the case throughout his turbulent presidency, and which would needlessly increase the ranks of his detractors, it was not so much what he did but the way he set about achieving it.

His autocratic performance had been like a red rag to a bull to Ecclestone and the constructors, who were further incensed by Watson being denied, despite repeated requests, the opportunity of a personal hearing to defend himself. Twenty-two years later, Balestre, invited to comment on the incident, declined to do so in any detail, other than to imply that he had, in fact, played no part in the proceedings. His only comment was: 'Please note that sanctions were taken by the race's stewards against Watson in Argentina because he cut the trajectory on the track.' Yet, despite this incomplete account of his involvement, he was back in the thick of the controversy two weeks later, at the Brazilian Grand Prix, when he declared that Watson would not be allowed to compete unless his fine was paid.

He also took the opportunity to publicly admonish Ecclestone for allegedly prohibiting drivers from giving evidence to the stewards' inquiry into the Watson incident. He further claimed that Ecclestone had approved the course of action agreed to be taken by the stewards and the FISA, but, fearing a backlash from drivers at Brazil and the potential threat to his commercial interests in the race, reversed his support. Ecclestone vehemently denied both claims. Balestre, intent on portraying the constructors' leader as a man the FIA had always claimed he was – a tyrant determined to squeeze every penny out of Formula One – continued his assault on Ecclestone's integrity by claiming that he had not only sold passes to the pit lanes while blocking officials from issuing free of charge International Press Racing Association (IPRA) badges recognised by the FISA, but had also imposed a mandatory £600 'tax' on foreign radio stations. They were charges to which Ecclestone declined to respond, at least publicly. However, a founder member of the International Press Racing Association, an organisation set up in the late sixties, gave credence to the charge by confirming that at one stage Ecclestone had attempted to charge IPRA members an annual fee of £5000 in return for a press pass, a move he was unsuccessful, for once, in enforcing.

Ecclestone was doubtless surprised by the ferocity of Balestre's high-profile intervention and accusations, courses of action that the more self-restrained and cautious Ugueux would never have dared to have expressed, at least not in public. Balestre clearly wanted the constructors to be in no doubt: it was no longer the FOCA that set the rules of the house but the FISA, which, under the leadership of Balestre, would not hesitate to act quickly and firmly in putting down any threat to its authority. But what went on behind the scenes was another matter. Privately, Balestre was about to face his first political challenge – and lose. In the basement of an office at Brazil's Interlagos circuit, Ecclestone and Mosley arranged a meeting with Balestre at which he was told that Watson would be competing without the fine being paid, a decision for which they had secured the support of the organisers, Ecclestone's financial stake in its promotion proving an influential factor. Unless Balestre wanted them to make the decision public, he would write and sign a statement that not only had Watson's fine been paid but that in future he would not act unilaterally. Balestre found himself alone, facing the very real prospect of having his newly acquired authority severely undermined. It was a risk he preferred not to run. Rather than lose face, he agreed.

Balestre composed the statement, written in green fountain pen ink, several times before the final version was accepted by Ecclestone. It read: 'The fine inflicted on Watson was paid by the FOCA within the delay prescribed by the sporting code. As a result, Watson, having satisfied the penalty, is disengaged from all obligations as far as the Automobile Club of Argentina is concerned. In the future all problems concerning the events counting for the Formula One championship will be looked at by the working group of Formula One and the sporting commission of the FIA.' Apart from the pleasing evidence it offered of the first blood going to the constructors, the statement was to prove of historical significance in that the working group, a body that Balestre had promised to set up shortly after his election to discuss and recommend proposed changes to rules and regulations, would pave the way for the formation of the powerful Formula One Commission of the future, which would be responsible for all matters other than the selection of stewards, circuit safety and discipline. It also, incidentally, contained a slight error of fact. Watson's fine was paid not by FOCA by the Automóvil Club Argentino, the organisers of the Argentine Grand Prix.

A few weeks later, at a meeting of the teams at Ferrari's headquarters in Maranello, Ecclestone went on the attack. He swept aside Balestre's proposed working group by declaring that the FISA would play no further part in the governance of the Formula One World Championship series. He proclaimed that all matters relating to Formula One – car specifications, safety, race regulations and matters of discipline – would be overseen by a committee appointed by the FOCA. It was an ambitious political move that had the support of probably the most powerful voice in Formula One after Ecclestone and Balestre, that of Enzo Ferrari. When asked if he believed in the necessity of the FOCA, he replied: 'By hook or by crook, I must believe in it.'

He also made a veiled criticism of Balestre for breaching the spirit and the letter of established conduct. 'The new president of the CSI [sic] ... must, with severe impartiality, impose on the organisers, on the competitors, on the drivers, on everyone, respect of the sporting code in force or else the FOCA will be compelled to acquire itself an autonomy that will bind its members still more to that self-discipline already provided in the association articles, which is the only serious guarantee of correct technical and sporting results.' It was, he confirmed, an ultimatum to the FISA. 'It is the last chance for the automobilistic sport of Formula 1.'[3]

Balestre's response to the FOCA's threat to usurp the FISA was equally unyielding, but demonstrated a degree of chutzpah which must surely have provoked a smile from Ecclestone himself. A statement was issued ostensibly on behalf of the FIA's executive committee, which, in noting the FOCA's beating of war drums, took the opportunity to 'renew its confidence in the President' and the members of the FISA, adding that it 're-affirms its approval of the reforms taking place within' the FISA. It appeared to be a resounding pat on the back for Balestre from the FIA President, Prince Paul Metternich, and his committee colleagues. Well, not quite. The statement was authorised and signed by Balestre himself, and issued through his office.

A month later, in April 1979, Balestre flew to London in an attempt to regain the initiative. He was there, said the FISA's publicity machine, to offer the British media 'a world-wide exclusive', which turned out to be a public roasting of the FOCA in general and Ecclestone in particular. He countered Ecclestone's declaration that the FOCA would take control of Formula One by reasserting the authority of the FISA as the governing power. He was, he said, prepared to allow the constructors 'a certain latitude' in making arrangements with the organisers, but he insisted they should have no further involvement, including matters of discipline and, most controversially, the negotiation of financial terms with the organisers or promoters. He claimed that the FISA had been forced to involve itself in the financial negotiations between the FOCA and the organisers because Ecclestone had allegedly failed to honour the financial terms of the three-year contracts agreed and signed in 1977, which had resulted from the ultimately unsuccessful efforts of World Championship Racing. He accused Ecclestone of going back to the Argentine Grand Prix organisers 18 months later to demand a 27 per cent increase in the teams' fees – to $900,000, plus television rights and hire cars – for the 1979 Grand Prix.

The financial details, which until then had been covered by a standard confidentiality clause in the FOCA's contracts, had come out at a meeting of organisers called by Balestre in Paris a couple of weeks earlier to discover how much each had been paying Ecclestone. Balestre also made covetous noises about the money the constructors were receiving through the sale to the European Broadcasting Union of television rights automatically acquired by Ecclestone from organisers and promoters as a condition of a race contract. As the FIA's modest income came principally from homologation fees, the thought that television rights revenue, generated by a sport that the FISA was supposed to be governing, was going into the constructors' pockets must have caused Balestre chronic dyspepsia. He implied that, in fact, the FIA was considered by the European Broadcasting Union, not to mention three American networks, who, he said, had made approaches earlier that year, as the rightful owner of the television rights. For good measure, he also claimed that a poll of sponsors had revealed a unanimous preference for the government of 'sporting power' rather than by 'the circus'.

It was becoming clear that Balestre, in his power battle with Ecclestone, was looking for ways to publicly challenge the FOCA leader at all and every opportunity. No sooner had the dust settled on the Argentine and Brazilian Grands Prix debacles than he attempted to bring him to heel over the Swedish Grand Prix, which was in danger of being cancelled due to the withdrawal of its cash-strapped sponsors. However, at the eleventh hour a Swedish oil company came to the rescue to cover the costs, including the FOCA's £25,000 advance payment. The race, Ecclestone announced, was back on. But then Balestre stepped in to insist that, as the race had been cancelled, it couldn't be immediately reinstated as a Grand Prix carrying World Championship points without the FISA's approval, which, unfortunately, was not possible due to lack of time. Despite protests by the organisers and the FOCA, the 1979 Swedish Grand Prix remained cancelled. Balestre had succeeded in making his point: once again, it was the authority of his word that counted, not Ecclestone's. The cancellation of the race at Anderstorp marked the end of the Swedish Grand Prix, which had begun in 1973 with Ecclestone the principal force, a factor that would have made Balestre's role in its demise all the sweeter.

Balestre attended the last Swedish Grand Prix, in 1978, but in accommodation that offence to his sense of dignity and importance of office. On his arrival in Sweden he was chauffeur-driven to a rather ordinary-looking house, arranged by the organisers, near the circuit. At the time the legality of Gordon Murray's 'fan' car was in hot dispute and Balestre arrived at Ecclestone's plush and spacious hotel room to clarify the FISA's position. He was in a foul mood, complaining, among other things, of the standard of his accommodation. The next day, while being driven to the circuit, he demanded of an accompanying Swedish motor club official to know why he had not been booked into the same hotel. Well, it was explained, Mr Ecclestone had booked all the rooms.

Such inferior treatment was guaranteed to be given his glowering disapproval, as were organisers or promoters who were known to be personal friends or allies of Ecclestone and the constructors. There was, for example, the experience of British-born businessman Chris Pook, who established the USA West Grand Prix at Long Beach, California, in 1976 with Ecclestone's encouragement, and who had sided with the FOCA in the dispute with Patrick Duffeler's World Championship Racing. Pook was forced to put back the April date of the 1979 Grand Prix by one week to meet television demands, which prompted a telexed reprimand from Balestre pointing out that the new date clashed with a Formula Two race at Hockenheim. He warned Pook that if Hockenheim incurred any losses as a result of the television coverage, he would be held liable by the FISA for the first $20,000.

More seriously, the Long Beach race itself came under threat shortly after

Pook signed a new three-year contract with Ecclestone at the Monaco Grand Prix. A team of FISA safety inspectors was sent to report on the road circuit. Their report was critical of the use of concrete blocks rather than Armco barriers, although the drivers at that time preferred the blocks to Armco, considering them safer. Pook flew to Holland the following month to protest to Balestre, who was attending the Dutch Grand Prix at Zandvoort, which, ironically, was considered to be one of the most dangerous circuits on the calendar as car speeds had become too fast for the track design, and which was blamed for a horrific first-lap crash between the Arrows team's Riccardo Patrese and Tyrrell's Didier Pironi at the 1978 Grand Prix.

Pook was not the only one who went to the Dutch Grand Prix with a grievance. Mal Currie, representing the organisers of the USA Grand Prix (East), wanted to find out from Balestre why the FISA was demanding safety changes at Watkins Glen that would cost £150,000 – with the race just one month away. The answer, it was widely believed, lay in the fact that, like Pook, Currie and his colleagues had sided with Ecclestone in the earlier battles against the FISA.

The threat issued by the FOCA to set up a breakaway Formula One World Championship series – not the first nor the last – was not put into action. The opinion within the ranks of the constructors, for the time being at least, was that the loss of the FIA's administration and endorsement might achieve more harm than good, especially with sponsors made more nervous by every hostile stalemate. In the meantime, Balestre, with baton in hand, was insisting that the FISA was now playing to 'new music and a new conductor'.

Part of the 'new music' was his proposed Formula One Working Group, which did little to impress Ecclestone. At a meeting in Paris he claimed that its proposed structure was unfairly balanced in favour of the FISA, and, suspecting that it was a devious ploy to straitjacket the constructors, counter-proposed that the two sides should come together to form a new body to replace the FISA. Balestre's reply was to produce a dossier of Ecclestone's alleged infringements of the FISA's authority. Ecclestone's reply was to refuse to attend any further meetings unless the constructors were more equally represented.

His suspicions about Balestre's motive may have been well grounded. The very next day Balestre let loose a devastating broadside intended to seriously destabilise the constructors: the FISA's Technical Commission issued a report proposing radical changes to the regulations of Formula One. The commission, under the chairmanship of Curt Schild, of the Automobile Club de Suisse, proposed reducing the length, height and width of Formula One cars, sustaining the 3-litre engine limit and increasing the minimum weight from 575 to 625 kilograms. It was, in effect, proposing a new Formula One, which would mean massive costs to the constructors, but to the considerable advantage of the French manufacturer Renault, which, over a four-year period, had invested more than £1 million in developing the heavier RS01, a turbocharged 1.5-litre V6 engine producing 510bhp, and whose power countered the cornering speeds of the lighter, nippier 'ground effect' car. The proposed new specifications fitted it perfectly. The RS01 first competed at the 1977 British Grand Prix but failed to finish. It competed in only three Grands Prix during the rest of the season and, again, through suspension and engine problems, failed to finish. It wasn't until the French Grand Prix in 1979 that Renault began to see a return on its money, when Jean-Pierre Jabouille and René Arnoux took first and third place.

But in that same year the constructors' adaptation of Chapman's Lotus 78 was proving highly encouraging. The first 'ground effect' or 'skirts' car of Ecclestone's Brabham team, the BT48 Alfa, driven by Niki Lauda in a test session, went round Silverstone in 1 minute 15.3 seconds, to record an astonishing average lap speed of 140.17mph, the first car to lap the 4710-metre circuit at over 140mph. To the constructors, switching to turbo made little sense. Keith Duckworth's Ford Cosworth DFV V8 had proved so successful since it first appeared in Colin Chapman's Lotus 49, with Jim Clark at the wheel, to win the 1967 Dutch Grand Prix in its maiden race that it made the opposition obsolete at a stroke. At a cost of £7500, it became the engine which the constructors built their cars around. But now the cost was £20,000 and to build and supply the constructors with a Cosworth turbo would have at least doubled that figure. The cost of repairs and a standard strip-down and service would also have escalated. The Cosworth DFV had brought a stability to Formula One which, the constructors argued, was being threatened by the turbocharged engine's superior horsepower, which would make Formula One less competitive and, therefore, less appealing to the public. Why, they chorused, change a successful show, which had been competitive, popular and relatively inexpensive to run?

Designers such as Brabham's Gordon Murray and Williams's Patrick Head claimed that to remove the 'skirts' from a car would adversely affect its centre of balance, which would mean a completely new design. Besides, others added, the removal of the 'skirts' would not slow down the speed of cars: new bodywork and aerodynamics, and the discovery of a comparable 'ground effect' system, would soon achieve similar speeds. It was an argument of clear logic. In an intensely competitive world such as Formula One, it was impossible to 'uninvent' something. And car designers were rather like successful tax accountants – constantly looking for ways around new laws. Once one loophole had been blocked, they simply worked to find another.

However, in the manufacturers' corner, the potential of the Renault turbo – following its success at the French Grand Prix, the RS01 scored six pole positions to the Cosworth's seven – was now considered a major contender for the 1980 World Championship (if, that is, technical director François Castaing and his team could cure the engine's occasional proneness to unreliability) and had prompted Ferrari to begin working on its own, a turbo engine to produce 600bhp, which compared with the Cosworth's 485bhp. Maserati and Ligier, following the latter's takeover by the French manufacturer Talbot, began similar development work, and the international high profile being enjoyed by Renault led to BMW announcing plans to return to Formula One with its own turbocharged cars, which took place in 1982 after an absence of 29 years.

The FOCA, which continued to oppose vigorously any attempt by the FISA to ban 'skirts', predicted fatal consequences for the constructors if it were to do otherwise. Said an angry Ecclestone: 'If ... FISA or anyone else wants to ruin racing, let them get on with it. Why should I spend so much time trying to make racing stronger and more competitive when we go and get a rule like this? What will happen is that my sponsor will come to me at the end of the season and ask what it takes to win races. I'll tell him "skirts" have been banned, and that we need another £4 million to develop a new turbocharged engine. And my sponsor, like a lot of others, will walk clean out of racing.'

Enzo Ferrari, though, was not impressed by this doom-filled prediction. In fact, the man who had not long earlier stated how 'by hook or by crook' he had to believe in the FOCA, had shifted his ground considerably. He was now fulminating that Formula One had 'deteriorated' because of the FOCA's 'machinations', adding that his company might well pull out of Grand Prix racing and transfer its money and resources to the revival of a world manufacturers' championship for sports cars.[4] It was considered more of a political statement than a genuine threat, and Ferrari himself was suspected of some Machiavellian intrigue when the Grand Prix Drivers' Association (GPDA), whose president, Jody Scheckter, drove for Ferrari, issued a statement claiming that its members were concerned about the cornering speeds of 'skirt' cars. The constructors were infuriated to see their drivers associated with such a statement. But how many had actually voted in its favour was uncertain. According to Williams driver Alan Jones, a senior member of the GPDA's safety committee, who would become the 1980 world champion, he had not given his support to 'anything that remotely resembled' a 'skirts' ban. It led to the resignation of several drivers from the GPDA, including Jones and Nélson Piquet, Ecclestone's lead driver.

Ferrari insisted that the constructors had been permitted to use 'skirts' because 'of the weakness of the FISA. They were illegal from the start.' He was, in fact, referring to a decision three years earlier by the Commission Sportive

Internationale (CSI) under Pierre Ugueux following protests that the cornering speeds of Chapman's Lotus 78 introduced new safety hazards. Its critics, principally Renault and Ferrari, were supported by a technical report issued by the Automobile Club d'Italia which, based on corner timing at a Fiorano test session, projected increases in cornering speeds as high as 40 per cent. But when Ecclestone successfully argued that the constructors were making huge investments in the new technology and that a ban would threaten the future of Formula One, Ugueux agreed to postpone a 'final decision' and, in the meantime, requested 'further information'. It had been the kind of vacillation that hastened Ugueux's departure from the presidency of the CSI. Shortly after his election, Balestre had made it clear that he would not be so obliging. 'If I have not done the job [of imposing a ban] in 12 months, then I will resign.'[5]

The report by the FISA's Technical Commission had been no less unwelcome with tyre manufacturers Goodyear and Michelin. It proposed that tyre and rim widths should be reduced from 21 inches to 18 inches. The two companies had earlier agreed with Balestre at a meeting in South Africa that tyre widths would not be reduced unless engine power and aerodynamic downforce were also reduced. Goodyear's racing division manager, Paul Lauritzen, alarmed by the increased dangers to drivers, described the proposal as 'lunacy' and warned that his company would pull out of Formula One if the proposals were adopted by the FISA. But Balestre, in full battle cry, paid no heed. Clearly he intended to use the divisive issue of 'skirts' versus turbo as a wedge to drive between the constructors and the manufacturers in a 'divide and conquer' strategy.

To provoke the constructors, he continued to pile on more aggravation. He decreed that they would no longer have the freedom to name their cars after sponsors, as with Lotus's 'John Player Special' or Williams's 'Saudi Leyland', a practice he denounced as excessive commercial exploitation. He also announced that drivers who failed to show up at pre-race briefings would be fined $2000 for the first offence and $5000 for the second. The briefings were generally considered by the constructors to be a waste of time and Balestre's insistence on their attendance seemed to be no more than yet another pretext to exercise his authority to their inconvenience. However, this seemingly petty edict would shortly bring about a major confrontation with the FISA and the manufacturers, and hasten an all-out war to threaten the future of Formula One itself.

At the end of February 1980 Balestre confirmed that, in the absence of the FOCA's acceptance of the proposed new regulations, a ban on 'skirts' would come into effect by 1 January 1981, a deadline which, as it had yet to be approved at the FISA's plenary spring congress due to take place little more than two months later, would fall considerably short of the two years' notice that the FISA was legally required to give. Balestre turned a deaf ear to the FOCA's vociferous protests, arguing that, as the ban was being imposed on the grounds of safety, the FISA was not compelled to give the statutory period of notice. It raised the ire of the constructors to a new level. They claimed that the FISA had no evidence that 'skirts' cars threatened acceptable standards of safety and that Balestre had deliberately misinterpreted the rule book to the advantage of the manufacturers.

At the FIA's plenary spring congress in Rio de Janeiro, where, predictably, delegates representing politically supportive motoring organisations, voted in favour of a ban on 'skirts', Balestre proceeded with the business of eviscerating the FOCA. After declaring that he intended to 'restore motor sport to its rightful place' – the headquarters of the FIA in Place de la Concorde – he sought, and received, the support of congress empowering him to draw up 'a list of measures ... so that in 1981 the FISA exerts full control over the World Championships belonging to it and which, at the present moment, are the object of a takeover by certain private associations [FOCA] foreign to the FISA'.[6] Those measures would 'guarantee' that each country's national sporting authority would hold 'absolute control of the entire sporting aspect of the Grand Prix', with the terms between the organisers and the FOCA fixed by a standard contract to be approved by the FISA. This was the very objective that Grand Prix International and World Championship Racing had signally failed to achieve. It was immediately rejected by the FOCA as being unworkable – a standard contract, it was pointed out, could not possibly meet the widely varying needs and requirements of the 18 or more organisers.

To what extent Balestre had the necessary support of the FISA's executive committee was a highly moot point. On the evidence of Basil Tye, the then chief executive of Britain's Royal Automobile Club, which as the FIA's national sporting authority and organiser of the British Grand Prix, represented the motoring organisation on its executive committee, it had been far from unanimous. Indeed, he revealed that other matters which had received the approval of the plenary congress had either not been agreed by the executive committee or not discussed at all. Balestre's premature announcement of a ban on 'skirts', which the plenary congress endorsed, had, for example, been a direct reversal of the recommendations of the FISA's executive committee.

Tye's account was confirmed by Max Mosley, who, as Ecclestone's deputy, was entitled to attend meetings of the committee. The pair argued forcefully, and successfully, in favour of 'skirts' being retained. There was, in Mosley's words, 'a tremendous confrontation' with Balestre, who was livid to see the vote go against him, a rare event indeed. Despite his defeat, he claimed at the plenary congress the next day to have the support of the executive committee.

As Mosley did not represent a club, he was not able to address the august gathering to inform them otherwise. Sir Clive Bossom, president of the RAC's Motor Sports Association and an FIA vice-president, was able to, and did. But, because he was widely viewed as an opponent of the FIA establishment, his words failed to bring about the defeat of the executive committee's so-called recommendation to ban 'skirts'.

According to Tye, Balestre neglected to consult the executive committee on another recommendation, which posed a direct threat to the very future of the South African Grand Prix. It followed an incident at the South African Grand Prix two months earlier, where Balestre claimed he had been 'the target of physical violence'. The 'violence' had apparently been no more physical than his unseemly elbowing off the overcrowded winners' podium. It was construed by Balestre, though, as an unpardonable offence to the dignity of his office. And it was compounded by another incident, which, this time, offended his national pride: the organisers had failed to arrange the playing of the French national anthem, La Marseillaise.

Balestre, who had instructed the FISA's lawyers to pursue legal redress for damages against the organisers, received the support of congress in demanding an inquiry 'aimed at establishing the responsibilities of the Grand Prix organisers'. It was agreed that, because of the 'seriousness of the matter and the legal action taken', the South African Grand Prix should be removed from the following season's calendar until the inquiry had been concluded. The legal action went no further, but the following year's South African Grand Prix, in 1981, did not take place as a World Championship race, although for reasons unconnected with this incident.

What Balestre, to this day, does not know is that his ejection from the podium was caused by a few mischievous words that Max Mosley had with the track's head of security. He was warned by Mosley before the race that Balestre would insist on getting on to the podium although he was not supposed to. 'Mr Mosley,' replied the burly no-nonsense official firmly, 'if Mr Balestre tries to get past me he will not succeed.' Mosley was in the nearby Kyalami Ranch Hotel, where the teams and officials stayed during the Grand Prix, having a cup of tea, when Balestre, unaware of Mosley's part in it all, stormed in, purple with rage, and, in between a stream of French curses, made known to one and all the terrible humiliation he had just suffered.

Twenty years later a senior FIA delegate spoke of Balestre's backroom manipulation of delegates to achieve his ends. '[Balestre] was a masterful politician. Before a vote came up, he would say, "Now we're all together in this, and if we stick together we're going to elect everybody just the way we say." He [would] say, "We must agree completely, right in this room, that we will all vote as we say we will." We represented maybe 25 per cent of the votes in there. It wasn't total control. You had to depend on the law of averages taking care of the rest of it, but he had it figured.'

In the early months of 1980 the constructors decided to take the battle to Balestre. A few weeks before the Belgian Grand Prix at Zolder in May, it was discovered that the supplementary regulations to the race did not oblige the drivers to attend the pre-race briefing, which presented the constructors with a tactical opportunity to defy a ruling introduced by Balestre not long after his appointment. It led to the drivers, acting on instructions, boycotting the briefing while those employed by the manufacturers – Ferrari, Renault and Alfa Romeo – turned up. For the first time, the teams were being forced to publicly nail their colours to the mast of either the FOCA or the FISA.

Balestre interpreted the boycott for what indeed it was intended to be – a slap in the face by the constructors. His response was to impose fines of $2000 on the drivers or face having their licences revoked. To no one's great surprise, his edict was roundly ignored. In this impasse the constructors, in combative mood, arrived two weeks later at Jarama in Spain for the Spanish Grand Prix, the deadline for the payment of the fines. Ecclestone called a meeting of constructors in the paddock. The only item on the agenda was the restoration of their drivers' licences. It ended with an ultimatum: unless the drivers' licences were restored immediately, the constructors would not take part in the race. The fact that the constructors had waited until then to issue such an ultimatum made it clear that Ecclestone and his colleagues were looking for a highly public fight. Balestre, who refused to back down, was ready to play his part.

With just two days to go before the race, and with no hope of a suspension of hostilities, high-level political discussions led to the personal involvement of King Juan Carlos, who, alarmed by the international embarrassment to Spanish pride and prestige that would be caused by the race's cancellation, issued an order to the organisers, Real Automóvil Club de España (RACE) – its president was Fernando Falco, Marqués de Cubas, a cousin of the king – that the race must take place. That it was issued to RACE rather than the FIA's national sporting authority in Spain, the Federación Española de Automovilismo, was in itself a snub to Balestre and the FIA's authority. Senior RACE officials held meetings with both sides through the night, with Ecclestone and Mosley, as usual, representing the constructors.

It was agreed that Ecclestone and Mosley would meet Balestre and senior FISA officials at seven o'clock in the morning in the slender hope of finding a solution to the deadlock. As the meeting proceeded Ecclestone and Mosley noticed that Balestre had placed on the table, among other papers, a list of his allies within the FIA. It was information that Ecclestone was very keen to have.

He turned to Mosley, and said *sotto voce*: 'If you can knock the table over, I'll get the list.' A moment or two later Mosley duly obliged – Balestre's papers went flying as Mosley clumsily got to his feet and stumbled, sending the table on its side. Ecclestone moved quickly to help Balestre retrieve his documents from the floor, at the same time pocketing the small piece of paper containing the list of names. A few minutes later, with order restored, Balestre became greatly agitated when he suddenly noticed its absence. 'Vair,' he demanded, 'ees may leest?' Ecclestone and Mosley appeared suitably mystified. It was not the best of times for Balestre. During the night, at Balestre's request, Marco Piccinini, Ferrari's sporting director, visited his bedroom. Engrossed in their talks, Balestre forgot that shortly before Piccinini's arrival he had begun to run a bath – until he saw the water seeping under the bathroom door.

The early-morning talks between the two sides ended, as expected, without solution. The RACE announced that the Spanish Grand Prix would be held. Their contract, it was pointed out, and as Ecclestone and Mosley had reminded them, was with the FOCA, and the FOCA was ready to honour it. Balestre, furious that the authority of the FISA had been overruled, retaliated by announcing that a race involving drivers not licensed to compete could not be a legal round of the World Championship series. It was shortly followed by the remarkable scene of FISA officials being marched from the circuit at gunpoint by Guardia Civil police officers on the orders of the organisers. Among them was Gérard 'Jabby' Crombac, who, as an FISA observer, had attempted to gain entry to Ecclestone's motor home, where he was having a meeting. Ecclestone, about the same size as Crombac, physically manhandled him off the premises to the protests of journalists that he was an FISA observer. 'Fine,' said Mosley, who was guarding the door, 'he can observe from out there.'

The events of the previous 24 hours had caused such disruption that the final practice session was put back by the FOCA from 10 a.m. to 11.30 am, a decision that Ferrari, Renault, Alfa Romeo and Osella chose to ignore. Their practice session duly began at 10 am, but within 30 minutes was brought to an abrupt end by a red flag, which caused the Ferrari team to declare that its 'arbitrary use' had made the race illegal. Joined by the other manufacturers, Ferrari expressed public support for the FISA by insisting that unless the fines of the drivers were paid, they would not compete in the race.

Later that day Ferrari and Renault held a press conference during which they claimed that they had had no alternative but to withdraw. As major manufacturers with responsibilities to all areas of motor sport, they believed that they couldn't run the risk of competing in an illegal race and lose their entrants' licences. Following an FISA executive committee meeting in Athens the following week, Balestre, attempting to restore some authority, declared that the race would not count towards the World Championship series. The

FOCA, which had reputedly put aside a £500,000 war chest to mount any necessary legal challenges to the FISA in similar future situations, believed it would. In fact, it did not. But, in addition to scoring an important political win, the constructors made also another turning point: with the absence of the turbos, the race at Jarama was described by commentators as one of the most exciting races of the season for lead changes and competitiveness.

An attempt by the teams to get the drivers' fines quashed by the FIA Court of Appeal failed on a technicality. Britain's Royal Automobile Club, which was representing the drivers, had not, in accordance with FIA rules, lodged the appeal with both the FIA and Belgium's national sporting authority, the Royal Automobile Club de Belgique. The embittered constructors, who believed they would win the day, were ordered to pay the fines on behalf of their drivers. The rapidly deteriorating relationship between the FOCA and the FISA was causing increasing concern to sponsors. Goodyear's head of racing, Leo Mehl, believed that the issue over the drivers' licences should have been resolved before the Spanish Grand Prix, or suspended until it was over. If their public wranglings continued, he warned, Goodyear would need to consider whether it should continue in Formula One.

It was such concerns that led, a few days after the Spanish Grand Prix, to Philip Morris hosting a meeting in Lausanne between Ecclestone, Max Mosley and Colin Chapman, and three FISA vice-presidents, Tom Binford, of the Automobile Competition Committee for the United States; Ron Frost, of Motorsport, New Zealand; and Joachim Springer, of the Allgemeiner Deutscher Automobil-Club, Germany. Held in Balestre's absence, the day-long meeting went well enough for an 11-point agreement to be reached, which, principally, proposed a review of the ban on 'skirts' and a reinstatement of the two years' notice rule in cases of changes to regulations. From the telex room at Geneva Airport Mosley faxed the agreement to every member of the FISA's executive committee. He wanted it to be seen as a *fait accompli* in order to make it very difficult for Balestre to attempt to reverse it. But the ploy backfired – it was leaked to the press, for which Balestre blamed Mosley. The backwash threatened the rapprochement almost before it had begun. Philip Morris and the FISA claimed that the agreement was supposed to have been confidential. In any event, it all turned out to be academic.

It was not possible, insisted Balestre, for him to rescind the ban because it had been approved by the FISA's executive committee, a claim which, according to Tye and Mosley, wasn't true. Balestre added that the committee would first have to meet to discuss the proposals and then any decision would have to go for approval to the FISA's plenary conference that October – a little more than two months before the ban was due to be implemented. This was Balestre mischievously allowing procedural technicalities to obstruct a possible settlement of differences, an indication of little enthusiasm for a settlement not of his proposal or approval. He also insisted that his right to issue short-notice changes to regulations was non-negotiable. Finally, he refused to agree to a request from the FOCA that the issues be referred to an independent arbiter.

At the same time, Balestre revealed that he had been busy with a meeting of his own. It had taken place in Paris on 12 June, about a week after the Lausanne gathering, to which, he said, he had invited representatives of the FIA's leading national sporting authorities. Apart from Britain, Brazil and the Automobile Competition Committee for the United States, which had yet to decide, he announced, they had all – that is, Argentina, Germany, Austria, Belgium, Spain, South Africa, France, Holland, Italy, Monaco, Portugal and Mexico – put their signatures to a statement supporting the FISA. It would therefore prove impossible, he said, for the FOCA to stage a breakaway World Championship series. The national sporting authorities of the French, German, Dutch, Austrian and Italian Grands Prix, he added, had gone a step further by offering to run races only for teams endorsed by the FISA, with their number being supplemented by Formula Two cars.

Balestre believed that, in one move, he had cleverly outmanoeuvred Ecclestone. With 12 races the minimum number to constitute a legal World Championship series, he appeared to have a strong hand, at least in theory. In practice, it was not necessarily so. As Balestre had been made humiliatingly aware at the Spanish Grand Prix, the national sporting authority did not have the final word on whether a Grand Prix would be held. The FOCA also had a further considerable factor in its favour. Ecclestone had sewn up contracts with every circuit bar one, and he had made it clear that he wouldn't hesitate to enforce their legality. Who then, in such an uncertain situation and under the threat of litigation, would stand four-square to the death with Balestre?

Balestre's peremptory rejection of the proposed agreement drawn up at Lausanne caused Sir Clive Bossom, the president of the British Royal Automobile Club, to express the RAC's 'deep concern' to the FIA's president, Prince Paul Metternich. 'We cannot emphasise too strongly,' he said in a statement, 'that if these [the 11 points listed] are not agreed, the permanent damage and harm that will be caused to motor sport in general throughout the world will be disastrous.'[7]

The constructors made a further attempt to resolve the differences with the FISA by proposing a meeting with the manufacturers – Renault, Ferrari and Alfa Romeo – and Balestre. Adopting a tone of compromise, Ecclestone made it clear that the constructors no longer had a problem with a ban on 'skirts' per se but with the way in which Balestre had attempted to impose it without consulting the constructors, and by ignoring the statutory two years' notice. Balestre agreed to attend the proposed meeting – but on one condition. He insisted that Ecclestone withdrew a threat to boycott the French Grand Prix, a tactic which he had used to focus Balestre's thoughts. He would not, he said, attend a meeting under the duress of a boycott. He agreed to attend a meeting therefore on 30 June – the day after the race.

Of all Grands Prix, Balestre wanted the French race to run smoothly. A repeat of the Jarama fracas was the last thing he wanted in his own country. There was a further, important imperative. Ligier was being sponsored to the tune of £333,000 by the manufacturers of Gitanes, which conflicted with the French government's policy on tobacco advertising. Balestre had thrown his weight behind lobbying efforts to persuade the government to grant Ligier an exemption, which, amidst much controversy, it finally agreed to do. For the French Grand Prix to be staged without the presence of such major players as Williams, Lotus, McLaren, Tyrrell and Brabham would cause him great personal embarrassment. As confirmation of his good intentions, Balestre gave his word of honour that if all the FOCA teams, including Ferrari, Renault and Alfa Romeo, were in agreement at the end of the meeting then the decision endorsed at the FISA's plenary spring congress in Rio de Janeiro to ban 'skirts' would be reviewed in favour of an acceptable period of transition. Ecclestone took Balestre at his word and the boycott was lifted.

The French Grand Prix – won by Williams's Alan Jones but with Ligier and Renault taking three of the first five places – came and went without incident. Balestre had had his trouble-free Grand Prix, and now it was time for a coming together of the warring factions, which took place at the Paul Ricard circuit, near Marseilles. Representing the FOCA were Ecclestone, Max Mosley, and Colin Chapman of Lotus; for the manufacturers, Carlo Chiti of Alfa Romeo, Marco Piccinini of Ferrari, Gérard Larrousse of Renault and Gérard Ducarouge of Ligier; and for the FISA, Balestre, Baron Fritz Huschke von Hanstein, Curt Schild, and three of its senior members – Enrico Benzing, Paul Frère and Gérard 'Jabby' Crombac, chairman of the Technical Commission of the Fédération Française du Sport Automobile.

The meeting quickly got down to business with Ecclestone's presentation of a series of proposals that came as part of a package, which had already been unanimously agreed by the constructors and the manufacturers during a 12-hour meeting at the Excelsior Hotel at London's Heathrow Airport a few days before the French Grand Prix. The proposals included a five-year postponement of the ban on 'skirts'; that cornering speeds – the central concern of the anti-'skirts' lobby – should be reduced by the use of less efficient tyres, possibly treaded or narrower tyres; that the constructors should have a greater say on whether a fuel flow system for turbos should be introduced; that the constructors should have more seats on the Formula One Commission, which had been formed in September 1979 following Ecclestone's rejection of

Balestre's Formula One Working Group; and that there should be greater stability of regulations. Perhaps to Ecclestone's surprise, the package, which was put forward as an all-or-nothing basis, received the enthusiastic support of Balestre and his colleagues. He publicly described the meeting as 'very constructive and very positive'. For the first time, it seemed there was good reason to believe that at last a peace formula had been found. It promised much, but, due to Balestre's duplicity, delivered little.

During the British Grand Prix at Brands Hatch, the tyre manufacturers Michelin and Goodyear met with representatives of the FISA's Technical Commission and voiced firm opposition to the proposed tyre changes: Michelin was not prepared to accept any tyre limitations, including tread design or reduction in tyre width, while Goodyear had proposed a reduction in tyre width and diameter, with treaded tyres being introduced at a later date. Balestre insisted that, due to their response, the all-or-nothing condition imposed by the FOCA on the package could not be maintained; it could not, therefore, be adopted. The ban on 'skirts', concluded Balestre, would therefore stand, unless, within two months, the constructors could submit a unanimously agreed solution to reducing cornering speeds.

The constructors were incensed. They had agreed to abide by any 'general agreement' reached between the FISA and the tyre manufacturers. The FISA, they believed, hadn't tried hard enough, and, in failing to find a solution, had given Balestre an excuse to throw out the entire package. He had given his word of honour that a set of proposals that had the unanimous support of the constructors and the manufacturers would be adopted by the FISA. Not without good reason, the constructors believed that they had been well and truly duped by Balestre to ensure the smooth running of the French Grand Prix.

During the eventful year of 1980 the FOCA claimed it had responded to more than half a dozen meetings proposed by Balestre in different parts of the world – South Africa, Monaco, Maranello, Nice, Madrid, Athens, Lausanne, Rio de Janeiro and Paris – to find a way of resolving their differences, but not one whit of progress had been made. Balestre, the constructors suspected, had simply been toying with them, like a cat with a mouse, as part of his personal power game.

Hopes of a rapprochement seemed as far away as ever. If the constructors were perceived as a motley crew of common arrivistes hell-bent on hijacking Formula One to their own avaricious ends, the FISA was seen as a bureaucratic administration more interested in political control and personalities than a more egalitarian division of power and authority. Balestre's leadership, they argued, had done little more than increase the number of commissions, conference and meetings, which, in Balestre's first full year of office, had resulted in a rise in FIA expenditure of 129 per cent. The constructors were also contemptuous of administrators and national sporting authority delegates who, with all expenses paid, would attend such glittering social occasions as the Monaco Grand Prix, yet could be relied upon to avoid the less attractive races.

Certainly Balestre, while supportive of all Grands Prix irrespective of their social allure, fully expected to be accorded the red-carpet treatment. Those who failed to rise to his expectations, said a former FIA colleague, did so at the risk of incurring his disfavour. 'If you [an organiser] wanted to be on good terms with Balestre, you would personally invite him to your Grand Prix and you would send a Rolls-Royce or a Cadillac to pick him up at the airport. The car would have a police escort and display FIA flags. He was not there [in office] for the money, but he enjoyed the power and all the trappings that went with it.'

An increasing sense of self-importance also came to demand, said his former associate, 'a whole suite of offices in a penthouse overlooking the racetrack. The smaller the country, the bigger the office, because every one of them was trying to impress him more than the next one.' At a Hungarian Grand Prix, Balestre 'went bananas' when he discovered his office was situated next to the toilet, accommodation deliberately arranged by Ecclestone. He insisted that he be transferred to another office, which was situated at a more respectable distance. He had one other demand that attracted critical comment from the constructors – an increasing supply of free Grand Prix tickets for his friends and business associates.

7

THE KEY TO RICHES – TELEVISION RIGHTS

As the 1981 season drew near, the relationship between the FOCA and the FISA progressed to one of entrenched hostility, with the rumblings of an all-out war becoming ever louder. While Ecclestone was advising one team boss, reluctant to proceed on the design of his car for the following season because of uncertainty over the regulations, to plan on 'skirts', Balestre was announcing in a press statement that teams wishing to compete in the following season's World Championship series would be required to register with the FISA by 1 December – a month in advance of the first race of the season, the Argentine Grand Prix – and, the statement stressed, their compliance would confirm acceptance of the FISA's ban on 'skirts'.

He further attempted to encourage a split in the ranks of the FOCA by announcing a restructuring of the Formula One Commission, which had been set up to examine and decide all matters relating to Formula One. In its original form its membership was intended to comprise three representatives from the FOCA, the FISA and the race organisers; two representatives from the major sponsors; and one racing driver. It would be chaired in rotation by the FOCA and the FISA representatives. It had been all but ignored by the FOCA. Now, announced Balestre, membership was open to 'all the Formula One constructors (without exception) who wish to be part of it'. The FOCA had, in fact, been looking for greater representation on the commission as part of the

11-point package agreed with the manufacturers to resolve the 'skirts' versus turbo dispute, but, given the way the constructors believed Balestre had sabotaged it, they had ignored the invitation to a man.

Of all Balestre's attempts to defeat Ecclestone and the constructors, the most provocative and determined effort came in August 1980, at the end of the Dutch Grand Prix, and through the columns of *L'Équipe*, the French daily sports newspaper. At its plenary conference in Paris in October, he confidently predicted in the newspaper that the FISA would be given the authority to take responsibility for the 'start' and prize money paid by the organisers to the teams, and for its distribution. The FISA would also become responsible for negotiating five-year contracts with organisers which would contain an inflation-linked clause to avoid 'excessive rises year after year'.[1] Acknowledging that it could not interfere with existing contracts between the organisers and the FOCA, Balestre insisted, however, that as the contracts expired it would be through the FISA that the organisers would be negotiating their renewal. The new arrangements, he said, would lead to a policy of greater accountability, with information on how much teams were receiving being made public.

There would also, he said, be more prize money available. It would come from abolishing what he described as the FOCA's 'black fund', a secret account whose purpose, he said, was to help teams through financial crises and which, as a result, worked to maintain the stability of the Formula One circus and its leading names. The FISA, he continued, would also eventually impose a limit of 14 Grands Prix to ensure the highest competitive standards, a move intended to appease those manufacturers who believed that the number of races being arranged by Ecclestone – in 1977 there were as many as 17 – was, though more profitable for the constructors and the sponsors, too punishing. In return for its organisational services, said Balestre, the FISA would retain no more than two per cent of revenue – estimated at about £100,000 per season.

The FOCA, he added obligingly, 'will still exist, if it wishes ... we will simply be distributing them [the teams] the money'. He added that a new rule book covering the sporting, technical and 'whole organisation' of Formula One would also be put before the conference for its approval. 'It is a real restoration of the sporting power, designed to forge a solid instrument. We want to take over full organisation of the World Championship and control the performance of the cars so that they do not exceed human capabilities – in short, to halt uncontrolled development. It is in no way breaking the imagination of the designers, but establishing a framework, setting limits.' Some saw it more clearly as an attempt designed to break the FOCA.

To be sure of the support of the manufacturers – Ferrari, Alfa Romeo, Renault and Ligier – in the major confrontation that Balestre surely knew was coming – indeed that he had been planning for – he persuaded them to agree to a secret deal. It took place during the autumn of 1980, when he invited senior executives of the manufacturers to his home at St Cloud, overlooking the Seine near Paris, where, after dinner, he promised that the FISA would continue its ban on 'skirts' if, in return, the manufacturers would give their word to back him in the make-or-break conflict that lay ahead. A senior FISA official who was present at the dinner table recalled: 'Balestre said, "Look, I am prepared to start this battle, but, before I do so, you have to guarantee me that you will support me throughout the war." They all agreed to support him.'

The article in *L'Équipe* led to an emergency meeting of the FOCA. It ended in perhaps the only way it could, with Ecclestone announcing that the constructors would be breaking away from the FIA. The FOCA, said Ecclestone, would be setting up the World Federation of Motor Sport (WFMS), which he described as 'an independent, professionally-run sanctioning body' to run a $10-million World Professional Drivers' Championship, with a guarantee of $1 million to the winning driver. The WFMS, said Ecclestone, would be 'made up of men with professional, commercial and sporting experience' and would give a better deal in return for 'the $70 million invested each year by the competitors and sponsors to produce the ultimate form of motor sport'. Balestre was quick to predict a brief and unhappy existence for the WFMS. 'Let me tell you something,' he warned through the media, 'those people don't know what they are in for, they don't understand power, they're just little men playing with toys, making cars in garages: who do they think they are?'

Ecclestone's reply was no less aggressive: 'Who the hell is the FISA? They are a bunch of nobodies, they appointed themselves and they think they own racing, when all they really have is a bunch of clubs around the world and self-important people living off the back of the sport.'[2] He also produced a stream of statistics to disprove Balestre's claim that the manufacturers were too important to be excluded from any World Championship series. Since the inception of the World Championship in 1950, the manufacturers – Ferrari, Honda, Porsche, Maserati, Mercedes-Benz, Renault, Alfa Romeo and Lancia – had, on average, produced only 1.6 cars per Grand Prix. And in that season, 1980, out of 80 starts by the major manufacturers – Ferrari, Alfa Romeo and Renault – only 30 had resulted in a finish, and out of that 30 only eight had competed on the same lap as the leader. His vituperative comments, plus the accompanying data, were, by the way, issued in a statement composed by Mosley, who was responsible for most of Ecclestone's more controversial public pronouncements.

The FOCA, whose members included seven of the top teams, and among whose ranks was the imminent world champion, Alan Jones, was certainly in a stronger position to fill the grid with more attractive teams. The FISA, on the other hand, had no more than four, without one driver in the top three of the 1980 championship. The FOCA had also legally binding contracts with virtually all the circuits. But in such a uniquely complex sport, in which so many financial and human elements had to work in unison for its successful exhibition, neither side, despite all the threats and belligerent rhetoric, could be sure of how the endgame would play out.

Despite the apparent tactical advantage of the constructors, during the weeks it soon became apparent that they were in a most financially vulnerable position. Sponsors such as Goodyear, who supplied most of the FOCA teams, had already withdrawn in protest at the split, and other sponsors, increasingly nervous about the future of Formula One, were ready to follow. Under increasing financial pressures, the constructors were forced to lay off mechanics, introduce a three-day working week and cancel test sessions to save costs. In the days when Formula One in Britain was more of a cottage industry, with engines and a wide range of component parts supplied by outside companies, the constructors, whose talents, in the main, did not include prudent financial planning, were soon beset by cashflow problems, with credit drying up overnight. The wealthy manufacturers, with their in-house production, faced no such difficulties.

The threat to the industries whose survival depended on the existence of the British teams was sufficiently serious for the conflict to be raised in the House of Commons. Tory MP Jonathan Aitken, who laid the blame at the door of Balestre and his associates, claimed that Formula One was heading towards a catastrophe of Grand Prix cancellations and company liquidations. Thousands of livelihoods would be lost and some famous small companies bankrupted. Unfair French tactics, he added, were being applied to Formula One through the FISA. Sports Minister Hector Monro responded by calling for an urgent meeting with his French counterpart to find a solution.[3] The response from the French was not encouraging. It was strange, said a French government spokesman, to find that the British, 'who do not normally mix sport with politics, [were now prepared] to change their policy'. There followed brief communications between the two governments that did nothing to resolve the conflict.

As the weeks passed, and as the political and financial pressures mounted, Ecclestone encountered two major obstacles that would bring an end to the FOCA's plans for a breakaway world championship series. It was unable to find the necessary insurance cover for its world championship, and circuits willing at first to work with the new organisation, even in the face of the threat of legal action by the FOCA, had a collective change of heart after Balestre warned of punitive disciplinary action against them. Through the national sporting authorities, the FISA made it clear to the circuit owners and promoters that if they sided with the FOCA they could forget about staging any other FIA-authorised motor sport event at their tracks. Without the revenue they generated during the rest of the year, the circuit owners feared the prospect of huge losses, if not closure. By the end of November 1980 the constructors were forced to accept the reality of their position. Six weeks after its birth, the World Federation of Motor Sport was no more.

It is worth noting that for some weeks the constructors, apart from Ecclestone's own Brabham team, had been testing cars without 'skirts', an indication that the constructors, without the financial resources to withstand a long-term war, were preparing for the inevitable. In announcing the end of the FOCA's plans for a rival championship series, Ecclestone, perhaps in an attempt to save some face, declined to say whether the constructors would rejoin the FISA World Championship series. It was a position that he clarified, though, less than three weeks later, when he confirmed that the constructors had decided to race in the first three meetings of the 1981 season – which would turn out to be the USA West at Long Beach, Brazil and Argentina – but with 'skirted' cars. The FOCA did have an important legal incentive for returning to the FISA fold.

As long as the constructors remained within the official World Championship series, the contracts that Ecclestone had with the circuit owners, which stipulated that races would be run to unchanged technical specifications, thereby allowing cars with 'skirts', carried the full force of law. Two weeks after Ecclestone had announced the end of the constructors' breakaway series, the FOCA went to the High Court in London to obtain injunctions against eight circuits – Kyalami (South Africa), Long Beach (USA West), Zolder (Belgium), Dijon (France), the Österreichring (Austria), Monza (Italy), Gilles Villeneuve (Canada) and Zandvoort (Holland) – which prevented them from entering into similar agreements with any other party. It was done with the circuit owners' knowledge, and indeed their support. It enabled them to turn to the FIA and say they had no choice but to side with the constructors.

The decision to race with 'skirts' defied Balestre's 1 December deadline, but in doing so the FOCA was shrewdly putting the pressure on him. The message was clear: let's race – and talk. If Balestre had insisted that the deadline was inviolable, he would have been pilloried as the person ready to bring down Formula One simply to make a political point. Balestre also had Renault to consider. The manufacturer would not have been happy at seeing Balestre enforce the deadline. Although over cognac at his St Cloud home Balestre had been assured of Renault's support, it was the more scheming Enzo Ferrari among the manufacturers who had been the driving force in favour of a 'skirts' ban, as well as an increase in the minimum weight, to give his turbo cars a significantly competitive edge over the constructors. If Renault were to back off, it might well have prompted Alfa Romeo and Talbot to follow suit, leaving only Ferrari to stand with Balestre. Indeed, Renault were to back off, but in remarkable circumstances that had nothing to do with the FOCA's decision or the FISA's deadline, but everything to do with the power of corporate image. It would bring about the beginning of the end of this most damaging conflict.

In addition to obtaining High Court injunctions against the circuit owners, the FOCA also had one issued against the FISA, as well as against every member of its executive committee, to block any attempts to interfere in the FOCA's contracts with the circuits. High Court injunction or no, it failed to dissuade Balestre from doing his best to disrupt the FOCA's plans. Accompanied by a senior FISA official and an interpreter, Balestre flew to America for a meeting in a New York hotel with senior members of the Sports Car Club of America (SCCA), who sanctioned the USA West Grand Prix on behalf of the national sporting authority, the Automobile Competition Committee for the United States (ACCUS). He wanted the SCCA to refuse to sanction the race, which was scheduled to open the season on 15 March – two months late due to the reigning mayhem. The race, he said, should not take place. Furthermore, he warned, if it went ahead, the manufacturers would not compete.

Farcically, Balestre attempted to get round the High Court injunction by looking on as his interpreter read questions from a list he had compiled. Apparently Ecclestone had been informed in advance of the meeting and requested that the list be covertly retained to be used, if necessary, as evidence of Balestre's breach of the injunction against him. By the end of the meeting, the list of questions, left on the table by the interpreter, had disappeared. The FOCA later pursued an action alleging against the FISA restraint of trade and interference with contract, although it was never heard. Balestre failed in his efforts to secure the support of the SCCA to get the USA West Grand Prix cancelled. But, more disastrously for him, a comment he made during the meeting resulted in a serious fracture, which in turn caused a fatal weakening in his relationship with Renault, which, in turn, led to a fatal weakening in the FISA's stand against Ecclestone and the constructors.

At that time Renault owned American Motors, and its senior management in America, fearful of the negative effect on its corporate image, were alarmed to hear the claim by Balestre that the manufacturers would not be racing alongside the constructors at Long Beach. A former FISA official who was at that meeting in the New York hotel said that from that moment 'Renault spread the word that, with or without Balestre, they would be at Long Beach', which was just weeks away. The decision by Renault proved a major blow to Balestre. It led to Enzo Ferrari deciding that his team, too, would race at Long Beach. Talbot and Alfa Romeo quickly fell in line to complete a full grid. The alliance between the manufacturers and Balestre was effectively over.

Renault had already stood by uneasily to watch the constructors score a major point by staging a race in South Africa. It was intended by FOCA to replace the Argentine Grand Prix, which was due to raise the curtain on the 1981 season, but which the FISA was forced to cancel after the constructors had refused to take part. The event was held to prove that the real balance of power lay with the teams – they could stage a race, the governing body couldn't. It was not only significant for the effect it had on Renault senior management, but also in seeding the ground for an historic Agreement, which would bring about a contractual and mostly peaceful alliance between the FOCA and the FISA. Its little-known inspiration was quite dramatic in its own right.

With Formula One in a state of chaos and confusion, and with the constructors trying to survive the severe financial strain it was wreaking, the future looked more than bleak as Colin Chapman, Max Mosley, Teddy Mayer and his wife, attending the Hahnenkamm downhill ski race at Kitzbühel, Austria, sat down for dinner at a restaurant in a nearby village. During the evening Chapman's curiosity had been aroused by a mural on a wall which depicted a scene of someone literally painting a cow as it grazed in a field. What did it mean, he asked a waitress. She explained that it was in remembrance of villagers who, under siege in a local battle and desperately low on food, attempted to deceive the besieging army into believing they had plenty of food by painting the same cow a different colour every day. Suddenly a light bulb came on in Chapman's head. That's it – the FISA, and Balestre in particular, had to be deceived into believing that the FOCA had the financial resources to stage its own races. At their hotel, they went to Mosley's bedroom and called Ecclestone. His response was instant: 'You're all pissed.'

In truth, that was not far off the mark, but the next day the idea was pursued, and Ecclestone, as he listened to the rationale of its guile, came to agree. Once the manufacturers, with all their tens of millions of dollars invested in Formula One, saw that the constructors could go it alone, the effect, it was calculated, could prove a decisive factor in weakening a resolve that was not very strong in the first place. The much-strapped teams were persuaded to go with it, and started to make arrangements for cars and personnel to be air-freighted with the help of some credit, while the tyres, no longer available from Goodyear, came from Ecclestone's International Race Tire Services. The South African Grand Prix, scheduled on the FIA calendar for 7 February, would take place, announced the FOCA.

Balestre attempted to scupper the FOCA's plans by the simple ploy of arbitrarily announcing that the date of the South African Grand Prix was being put back to 11 April, which created a serious problem for the circuit owners, Kyalami Enterprises. Far from the most financially stable of Formula One Grands Prix, Kyalami Enterprises had succeeded in securing a lucrative sponsorship deal with office-equipment manufacturers Nashua, which had geared its promotional plans for 7 February, and whose financial support was contractually contingent upon that date. For that reason, and because of the uncertain state of the 1981 season, Kyalami Enterprises had sought from the FISA, and received by telex in early December, confirmation of the February slot.

Following talks with Ecclestone, Kyalami Enterprises refused to accept the FISA's decision. They also reminded Balestre, at Ecclestone's suggestion, that there was a High Court injunction compelling the circuit owners to fulfil the conditions of the contract with the FOCA on the agreed date. Balestre's response was to downgrade the race to a Formula Libre event, which, stripped of its Grand Prix status, could not count for World Championship points. Nevertheless, the race, which was won by Carlos Reutemann in a Williams FW07-Ford, went ahead, albeit in appalling weather conditions. The absence of the manufacturers, not least the crowd-pulling Ferraris, combined with poor advance publicity and promotion caused by its uncertain fate, resulted in a poor spectator audience. But, crucially, it received international television coverage, leaving senior Renault executives to consider the cost to the company's image and massive team budget of playing in Balestre's power battle. By the time Balestre went to New York, his gaffe in stating that Renault would not be taking part in the USA West Grand Prix was enough to cause the manufacturer to switch sides.

Renault's decision hit Balestre all the harder because he had been convinced that the solidarity of the FISA and the manufacturers would win the day. A former senior FIA official said that Balestre believed that, but for Renault breaking ranks, 'the constructors would have had to say, "OK, [we] will sign with the FIA." This is how the war would have been won if Renault had not betrayed Balestre.' Victory for the FISA on Balestre's terms, he added, had been 'very close'. Indeed it had. Said Mosley: 'We were absolutely skint. If Balestre could have held the manufacturers' support for a little bit longer, the constructors would have been on their knees. The outcome then could have been very different.' The decision to stage a race in South Africa had been, he added, a 'masterstroke'.

But even before Kyalami, Balestre was being edged out into the cold. Enzo Ferrari, a principal protagonist who was now keen to be seen as a peace-maker, invited Ecclestone, Mosley and the 'grandis' to a meeting at his factory in Maranello on 16 January. Over the next few weeks it led to a series of meetings between Max Mosley, for the FOCA, Marco Piccinini, for the manufacturers, Renault's lawyer Ronnie Austin and a lawyer from the FIA, from which emerged a peace agreement that came to be known as the Maranello Agreement. Piccinini, with his faultless French, reported the discussions to Balestre.

The proposals gave the constructors and manufacturers what they had always wanted: for the FOCA, which accepted without qualification the banning of 'skirts', a minimum period of two years' notice to cover technical rule changes, plus a minimum of four years' stability on all major changes; and, for the manufacturers, that the technical rules should be the exclusive governance of the FISA. It was all as simple as that, and yet had been so difficult and costly to achieve.

It led to a revamping of the Formula One Commission, which gave greater representation and power to the constructors and manufacturers. It was agreed that the Commission would comprise three constructors and three manufacturer representatives; four race organisers – two European and two overseas; two sponsors – one constructor and one manufacturer; and one FISA representative. The FISA's executive committee could accept or reject the Commission's recommendations, but it couldn't amend them. (Four years later the work of the new Commission was complemented by a Permanent Bureau consisting of Balestre, Ecclestone and Marco Piccinini, Ferrari's team manager, to respond to problems requiring immediate resolution.)

The FOCA retained the right to negotiate freely with organisers and promoters in all areas of its commercial activities. In a separate document it was agreed that Ecclestone would receive eight per cent of the gross – 'less than a standard agency commission,' he said[4] – which, given an estimated $500,000 from each of the season's 15 races, represented an attractive cut nonetheless. Most importantly, though, the agreement left the teams with what would turn out to be the most valuable asset of all, the jewel in the Formula One crown – the marketing of the television rights, which were now being sold in 95 countries with a global viewing audience, according to FOCA figures, exceeding one billion. It was agreed that while the FIA would have sole and exclusive proprietorship of all broadcasting rights, they would be assigned to the FOCA for Ecclestone to market, the proceeds of which would be distributed among the teams. Surprisingly in the circumstances perhaps, the FIA didn't receive a sou. It wasn't until 1987, with a share of 30 per cent, that it began to enjoy a share of the proceeds. Certainly Balestre had coveted the revenue of the television rights for the FIA's coffers. They had been, it was suspected, his primary motive in his bid to seize control of the FOCA's commercial interests. At the height of the war with the FOCA he had actually tried to negotiate the sale of television rights to two major networks through the public-relations division of the French oil company Elf. His efforts came to naught after the constructors' withdrawal from the World Championship series caused the marketable value of the rights to plunge.

There was one other, little-publicised condition, but it was to the immense benefit of the teams. Unless an organiser first agreed financial terms with the FOCA, the FIA would not grant the organiser the right to stage a Grand Prix. It was done, at the FOCA's insistence, to ensure that the FISA could not enhance the bargaining position of an organiser by including an event in the calendar before terms had been agreed with the teams. It put Ecclestone very much in the driving seat in negotiations, and would prove a seminal stage in his increasing control of Formula One. As for Balestre, he appeared pleased with the deal because it was his hope to take back all of the rights at the end of the four-year agreement so that the FIA could run its own championship, as it ran the rest of the world's motor sport, an ambition which, in his negotiations with Ecclestone, he would never succeed in achieving.

This was the essence of the Maranello Agreement, which was agreed by Ecclestone and Mosley with Balestre over breakfast in the Hôtel Crillon next to the FIA headquarters, which were situated in the Automobile Club de France's offices in Place de la Concorde. Balestre had one stipulation – he wanted the document to be known as the Concorde Agreement, a matter that was of complete indifference to both Ecclestone and Mosley. It was agreed that he would sign the agreement by 8 February, only a matter of days away. But the petulant Frenchman, hoping perhaps to restore some lost pride, if not authority, was not done with his power games. He suddenly objected to the proposed number of FOCA seats on the Formula One Commission. On 20 February Ecclestone and Mosley flew to Paris to discuss his concerns. The issue was resolved, but Balestre continued to withhold his assent.

First, he insisted, Ecclestone had to bring an end to the FOCA's High Court injunctions against the FISA and its executive committee members which prohibited him from interfering with the FOCA's contracts with the circuit owners. He argued that to sign the agreement while the injunction was still in place would be tantamount to violating it. Balestre telexed his terms to Ecclestone at the South African Grand Prix, but at that time he was, in fact, in Rio de Janeiro negotiating sponsorship for the Brazilian Grand Prix. Ecclestone replied that the injunction would be lifted once Balestre agreed to put his signature to the agreement. At last Balestre agreed to do so. His delaying tactics had achieved little, other than to cause the constructors and the manufacturers to seriously consider joining forces to stage and govern their own World Championship series.

On 11 March 1981 the Concorde Agreement was formally signed at the headquarters of the FIA in Paris, to take effect from 1 January for a period of four years. Yet even then, there was one signature missing, that of Enzo Ferrari, who, at the last minute, dramatically decided to withhold his blessing after claiming there was still a number of questions to be answered. It was added to the agreement two weeks later, accompanied by the observation of some commentators that it had been a theatrical stunt by Ferrari to steal the limelight as the man who had formally brought an end to the longest on-off suicide attempt in sporting history.

So who won the war? It seemed at the time that neither side had emerged victorious. All that had been established had been the boundaries of each other's turf. The FOCA had established the right to continue, through Ecclestone, to control all financial matters relevant to the constructors' interests, while the FISA had established the right to continue to be responsible for the rules and regulations, with a say in proposed changes going both to the constructors and the manufacturers. The constructors no longer had their 'skirts', although future events would prove otherwise, but they had been prepared to give them up, and they had got what they wanted anyway – an acceptable period of notice before new technical rule changes were introduced.

If the war exposed the constructors' financial vulnerability, it also revealed the FISA's political vulnerability. The governing body had failed to bring the constructors to heel, and was forced to realise that without them it could not effectively stage a World Championship series and that, consequently, they had to be accepted on equal terms. Divided, the two were a far lesser force, a fact that over the years, which had seen so much time, energy and money expended, had become blindingly obvious to those in the ringside seats. At that time there appeared to be no apparent victor, although the chief beneficiary, over the years ahead, would prove to be Ecclestone, who would go on to exploit the television rights so shrewdly. Said the former FIA official: 'It was Ecclestone who won the spoils of the war. He got the television rights, which, as things turned out, would be the true prize.'

Peter Warr, who took over the running of Team Lotus in December 1982 following the death of Colin Chapman, believes that Ecclestone's great skill was in playing to Balestre's megalomania. The Frenchman saw himself, said Warr, as 'the all-singing and all-dancing dictator, with nothing happening unless he said so. One of Bernie's great achievements was to allow Balestre to continue thinking that, while in reality it wasn't true. He basically said, well, let's keep humouring him and keep him believing that he is the one that matters, and we'll get on and do our own thing and make sure it happens. Balestre, to whom adornments were so important, got the trappings of office but none of the substance. Certainly, he could go into the FIA headquarters and throw the most huge wobblies and he could come to circuits and interrupt stewards in the middle of drivers' briefings and he could go out on the track and shout at individuals but all that was huff and puff. It was Bernie who really won the war against the FISA.'

So, at last, peace and goodwill had been restored to the turbulent world of Formula One. At least, so it appeared. There were fresh storms brewing, even before the ink on the Concorde Agreement had dried. But this time it was between the constructors, and would reveal yet again how the forces of self-interest that had united them in their battles against the FISA would now work to divide them, with two of their leading personalities – Ecclestone and Colin Chapman – once more the target of each other's wrath.

Centre stage in the first split was a car with a twin-chassis body, known as the Lotus 88. It was Chapman's innovative solution to a problem caused by the massive downforce created by the development of 'skirts', which required heavier suspension springs. The almost solid suspension, not to mention the much increased cornering G-force, gave the driver quite a buffeting and affected a car's drivability. Chapman's answer was to suspend the body unit and undertray as a separate downforce-creating assembly, with linkage to the outboard ends of the front and rear lower wishbones. As the downforce created by the body unit passed directly to the wheels, it bypassed a conventional chassis, which carried the engine, gearbox and driver on lighter springing to achieve comfort, traction and drivability. It was ingeniously clever, and led a number of teams to pursue the time-honoured course of action when faced with a car which threatened to make theirs uncompetitive: if time or money made copying impossible, get it banned on the grounds that it broke the rules.

The protests began at the USA West Grand Prix at Long Beach, the first race of the 1981 season, despite a ruling by the scrutineers that it was perfectly legal. Nevertheless, the opposing teams – ten backed a ban, five did not, including Tyrrell and Fittipaldi, while Ferrari merely objected to the decision of the scrutineers – claimed it violated article three, paragraph seven of the FIA's technical regulations, which stated that all parts of a car having an influence on aerodynamic performance had to remain immobile in relation to the sprung part of the car. Chapman argued that the aerodynamics of the twin-chassis were immobile to at least one of them and therefore fully conformed to the regulations.

After his argument failed to stifle protests at an emergency meeting of the teams, he lodged an appeal with the Automobile Competition Committee for the United States (ACCUS), which, after hearing technical submissions from chief aerodynamicist Peter Wright at a two-day hearing in Atlanta, Georgia, backed the scrutineers and ruled it legal. However, the constructors refused to withdraw their threat, which Chapman believed to be no more than a bluff, but the organisers weren't prepared to call it. During an untimed practice session the car was 'black-flagged'. At the Argentine Grand Prix the following month, where once again it was excluded from the race following protests from the teams, Chapman was so incensed that he issued a statement critical of Balestre and Ecclestone. He suspected that Balestre had given support to Ecclestone's efforts to kill off the Lotus 88.

The statement had been written by the convivial and widely respected Gérard 'Jabby' Crombac – the then French representative on the FISA's Technical Commission, a French motor sport magazine journalist and a lifelong admirer of Lotus – who believed the design of Chapman's car was in accord with the letter of the rule book. However, after Balestre was given a copy of the statement, his translator, Dublin-born David Waldron, pointed out that it had not been written by an Englishman. Balestre made enquiries and became enraged on discovering that Crombac was the author. Chapman, rushing to catch a flight to Cape Canaveral to watch a missile launch, had dictated the statement to Crombac, whose hurried notes led to mistakes noted by Waldron. On returning home, Crombac discovered that Balestre's punishment was swift: he had been sacked as chairman of the Technical Commission of the Fédération Française du Sport Automobile, which automatically disqualified him from the FISA's Technical Commission. When Chapman heard what had happened, with typical panache he threw Crombac the keys to his own Lotus Eclat 2.2, with the comment: 'That's the least I can do for you.'

For the record, Chapman went to the FIA's Court of Appeal in Paris for a final judgement, which he lost. Apart from a practice session at the British Grand Prix at Silverstone that year – it was prohibited from taking part – the Lotus 88 did not appear again. The incident, however, illustrated the double standard which prevailed among the teams due to the intense rivalry. Also competing in the Argentine Grand Prix had been the less spectacular Ferrari 126CK. Contrary to the FISA's rule book, the side pods touched the ground at more than one point of the circuit on a full fuel load. But, unlike Chapman's twin-chassis design, the car did not pose the same competitive threat. Its illegality was not pursued.

Ecclestone believed that Chapman had been the architect of his own misfortune. He made a fundamental mistake in not notifying the teams in advance of his new concept. In a forthright and affable face-to-face meeting, the teams who came out in opposition would have found it difficult to go against good ol' 'Chunky' Chapman. By keeping it under wraps, until its performance spoke for itself during a practice session at the USA West Grand Prix, Chapman was giving a clear signal that he didn't give a damn what the other teams thought. The teams' response, opined Ecclestone, was: 'OK, we'll attack it through the rule book.'

Balestre was extremely embarrassed by Crombac's involvement in the Lotus statement because, as Chapman had suspected, he had indeed assured Ecclestone of his support in formally objecting to the Lotus 88. Accordingly, Balestre insisted that if it didn't contravene the letter of the law, it did so in spirit. The incident so angered Basil Tye, Managing Director of the British Royal Automobile Club's Motor Sports Association, which had sanctioned the entry of the Lotus 88, that he had a stand-up row with Balestre at the British Grand Prix. It resulted in Balestre's exclusion from the RAC's hospitality suite. Balestre responded by withdrawing an invitation to the Englishman to serve as a steward at the Dutch Grand Prix. Tye, not given to personal animus, nevertheless believed that Balestre's autocratic and bombastic style vitiated any sense of fair play, and that his intention to stand that October for re-election as president of the FISA for a further four years could not go unchallenged. Despite some encouraging early support, but without the political resources and allies, not to mention guile and influence to win wider backing, his efforts came to naught. A widely respected figure who had been involved in motor sport for more than 30 years, and who was said to have been bitterly disappointed when promised support for his candidature failed to materialise, Tye collapsed and died six months later while sailing his motor yacht, *Mosport*, near his home in Poole, Dorset.

According to a senior FIA representative at the time, Ecclestone had urged Balestre to oppose the Lotus 88 because he wanted the stage cleared for the latest Brabham car – the BT49C – which was about to be unveiled, and which was no less inventive. For some months Brabham's chief designer, Gordon Murray, had been working on ways of getting round the FISA ruling preventing the use of 'skirts', which stated that at the start and end of a race there had to be a 6-centimetre gap between the track and car and that there should be no systematic contact with the track while the car was in motion. Anticipating the imaginative efforts of designers to get round this obstacle, the ruling also prohibited any driver-operated system that enabled the lowering of the car during a race. Murray's clever solution was the BT49C's complex hydro-pneumatic suspension system, which used aerodynamic force to pass fluid from the suspension through a series of tiny valves and into a central reservoir which 'pulled' the car down as long as it was travelling at speed.

When the driver slowed down at the end of the race, compressed air returned the fluid through the valves and back into the suspension, causing it to rise to the minimum ride height of 6 centimetres. The car further complied with the new rule in that its 'skirts' did not systematically make contact with the tracks, as the condition of the 'rubbing strips' proved. It was estimated that the system gave the Brabham cars 80 per cent of the downforce of the banned 'skirts' while rival teams had no more than 40 per cent. At the Argentine Grand

Prix, Nélson Piquet, Brabham's lead driver, took the chequered flag, pole position and the fastest lap.

Predictably, the BT49C raised howls of protests from the other teams, which were led with some enthusiasm by a Colin Chapman still smarting from Ecclestone's successful efforts in the banning of his Lotus 88. No less enthusiastic were the manufacturers, who claimed it made a mockery of the Concorde Agreement, and that the costly war between the FOCA and the FISA over 'skirts' had all been for nothing. Unable to figure out how the system worked, some claimed that it was illegal because it had to be driver-operated. To keep them off the scent, Murray mischievously got his mechanics to build a little aluminium box and put it under the bodywork with some wires coming out leading to the gearbox. 'Everybody concentrated on the box and nobody looked at the valves,' recalled Murray.

By the fifth round of the 1981 World Championship series, the Belgian Grand Prix, by which time Piquet had taken two firsts and a third, it became clear that it was in danger of becoming a one-horse race. The Formula One Commission, alarmed that the disadvantage to the other teams would harm the championship's competitive appeal, came up with a political compromise that sanctioned Murray's hydro-pneumatic system, which became known as Automatic Ride Control. It allowed the other teams to introduce a similar system operated by the drivers. It resolved an increasingly threatening situation – at one stage Enzo Ferrari threatened to revert to the banned 'skirts' unless the Brabham team's hydro-pneumatic system was declared illegal – but it was a solution that left him and Ecclestone spitting feathers. 'Suddenly everybody got let off the hook,' said Murray. 'Bernie and I went bananas because, again, [a reference to the controversial 'fan' car of 1978] they had taken this big advantage from us.' All the same, he remained optimistic. 'I knew it would take four or five races before they would get it anywhere near right, by which time we would have the Championship sewn up.' Indeed it would. Piquet went on to win the first of his two World Championships with Brabham after outmanoeuvring Carlos Reutemann in the final race of the season at Las Vegas.

By the end of the year the FISA had formally scrapped the 6-centimetre ride height, which ended the future of Murray's hydro-pneumatic system, and had approved the use of 8-centimetre deep 'skirts'. All in all, a season that had begun so ominously ended well for Ecclestone, both politically and on the circuit. And he also had acquired in Balestre a new friend – the same man who shortly after his election as president of the CSI had pledged to resign if, in his mission to bring the FOCA to book, he had not banned 'skirts' within 12 months. To the constructors' great advantage, and Ecclestone's in particular, he had achieved neither.

That a new day had dawned in the relationship between Balestre and the constructors, one that coincided with the signing of the Concorde Agreement, was indicated by his response to protests by the manufacturers at another masterly attempt by the teams – notably Williams and Brabham – to counter the power of the turbos by bending the rule which stated that the minimum weight of a car at the beginning and end of a race had to be 580 kilograms. This, the constructors argued with some justification, favoured the heavier, turbocharged cars. Williams and Brabham rose to the challenge by installing 'water-cooling' brake reservoirs in their cars, which, when topped up with water, complied with the minimum weight rule. But, once on the track, the water was dispersed, enabling the cars to run at a considerably lighter weight. At the end of the race the reservoirs were topped up to meet the minimum weight requirement. To the fury of the manufacturers, and Ferrari in particular, it was perfectly legal, complying precisely with the letter of the FIA's rule book.

The effect of the super-lightweight cars became apparent at the 1982 Brazilian Grand Prix, the second race of the season, when Brabham's Nélson Piquet and Williams's Keke Rosberg finished first and second after Gilles Villeneuve in a Ferrari spun off. Ferrari and Renault, insisting that Ecclestone and Williams had raced illegal cars, protested to the FIA's Court of Appeal. Enzo Ferrari went one stage further by blatantly challenging the rule book himself. Ferrari's two cars – driven by Villeneuve and Didier Pironi – appeared at the following race, the USA West Grand Prix at Long Beach, with two rear wings to increase downforce. Villeneuve, who finished third, was duly disqualified, while Pironi, academically, spun off. Soon after the USA West Grand Prix, the FIA's Court of Appeal announced its decision on the Brazilian Grand Prix. It stated that the 'normal level of lubricant and coolant is that which is in the car when it crosses the finishing line, therefore no topping up of any kind is permitted'. With that, it retrospectively closed the loophole and disqualified Piquet and Rosberg. Alain Prost, in a Renault, who had come third, was classified as the winner. The decision incensed Ecclestone and Williams – and prompted Balestre, as quoted in a motor sport magazine, to issue a statement highly critical of the appeal court members.

The FOCA requested the FISA to postpone the next race, the San Marino Grand Prix at Imola, to give the constructors time to study the implications of the appeal court's decision. The FISA rejected the request, which led to Ecclestone announcing that in that case the constructors would boycott the race, which, it was suspected, had been their protest plan all along. But it proved not to be the smartest of moves, given the fact that the Italians would turn up in their droves simply to watch the Ferraris in action. Indeed, record crowds attended the race, which saw Ferrari take first and second place, with Tyrrell third. While he fully supported the principle of the boycott, Ken Tyrrell decided to compete because, after the USA West Grand Prix, he had landed a three-race sponsorship deal – plus a one-off with an Italian ceramics company for the San Marino Grand Prix – which, with pressing bills to pay, he couldn't afford to turn down. Tyrrell's decision to race was of some historical importance, in that, for the first time, the great strength of the FOCA – its unity – had been weakened. It proved that the constructors' power base was not invincible. For the teams who stayed away the boycott proved a political as well as a PR disaster.

The constructors had also voted to boycott the Belgian Grand Prix at Zolder, just two weeks away. But, in the meantime, the FIA's spring plenary conference was due to be held in Casablanca, which, with Balestre's support, Ecclestone and Williams seized as a final opportunity to plead their case, alleging that the appeal court's decision had, without the power or authority, introduced a change to the rule book. They were looking for a suspension of the appeal court's decision pending an inquiry. Balestre had another agenda: a ten-point list of sweeping changes supposedly intended to unify Formula One. If they were not adopted, he warned, he would resign.

It was seen as a hollow threat to mask a political ploy: their acceptance, of which he had every reason to be confident, would confer on him the tribute of the man who saved Formula One from self-destruction. The most controversial proposal, which was aimed at reducing the speed of turbos, was to impose a 200-litre fuel tank capacity. As turbos ran at that time on 215–230 litres such a ruling was predicted to be their death knell. It was further evidence, if any were needed, of the degree to which Balestre, who not so long ago had been behind the increase in the minimum car weight to the disadvantage of the FOCA teams, had turned to Ecclestone's corner. So much time was spent discussing Balestre's proposals that there remained little energy or interest to consider a plea on behalf of Ecclestone and Williams, for which few delegates had much sympathy anyway. The best that Balestre could achieve was to persuade the conference to agree to a seven-man committee to hear their arguments, which, after a two-hour hearing, duly rejected them. Balestre fared better with his onslaught on the turbos: the conference agreed to the implementation of the ten-point programme but that it should be postponed for six months.

With immense commercial pressure on the constructors to get back to business, the FOCA voted to turn up at Zolder, with their cars ballasted to make the weight. With the memories of the great war still fresh, they had no stomach for another protracted and costly showdown with the manufacturers. Said a constructor: 'We need to go racing because we are dependent on sponsorship. It is only the manufacturers that can afford a long-term boycott.' Certainly the constructors had good reason to be concerned by the progress of the turbo engines. By now, Renault's technical director, François Castaing, had overcome earlier problems that had caused more than one engine to blow, and, while Williams's Rosberg went on to become the 1982 world champion despite winning only one Grand Prix, Renault and Ferrari came first and second in the Constructors' Championship, with Pironi and Prost, of Renault, coming second and fourth in the World Championship title race.

It was believed that qualified opposition at the conference to Balestre's proposals was in no small part due to the influential and determined efforts of the Automobile Club de Monaco (ACM), the organisers of the Monaco Grand Prix and the Monte Carlo Rally, as well as manufacturers protecting their millions of dollars of investment in turbo engine development. Senior officials were far from pleased at the prospect of losing the following year their historical right to negotiate a highly lucrative contract with the American television company ABC TV, which it had enjoyed for 20 years, due to the Concorde Agreement giving the marketing of television rights to Ecclestone. The ACM, it was said, were not alone among the organisers in hoping that defeat for Ecclestone and Tyrrell at the conference would bring about their threat to boycott the Belgian Grand Prix, which, hopefully, would lead to a fresh conflict and result in a new peace pact, one which would restore television rights to the organisers.

Hopes for the restoration of television rights to the ACM did not end with the conference at Casablanca. Rather, it was the beginning of notable public discord between the club's president, lawyer Michel Boeri, and Balestre, which was said to have been enflamed by the Monégasque's opposition to Balestre's ten-point proposals. It was a confrontation which would lead to lawsuits, the involvement of President Mitterand of France and Prince Rainier of Monaco and an extraordinary statement by Balestre intended to demonstrate his independence of Ecclestone.

A once active supporter of Grand Prix International, the organisation that had been set up by the Commission Sportive Internationale to break Ecclestone's grip on the organisers, the ACM saw its troubles begin when Boeri signed a new five-year contract with ABC TV following the expiry of the contract at the end of 1983. Once the news reached Balestre's ears, he moved to ensure that the Monaco Grand Prix, the glamour event of the season and of more promotional value to the sponsors than all the other races put together, was absent when in October 1984 the FISA announced the following season's World Championship schedule. Balestre turned the screws tighter by threatening to expel the club from the FIA, thereby endangering even the future of the Monte Carlo Rally.

Balestre explained his decision by stating that in signing a new contract with ABC TV, the club had pointedly ignored a warning issued at the FISA plenary conference in Paris two months earlier to the effect that any country not respecting the FIA's television rights would not be given a World Championship round. Boeri believed he had done that by consulting Ecclestone as the FISA's television rights negotiator, who, he said, had approved the terms of the contract signed in January 1984 between the television network and the FOCA. It had, he added, cost the ACM $300,000 to buy the rights back from ABC TV to cede them to the FOCA. Balestre remain unmoved. He argued that the contract was invalid for two reasons: it should have been for three years – not five – and, rather than ABC TV, the FISA might well have wanted another US network to cover the Monaco Grand Prix.

Balestre was right – Ecclestone had jumped the gun in agreeing the deal with Boeri. The television rights, under the terms of the Concorde Agreement, returned to the FIA at the end of 1984. At the same time Balestre seized the opportunity to make the following statement on his relationship with Ecclestone: 'Some people ... suggested that Balestre was in Ecclestone's pocket, that all that was needed was to get Ecclestone's agreement and Balestre would fall into line. When I got the agreement [between the ACM and the FOCA] on my desk, I sent a telex to Bernie telling him very strongly that he had no powers to deal with the FIA's property – and that the agreement did not restore the FIA's rights.'[5]

It was, even by Balestre's standards, an odd statement to make. It simply drew attention to what many people suspected to be the reality of their relationship. Those close to Balestre insisted that the statement was not, in fact, intended, as a rebuke of Ecclestone, but, rather, aimed at putting the ACM in its place for Boeri's opposition at Casablanca. Said a former colleague: 'Balestre wanted to do everything he could to damage Boeri [after the Casablanca conference], and one way was to stop the Monaco Grand Prix and the Monte Carlo Rally.'

The ACM proceeded to issue a series of lawsuits against the FISA to test the legality of the FIA's ownership of television rights, as claimed in the Concorde Agreement. Ensuing talks between the two sides failed to resolve the dispute, which rapidly escalated into a crisis leading to diplomatic discussions between senior officials of the Monaco government and senior aides to President Mitterand. Prince Rainier became personally involved by insisting that only he could take the final decision for the principality of Monaco. Five months later, in February 1985, three months before the Monaco Grand Prix was scheduled to take place, Boeri, accused by Balestre of involving the ACM in 'suicidal madness', was forced to concede defeat when a High Court of Justice in Paris refused to order the FIA to reinstate the Monaco Grand Prix on the calendar of the Formula One World Championship. The ban on the Monaco Grand Prix and the Monte Carlo Rally was lifted when Boeri agreed that TV rights would revert to the FIA, that all legal action against the FISA would be dropped and that the Automobile Club de Monaco would pay all the FISA's legal costs.

Boeri claimed that he had 'not surrendered but signed a peace treaty'. Many years later he appeared to remain less than satisfied with the terms of that treaty, arguing that the organisers' loss of TV rights led to a 'uniformity' which 'resulted in a less efficient structure, at least as far as the Monaco Grand Prix was concerned'. At the same time, giving a forelock-tugging nod in Ecclestone's direction, he conceded that 'after 20 years of central marketing of the Formula One TV rights by Bernie Ecclestone, the exposure and success of this championship have achieved levels which were unthinkable only a few years ago, and this is advantageous for everybody, including the organisers'. As in all political wars, when the blood had been mopped up and egos restored to their former glory, it was not long before Balestre and Boeri became as one in the common political cause of Formula One. Boeri was appointed, with his former adversary's endorsement, a vice-president of the FISA and, later, of the FIA.

After the conference in Casablanca a disappointed Ecclestone, Mosley and Williams flew back to England in his hired Citation jet. (Disappointed, but not humourless – Ecclestone bought three sets of Arab robes complete with sandals and fez hats. It was agreed they would turn up at the next FOCA meeting dressed in the clothes to report on their trip to Casablanca, and they duly did.) The unresolved problem of turbos put Ecclestone in something of a quandary. For he had signed an exclusive 12-month agreement with BMW to use their turbocharged engines, and a series of tests at Silverstone had revealed that the Brabham BT51 BMW ran fractionally faster than the latest edition of the Cosworth-powered skirted BT49. In fact, Gordon Murray had been working on the BT50 BMW turbo, in which Nélson Piquet would win the 1982 Canadian Grand Prix, 12 months earlier. It was believed that Ecclestone was covering all options – if efforts to limit fuel-tank capacity of the turbos failed and the constructors had to run at a minimum weight of 580 kilograms, the turbo would prove Brabham's salvation. Uncertain of which endgame Ecclestone was playing, BMW took the highly unusual step of issuing him with a public rebuke – that he should return Formula One to 'responsible sports management' – and an ultimatum: either use BMW engines or the company would terminate its co-operation with the team.

Sponsors Marlboro and Elf were also concerned by Ecclestone's activities, but for different reasons. As the tensions continued to mount between the constructors and the manufacturers over the minimum weight rule, they warned that their levels of sponsorship could only be maintained 'within the framework of a stable sport'. They had good reason for such concern. With Balestre seemingly in Ecclestone's camp and 'skirts' back on the cars, and the Concorde Agreement effectively not worth the paper it was written on, the idea was even mooted of two World Championships – one for FOCA constructors and the other for the turbo manufacturers – which, for the benefit of television, would run at the same race with separate prize money. Happily for Formula One, the idea was not pursued.

Both sides eventually came to agree that 'skirts' should be banned and that there should be a reduction in the cars' total plan area from 4.5 to 3.5 square metres, to produce narrower cars which, with rear wings moved forward, would generate less downforce. The manufacturers had earlier favoured a full flat bottom to reduce cornering speed but realised it would still generate 'ground effect'. It was a dilemma that remained unresolved until October 1982, when Balestre obtained a *force majeure* mandate to issue a 13-point list of changes aimed principally at reducing speeds, and which would bury whatever remained of the Concorde Agreement.

Included in the changes, which were to be introduced by the beginning of the following season, Formula One cars would, in opposition to the general consensus, have full flat bottoms; 'skirts' would be banned; the width of the rear wing and overhang would be reduced to decrease downforce; the minimum weight would be reduced from 580 to 540 kilograms; and fuel tank capacity would be reduced from 250 to 220 litres in 1984 and to 200 litres in 1985. The full flat bottom was the most radical change since the introduction of the 3-litre Formula One engine and, combined with the other rule changes, was greeted with almost universal criticism. The changes meant new designs, new cars and a lot more money. But Balestre, citing a number of accidents, claimed to have the public and drivers behind him. Ecclestone, Mosley and several leading constructors met with the manufacturers at Ferrari's factory in Maranello and, contrary to expectations, agreed to the rule changes.

There was one constructor, though, who would benefit from the changes – Bernie Ecclestone, who had committed the Brabham team to BMW's turbo engines the previous year. Although McLaren, Williams and Lotus had by now agreed turbo deals with, respectively, Porsche, BMW and Renault, Ecclestone was at least a couple of laps ahead. As one constructor said: 'We don't know what is going on but ... we've got a sneaking suspicion that flat bottoms fit very nicely into Brabham's plans for 1983.'[6] His suspicions, it seems, were not unfounded. Work on the flat-bottomed turbo BMW BT52 was by then well under way and completed with time to spare for the Brazilian Grand Prix in March, the first race of the 1983 season, which ended with Brabham's Nélson Piquet winning his second World Championship title.

The irony was that after all the bloody battles, after all the destructive upheaval and costly consequences, four years later, in October 1986, the FISA announced that turbo engines would be phased out of Formula One for safety reasons. It would also, added Balestre, give 'a new boost' to the World

Championships and reduce costs. During the 1987 and 1988 seasons teams were given the option of using atmospheric engines of 3.5 litres and up to 12 cylinders, with a total ban on turbos beginning in the 1989 season.

The relative peace brought to Formula One through the Concorde Agreement and Piquet's World Championship title would soon be followed by another major event in Ecclestone's life. Dora Tuana Tan, who years later became a born-again Christian at Holy Trinity Brompton Church in London, had long departed from his life when he met his future wife in the paddock at the 1982 Italian Grand Prix at Monza.

She was a stunningly elegant and beautiful young Croatian model of twenty-three, Slavica Malic, who that year had joined the fashion house of Giorgio Armani, although she was at Monza to promote a range of Fila sportswear. Five feet eleven inches tall and twenty-eight years younger, she towered over the 5ft 6in-tall man by her side, with whom she seemed to have little in common, not least the ability to converse: she could speak hardly any English and Ecclestone wasn't too fluent in Croat. With the aid of a language dictionary, she understood his invitation to have a Coca-Cola and to take refuge from the sun in his motor home. Accompanied by a colleague, a Dutch model who spoke fluent English, Slavica agreed. It was a brief meeting that came to a close with her giving him, at his request, her phone number, which, as he soon discovered, turned out to be a wrong number. She said: 'I was young. I didn't know him. I didn't give my phone number to anyone.'

Ecclestone, though, was smitten. He made enquiries and, through a photographer, tracked her down within a matter of days. This time, she not only gave him her correct phone number but also accepted an invitation to accompany him in his private jet to the Las Vegas Grand Prix a few days later. But not before having her nervous doubts calmed by a make-up artist friend. 'I thought I was so young ... and going to America? Can you imagine?' But, despite suddenly being catapulted into a social stratosphere that she might have once only dreamt about, she did not care for the experience, or the inevitable sidelong glances. 'I hated it, going out for stupid dinners with different people, business people, not talking ... everybody giving me the dirty look ... young girl, you know.'

Shortly after arriving at Caesar's Palace, she also began to have doubts about the sexuality of the worldly-wise, jet-hopping businessman. When they arrived at the luxurious hotel, its president, Billy Weinberger, greeted them personally and accompanied the couple to their huge suite comprising a living room, two bathrooms and two bedrooms. Weinberger followed Ecclestone into one of the bedrooms and closed the door. The two men remained in the bedroom for some while, but engaged in nothing more passionate than business. Slavica, though, unused to Ecclestone's love of business regardless of the hour of the day or circumstance, suspected the worst. With the business finally done, followed by Weinberger's departure, Slavica kept her fears to herself. It was some time before she shared them with a much-amused Ecclestone, who, by that time, had long proved himself to be soundly heterosexual.

Two years later Ecclestone, at the age of 54, became a father for the second time. Slavica gave birth to Tamara, the first of their two daughters, in Milan. Three months later she arrived in England to set up home with Ecclestone in a rented apartment in Pier House, Oakley Street, Chelsea, which Ecclestone subsequently bought and sold to his friend Flavio Briatore, the then Benetton team boss. The following year, on 17 July 1985, the couple were married at Kensington and Chelsea Registry Office, after Ecclestone, in a by-the-way proposal, said they should get married, a solemn occasion which didn't quite go as planned.

Ecclestone made arrangements for the wedding to take place about a week later, which included a phone call to Mosley asking him if he had a few minutes to spare on the allotted day. He was getting married, he explained, and needed a witness. Mosley readily agreed and arrived to notice that a second witness, as required under UK law, turned out to be a home help employed by Ecclestone. Everything went smoothly until the registrar noticed that she didn't speak English, a factor which immediately disqualified her. Mosley came to the rescue with an urgent call to his secretary, Jacqueline Self, who arrived by taxi 20 minutes later for the ceremony's successful completion. Then, for Ecclestone, it was back to business. There was no honeymoon. Nor, come to that, was there a photographer to record the joyful occasion.

In December 1988 Slavica gave birth to their second daughter, Petra, and settled down to a life much devoted to the care of her children. By the end of the next decade, she would be the richest woman in Britain.

8

BRABHAM TAKEN FOR A SWISS ROLL

There have not been many events in Bernie Ecclestone's life that have not been tainted by controversy. And it was so when Brabham lead driver Nélson Piquet won his second World Championship title in 1983, and the team came third in the Constructors' Championship. Piquet's success had been achieved, it was later alleged, by the use of illegal fuel, most effectively at the Italian Grand Prix at Monza and the European Grand Prix at Brands Hatch, which he won with octane levels of 102.8 RON and 102.9 RON respectively, well over the legal limit of 102 RON. It was also alleged that Piquet's fuel had been 0.5 RON over the legal limit at the British Grand Prix, where he came second, and 0.8 at the German Grand Prix, where an engine fire caused his retirement. In the final race of the season, the South African Grand Prix, Piquet came third, which gave him sufficient points to sneak the title – 59 to Prost's 57.

Protests by Renault and Ferrari were dismissed by Balestre as 'contradictory and unfounded', a statement that demonstrated yet again the remarkable entente cordiale that now existed between the FISA's president and Ecclestone, made all the more remarkable by the fact that the zealously patriotic Frenchman was standing against the interests of a French team and driver. Such was his enthusiasm to defend the Brabham team that he produced what he described as an official telex from the Institut Français du Pétrole, which stated that for an octane rating of 102, 'a value of 102.9 was proper'. Britain's Royal Automobile Club, asked to undertake analyses for the Grand Prix of Europe, confirmed 'a tolerance of 0.9 at 102 RON'. But Renault claimed that the FISA had supplied 'inaccurate or distorted' data. A tolerance of 0.9, the company argued, applied to 'the co-efficient of repeatability' and was often confused with the 'accepted tolerance'. Neither Renault nor Ferrari pressed for Piquet's disqualification; rather, they wanted clarification of fuel regulations. That finally came 11 months later, and merely served to underscore Balestre's inconsistency. He insisted that fuel octane levels must not exceed 'as it frequently does now -102 RON, as defined in the FIA rule book'.

Prost, who went on to win four World Championship titles, viewed the defeat as the biggest regret of his career. 'To this day I still consider we won. Everyone knew the fuel used by Piquet's Brabham was not legal and, from the summer onwards, the lead we had was steadily nibbled away. We could have protested: I wanted to, but Renault management didn't, and at that time I didn't have enough weight to influence the decision. Renault deserved the title.'[1] A former senior technical adviser to the FISA confirmed the existence of a report based on the analyses of fuel used in the Brabham car. It was deliberately suppressed, he added, to prevent it going through 'the normal channels, as a result of which Brabham would have been disqualified. Renault could have lodged a protest and they would have won, but they dropped the matter because they wanted to become champions "on the green carpet" – in other words, on the track, rather than the boardroom.'

The next couple of seasons proved mediocre for Brabham, with Piquet finishing fifth and eighth in the World Championship. Designer Gordon Murray was also having problems with his latest design, the BT53, which, in the middle of the 1984 season, underwent major surgery with new bodywork, aerodynamics and cooling system. But the team was dealt a major blow when Piquet, who had been with Brabham since 1978 to team up with Niki Lauda, decided to quit at the end of the 1985 season. It was over something very close to Ecclestone's heart – money. The relationship between them had been strained for some time over the issue. Ecclestone was incensed when Piquet, at the South African Grand Prix in 1983, the last race of the season, allowed teammate Riccardo Patrese and Alfa Romeo's Andrea de Cesaris to overtake him, knowing that the World Championship title was in the bag. Fumed Ecclestone: 'I don't pay drivers to lose races.' To which Piquet responded: 'You get paid so little by Bernie that you have to get something else out of it – and [all] I wanted was the World Championship.'[2]

But Piquet's demand for a substantial increase in his retainer left Ecclestone unmoved. Like Enzo Ferrari, he believed it was the car and not the driver that won a race, and refused to budge. It was, recalled a member of the team, a row over 'peanuts'. He added: 'It was a really stupid argument over a tiny bit of additional money, but Bernie wouldn't back down. Piquet was a brilliant driver, and he was part of the core of the team. It was a pretty bitter pill to swallow because we had no one else to replace him.' It was a predicament that Ecclestone attempted to resolve by making an approach to Niki Lauda, who had announced his retirement by walking out on Brabham six years earlier only to return to win his third world title with McLaren the previous season before announcing that he was retiring once again, but this time for good.

Ecclestone attempted to dissuade him with an offer that was substantially more than what Piquet had been looking for, but far short of what would satisfy Lauda, which was an annual retainer of £5.5 million. The main sponsor, Olivetti, willing to pick up half of what Ecclestone was offering, declined to dig deeper to satisfy Lauda's demand. It brought their negotiations to an abrupt end. According to a senior member of the Brabham team, Ecclestone's obduracy in his negotiations with Piquet was a major miscalculation, and would prove a significant factor in the team's future.

Piquet, who joined the Williams team to finish third in the 1986 World Championship and take his third World Championship title the following year, was finally replaced by Elio de Angelis, a 27-year-old Italian, who, after just four races with Brabham, was killed in a 180mph crash while testing at the Paul Ricard circuit on 15 May 1986. The cause of the crash was a suspected component failure. The car went out of control through the second, right-hand half of the Verrerie S-bend at the end of the pit straight. De Angelis died hours later in hospital.

The news hit Murray badly. Of all the cars he had designed there had barely been a serious injury to a driver. De Angelis was killed in Murray's latest car, the revolutionary 'low-line' BT55, which positioned the driver in a far more horizontal position. The central problem was that the design of the car, the first all-carbon, was too radical for the installation of the BMW engine – redesigned so that it could lie almost flat in the chassis – to work. Years later Murray blamed himself for the car's lack of competitiveness. 'We could never get the engine installation to work, and, in retrospect, it was totally my fault. It was far too much to try and do in the few months we had to design and get it ready ... it was a very, very radical car.' But the death of de Angelis proved to be the final straw for Murray.

The departure of Piquet, and now the death of the young Italian, caused Murray to suffer a massive loss of interest in his work. There was also another factor: his relationship with Ecclestone had become increasingly strained. For the first time he seriously began to consider his future at Brabham, even in Formula One itself. 'I was beginning to think that we were going nowhere as a company. Bernie, with his other activities, was not concentrating on getting ongoing sponsorship contracts and replacing Nélson Piquet.' It seemed to Murray that the good times, the giant-killing days, when Brabham, with a small budget and team, took on, and beat, the likes of Ferrari, McLaren and, later, Williams, when Ecclestone would hold 'board meetings' with him and team manager Herbie Blash over a pint and a sandwich – or Ecclestone's favourite, egg and chips with lashings of brown sauce – in the Star pub in Leatherhead Road, Chessington, down the road from the works, were long over. (It was not unusual for Ecclestone to use the pub for a working lunch with international businessmen and politicians. According to Blash, it was the setting for negotiations between John Bannon, the then prime minister of South Australia, and Ecclestone for the first Australian Grand Prix, in Adelaide in 1985.)

In this deeply unsettled frame of mind, Murray, after playing a major role in Brabham's two World Championships and 22 Grand Prix wins, decided it was time to move on. When he broke the news to Ecclestone, he believes that it came as no surprise. 'I was pissed off, and I could see he was pissed off. I said I was going to stop, and he said, "Fine." That was it.' There was no attempt by Ecclestone to change Murray's mind. It was never his style, not even for someone so crucial to the team. His departure, in November 1986, brought to an end an association of 14 years, many of them as a director of Motor Racing Developments, owners of the Brabham team. Murray's decision to leave Brabham was one of the toughest of his career, but he had reason to believe that at least he would not suffer financially. For on the strength of a handshake given some years earlier, Ecclestone, said Murray, had 'talked about' a share in the company. But he was to be seriously disappointed.

Ecclestone managed to persuade him that the company was worth little. Murray found himself agreeing to a one-off payment of £30,000, and signing a document relinquishing all further interest or claims on the company. 'I was very disappointed with the financial settlement after all those years of hard work and all the success, but on the positive side it taught me a valuable lesson for the future – I would never enter another working relationship without a well-constructed written contract.' He added philosophically: 'I have no regrets. I should have known better.'

In Ecclestone's view, 'dear old Gordon' had been a tad unfair in his interpretation of events. 'Actually, it [£30,000] was a large chunk of money [in those days].' (In 2002 it would have been worth £55,800.) He claimed at first that it had been Murray who had 'established' the sum of £30,000, 'not me'. But added a few moments later: 'If I told you I could remember, I would be lying. But it wasn't a "take this or get nothing" offer, OK? Because that is not my style. I wouldn't do that.' Murray was also given, at his request, the BT49 car in which Piquet won the 1982 Grand Prix. 'He said he would never sell it, but subsequently did.'

Some nine months later Ecclestone reportedly received an offer of £15 million from Jesús Gil, the president of Atlético Madrid football club, shortly after Gil, as Ecclestone's VIP guest, visited the 1987 German Grand Prix. It is Ecclestone's recollection that no figure was mentioned by Gil, although he was quoted as saying at the time that 'there may have to be an adjustment to the sum suggested ... but there is no way I will be persuaded to dispose of it unless I have the assurance that it will continue to be operated in its present form and with the same efficiency and dedication which my staff have shown me for so many years.'[3]

Although the proposed deal fell through – a condition of its purchase was that Ecclestone would invest the money in Atlético Madrid – it gives ground to believe that the company was worth considerably more than Murray had apparently been given to understand. Murray went on to join McLaren International to lead its restructured design team, where he negotiated a contract so detailed that it covered even the style of clothes he could wear.

As with Ron Tauranac and Colin Seeley before him, Murray had the cold comfort of knowing that smarter businessmen than he had come off second best in dealing with Ecclestone. Their skills and expertise are in design and engineering. Give them a profit-and-loss account and the shutters come down. In Ecclestone's hands, they were innocents abroad. The evidence of their experiences does little to confirm his oft-quoted comment in media interviews that his word and his handshake are sounder than any contract. 'What I've done,' he said in one newspaper interview, 'I've done honestly and correctly. I've never done anything bad to anyone in my life. I've never cheated anybody. If I do a deal, I don't need to write it down on paper. Everyone knows I won't go back.'[4]

Ecclestone's response to the offer from Jesús Gil confirmed what some had suspected for some time, that he was ready to sell the Brabham team for the right offer. There had been rumours a couple of years earlier that he had had talks with Ford, which, if true, came to nothing. But Murray's departure – Ecclestone was once quoted as saying that he would sell the team if Murray ever quit – added considerably to his problems. Three months earlier BMW had announced that it would be ending its four-year association with the Brabham team at the end of the year, explaining that if it were to remain in Formula One it would want to build its own car, rather than be a supplier of engines, which was too costly; instead, it intended to concentrate on saloon-car racing. But things for Ecclestone would get worse.

The 1987 season was humiliatingly dreadful for Brabham. Lead driver Riccardo Patrese came thirteenth in the World Championship and the team eighth in the Constructors' Championship. Brabham's tyre contract with Pirelli was coming to an end, the team's major sponsorship deal with Olivetti was running out, and Patrese and his fellow Italian Andrea de Cesaris were on the move – respectively to Williams and German millionaire Hans Gunther Schmidt's new team, Rial. Confirming Murray's claim that Ecclestone had begun to show increasingly little interest in getting new sponsors, a former senior member of his staff said: 'We used to get people phoning up and say, "We are giving you all this money, could we have a photograph of the new car, please," and they would end up being put through to the receptionist, who had no idea what they were talking about. That was about our level of commitment to the sponsors.'

It was believed the moribund state of the Brabham team had come about because Ecclestone, now 57, was finding greater pleasure and personal profit in pursuing the riches of Formula One's commercial activities, which was taking him into the centre of the FIA establishment he had once so openly despised. Ownership of the Brabham team had served its purpose in establishing his power base, but he was a businessman first and a frustrated racer second, and he was, said a former team manager, 'no longer interested in knowing whether there were three engines ready for the next race, or why they blew up at the last one'. For Ecclestone it was time to move on. By the beginning of 1988 he had still to find replacements for Patrese and de Cesaris, as well as a new engine supplier. There had also been little progress made on replacing the BT56 built by David North – a long-standing colleague of Murray who was now the team's chief designer – and designed around the unsuccessful BT55. The fortunes of Ecclestone's Motor Racing Developments, which owned the Brabham team assets, were also dipping sharply. Company returns for that year showed a net loss of £3.63 million compared with net profits of £2.5 million two years earlier.

Although there was no official word from the Brabham team's Chessington works, the deadline for entries in the 1988 World Championship series – 31 January – passed without the FISA receiving an application from Ecclestone, the first time Brabham had missed the line-up in 26 years. It wasn't until the Brazilian Grand Prix in April that Ecclestone announced that the team would be pulling out of Formula One after two 'disastrous years' with the BMW engine. Ecclestone gave no indication of his personal plans, but the pit gossip was that, whatever the future of the team, he wouldn't be at the wheel. It proved to be accurate: Ecclestone sold Motor Racing Developments to Alfa Romeo for an undisclosed sum. It was Alfa Romeo's plan to design and build, with the Brabham team's expertise, a car to take part in a much-hyped new event for manufacturers called the Production Car World Championship, and which was due to start in 1990. With the support of both Ecclestone and the FISA president, Jean-Marie Balestre, its success was considered assured.

For Alfa Romeo and other major manufacturers, though, who were expected to finance the event, it turned out to be a short-lived and highly expensive disaster. The new formula, amid much controversy, failed to materialise. Alfa Romeo, which had been taken over by Fiat in December 1986, decided to dispose of Motor Racing Developments in late 1988 to what a press spokeswoman described as 'some Swiss interests'. The man who brokered the deal was Ecclestone. It would lead to the eventual financial collapse of the Brabham team, a fall from grace made all the more tragic by its fraudulent exploitation.

The circumstances had been set in train a couple of years earlier, when world champion golfer Greg Norman met Nigel Mansell at a ProAm tournament in Australia. Over the next 12 months a friendship developed between the two men with Norman becoming increasingly interested in getting involved in a Formula One team. At this stage a meeting was arranged in Adelaide between Norman and Peter Windsor, a former motor sport journalist and the Williams team's manager of sponsorship and public affairs, who was ambitious to run his own team. The meeting with Norman was sufficiently encouraging for Windsor, when Ecclestone officially broke the news of the Brabham team's immediate future at the Brazilian Grand Prix, to begin looking for a merchant prince with the necessary finance to buy Motor Racing Developments Ltd.

The man he decided to approach was Swiss millionaire Walter Brun, who had made his fortune in slot machines and in 1986 won the World Sport Prototype Championship, and who that season had launched the EuroBrun Formula One team, which would appear in 14 Grands Prix before pulling out of Formula One two years later. Windsor also approached Sir Jack Brabham for his assistance in the successful negotiation of a Judd engine deal. By early November 1988 Windsor believed he was in a position to confidently announce that the Brabham team would be back on the Formula One grid in time for the following season. He confirmed the involvement of Brun and also an 'anonymous' Swiss banker. That banker was Joachim Lüthi, who owned a financial investment firm called Adiuva Finanz AG, based in Zurich, and also had a 50 per cent interest in a company called Kingside Establishment, based in Liechtenstein. In an agreement with Brun, Windsor, who had quit Williams to become managing director of Motor Racing Developments, was due to receive a 20 per cent stakeholding in the company.

However, shortly after December 1988, when Brun and Lüthi were registered as directors of Motor Racing Developments, Brun decided to sell his interest in the company to Lüthi, who, according to High Court documents following subsequent litigation by Windsor, paid £5.5 million for the Brabham team. The sale by Brun of his interests in the company to Lüthi brought an abrupt end to Windsor's Formula One aspirations. One of Ecclestone's close associates said Windsor had a meeting with Ecclestone at the Brabham team factory in Chessington – 'I think there was only one meeting' – to discuss the sale of Brabham, which was followed a short while later by a similar meeting between Lüthi and Ecclestone. 'He [Lüthi] didn't want Windsor involved,' added the associate. Windsor, after bringing the deal together, was being elbowed out.

In early January Windsor confirmed that he and Greg Norman were no longer involved in the Brabham team. But, angry at Brun's dealings with Lüthi, he went to law for clarification of his agreement with Brun and its effect on Lüthi's acquisition of Motor Racing Developments. He successfully applied for a High Court injunction freezing his 20 per cent interest in the company. By then, however, Lüthi had already effectively removed ownership of the shares – and the company – out of the country. Retaining one ordinary share, he transferred the remaining 999 to the Liechtenstein-based Kingside Establishment. The transfer was all part and parcel of Lüthi's real interest in Motor Racing Developments – to use the company as a cover for a major fraud.

On 23 December 1988, just two weeks after acquiring the company, he arranged a loan of £2 million to be made by Motor Racing Developments to Kingside Establishment, which then went into liquidation – but not before transferring its funds to a newly opened branch office in Zurich from where it was transferred on to Lüthi's Adiuva Finanz AG before it, too, went into liquidation. Accountants Robson Rhodes subsequently reported that 'no details have been found ... to confirm the purpose, terms or recipients' of the £2-million transfer. Motor Racing Developments also paid £250,000 to an unnamed director for loss of office and the company chairman, namely Lüthi, received a payment of £291,000. To cover the transfer to Kingside Establishment, Lüthi arranged for Motor Racing Developments to receive loans totalling £2.285 million from Adiuva Finanz AG. By now, Brun – there is no evidence to suggest he was aware of Lüthi's activities – was no longer involved in Motor Racing Developments, having resigned his directorship on 28 January.

To all the world, Lüthi, who in early 1989 flew to Japan reportedly to discuss an engine deal with Honda, appeared to be genuinely committed to the future of the Brabham team. Martin Brundle, the World Sportscar Champion, and promising young Italian Stefano Modena were contracted to drive the BT58 Brabham-Judd. Teddy Mayer, a co-founder of McLaren, was appointed managing director, with Herbie Blash as team director. Hardly surprising in the circumstances, Lüthi was keen on keeping a low profile and tried to persuade Blash, who had no idea of his boss's grand fraud plans, to act as his front man while he remained in Zurich. Blash declined. Lüthi told a senior associate that 'if anybody finds out what I'm up to, I'm going to be in trouble'. The associate added: 'What he was concerned about was that he was in the money business and, basically, if all of a sudden he was being seen to be spending millions and millions, people who were investing money with him might wonder what the hell was going on – where's the money coming from. Then they would have asked for their money back and he would have been in trouble, which is exactly what happened.'

Indeed it did. Less than a month after failing in an attempt to get Windsor's injunction lifted, Lüthi was back in court – but this time in the dock. He was arrested in Zurich in connection with the suspected embezzlement of clients' funds totalling $100 million, which had been invested in Adiuva Finanz AG. His arrest followed an investigation by the Swiss Federal Banking Commission after complaints from clients unable to withdraw their funds, and, following further allegations, a separate criminal investigation into his business activities by an investigating magistrate in the Swiss canton of Aargau. Before his case could come to court, Lüthi, who was finally charged with embezzling $133 million from 1700 investors, fled to America, where he lived under the name of Terry Sexton. He was arrested by US Marshals in Marina del Rey, California, in 1995 after being located and identified, with the help of the authorities in Switzerland, by fraud investigation specialist Gary Bleakley, of Houston, Texas, who had been hired by one of Lüthi's victims in the States. He appealed unsuccessfully against an extradition order, and in May 1996 was extradited to Switzerland to complete a seven-and-a-half-year jail sentence.

Teddy Mayer, who was appointed managing director on 3 June 1989, remained for just one month before resigning. Following a request from Ecclestone, who felt Lüthi needed some help in running the team, Mayer agreed to take leave of absence from his directorship of Penske Cars in Poole, Dorset. Rumours at the time put down his short stay to a clash of management style with Lüthi. More accurately, said Mayer, it was due to inadequate financial resources. 'It became obvious very quickly that they didn't have the money to be a serious contender, so I resigned and went back to Penske. The finance wasn't there to produce a winning car. By the time Lüthi was on fraud charges, I was long gone. I didn't know what it was all about [Lüthi's fraudulent activities] ... but I soon discovered that as a financier he wasn't going to do anything that would bring them [the Brabham team] back to their days of glory. It was pretty hopeless.'

Blash claimed to be not at all surprised by Lüthi's arrest. He suspected for some weeks that Lüthi was in financial trouble. 'It was always a case of the money was coming, and then we could see that there were strange manoeuvres going on, and it didn't come as a shock that we had problems. The trouble was his heart was in the right place but his wallet wasn't.' Blash remained with the Brabham team, successfully persuading the team's one and only sponsor, a Japanese credit-card company called Nippon Shinpan, to continue its support. Said Blash: 'The company president was fantastic, to stand up in front of his board and convince them that they should stay with a team whose owner was in prison on fraud charges.'

Ecclestone believed that Lüthi had tried to do his best for Brabham 'and keep the old tradition going'. He had been keen 'to put Brabham where it belonged – on the front row of the grid'. He promised to help Lüthi in that aim, and did so until the end of the Brazilian Grand Prix in March. Ecclestone's reported observation on Lüthi's fraudulent activities was oddly sympathetic. 'As I understand it, I don't think he [Lüthi] used other people's money in Brabham. What he used was sponsorship money.'[5]

The decision by Nippon Shinpan to remain with Brabham kept the team afloat until the Middlebridge Group, of Japan, bought Motor Racing Developments in March 1990. It switched to a Yamaha engine but neither a change of company nor engine could reverse the team's fortunes, particularly when Middlebridge began to suffer financial problems due to underestimating the costs of running a Formula One team. Its plight led to Ecclestone, who was negotiating the sale of the Chessington factory to Middlebridge, locking out the team because the company had failed to meet the agreed sale deadline. Yamaha bought the factory, with team manager Herbie Blash remaining as the company's sporting director, while Middlebridge, after virtually laying off all its staff, moved to Milton Keynes to cut costs.

The Brabham team staggered on until the Hungarian Grand Prix in 1992, where Damon Hill, a new name on the Formula One scene at the age of 32, had the distinction of driving the last Brabham car to compete in Formula One, finishing in eleventh position, before joining the Williams team the following year. The Brabham team became so short of cash that a Japanese heavy-metal rock star set up a money-raising appeal in an unsuccessful attempt to keep it going.

Once again, for the second time in five years, Brabham failed to meet the FIA's registration deadline point. In March 1993 Brabham was effectively laid to rest in a terse statement by the FIA's World Motor Sport Council which ruled that, unless the team's debts were settled, it would not be allowed to enter the 1994 World Championship series. It brought to an end a tardy and undignified period which should have had no place in the history of one of the great Formula One racing teams, whose roll of honours reads: 394 Grands Prix, 35 wins, three drivers' World Championships and two Constructors' Championships. But they tell little of the insane passion and bloody-minded commitment, the constant roller-coaster ride of chaos and crises, the failures and triumphs from which they were wrought, and which began 31 years earlier when Ron Tauranac arrived in Britain to join Jack Brabham in creating one of Formula One's legendary teams.

Peter Windsor's legal action against Motor Racing Developments was resolved in September 1991 when he was awarded an agreed sum of £450,000. It brought to an end an unhappy – and painful – period in his life. Six months earlier he had been bundled into a van by two men as he left the Williams team factory in Didcot, Oxfordshire. Employees who went to his aid were threatened by what appeared to be a gun. Handcuffed and blindfolded, he was driven to the countryside, beaten up and later dumped by the roadside. He was taken to hospital for treatment to cuts and bruising.

Windsor declined to comment on the incident, his legal action against Motor Racing Developments or the agreed payment. 'I'd rather not co-operate on the subject you want to talk about.'

PART 2

9

BERNIE GOES WEST – AND MEETS HIS MATCH

With the sale of the Brabham team behind him, Ecclestone was now free to commit more of his formidable energy and shrewdness to exploiting Formula One's commercial assets. A critical constituent to the stability of the golden triangle – the teams, television and the circuits – on which balanced the global marketing platform of Formula One was his control of the organisers and circuit owners. It enabled him to dictate each and every detail from the financial package, which included track signage, corporate hospitality and television rights, to the standard of medical facilities and layout of the paddock and parking areas. (At one Grand Prix he took to the air in a helicopter to check the herringbone pattern of the spectators' parked cars.)

According to Patrick Duffeler, who headed the aborted World Championship Racing, set up by the Commission Sportive International to represent organisers in their negotiations with Ecclestone, his technique in imposing his will on organisers whom he considered inefficient or incompetent was simple but effective: he increased the FOCA's fees to a level he knew they would be unable to afford. 'His view was that some of those organisers were completely ill-organised ... and they were not therefore competent business people and ... he felt he could do a better job. So for him to do a better job he said, "I'm going to dictate the [financial] terms and I'm going to make sure this is the way it's going to be done."' Ecclestone would make the financial terms so difficult to meet, added Duffeler, that he would then step in with a financial package to give him control.

It was certainly in Ecclestone's personal interest to squeeze promoters for the highest dollar. Once the teams' prize fund and travel expenses had been covered, whatever was left over was his profit. He was able to produce a flexible financial package to suit almost any situation, as these following examples, which all took in place 1982, illustrate. When the financially strapped owners of the Österreiching, the home of the Austrian Grand Prix, were unable to meet his demands, Ecclestone offered to pay £105,000 to rent the circuit for eight days and take over all promotional rights; when the Argentine Grand Prix, whose sponsors were frightened off by the threat of a drivers' strike, faced cancellation, he offered to 'buy' the race, past losses and all, if a multi-year contract could be agreed; when he negotiated a street Grand Prix in Detroit it was based on a seven-year contract – four years direct and three years option – with the FOCA taking a healthy percentage of the race revenue; when the Brazilian Grand Prix, hit by a falling dollar, was in great danger of being called off, Ecclestone agreed to reduce the FOCA's prize-money fee by about 30 per cent. The uncharacteristic largesse was due to the fact that on this occasion Ecclestone was the promoter with a significant financial interest in the race.

For those unable, or unwilling, to meet his terms, the alternative was bleak. When the organisers of the Argentine Grand Prix declined Ecclestone's offer, the race remained off the calendar until 1995. The Spanish Grand Prix suffered a similar fate when the organisers were unable to raise only $300,000 of the $680,000 he was demanding. The race disappeared from the Formula One scene until 1986. It is significant that Ecclestone's move to take over the circuits themselves took on a new energy following the Concorde Agreement some 12 months earlier, when he was appointed to market the television rights. Not unnaturally, it was seen by organisers, circuit owners and promoters as formal approval of the one person the FIA had once wanted to see driven out of Formula One. Ecclestone was now an influential member of motor sport's governing body, which emboldened him to act even more forcefully.

According to Max Mosley, in the early days the teams had every opportunity to share the rewards of promoting a race if they were prepared to share the risks. If, for example, the gate receipts were on offer because a promoter of a less successful race couldn't meet Ecclestone's prize-fund figure, he would first offer a co-deal to the teams. The teams, recalled Mosley, would always decline. 'They would say to Bernie, "If you want to take the gate receipts, that's up to. You pay us, and if you win, you win. If you lose, you lose. We don't care. We're not race promoters.'" Over a season Ecclestone always came out on top, ensuring that any unlikely loss on a race was more than covered on the next. In this way, long before mammoth television deals starting to yield their own fabulous rewards, he added considerably to his personal riches.

By the mid-eighties he was known to have had a financial stake in the Grands Prix in Brazil, Portugal, Belgium, Austria and South Africa, as well as a financial interest in Long Beach and Mount Fuji. Prior to Ecclestone's arrival at the FOCA in 1972, 18 countries had hosted Grands Prix – Argentina, Austria, Belgium, Canada, France, Germany, Great Britain, Indianapolis, Italy, Mexico, Monaco, Morocco, Holland, Portugal, South Africa, Spain, Switzerland and the USA. By the end of the eighties, his efforts had been responsible for increasing that number by a further six – Australia, Brazil, Hungary, Japan, San Marino, and Sweden. To complete the record, by the year 2000 Ecclestone had increased the number of host countries by a further two – Malaysia and America (Indianapolis) which, following the demise of the US Grand Prix at Watkins Glen in 1980, had proved a difficult and uncertain market.

In the days when Formula One had yet to become established as a transnational brand image oozing technological sex and drama, with countries queuing up for the international prestige of being associated with the bold and thrusting new world that a racing car phallically symbolises, what Ecclestone achieved, whatever his method, was an extraordinary example of dogged and determined effort, as he jetted round the world cutting deals with senior government officials and industrial leaders to add another circuit, with all its immensely complex planning and construction at a cost of many millions of dollars, to the Formula One calendar. In the days of the Berlin Wall, he was not deterred either by the political limitations imposed by a deeply divided Europe, nor by unfavourable economic conditions or currency regulations. Ecclestone, as ever, would do whatever it would take to broaden Formula One's global image for the benefit of sponsors, television and his profit margins.

It led in 1986 to the first Grand Prix in the Eastern bloc, in the Hungarian capital of Budapest, although it came about through a series of fortuitous events. Ecclestone had actually set his sights on a country further east still – in Moscow itself. However incredible at first sight such a prospect seemed at the time, it had a major factor in its favour: the Soviet president, Leonid Brezhnev, was a keen car-racing fan. Ecclestone had made a number of trips to Moscow and talks with senior government officials got as far as discussing a road circuit near the Lenin University of Technology. They came to an abrupt end following the death of Brezhnev in 1982. Yet out of these negative circumstances came a chance meeting that would lead to the launch of the Hungarian Grand Prix.

While returning on a flight from Moscow, after discussions had finally collapsed, Ecclestone renewed an acquaintanceship with Budapest-born Tamas Rohonyi, a resident of São Paulo, who had helped him to organise the Brazilian Grand Prix. When Ecclestone told Rohonyi of what had happened to his plans for a Moscow Grand Prix, his fellow traveller suggested that if he was keen to break into eastern Europe, Hungary, one of the more progressive and 'westernised' communist countries, would prove a relatively easier nut to crack. In London, Rohonyi telexed the country's Minister of Foreign Affairs, who passed a request for a meeting on behalf of Ecclestone to the Ministry of Sport and a senior official of the state-run Hungarian television network. Within a week or two it had been arranged, and Ecclestone flew to Budapest, where he booked into the Hotel Inter-Continental overlooking the Danube, in the suite where Elizabeth Taylor celebrated her fiftieth birthday. A series of preliminary meetings took place but proceeded no further due to difficulties in finding the commercial partners able to raise the necessary investment capital for, among other necessities, the construction of a Formula One circuit.

Any further thoughts of a Hungarian Grand Prix gathered dust for two years until the vagaries of fortune intervened. Following a game of tennis between a senior official of the Ministry of Sport and an adviser to the deputy prime minister, Ecclestone's proposal was raised in casual conversation. Enthused, the adviser mentioned it to another tennis-playing friend, an adviser to the Ministry of Transportation, who said he would try to bring together a group of companies prepared to fund the construction of the circuit if the deputy prime minister gave his approval. He did – and, under the aegis of the Ministry of Transportation, a co-operative of Hungarian companies pledged to provide the necessary capital was established.

A five-year contract between the FOCA and the Magyar Autoklub was signed in London in September 1985. Ecclestone had negotiated a payment of $3.5 million, 60 per cent of the revenue from the first 10,000 tickets, 2000 free nights in top Budapest hotels – a device to avoid the organisers paying out hard currency and which he converted into cash as part of a travel package sold by his company, FOCA World Travel – and the obligatory track signage and hospitality rights for the benefit of AllSport Management. Eight months later, at a cost of more than £5 million, the 2.5-mile Hungaroring track, 12 miles north-east of Budapest, was ready, and in August 1986 the first Hungarian Grand Prix took place before a track capacity of 130,000 spectators, and, through co-operative television arrangements, a television audience of an estimated 500 million. Ecclestone consolidated his personal financial interest in the Hungarian Grand Prix when its contract came up for renewal by insisting that a company be formed to promote the race. As part of a new deal, Hungarian Formula One Grand Prix KFT came into existence, with 25 per cent of its income going to the organisers and the rest to Ecclestone.

But, by 2001, the future of the Hungarian Grand Prix was under serious threat. While in 1986 a Grand Prix in an Iron Curtain country was a politically prestigious breakthrough for Ecclestone, 15 years later it was in danger of being dropped in favour of a venue that would prove more popular and which Ecclestone had originally targeted – Moscow. In early 2001 he returned to the Russian capital for negotiations with mayor Yuri Luzkhov, whose city council had earlier given its approval to a £70-million development of Nagatino Island, a few kilometres south of the Kremlin and Red Square, where the first Russian Grand Prix is scheduled to take place in 2003. However, its inclusion in a Formula One calendar will exceed the limit of 17 races, which means that an existing race will have to go. The axe was tipped to fall on either the Italian Grand Prix at Imola, Hungary or Brazil, although the FIA was said to be reluctant to lose the South American event. Hungary, seen as the least glamorous, was expected to be axed.

An agreement for the construction of a circuit on Nagatino Island was signed at the Russian Embassy in London in November 2000 between Arrows team boss Tom Walkinshaw, on behalf of his TWR Group, which was awarded the contract to carry out the construction work, and the deputy Premier of Moscow, Iossif Ordonikidze, and the chairman of the Committee for Tourism, Grigori V. Antioufeev. The attraction of a Russian Grand Prix was seen as a major boost to promote desperately needed tourism, trade and commerce. Ecclestone strongly favoured Moscow over eight other venues said to be seeking a Grand Prix because it is more beneficial to Formula One's global marketing platform. In line with Ecclestone's obligatory contractual restraint, what it will cost the Russians was not made public. Such secrecy is to his advantage in negotiations, in the same way that the organisers in the pre-FOCA days insisted on confidential one-to-one deals with the teams. It is a restraint that has provoked little public concern. The one exception has proved to be the Melbourne Grand Prix, where protests over the secrecy surrounding the cost to the taxpayer, and ecological damage caused by circuit construction, continue to this day.

Ever since its debut event in 1996, the government of Victoria, Australia, has, despite repeated requests, failed to put full financial contractual details in the public domain, fuelling criticism of the clandestine relationship that can exist between Ecclestone and politicians at the highest level. The driving force behind the move for a Grand Prix in Melbourne was business tycoon Ron Walker, a controversial and entrepreneurial character in the swashbuckling Ecclestone mould. It was with the blessing of his good friend, Jeff Kennett, Premier of Victoria's Liberal–National government, that Walker, the Liberal Party's Federal treasurer and fund-raiser, set to work in 1993 on a business proposal to persuade Ecclestone to agree to switch the

Australian Grand Prix from Adelaide to Melbourne. Walker was both determined and optimistic.

His determination was spurred by a desire to avenge the defeat of former Victorian Premier John Cain, who had been outmanoeuvred by John Bannon, the Premier of South Australia, to get Ecclestone's signature on a contract for the staging of the first Australian Formula One Grand Prix at Adelaide in 1985, where it had been held ever since. He was optimistic because he was convinced the time was right. With a government election looming, Bannon's popularity was on the wane largely due to the collapse of the State Bank. His future was thrown into further doubt by the success of the opposition Liberal Party in its running criticism of fat-cat salaries enjoyed by the Grand Prix organisers while the taxpayer bore the cost of its losses.

Bannon had been a keen supporter of the Grand Prix, and it was thought probable that his departure would seriously threaten the continuation of the Grand Prix. Up until then, Ecclestone, in turn, had been a keen supporter of Bannon, assuring him that as long as he was premier the Australian Grand Prix would stay in Adelaide. His admiration was founded on Bannon's willingness to jump on a plane and fly halfway round the world to Ecclestone's office, then based in Chessington, Surrey, to state the case for Adelaide. 'I thought that anyone who bothered to do that should be looked after,' said Ecclestone, who has nothing but contempt for the establishment snob. The deal was agreed in principle in Ecclestone's local pub, the Star, near to the Brabham works. 'If anyone was too stuck up to go to the local pub, I probably wouldn't want to do business with them,' he said.

Now it was Walker's turn to take a plane to the UK, this time to Ecclestone's office in London's fashionable Knightsbridge in September 1993 – he had moved out of Chessington five years earlier – where he put forward a proposal that immediately had his interest. Within ten minutes it was agreed that the Australian Grand Prix was on its way from Adelaide to Melbourne for 1996. While the details of the deal were known only to Ecclestone and one or two people close to Kennett, it was understood to have been based on a ten-year contract worth A$15 million a year. With an estimated guaranteed minimum A$150 million in the bank, it had proved a good day's work for Ecclestone – he had been receiving a mere $9 million a year from the Adelaide organisers, on behalf of the South Australian government. Walker flew back to Melbourne a happy man. But the cloak-and-dagger manner in which payment was agreed, and the use of legislation to block opposition to the Grand Prix, became quite extraordinary.

The contract Ecclestone put his signature to was with a company called Melbourne Grand Prix Promotions Pty Ltd (MGPP) – later to be succeeded by the Australian Grand Prix Corporation (AGPC) – after a semi-government company called the Melbourne Major Events Company (MMEC), of which Walker was the chairman, approached the government on 13 April of the previous year to set up a wholly owned subsidiary company to help finance bids for major events. State Treasurer Alan Stockdale, a friend and confidant of Kennett, approved the move on 30 April. A 21-page report was submitted by MMEC on the economic implications of staging a Grand Prix at Melbourne's Albert Park, but it was accepted without being submitted for Cabinet approval or Treasury evaluation of its key cost-benefit analysis.

Within a week of Walker's return to Melbourne, Kennett, after consulting with no other Cabinet minister than Stockdale, confirmed for Ecclestone's benefit that the total payments would be underwritten by the taxpayer and made through MGPP, or its successor, AGPC, Walker being the chairman of both. He later justified such secrecy by citing Ecclestone's 'commercial confidentiality' clause, which, he said, had made it impossible for the contract's financial implications, including the full details of the deal and the liabilities of MGPP (or the AGPC), to be studied by the Treasury and the Auditor-General. At an Administrative Appeals Tribunal held in July 1994, where an unsuccessful attempt was made by the opposition Labor Party to force the government to release contractual information about the Grand Prix, Jeremy Kirkwood, the chief of staff of the Treasurer's Office, said that the government had taken the 21-page report submitted by MMEC 'at face value'.

Kennett's zeal for a Formula One Grand Prix began to take on an autocratic dimension soon after MGGP began discussions for the construction of a circuit in Albert Park, one of Melbourne's most attractive parklands, at an estimated cost of A$60 million (although as it was largely designed as a temporary circuit, it would require a further average annual expenditure of A$14–16 million to cover the cost of erecting, dismantling and storage of grandstands, overpasses, concrete crash barriers and other standard Formula One requirements such as medical and media facilities). When opponents claimed the government was in breach of planning regulations and environmental laws, moves to take their case to court were blocked by Kennett amending legislation – the Australian Grands Prix Act 1994 – to exempt the Grand Prix from such considerations. This Act was also invoked to prevent claims by members of the public seeking compensation in the courts for damage caused to their homes by dynamic compaction of part of the park for construction of the racetrack. A test case brought by one resident whose house had been damaged was unsuccessful, with costs of A$120,000 awarded against the plaintiff.

Kennett was no less obstructive when members of the public sought to obtain details of the contract with Ecclestone under the state's Freedom of Information Act. He simply made use of the Australian Grands Prix Act 1994 to block applications for any information under the Act relating to the contract with Ecclestone or the Grand Prix. And in a series of protest actions in the park by thousands of protesters against construction of the racetrack, which included the cutting down of over 1000 trees, more than 600 people were arrested. After a court ruled that they had broken no law by protesting on public land, Kennett pushed through amending legislation making it a trespassing offence for the public to enter sections of the park, which were sealed off for 17 weeks, to allow the development of the site to continue free of protests.

Such was the strength of opposition that Ecclestone received threats to his life if ever he dared to visit Melbourne. It was for this reason that Kennett, who was driving the car, refused at first to stop when so requested by Ecclestone while driving through Albert Park, which, with yellow ribbons tied to trees, was witnessing yet another protest by demonstrators. Ecclestone insisted on speaking to a group of protesters to try to persuade them, in vain, of the recreational benefits the new circuit would bring. Instead, he was warned to 'watch out' for his health. But, says Ecclestone, he wasn't concerned: 'Anyone who threatens to do something, never does it.'

Two days later, while flying on a Shell Group private jet to Adelaide because he couldn't get a flight out of Melbourne, a 'massive explosion' occurred at 2000 feet. An engine was put out of action and, with the hydraulics also damaged, the pilot made an emergency landing. First thoughts were of an attempt on Ecclestone's life. It was an incident to which, Ecclestone claimed, he was indifferent. 'He [the pilot] said to me, "I looked round and you were reading a magazine." Well, I said I couldn't fix the engine, what could I do? They were paid to worry about landing the plane, not me. That was their problem.'

Ecclestone got on as well with Kennett as he had with Bannon. Once again, it was the matey, down-to-earth attitude that appealed to him. When the news was announced that a circuit was to be build in Albert Park, Kennett agreed to do a photo-call and pose in the park with a chequered flag. While the television cameras were rolling, a member of the public rode by on his bike, shouting: 'Fuck you, Kennett.' To which the Premier of Australia replied: 'Fuck you, too.' At the end of the story, told by Max Mosley, Ecclestone commented: 'He's a great guy. We could do with him being Prime Minister of England.'

Despite the Government's confident expectations, it is claimed that the Melbourne Grand Prix has hardly proved a financial success, failing even to meet the initial requirements of the Treasury to break even. While Ecclestone has done extremely well, the first Grand Prix in 1996, according to the Auditor-General's report, cost the taxpayer close to A$60 million. This was set against an economic impact assessment report issued by the government's Department of State Development, which claimed the race had generated economic benefits to the State of Victoria totalling A$95.6 million.

However, an independent economic report commissioned by the Save Albert Park protest group counterclaimed that the figure was misleadingly based on gross economic impact as well as exaggerated or non-existent benefits.[1] It estimated that the net economic impact of the 1996 race, after allowing for the government-funded capital costs, was no more than A$23.67 million. Using increased wealth as the performance benchmark, the report forecast that the Grand Prix would generate for the Victorian economy as little as A$21.87 million over the ten years of the contract. It claims the same capital invested in an equivalent commercial project may well have accrued over the same period net profits as high as A$500 million. By the end of the Melbourne Grand Prix in 2000, accumulated operating losses, which include depreciation, based on figures released by the Australian Grand Prix Corporation, had reached a total of A$31.6 million. The operating cash deficit on the 2000 Grand Prix alone totalled A$3.995 million. These figures do not include costs to the taxpayer incurred by the park, transport and police authorities, nor a total of A$747,000 for the cost of Royal Australian Air Force fly-overs.

Ecclestone claims to have made it a business principle to alert organisers of new Grands Prix, as in Malaysia, China and Bahrain, to the probability that they will not make money. 'I tell them upfront, "You are going to lose money running this event. You will not make money." I know how many people are going to be there. There is no bullshit. I would not ever tell them that this is fantastic, that they are going to make a fortune. If they don't [know], they come crying to me.' Did he so warn Jeff Kennett? 'He had enough brains to know that he wouldn't.'

When Kennett's Liberal–National coalition was replaced by the Labor Party following the State election on 18 September 1999, newly elected Premier Steve Bracks announced that details of government contracts involving billions of dollars would be made public to end 'a culture of needless secrecy'. The financial details of 76 contracts were made available to the public – except for the Grand Prix contract with Ecclestone, which was renewed for a further four years in August 2000. Dr Ross Ulman, president of the Save Albert Park group, said: 'The Melbourne Grand Prix makes a huge loss year on year. We want to know how much is ending up in Ecclestone's pocket and how much is tax exempt. The Grand Prix, which doesn't attract that many tourists, generates little economic benefit to the State. To make public the details of all contracts other than the Formula One contract is rank hypocrisy, to the detriment of the taxpayer and the benefit alone of Bernie Ecclestone.'

The Melbourne Grand Prix provides an illuminating example of the political level at which Ecclestone negotiates, of the inviolable secrecy that surrounds his contracts, and the extreme measures, even to the apparent detriment of democratic rights, that will be taken to protect them.

The penalty for refusing to accept Ecclestone's contractual terms is severe, as German businessman Rainer Mertel, the then manager of Germany's Nurburgring circuit, was to discover. It cost the Nurburgring the German Grand Prix and Mertel considerable professional anxiety. The circumstances that led to their confrontation came together following the horrific near-fatal accident of Niki Lauda in August 1976 when his Ferrari struck a high kerb at the circuit's Bergwerk left-hand corner, causing him to lose control and hit a rock-face wall before the car burst into flames.

The 14-mile track, long criticised by drivers for the dangers of its 174 corners and the jumps of Pflanzgarten and Flugplatz, was removed by the FISA from the Formula One calendar until it had undergone a major redesign. It was announced that the 1977 Grand Prix would be staged at Hockenheim, a move that was generally attributed to Lauda's accident. In fact, Ecclestone had already agreed with Germany's national sporting authority, the Automobil-Club von Deutschland, at the Monaco Grand Prix the previous year, that the Grand Prix would be transferred to Hockenheim beginning in 1976. Certainly the drivers considered the Nurburgring to be hazardous, but there was another reason – the length of its track made for poor television. The result of the redesign, at a cost of £18 million, was a shorter, safer, 12-corner complex able to accommodate 120,000 spectators, which earned the praise of teams and public alike. Work was completed in May 1984 and the German Grand Prix was ready to return to the Nurburgring the following year. But it was a prospect viewed with dismay by the Automobil-Club von Deutschland. Keen to retain it, senior officials attempted to prevent its return to the Nurburgring, and the fold of its rival, the Allgemeiner Deutscher Automobil-Club, by making heartfelt entreaties to Ecclestone.

But their best efforts came to naught. Ecclestone believed the Nurburgring, the cradle of German motor sport, and where the German Grand Prix had been staged since its inception in 1951, to be the superior circuit since its redesign. He was soon to be forced, though, to reverse his decision when the time came to agree the terms of the contract, a matter he had doubtless considered to be a formality. Mertel was not prepared to sign over the circuit's advertising rights to be marketed by AllSport Management, the company in which Ecclestone has consistently claimed to have no interest. Mertel, employed by the State of Rheinland-Pfalz, which owned 90 per cent of the circuit, said: 'Mr Ecclestone said that if I were to go with him, then the Nurburgring would be successful. If not it [the German Grand Prix] would go to Hockenheim. But first I had to give him the advertising rights, which I could not do. It was a matter of doing the honourable thing. The organiser had to have the advertising rights, because without these the organiser could not afford to organise his race.'

The organisers of 56 other national and international races held at the

Nurburgring, he added, would also have suffered. Ecclestone, said Mertel, reassured him that the Nurburgring would gain financially by the deal. 'He offered money to the Nurburgring to give him the advertising rights, but I had to have respect for the purses of the organisers.' The 1985 German Grand Prix was the last to be held at the Nurburgring. Hockenheim became its new home. The loss of Formula One hit the circuit's revenue hard. It was, said Mertel, 'a very, very dramatic [financial] situation', a dilemma that led to a host of new events, from rock concerts to truck racing, in an attempt to restore its profit level.

But while Hockenheim got the German Grand Prix, it also got increased financial demands from Ecclestone, which led to a massive hike in ticket prices – along with highly expensive corporate hospitality facilities, again for AllSport Management's benefit – that at one stage threatened the future of the event. One Grand Prix attracted no more than 49,000 spectators, and the Automobil-Club von Deutschland warned that the race might no longer be financially viable. The promoters, Formel Eins Gesellschaft für Motorsport MBH, denied at the time that the German Grand Prix was in any financial danger. However, the financial pressures persisted and in August 1990 the company was acquired by Ecclestone, which gave him an increased financial interest in the well-being of the German Grand Prix. As elsewhere, when it came to settling the FOCA's package for racing at the Nurburgring, he was effectively negotiating with himself.

Mertel had another reason for opposing Ecclestone's demand for the advertising rights. As president of the Association Internationale des Circuits Permanents, or Circuits International, established in the early fifties to represent the interests of circuit owners, now numbering 39, he had been urging them to stand firm against Ecclestone's tactics, which, he claimed, had became so threatening that in December 1987 Circuits International threatened legal action against the FOCA to prevent its 'interference' in 'curtailing' the advertising rights of its members, 'an indispensable source of income for each race track operator' in 'maintaining and improving modern motor-racing facilities'. However, as Mertel acknowledges, it was a threat of little substance. One by one the organisers capitulated. 'They were all angry about Bernie, but none had the courage or the power to say no. That was the problem.' He had learned the lesson known to Duffeler, Ugueux and Treu. He also confirmed the charge that Ecclestone gained control of certain circuits by imposing financial demands that organisers or promoters couldn't meet. 'That's true. And he always said, "Who has obliged you to sign my contracts? It was your free will. You are over 21, you know what you are doing."' Negotiations were also difficult. 'If he was on position A, he would then move to position B, and then to C and so on. It was nearly impossible to find a conclusion.'

The two men were destined to clash again, but this time over Grand Prix motorcycling. And Ecclestone would be exclusively representing his own interests, rather than those of the FOCA, through the activities of a marketing company called International Sportsworld Communicators (ISC), which he had set up in 1982, shortly after the FIA, through the Concorde Agreement, leased its commercial rights to the FOCA for Ecclestone to market. He was not slow, naturally, to appreciate that such authority put him in a unique position to exploit the business potential of non-Formula One events, too, although ISC remained more or less dormant until 1985, when his new ally, Jean-Marie Balestre, as president of the FISA, appointed the company to market the television rights of the Formula 3000 International Championship.

ISC went from strength to strength. The International Race Teams' Association, World Championship motorcycle racing's equivalent of the FOCA, and the Fédération Internationale Motocycliste, its governing body, agreed that they wanted its boss to do for their sport what he had been doing so successfully for Formula One – the marketing of its commercial interests. In December 1988 ISC was awarded a four-year contract. However, the staging of a round of the World Championship series at the Nurburgring, co-hosts on alternate years with Hockenheim, raised once again the issue of advertising rights and Mertel's troublesome principle. Ecclestone disposed of the problem by announcing that from 1990 the round would be exclusively staged at Hockenheim.

One of his first moves was to get the motorcycle teams to sign contracts with ISC and, with those in his hand, he negotiated on their behalf with the organisers. It was similar to his iron-grip control of Formula One, with the organisers compelled to agree to his terms. Mertel, as president of the Association Internationale des Circuits Permanents, had a brief meeting with Ecclestone at the 1991 Spanish Grand Prix to plead the case of his members, who wanted the freedom to negotiate their own contracts. 'I told him that, as with Formula One, we did not want a monopoly of motorcycling. He was not interested.'

The loss of the world motorcycle-racing championship series was another significant financial blow for Mertel. After seeking legal opinion he decided to retaliate with a strategy that in later years others would pursue with equal success, and much to the frustration of Ecclestone's financial ambitions. In 1992 Mertel filed a complaint to the Directorate-General IV of the European Commission in Brussels, which is responsible for competition policy, alleging that Ecclestone's monopoly of both Formula One and the world motorcycle championship series constituted unfair competition. The effect, said Mertel, was quite dramatic. Ecclestone agreed that the Nurburgring could be reinstated on condition that the complaint to the European Commission was withdrawn.

'He said if [we] wanted a motorcycle Grand Prix ... then [we] would have to withdraw this complaint.' He added: 'He was absolutely fearful of a complaint ... which has to do with lawyers or courts and so on [because] he knew that he [did not have] the [commercial] rights of the racetracks.' The complaint was subsequently withdrawn – and in 1995 the Nurburgring began staging not only a round of the world motorcycle championship series but also became the host venue to the European and Luxembourg Grands Prix, with, of course, the stipulation that Ecclestone had the advertising rights. By then, Mertel's interest was academic. Twelve months earlier he had resigned as manager of the Nurburgring to accept a senior position in the leisure industry.

Ecclestone didn't remain marketing supremo of the world motorcycle championship series for long. He had a major skirmish with the Fédération Internationale Motocycliste after it agreed a £30-million contract with a Madrid-based marketing company called Dorna Promoción de Deporte SA. The arrival of Dorna led to his loss of the television rights in a tripartite agreement which conflicted with Ecclestone's need to be in absolute control. In April 1993 he sold Two Wheel Promotions, a company he set up in September 1991 to take over the marketing from International Sportsworld Communicators, to Dorna for a reputed £50 million. Out of accumulative profits in 1993 of no more than £554,000, in 1992 and 1993 he paid himself a total of £501,000 for his management services.

Until November 1998, when a £30-million deal with Tony George, the billionaire president of the Indianapolis Motor Speedway, heralded its return to America after an absence of almost ten years, Ecclestone had failed with distinction in making Formula One a truly global marketing platform. Ceaseless efforts during the eighties had been largely frustrated by inconsistencies of venue and television coverage. Its total absence during most of the nineties prompted Jacques Nasser, the then president of Ford, to remark: 'It seems to me it's difficult to portray Formula One as a world sport without having an event in the world's largest market.'

It was an absence that plagued Ecclestone. In his mind there was no question where the problem lay. It was 'because the people who do business there seemed to have failed to understand what a contract is, and to respect it'.[2] To others, however, there was a more familiar reason – demanding contractual terms, particularly in respect of television rights, that circuit owners and promoters were not prepared to accept. In a country where there were more than 60 major motor sport events at 45 tracks attracting 12 million spectators, he was discovering that he was not dealing with a European organiser or promoter in fear of his every word and move. For the first time he was dealing with equally hardheaded businessmen whose commercial success did not depend on the patronage of Formula One.

The beginning of Ecclestone's problems in America began when, in pursuit of bigger bucks, he turned his back on the venue where Formula One had been consistently successful for almost 20 years – Watkins Glen, a purpose-built circuit situated about 300 miles north-west of New York in a small town of about 3000 people. It had been built in 1956 on 680 acres of land – later extended to 1180 acres – acquired by the Watkins Glen Grand Prix Corporation to replace the 6.6-mile course on which the first American road race was staged in 1948, founded, and organised until 1970, by a young lawyer, Cameron Argetsinger.

The first two United States Grands Prix, in Sebring, Florida, in 1959 and Riverside, a suburb east of Los Angeles, in 1960, proved financial disasters. But Watkins Glen, from its debut event in October 1961, won by Innes Ireland in a Lotus, proved an immediate hit with the teams and public alike. In 1966 it put up a record prize purse of $100,000, increased four years later to $250,000. However, its popularity made it a victim of its own success. Following discussions with the FISA, the corporation had to find $3.5 million to extend the circuit by a mile and improve team and public facilities. To raise the money, a high-risk quasi-municipal bond was floated, with the Bank of New York, as trustee, securing the mortgage on the land as security. It was an ambitious sum incurring a debt service charge of $1000 a day, payments which the organisers found increasingly difficult to meet.

According to hotelier Vic Franzese, chairman of the Industrial Development Agency responsible for issuing the quasi-municipal bond, and the then president of the Watkins Glen Chamber of Commerce, of which the Watkins Glen Grand Prix Corporation was a subsidiary, the causes of the problem were safety demands by, initially, the Grand Prix Drivers' Association for safety improvements, and, latterly, Ecclestone's financial demands on behalf of the FOCA. 'The new track was very smooth and much faster. This enabled the cars to sustain much higher speeds – by the mid-seventies they were completing the 3½-mile laps in about 1 min 34 secs – but they were too high for the safety factor in the construction of the cars. We tried slowing down the circuit by adding, for example, chicanes, but it didn't work because the cars were still getting faster. So each year the Grand Prix Corporation was forced to add or remove from the track whatever the Formula One powers decided they wanted to try next. To cover the cost we were shelling out perhaps $200,000 every year. That was in addition to about $3 million the Grand Prix was costing towards the end of the seventies. Much of that went on flying the teams in, and the prize money, which, by then, was a closely guarded secret between the Pied Piper [Ecclestone] and one or two others.'

No longer able to service the debt, the Bank of New York foreclosed on the property, forcing the Grand Prix Corporation to declare itself bankrupt in 1981 with assets of $3.5 million against debts totalling $5.9 million. Of that sum, $800,000 was owed to the FOCA. It could have been paid, says Franzese, if Ecclestone had responded more positively to efforts to refinance the Grand Prix Corporation. 'The Formula One group was prepared to swallow that loss because they were committed to go elsewhere for more money. He [Ecclestone] was looking for millions of dollars, which he thought couldn't come out of here. He figured there were cities where they were going to throw millions at them. Watkins Glen no longer fitted in with Ecclestone's plan for the future of Formula One.'

The last Grand Prix at Watkins Glen, won by Alan Jones in a Williams-Ford, took place in 1980. The economy of the community of Watkins Glen, which over nearly two decades had invested a good deal of effort and money in the Grand Prix, was hit badly by Ecclestone's decision, which also hurt fan support of all American road race sports, said Franzese. 'Only now is the support for road racing starting to pick up a little.' But he insists that it was Ecclestone and the teams who were the losers. 'Watkins Glen hosted 20 successful Formula One Grands Prix that were basically financially profitable. Bernie and company had ten years of failures and ten years of no races in this country after leaving Watkins Glen. They didn't understand what American fans will support, and where they will spend their money. The new track owners are enjoying a very profitable business. Bernie should have taken a second look before jumping ship. He and the Formula One group miscalculated badly.'

A few years later Ecclestone blamed the backwoods image of Watkins Glen for the teams' departure. 'It was in the wrong place,' he said. 'Everything was wrong with it. It wasn't the image we're trying to project. Didn't do anything for us.'[3] Its image was seriously tarnished, said Max Mosley, by a series of incidents involving locals allegedly setting light to a bus containing the luggage of Argentinian tourists and a car being set alight, which caused its two sleeping occupants to be burnt to death. They were incidents that 'dear old Vic' had forgotten about. 'It got to the point where it really wasn't good for the image of Formula One,' said Mosley. And Ecclestone commented: 'If that wasn't bad enough, they forgot to pay us $800,000.'

Cameron Argetsinger, who left the Grand Prix Corporation in 1970 and became president of the Sports Car Club of America in 1974, expressed a different point of view. 'That's bullshit. Watkins Glen was the right place at the right time, as its success over almost 20 years proved. It is the only circuit in America where a United States Grand Prix has been successful. I think his comments might be coloured by the fact that he got stiffed for $800,000.'

In an era when the global monetary system was less efficient and cheques were not always to be trusted, the financial arrangements between the Grand Prix Corporation and the teams were, as elsewhere, strictly cash only. Michael Tee, then vice-chairman of Champion Sporting Specialists International, which was extensively involved in promoting Grands Prix, was present when an FOCA associate of Ecclestone's made a payment in cash to one of the team bosses. He said: 'He came in and said, "Look, can I just have a moment?" I got up [to leave] and he opened a case and it was a mass of dollar bills. He said, "I think you will find everything is there." He just handed over a wad of notes, closed the case and walked off. He was doing the rounds of the various teams and handing over their "start" and prize money. It was entirely up to them how they put it through their books. In those days everything was cash.' Such deals, he confirmed, were an intrinsic part of the Formula One culture. He was paid $7000 cash to produce a series of promotional articles and programmes. 'That, in a minor way, was what was happening [throughout Formula One],' he said. 'Now, of course, it doesn't have to be that way, because money can be put in and moved about so easily from overseas banks ... but the amounts now are ridiculous.'

In moving out of Watkins Glen, Ecclestone began looking for somewhere like Long Beach, California, where since 1976 he had also been staging the USA West Grand Prix. He believed he had found the ideal venue in Nevada when he struck a deal with Clifford Perlman, the chairman of Desert Palace Inc., owners of Caesar's Palace in Las Vegas. Billy Weinberger, the president of the casino, believed the glamour of a Grand Prix would help pull in the gamblers, and he drove Ecclestone to a board meeting where the deal was agreed in record time. Ecclestone was escorted to a vault-like soundproof room deep below ground level where he was introduced to members of the board.

'This is Bernie Ecclestone,' Perlman announced. 'We want to have a Grand Prix here at Caesar's Palace and this is the guy who is going to fix it. Are you in favour?' A voice to Perlman's right broke the silence with a solitary yes. 'Congratulations, gentlemen. Done.' A Las Vegas Grand Prix was staged in 1981 and 1982 in the casino's huge car park, but both events proved financial disasters. They failed to attract the crowds or the interest of the major television companies on which their success had essentially depended. They heralded, in fact, the beginning of a series of similar disasters.

In the same year that Las Vegas was hosting its second and last Grand Prix, Ecclestone had moved east to stage a Grand Prix in the streets of Detroit – an unusual choice for someone keen on an image more glamorous than Watkins Glen – which, with Long Beach, meant that during 1982 there were three Grands Prix in America, a number which Ecclestone believed the size of the country could support. The deal that he cut with the organisers – four years and three on option – was a confident one. The length of the contract could be guaranteed, he said, because, rather than a flat fee, the teams would be taking a percentage of the race earnings. It was structured to give the FOCA the first $500,000, with the next $1.2 million going to the organisers and the next $500,000 to the FOCA; after that, the receipts would be split down the middle.

However, long before the contract had expired, his relationship with the organisers of the Detroit Renaissance Grand Prix, so named because the street circuit looped round the city's huge Renaissance Center, had turned sour. Ecclestone claimed the organisers had failed to provide the standard of facilities necessary to maintain a successful Grand Prix, including adequate garage facilities for the teams, media and sporting control centres, and on-track medical units, while the organisers reportedly claimed that Ecclestone made so many last-minute financial demands to increase his share of profits that budgeting became a nightmare.

By the time the Grand Prix in Detroit was in its second year, the USA West Grand Prix was bringing the shutters down for good due to the financial demands made by Ecclestone of organiser and promoter Chris Pook, a Somerset-born businessmen who had arrived on the Pacific coast in 1963. Ten years later Pook began discussions with the City of Long Beach to permit a Grand Prix street race, which led, in 1976, to the first of eight Grands Prix. However, despite every effort by Pook – not averse to rolling his sleeves up, as witnessed at the 1977 Grand Prix, when, with the installation of safety fencing behind schedule, he assisted crews in its construction, and, during the second practice session, manned one of the pit access gates to check credentials – the event became so unprofitable that he was forced to drop Formula One for the more popular Championship Auto Racing Teams (CART) series.

He said: 'We were running this huge race every year and only making $80–100,000 profit, and if we had a bad, rainy weekend our company would have been upside down. We could not see the light at the end of the tunnel to be able to build our company, and that is why we had to change.' It was brought about, he said, by the size of the prize money expected by Ecclestone and the cost of the teams' transportation. Advertising and hospitality rights had also been a factor. 'F1 was growing in a certain direction and wishing to maintain control over certain assets that it saw [for] itself, and, quite candidly, in the US the market is so fierce for similar assets that F1 wanted ... that those of us who were promoting it [Formula One] couldn't see a way through the maze.'

Coverage of the last Long Beach Grand Prix, produced by Grand Prix Teleproductions, was syndicated through cable television. Network television companies, in a country where Formula One attracts a quarter of the television audience of IndyCar racing and up to eight times fewer than NASCAR (North

American Sports Car Racing), argued that viewing figures simply didn't justify Ecclestone's financial terms. For Pook, as with others, it meant only one recourse – to hike up ticket prices, which did nothing to improve the prospects of Formula One's success. Said Pook: 'There is huge competition [in the USA] for the leisure dollar, and if you start to charge $150–200 for a ticket, your market diminishes very, very fast. It wasn't that Americans didn't embrace Formula One. It was a commercial issue.'

Lest he should appear too critical of Ecclestone, Pook, who, like many others in Formula One, has a healthy respect for his power and favour, later insisted that his comments should include reference to Ecclestone's 'incredible negotiating ability, his brilliance, his quickness and [that his] word is his bond'. He failed to mention, though, that Ecclestone's recall of detail apparently falls somewhat short of his. The demise of Formula One at Long Beach, according to Ecclestone, had nothing whatsoever to do with any commercial factors, but 'because we were told by Chris Pook that there was going to be major developments in the city which would necessitate the shortening of the circuit, which would not thereafter comply with the FISA regulations'.[4] Following the departure of the teams, Pook nevertheless continued to use the appeal of Formula One to pull in the crowds, said Ecclestone. 'We built up Formula One and it was called the Toyota Long Beach Grand Prix. It never mentioned Formula One. When we left, and they went to CART cars, Chris still called it [Toyota Long Beach Grand Prix]. In fact, so many people complained to me that they had gone to see Formula One and it wasn't Formula One.'

With the split at Long Beach, and Detroit falling short of expectations, Ecclestone attempted to strike oil in Texas. After much haggling in a deal brokered by Chris Pook, the financial terms were finally agreed with Dallas real-estate developer Donald R. Walker, who ran Dallas Motorsports Inc. from a plain, unmarked warehouse north of the city near LBJ Freeway and Interstate 35. The Dallas Grand Prix, which cost co-promoter Walker and his associates an estimated $6 million, proved to be one of the most short-lived US Grands Prix. Ecclestone's negotiating tactics, according to Walker, caused an intensity of conflict that seriously threatened cancellation of the race. He complained that Ecclestone avoided agreeing specifics until he had had become committed to heavy investment. 'Then, once he knows you're committed and have a heavy investment, he'll then use the leverage of cancelling your race to get the specifics the way he wants them.'[5]

It was a charge rejected by Ecclestone, who denied that Walker had invested heavily. 'The only investment he had ... it was a street circuit.' He added: 'The only complaint we ever had with him was that, firstly, he would have to respect FOCA passes, and, [secondly], the track broke up in the heat. All the drivers wanted to cancel the race. I pushed them to make the race go on.' Italian Michele Alboreto, who drove for Ferrari, was particularly alarmed, said Ecclestone. 'On the starting grid, he came to me and said, "I am going to die in this race, and you are going to be the one that's murdered me." I said, "Well, the easiest thing is don't race, if that's what you believe."' Tragically Alboreto, who spun off during the fifty-fourth lap, did die on the track – he was killed on 25 April 2002 at the Lausitz circuit, Germany, when his Audi test car had a puncture at 200mph, causing it to hit a crash barrier.

For all his criticism of Ecclestone, there were others who had cause to complain about Walker's business methods. By the following March he was forced to file for bankruptcy proceedings following a $17-million tax dispute with the Internal Revenue Service, who claimed that between 1982 and 1984 he had understated tax liabilities to partners involved in real-estate developments totalling $165 million. He and his wife, Carol, were later charged with owing $85 million in taxes, interest and penalties dating back to 1981. In January 1988 Walker was jailed for seven years after pleading guilty to three counts of felony tax fraud related to three limited partnerships in 1982.

The 1984 Dallas Grand Prix, won by Keke Rosberg in a Williams-Honda car on his way to a World Championship title, proved to be the first and last. Attempts by other businessmen to fulfil the four-year contract with Ecclestone were thwarted by the sheer cost of the event and legal difficulties, including a lawsuit for damages by residents living near the Fair Park circuit against the City of Dallas and Walker. It was Chris Pook's opinion that the Dallas Grand Prix would have proved to have been 'an incredibly successful venue' but for the downfall of Walker. But to seasoned sports reporter Gene Wojciechowski, with the *Dallas Morning News* at the time of the Grand Prix, 'it was the wrong place and the wrong time. It was novelty, something different. Dallas considers itself world-class but it is very provincial. They don't go to the sports pages looking for the results of Formula One. Bernie Ecclestone's style didn't go down too well, either. It was "my way or the highway", and with so many other motor sports around that wasn't the smartest approach with people who wanted to see Formula One succeed.'

Ecclestone's attempts to establish a long-term Grand Prix venue in America proved no more successful when the Formula One big top rolled on to Phoenix, Arizona, several years later. In 1989 the city council members gave their 7–1 backing to the plan, along with a one-off $2.9-million grant towards the cost of building and maintaining a 2.2-mile, 13-turn street circuit, and an annual $1.6-million grant thereafter. But, three years later, the Phoenix Grand Prix was no more. The first race was staged in June, a time of blistering heat when the city attracts few visitors. It was a disaster, with no more than an estimated 13,000 spectators going through the gate. It proved particularly costly for Ecclestone, who, as the promoter, ended up with a bill totalling £12 million.

He decided to stage the following year's race in March, but, while the attendance figure marginally improved, the layout of the track was widely criticised by spectators who had paid more than $200 for grandstand seats and could see little more than the drivers' helmets.

At the end of the race, a disgruntled spectator, intent on making his dissatisfaction known to the organisers, came across by chance a diminutive figure wearing an accreditation tag around his neck. Assuming him to be merely an official, and unaware that he was addressing the head honcho himself, he complained long and loud about the restricted view. Ecclestone waited until he had finished and then asked to see his ticket. Appearing to examine it, he replied poker-faced: 'Yes, I can see the trouble. You bought a "listening" ticket. Next time you should buy a "watching" ticket.' He then walked smartly away, leaving the complainant somewhat puzzled.

The third race, in 1991, proved no more popular. Won by Ayrton Senna, who dominated the race from start to finish to take his fifth US Grand Prix win, it turned out to be last Grand Prix to be held in America for the next nine years. Describing the Phoenix Grand Prix as 'a debacle', Chris Pook said that Ecclestone 'really did himself some harm, or Formula One did themselves some harm, because it just didn't work. The circuit wasn't compatible, the spectators couldn't see. It was a non-event. Unfortunately, Bernard received some very bad advice, very bad advice. The dilemma was that Formula One came to be seen as an anchor around the neck [of promoters] ... trying to swim.'

Ecclestone attempted that year to set up his own Grand Prix base in America by making a $4-million offer for the 12-turn, 2.52-mile Road Atlanta track in Georgia, which had hit financial difficulties. He said he agreed its purchase on a handshake, but when another interested party offered $100,000 more, he was invited to top it. 'The guy came back to me and said, "Do you want to give another $500,000?" I said no. You can't sell it twice. You'd be put in prison for that.' Twelve months later the owners filed for bankruptcy. Ecclestone and a New Hampshire businessman bid $2.6 million against bids of $3.2 million from a tyre corporation and an Atlanta-based group of companies. Ecclestone's bid was unsuccessful; the track was sold but reportedly failed to reach its investment potential.

By February 1996, its new owner, multi-millionaire Don Panoz, who had made a fortune in pharmaceutical research, was talking to Ecclestone about hosting a Formula One Grand Prix. Widely considered to be one of the best tracks in America, Panoz, the kind of businessman who established a successful vineyard in Georgia when the experts said it couldn't be done, spent $30 million improving the circuit to Formula One standards and facilities. But it all came to nothing. Although Panoz had committed $30 million to bringing Formula One to Georgia, he was not prepared to back down over the financial terms. Ecclestone insists the issue was safety, not money. 'There was a bridge with concrete on either side of the track, and when I agreed to buy it, I agreed to knock it down. It was dangerous. There was no way we would race there.'

Ecclestone became so desperate to break into the American market that he was willing to do so on the back of the hugely popular Indy 500 series. He supported an FISA proposal, mooted by Max Mosley in 1993, that oval races of up to 500 miles be allowed into the Formula One World Championship series, with slightly modified Formula One cars competing against IndyCars. As the United States Auto Club, the then organisers of the Indy, is sanctioned by the FIA, it was theoretically possible. But, across the Atlantic, it was rejected out of hand. The technical differences between the two cars apart – the lighter, nimble Formula One cars with their carbon brakes would have had an overwhelming advantage over the heavier, turbocharged IndyCars and their steel brakes – it made no sense for the owners of the top-class ovals, strongly committed to the IndyCar and the NASCAR series, to threaten that profitable relationship by getting involved with a formula that had little following. The proposal, criticised by the American motor sport media as 'silly and irrelevant', was dismissed as a headline-grabbing stunt to raise the profile of Formula One in America. More crucially, the teams themselves were far from keen.

A few months later similar judgement was accorded a challenge Ecclestone issued to IndyCar team owners: a £5-million showdown between Formula One cars and IndyCars on the streets of Adelaide the week before the Australian Grand Prix. Probably to his surprise, the challenge was accepted. Roger Penske, owner of Marlboro Team Penske, and the Michigan International Speedway, which accepted on behalf of another team owner, and between them they agreed to supply eight IndyCars to race against four Williams and four McLarens in a road race one day and on an oval circuit the next. Fine, responded Ecclestone. The race was on. But there was a qualification. The Formula One cars, he insisted, would race only on an FIA-approved track – and when one was built in Europe. Ecclestone had grabbed the headlines, and his £5 million was safe.

He had consistently refused to have a US Grand Prix as a separate event on an IndyCars programme. It was either a head-to-head, he insisted, or nothing, otherwise the television rights would be devalued, along with the level of his profits. 'Television coverage would be confused,' he said. 'No mileage in that for anyone.' It had probably proved the stumbling block when Ecclestone and Tony George had talks at the last US Grand Prix at Phoenix in 1991. But that was then, in the days when Ecclestone probably still believed that America was there for the taking. Now, after several years of varying degrees of failure trying to replicate the long-term success of Watkins Glen, he was ready to meet again with George – after talks, which involved Chris Pook, with Willie Brown, the controversial mayor of San Francisco, to stage a street race similar to Long Beach floundered.

During the weekend of 13–14 September 1997, George, accompanied by his executive vice-president, Leo Mehl, flew to London to discuss once more the obvious synergy of a commercial alliance at the Indianapolis Motor Speedway. George, from one of the richest families in the USA, said to be worth more than $9 billion, guaranteed a level of professionalism to ensure a stable Grand Prix home for Formula One. A further three meetings took place during 1998 to see a conclusion to the negotiations that had stalled seven years earlier in Phoenix. On 2 December it was announced that a $30-million multi-year contract had been agreed to stage a US Grand Prix beginning in 2000 at the speedway.

It took place on a 2.606-mile circuit combining an infield loop with a mile-long section of the storeyed oval and before a record crowd of more than 250,000. The US Grand Prix, won by Ferrari's Michael Schumacher, had, in a sense, returned home after a 40-year absence. Until 1960, the Indy 500 had been included in the Formula One calendar to justify the World Championship series title. The Indianapolis circuit had been bought by George's grandfather, Tony Hulman, as a derelict speedway in 1945 for $500,000 to save it from housing development, and now George described the return of Formula One to the venue as 'the realisation of my dream'. After nine years in the American wilderness, it was probably no less a dream come true for Ecclestone.

Before his link-up with Tony George there was one other Stateside deal that went sour for Ecclestone. This time it was with Hollywood star Sylvester Stallone, who was keen to direct and star in a film on Formula One. At the Italian Grand Prix at Monza in 1997, Ecclestone signed, for the benefit of Stallone's backers, an agreement provisionally granting him the film rights.

For the next two years, Stallone claimed he worked hard with lawyers and producers to formalise the financial arrangements. 'I thought we had a deal but, every time I went to sign, Bernie would raise the price.' Ecclestone claims he had been advised that the terms provisionally agreed with Stallone were too generous. The project went no further. But even if Ecclestone had been willing to proceed, it seems the project would have run into a major obstacle with the FIA. Stallone wanted the rights to the film for infinity, something that Ecclestone couldn't guarantee, as the Formula One commercial rights will revert to the FIA on the termination of his contract with the governing body in 2010.'

Mosley wanted to check the script. He explained he had to be sure that Formula One would not be portrayed in a sensational plot that was detrimental to its image. Stallone refused point blank, and phoned Ecclestone to express his anger at that 'fugger Mosley.'

10

HOW CANADA LOST ITS NSA – AND BRANDS HATCH THE BRITISH GRAND PRIX

By the mid-eighties the single most powerful voice in Formula One belonged to Bernie Ecclestone. He now assumed all authority in dealing with the teams, television broadcasters, sponsors, promoters, circuit owners and the FIA. By extension of his influence within the FIA, national sporting authorities (NSAs), invariably a country's principal motoring organisation appointed by the FIA to ensure Grands Prix were run in accordance with its rules and regulations, also became subject to his control.

The NSAs discovered how vulnerable they were to the new rule of order through the examples of the Canadian Automobile Sports Club (CASC) and Britain's Royal Automobile Club (RAC) – that it was no longer the FISA to whom they were answerable, which had been the case for more than 30 years, but to Ecclestone. The manner in which he removed the CASC as the national sporting authority of the Canadian Grand Prix, and replaced it with his own NSA, is particularly illuminating as an exercise in legal and political expediency. The message it sent out was clear: do not incur Ecclestone's displeasure.

The conflict began, like so many others, over his financial demands on behalf of the FOCA. The sponsors, the Canadian brewery Labatt, who had promoted the Canadian Grand Prix since 1978, when it financed the construction of the Gilles Villeneuve circuit in Montreal, claimed to be so concerned by Ecclestone's increased demands, principally over the prize money, that the company expressed serious doubts to the CASC's executive director, Bob Hanna, that it could agree terms for the renewal of its six-year contract with the FOCA to begin in 1985. It was already losing annually one or two million dollars, which was acceptable due to the promotional value of the Grand Prix, but Ecclestone's demands threatened to double those losses.

The discussions between Labatt and Ecclestone during 1984 finally ground to a halt. The company informed the CASC, on 31 August, that it was serving notice of its intention to terminate its five-year agreement as sponsors, which had been renewed in 1983, because it had been unable to agree terms with Ecclestone. Its contract with the CASC was conditional on such an agreement. Hanna phoned Ecclestone, who told him that he was continuing to talk to Labatt, but, if a deal couldn't be done, they would work together to find another sponsor/promoter. On 9 November Ecclestone contacted Hanna to tell him that he was close to concluding a deal. He had also advised Labatt that, despite the fact they had terminated their agreement with the CASC, the club must continue to be involved as the organiser. On 13 November Hanna received a telex from Labatt claiming that an agreement had been reached with Ecclestone and requested the CASC to sanction the race.

But what followed suggested to Hanna the real reason why Labatt had terminated its contract with the CASC. During its negotiation the company had applied considerable pressure on him to agree to sign over all commercial and sporting rights. This was not in Hanna's power to do, even if he had so wished. The Concorde Agreement made clear that the sporting function of a Grand Prix, in ensuring that the FIA's rules and regulations were observed, was the obligation of the national sporting authority, while the commercial activities were the responsibility of the promoter, who could have no control over the sporting role.

Now, in negotiating a new contract, Labatt tried to gain complete control of the event through its influence within the CASC. During the negotiations it stipulated that it would pay only a limited amount of out-of-pocket expenses for a few senior CASC officials, and it would also arrange for the Fédération Auto Québec, the Quebec branch of the CASC, to provide the necessary officials to look after the sporting activities. Hanna resolutely refused to agree to Labatt's terms. But it seemed to confirm what he had suspected – that an influential Quebecois faction on the Labatt board of directors was pulling the strings.

It was given credence by events at a CASC board meeting on 7 December, when a stage-managed revolt, led by the Quebec region delegate, who later went on to join Labatt, resulted in a vote of no confidence being passed in the president, John Magill. The board directors – described by a senior official of another national sporting authority as 'amateurs frightened of losing the Grand Prix' – had been persuaded that he and Hanna had been the problem in negotiating with Labatt and, as a result, had put the race at risk. The board then appointed a committee, consisting of three directors, none of whom had any experience of Formula One negotiations, to conclude talks with the brewery, which led to the CASC signing over the sponsorship rights to the Canadian Grand Prix for five years, followed by a five-year option and then a five-year first refusal, and on terms advantageous to Labatt.

Labatt now believed that it was in a very strong bargaining position in concluding its contract with Ecclestone, which had yet to be signed. For a senior executive had contacted a leading figure of a national sporting authority outside of Canada to confirm if it was correct that, under FIA rules, a Grand Prix could not be held without the approval of the national sporting authority. He was told that this was so. With, as it thought, the CASC safely in its corner, and with a contract to prove it, Labatt believed that Ecclestone would have no alternative but to accept its financial terms. This was to fatally underestimate the man, or the power that he wielded within the FIA. Balestre apart – and he was now very much on Ecclestone's side – he was the one man who could tear up the rule book.

The CASC would also have been unaware that during this time Ecclestone had been busy behind the scenes opening up his options. As an insurance policy, he had been talking to an American called Jack Long, whose motor sport marketing company, Long-Dilamarter Inc., represented a rival brewery, Molson, which had been standing on the sidelines, ready and willing to sponsor the Canadian Grand Prix. When news of Labatt's sponsorship deal with the CASC reached Ecclestone, he was furious at what he saw as a blatant attempt to outsmart him. He picked up the phone, called Long and agreed to sign a six-year contract with Molson.

When Labatt heard of Ecclestone's deal with Molson, it remained defiantly chippy, insisting that it had the one contract that mattered – with the national sporting authority, the CASC. The company had seriously miscalculated, though. While a Grand Prix could not be held without the approval of the national sporting authority, an organiser or promoter first had to have an agreement with the FOCA before the FISA would approve a Grand Prix. It was a lock-up clause introduced in the first Concorde Agreement. The dispute between Labatt and Molson became so vexatious, with an exchange of writs between the breweries claiming the right to stage the 1987 Canadian Grand Prix, that it was cancelled, the first time it had been absent from the Formula One calendar since its inception in 1967. But while the two companies were preparing to square up in court, Ecclestone was quietly planning retribution.

With Balestre's support, the plenary conference in Paris that October overwhelmingly backed a proposal that the CASC should be stripped of its national sporting authority status for failing to defend the 'sporting interests' of the FIA, namely by entering into a contract contrary to the terms of the Concorde Agreement, which allowed Ecclestone alone the authority to negotiate the FIA's commercial interests. The decision, which made its contract with Labatt null and void, led to the expulsion of the CASC from the FIA. Labatt initially decided to challenge the decision in court but, two months later, withdrew the action. The company, said a spokesman, was left with the choice between protecting 'our rights in the courts and risk the future of the Grand Prix for the next five years, or pull out'.

Labatt had learnt the hard way what was becoming universally recognised in Formula One – that the only contract that mattered was the one with Ecclestone's signature on it. But there was now the question of who would replace the CASC as Canada's national sporting authority. Ecclestone came up with a simple solution: he arranged the setting up of what was effectively his own national sporting authority. Its first president was a French-Canadian building contractor, a former CASC member, whom Ecclestone had come to know through the construction of the teams' garages at the Gilles Villeneuve circuit. At that time, said a senior member of the FIA's World Motor Sport Council, the rest of the executive committee consisted of a couple of his friends. Canada's new national sporting authority, the Autorité Sportive Nationale du Canada FIA Inc., was given the rubber-stamp endorsement of the FISA's executive committee.

A senior member of the World Motor Sport Council who attended the meeting commented: 'I said to some of my friends, "Do you realise we have just given Mr Ecclestone a national sporting authority of Canada, because that man [the French-Canadian] is his front there."' Staff at the new national sporting authority came to include many of those who had actually worked for the expelled CASC, including its president, who replaced the French-Canadian – he quit after allegedly failing to persuade Ecclestone to invest in his business – before becoming chairman of the FIA's Circuits and Safety Commission in 1998.

Jack Long went on to become Ecclestone's representative in North America to promote the disastrous Grands Prix at Phoenix and Las Vegas. In April 1989 Ecclestone acquired Long's Long-Dilamarter Inc., which, through a subsidiary called Canadian Grand Prix Enterprises, he would promote as well as organise the Canadian Grand Prix. It opened up a new enterprise for Ecclestone, which he was able to extend to America, although less successfully, through General Promotions Inc. in May 1989; to Belgium through Racing Francorchamps Promotion SPRL, which became Spa Activities in 1997; to Germany through Formel Eins Gesellschaft für Motorsport MBH in 1990; and to Hungary through Hungarian Formula One Grand Prix KFT, of which he owned 75 per cent, in 1991.

Ecclestone's thwarting of the Royal Automobile Club (RAC), Britain's national sporting authority and arbiter of the venue of the British Grand Prix, is no less fascinating, not least for the example it provides of his controlling influence over Balestre as the president of the FISA. It all began around mid-1985 when Ecclestone made it known that he wanted to bring to an end the practice of alternating the British Grand Prix between Brands Hatch and Silverstone. He believed it was necessary in order for the selected circuit to generate the level of profits required to fund the major track, media and spectator improvements that the standards of Formula One demanded. But, as events unfolded, it was a plan that suited well Ecclestone's commercial ambitions towards the British Grand Prix.

The only other countries to have alternating venues – France and Belgium – had already fallen into line. Balestre, as president of the French national sporting authority, the Fédération Française du Sport Automobile (FFSA), had agreed that the French Grand Prix, which since 1973 had alternated between the Paul Ricard circuit at Le Castellet, near Marseilles, and Dijon, south-east of Paris, would be held for the last time at Dijon in 1984. It remained at Paul Ricard for six years, until President Mitterand intervened to have the event switched to the Nevers Magny-Cours circuit, some 160 miles south-east of Paris and in the heart of his political powerbase. During the eighties the one-time club racing circuit underwent a series of extensions to double its length. Mitterand decided that the region would be regenerated with a highway from the centre of Paris to the circuit, along with the construction of hotels and an airport.

In 1996 the FFSA wanted the French Grand Prix returned to Dijon, a request that, with Ecclestone's support, was refused by the FIA because the circuit failed to comply with Formula One safety standards. (Three years later, incidentally, Ecclestone added the Paul Ricard circuit, complete with airport and hotel, to his portfolio for £11.5 million.) The Belgian national sporting authority, the Royal Automobile Club de Belgique, was similarly compliant. The introduction of Zolder in 1982 as an alternating venue was short-lived – it, too, came to an end in 1984. Spa-Francorchamps, where Ecclestone had substantial commercial interests, became the chosen circuit.

But Ecclestone's proposal was received less submissively by the RAC, whose Motor Sports Association had been responsible since 1964 for organising the British Grand Prix alternately between Brands Hatch and Silverstone. It insisted that the well-established practice of rotational venues was in the best interests of British motor sport and preferred, in particular, by Formula One fans. It was made clear that the RAC would firmly oppose efforts to bring it to an end. As for Brands Hatch, its senior management was puzzled by Ecclestone's claim that his proposals were necessary to finance improved circuit facilities – there was access to virtually unlimited funds provided there was adequate security of tenure.

Far from wanting a monopoly, the RAC's Motor Sports Association's management committee was actually keen to see the number increased. In 1983 building company boss Tom Wheatcroft, the millionaire owner of the Donington Park circuit in Leicestershire, was given an indication that he could stage the 1988 British Grand Prix. On the strength of that understanding he proceeded to spend £850,000 on track improvements in order to obtain a Formula One track licence from the FISA. The Motor Sports Association had good reason to believe that it was in a strong position to win the day. It not only had ownership of the British Grand Prix title but also the comfort of a long-standing relationship with Silverstone and Brands Hatch in organising the event. It was a united force, it was confidently believed, that would see the status quo maintained. It had yet another, weightier reason for presuming a favourable outcome – the support of Balestre, whose authority at that time was still widely considered to be greater than Ecclestone's.

It was given following a series of inconclusive meetings between Balestre and Jeffrey Rose, the chairman of the RAC, who was leading the discussions with the support and approval of the Motor Sports Association, at the FIA's headquarters in Paris. At the Italian Grand Prix at Monza in September 1985, Balestre finally agreed with Rose that, subject to the approval of the World Motor Sport Council, the British Grand Prix could continue to alternate between Brands Hatch and Silverstone. A letter was drafted by Yvon Léon, the general secretary of the FISA, signed by Balestre and delivered to Rose at the RAC in London. It seemed that, bar the formality of the council meeting – it was hardly likely to vote against its president's recommendation – the RAC had triumphed. But Balestre had erred. He had failed to consult Ecclestone.

Shortly before the opening of the World Motor Sport Council in December, Ecclestone, without explaining his reasons, made it clear that he couldn't accept Balestre's recommendation. Balestre, who was present, said nothing. When the time came to discuss the resolution to allow the British Grand Prix to be staged at alternating venues, Balestre, with reference to his recommendation, said he could speak only as the representative of the Fédération Française du Sport Automobile. With an obvious lack of enthusiasm for his own recommendation, the resolution failed to attract a majority vote. It was subsequently announced that from January 1986 there would be a policy of one country one circuit. The RAC came in for considerable flak from the UK motor sport media, which accused the motoring organisation of failing to do enough to block the move.

As Brands Hatch dominated the motor sport scene and homologation fees were a major source of income for the RAC, John Webb, the managing director of Motor Circuit Developments Ltd (MCD), which ran Brands Hatch, was in a position to urge the Motor Sports Association to throw its weight behind Brands Hatch as its choice of circuit for the British Grand Prix, which it duly did. But whatever influence it might have once wielded within the FISA, it was now of little force. As the Canadian Automobile Sports Club was also to learn, it was Ecclestone's view alone that mattered. It would be he who would decide which circuit would get the British Grand Prix. The precedent had been established: the authority of the Royal Automobile Club as Britain's national sporting authority, which had been considered one of the strongest and most influential in Formula One, was now subject to Ecclestone's wishes.

Around this time Webb had other pressing matters on his mind – he was busy looking for heavyweight investors to back a rescue of MCD, a quest that would come to involve the omnipresent Ecclestone, and which may have explained his enthusiasm for the introduction of a one-country-one-circuit ruling. Webb, who had joined Brands Hatch as a contracted press officer in 1954, was perfectly suited to the task before him. He had played a leading role, at the request of the then managing director, in the sale of Brands Hatch to Grovewood Securities, an investment company, in 1961, which led to his appointment to its board as a director. He began negotiations with the RAC that led in 1964 to the circuit staging, on alternate years with Silverstone, the British Grand Prix, and was also responsible for the acquisition of Mallory Park, Snetterton and Oulton Park. MCD was formed as a centralised operational company to run the circuits.

Grovewood Securities was taken over in 1972 by Eagle Star Holdings, a financial investments company which, in turn, was bought by British American Tobacco (BAT) in the early eighties. By late 1985 BAT decided that motor sport no longer suited its long-term group business activities and made it known that it wanted to sell its assets, possibly to property developers interested in developing, for example, Brands Hatch as a supermarket complex. Webb, president of the Association Internationale des Circuits Permanents (Circuits International), the organisation representing the interests of circuit owners worldwide and which Rainer Mertel would subsequently lead, was a much-respected figure in British motor sport and became determined that Brands Hatch should remain a major motor sport circuit. He wrote to Patrick Sheahy, chairman of BAT, requesting first option on Grovewood's motor-racing interests.

Sheahy agreed, and Webb, aided by his wife, Angela, who had been appointed a director of MCD by Grovewood Securities in 1976 and its deputy managing director in the early eighties, put together a buy-out plan, which required considerable capital investment. By February 1986 – a month after the one-country-one-circuit ruling had been introduced – Webb had found two interested parties. The first was 38-year-old John Foulston, multi-millionaire founder of Atlantic Computers, a computer leasing company, whom Webb knew well as a sponsor and a participant in Historic Sports Car Club championships at Brands Hatch. The other was Ecclestone.

In either late March or early April, following a preliminary round of discussions, Foulston, Ecclestone and the Webbs met at Fairoaks Aerodrome, Surrey, where the Webbs' proposal was verbally agreed. Foulston and Ecclestone would go 50-50 to buy the circuit's freehold through a holding company, later to be known as Brands Hatch Leisure Plc, while the Webbs would have a 20 per cent stake in an operational company, which would come to be known as Brands Hatch Circuits Ltd, and which they would be left to run. The sum involved, or so Webb confidently believed at the time, was about £3.5 million. Both Foulston and Webb proceeded with some confidence. At that meeting Ecclestone had reassured Foulston and the Webbs that the Grand Prix would be going to Brands Hatch.

Webb informed Eagle Star that his act was in place and it was informally confirmed that the price would be about £3.5 million, although Webb was informed that, to protect shareholders' interests, a consultant would be engaged to revalue the assets. From that point, he noted, another party became interested in buying the company. That party was British Car Auctions (BCA). Its involvement hiked up the price dramatically. Then, shortly after the Monaco Grand Prix on 11 May, Webb received a phone call from Ecclestone. He'd gone cold on the deal, would he mind explaining to Foulston? Webb declined, and told Ecclestone to tell Foulston himself. Foulston later called Webb to say that he had heard from Ecclestone but was prepared to go it alone. However, due to the intervention of British Car Auctions, the price of MCD soon reached £5.25 million – £1.75 million more than the initial valuation. If it went any higher, said Foulston, he would pull out. It didn't – and he got the company.

At a board meeting of Brands Hatch Leisure Plc, which included Tory MP Sir Geoffrey Johnson-Smith and Sir Jack Brabham, Foulston was asked how he had reacted to Ecclestone's call. His answer, which was not minuted, was that Ecclestone said he was prepared to go with the latest increased figure – it had yet to get to £5.25 million – only if he, Foulston, loaned him his 50 per cent. Foulston said that he would, but at some rate of interest. Ecclestone said no, he wanted it interest-free. Foulston replied that there could be no deal on that basis. After that, Foulston reported, 'Bernie threw his toys out of the pram.' Their business association came to a sudden end.

Given his wealth and his usual method of business, Ecclestone's request was implausibly out of character, as if he were deliberately creating a reason to pull out of the agreement with Foulston, which was more than likely. For unknown to Foulston, Ecclestone had also been talking to David Wickins, founder and chairman of BCA. Ecclestone had come to an 'understanding' with Wickins: if BCA's bid was successful, the company would lease the track to him. Ecclestone, as ever, had done his sums and had doubtless found this proposition more appealing, not least because, without the hindrance of a partner, particularly one as potentially troublesome as Foulston, he would be in complete control.

Commenting on the 'understanding' with Ecclestone, Wickins, who headed BCA from its founding in February 1946 to his retirement in 1988, said: 'I am not sure there was anything firm or fixed about it, but when you gave your word, you'd given it. We were only interested in Brands Hatch as a site for an auction centre. It wouldn't have interfered with the racing. I was certainly not interested in running Formula One. I tried never to get involved in things outside my particular knowledge.' BCA, he recalled, had bid £250,000 more than Foulston but it was conditional on planning permission being granted for the construction of offices. 'I don't know what happened after that. I went to America and started buying auctions there.' Ecclestone, he said, had had no personal stake in BCA's bid, nor did he do anything to promote it.

With Foulston's successful acquisition of Brands Hatch, Ecclestone's interest switched to Silverstone, the former military bomber base in Northamptonshire whose original x-shaped circuit hosted the first British Grand Prix in 1950, and which was owned by the British Racing Drivers' Club, a mutual organisation of some 800 members. He had secret talks with managing director Jimmy Brown, and, on 21 May, within weeks of the partnership with Foulston breaking down, a contract was signed between Ecclestone, on behalf of the FOCA, Balestre, on behalf of the FISA, and Brown, which led to Silverstone getting the British Grand Prix for the next five years. With few aware of what had been going on behind the scenes – as well as the RAC, as the national sporting authority, whose senior officials were livid at being kept in the dark – Ecclestone explained that the contract had gone to Silverstone 'because there is room to build the kind of facilities necessary'. In an off-the-record comment, which he refused to enlarge, he said he had been involved in 'the early stages' of the sale negotiations of Brands Hatch.[1] The news was announced by Balestre during the Belgian Grand Prix at Spa-Francorchamps. It was relayed to Webb in a phone call from the motor sport correspondent of the British daily newspaper *The Guardian* at 9 a.m. on Saturday 24 May. He was stunned, at least briefly.

Six days earlier, on 18 May, a statement had been issued announcing the change of ownership of Brands Hatch through the acquisition of Motor Circuit Developments Ltd by Foulston, with the Webbs in operational control. The future of the British Grand Prix at Brands Hatch was secure, Webb had declared. But if Foulston was deeply concerned by the news about Silverstone, he appeared unperturbed. 'In a financial sense there was no reason why he should be,' said Webb, 'because in those days one made very little money out of a Grand Prix. He took it very well, and simply got on with business.' The 1986 British Grand Prix, won by Nigel Mansell in a Williams-Honda, was the last one to be staged at Brands Hatch. Foulston later added Cadwell Park – Mallory Park was sold in 1983 – to his stable of circuits, which underwent extensive improvement programmes. 'In fact, we went on to make some of our best profits,' added Webb. 'If anything, a Grand Prix can cloud one's mind and distract attention from other opportunities. So when we had to start thinking hard, it went well.'

In blithe ignorance of all that had been going on between Ecclestone, Brands Hatch and Silverstone was the RAC's Motor Sports Association, and the hapless Tom Wheatcroft, who had spent a fortune on his hopes for a Grand Prix at Donington. The general reaction of senior RAC management, as reported at the time by the motor sport media, was one of disquiet, although Peter Cooper, the then chairman of the Motor Sports Association, claims today that he had not been surprised by the news. 'I was not surprised by anything that Bernie did.'

Wheatcroft issued a High Court writ against the RAC for damages of £1.25 million, a legal action which progressed no further. But he finally got his Grand Prix, even though he incurred heavy losses. It took place in 1993 – 50 years after the Leicestershire circuit, a one-time pre-war motorcycle track, held its first Grand Prix – after Ecclestone backed his application to the FISA to stage a one-off European Grand Prix following the cancellation of the Asian Grand Prix in Japan. Given just 12 weeks' notification, Wheatcroft, then aged 71, worked furiously to get everything ready for the Easter weekend event.

But his long-awaited dream, at least financially, was washed down the drain as rain fell for three days. Attendance figures were disappointingly low, leaving him with a bill of more than £3.5 million, much of which, of course, was Ecclestone's cut for the FOCA. How much Ecclestone actually received, Wheatcroft declined to say. 'When you sign a contract, there are two things you can't talk about – how much you pay for the race and where the money goes.' Whatever happens, though, Ecclestone, he said, 'can't lose'. Wheatcroft had the opportunity to stage a European Grand Prix the following year but was thwarted by a heart attack. All the same, he had no regrets that it didn't take place: he conceded that Donington needed 'a lot more infrastructure'. But, for one of motor sport's rare nice guys, the experience of staging a Grand Prix prompted the comment, which he declined to explain: 'You can watch racing all your life, you can enter cars, but when you own a circuit you get into the political side, which I call the "dirty tricks" side. People are nice to your face ... [then] stab you in the back.'

With an estimated personal fortune of £40 million, John Foulston had funded the acquisition of Motor Circuit Developments Ltd through a mix of ready cash and the proceeds of the sale of a minor part of Atlantic Computers, which he co-founded in 1975. But he would have little time to fully achieve his ambitious expansion plans for his circuits. Sixteen months later, in September 1987, he was killed instantly, and ironically, at Silverstone. In a test outing, a component failure caused him to lose control of his prized 1970 McLaren-Offenhauser M15, a powerful 1000bhp IndyCar, and crash into barriers at Club Corner. His death, at the age of 40, led to the sale of Atlantic Computers, which, considered to be very much a one-man show, would, it was feared, soon plummet in value.

It was sold to British & Commonwealth Holdings Plc, whose activities included banking, shipping, securities and investments. The sale, now in the name of Mary Foulston, who had inherited her husband's holdings, went through the following year, but in late 1989 the company collapsed, pulling British & Commonwealth into liquidation with debts totalling £1.3 billion. A report published by the Department of Trade and Industry in July 1994, following an investigation into Atlantic Computers, criticized Foulston for misrepresentation over the number of lease contracts with 'walk' clauses in the event of the company's sale, the cause of its downfall.

As for John and Angela Webb, two years after Foulston's death they withdrew as chief executive and managing director respectively of what had now become the Brands Hatch Leisure Group. They were unable to get on with Foulston's intensely ambitious daughter, Nicola, who, at the age of 18 had been appointed managing director of Haslemere Sports Cars Ltd, which ran her father's historic Formula One and CanAm cars. In September 1989, at 21, she was appointed commercial director, a move which was said to have had the support of John Webb in order that he could 'keep an eye on her'. But within just four weeks the friction was such that the Webbs decided they couldn't continue.

John Webb told Mary Foulston that either her daughter had to go or he and his wife would resign. Mrs Foulston, who believed the Webbs had done an excellent job for the group, was reluctant to lose them, but nevertheless was persuaded to let them go. She agreed to buy out their 20 per cent share – as long as the news was broken to them by one of the company's advisers. In 1990 a press statement was issued stating that the couple – he had been at Brands Hatch for 36 years and she for 18 – were retiring to Spain.

Six months after her appointment as commercial director, the feisty Nicola Foulston took on a new role as chief executive and set off on an ambitious expansion programme to raise Brands Hatch's motor sport profile and revenue, which topped £10 million a year but with minimal profits. For her more cautious mother it proved more of a white-knuckle ride – she saw her daughter as 'a ridiculous risk-taker' – which led to increasing friction between them. The relationship became so strained that in January 1991 Foulston offered to buy her mother out. Through Baring Brothers, she was backed to the tune of £6 million to buy the company in February 1992, following 12 months' negotiations – a protracted period that gave rise to reports of deep acrimony between mother and daughter – which resulted in the final purchase taking place through offshore trusts rather than with debt provided by Barings.

Over the next decade Foulston transformed Brands Hatch, with the building of new headquarters and conference centre, new pits, renegotiation of television contracts and lucrative diversification into exhibitions and corporate hospitality. In 1995 she organised a £15.5-million management buy-in of the Brands Hatch Leisure Group – enriching herself by £1.55 million through a ten per cent stake, the purpose of which was to raise finance to buy out the freeholds of the circuits from her mother's trusts – and in November 1996 went public, adding considerably to her personal wealth, but also enabling the funding of further expansion. Foulston, who won the Veuve Clicquot Businesswoman of the Year award in 1997, had achieved one of her father's plans – to see Brands Hatch successfully floated. But it had all been part and parcel of her own grand plan. For Foulston, perceived as a hard, ambitious and ruthless operator in the genetic strain of Ecclestone, was working to a hidden agenda that had driven her throughout her mercurial career, one which, if all went to plan, would bring her sufficient riches for the rest of her life. The key to its success was the acquisition of Silverstone.

It led in mid-1998 to a series of exploratory talks with Denys Rohan, the chief executive of Silverstone Circuits Ltd, the track's commercial subsidiary, to discuss ways of bringing Brands Hatch and Silverstone together. The thought of contacting Rohan in the first place had been prompted by the unsuccessful efforts of an American company to acquire RAC Motoring Services, which was finally bought by Lex Service, a UK motoring and related businesses group, in July 1997 for £437 million after the 11,000 members of the mutual organisation agreed to accept payments of £34,000 each. Its structure was not dissimilar to the British Racing Drivers' Club, whose 838 members owned Silverstone. Founded in April 1928, with membership restricted to established racing drivers, by 1931 the club had proven so popular that it became registered as a company limited by guarantee. BRDC Ltd bought the lease of Silverstone from the RAC in 1952 and the freehold from the Ministry of Defence in 1971.

It was Foulston's initial gut instinct to launch a surprise attack on Silverstone, one that would have enriched each member by a figure in the region of £100,000. She believed that a sufficient number of members would agree to the proposal before BRDC's 12-strong board of directors could muster a counter-attack. She held back because she had been advised that if she moved too quickly she could risk inadvertently breaking City codes, such as the listing rules of the Stock Exchange and the Financial Services Act, which govern a plc's offer of shares to members of the public who form a co-operative such as the BRDC. By late autumn Foulston was proposing a more formal approach – a straightforward takeover of Silverstone, a move that Rohan was said to have greeted positively. But, by now, the future of Silverstone had attracted the interest of another party, prompted by an inevitable leak of Foulston's covert meetings with Rohan.

In November property developer and BRDC member John Lewis, a former non-executive chairman of Silverstone Estates Ltd, which managed the assets of the club's industrial property, made a £41-million offer, backed by HSBC Private Equity, for Silverstone. He believed that the BRDC would be more receptive to a known face, someone who respected the culture and traditions of Silverstone, rather than Foulston, who, in the eyes of her critics, would race jam doughnuts if the bottom line was sufficiently attractive. Lewis's bid subsequently attracted the interest of another property developer, Essex-based Colin Sullivan, who put up a figure of £45 million. Bids from other parties were also put on the table.

Foulston now found herself somewhat on the back foot as the board directors began to set the agenda. It hired the services of merchant bankers Dresdner Kleinwort Benson (DKB) as financial advisers to review all the options open to the club. In reply to a letter from DKB to all interested parties, Brands Hatch Leisure Plc, the holding company of the Brands Hatch Leisure Group, confirmed its interest in buying Silverstone for a figure later put at £47.9 million. An information pack on Silverstone, containing financial detail not publicly available, was offered by the bankers on condition that Foulston signed a confidentiality agreement, which also included a lock-out clause preventing a direct approach to BRDC members. Foulston declined to have her hands tied by the clause, but it confirmed in her mind that her early instinct to make a direct approach on day one would probably have proved successful.

Brands Hatch Leisure now seemed to be out in the cold. Until, that is, Foulston decided to seek the support of the one person who could snatch victory from the jaws of defeat. In early December she arrived at Ecclestone's office in Knightsbridge with nothing more than a book to read while he kept her waiting for his usual obligatory period. She had deliberately left her briefcase at her office, along with a sharp business attitude that might work against her. She knew that Ecclestone, like her father, had an ego easily rankled by an attitude suggesting peer equality, particularly from someone so young.

Inside his office, Foulston immediately got down to explaining the reason for her visit, of her interest in Silverstone, of the proposed takeover talks she had had with Denys Rohan, and now the hiring of Dresdner Kleinwort Benson, whose services had been engaged, she believed, in order to bring about a merger between Brands Hatch and Silverstone. As she unfolded the events, Ecclestone was said to have become increasingly angry. It became apparent that he had had no idea of what had been going on. Foulston believed that the BRDC board had made a major tactical blunder. A 'change of control' clause in Ecclestone's contract with Silverstone allowed him to pull the Grand Prix if its management was in any way reconstructed or the company taken over without his approval. Foulston found she had Ecclestone's undivided attention as she set about negotiating in effect an option agreement: if the BRDC sold to her, the British Grand Prix would stay at Silverstone. But if it was sold to anyone else it would lose the Grand Prix.

While Ecclestone was incensed by what he had heard, it did nothing to diminish his insistence on a top-dollar deal. To secure the contract, Foulston had to offer a most attractive incentive: $10 million a year – $4 million more than he was getting from Silverstone – for a ten-year contract with an annual compound increase of ten per cent. The first payment would also fall due upon acquisition of Silverstone, not when the contract with Silverstone expired two years later, an incentive designed to encourage Ecclestone's further support to make it happen. Foulston left his office with a provisional agreement, which was known as the Number One Silverstone contract.

DKB believed that Ecclestone had, in fact, been made fully aware of events. As a BRDC member, he had been informed by letter in November, following the bid from John Lewis, that the board of directors had decided to consider a review of the options, including a possible restructuring – but it gave no hint of a merger that the board was apparently seeking as relayed by Foulston. DKB also believed that, beyond progress letters sent to members, which included Ecclestone, it had had no reason at that stage to seek his stamp of approval. Nothing had been formalised by the board or put before the members for their endorsement. Until that stage had been reached, everything was in the air. Nevertheless, Ecclestone would have interpreted the absence of his involvement as a personal snub by a clique of board members who continued to see him, despite all his achievements, as a second-hand-car dealer with too much money for his own good. He, in return, saw them as old school-tie fogies interested only in self-glory.

However, Foulston and her finance director, Rob Bain, believed that Lord Hesketh, the then president of the BRDC and the former Hesketh team owner, and DKB had another, more tactical reason for not going to Ecclestone. They were hoping that Foulston would agree to a merger with Silverstone to give them the whip hand in negotiating with Ecclestone the terms of the British Grand Prix contract. With such an alliance, who else could realistically stage it? Foulston had now regained the initiative. In January 1999 she received an invitation from Lord Hesketh for a meeting at his private office in London. Over tea she listened to a subtly worded overture which, in her mind, confirmed her and Bain's suspicions of the BRDC's strategy. Hesketh indicated that, rather than a messy takeover of Silverstone which, in his opinion, was unlikely to succeed, a merger between Brands Hatch and Silverstone would be to everyone's advantage, if, that is, she would accept a diminution of power. Foulston declined to be drawn and left the meeting an hour later, unimpressed by what she had heard. Lord Hesketh declined to comment on Foulston's account.

It was shortly followed by another invitation, this time from DKB to discuss her company's offer in more detail at Brands Hatch Leisure's offices in Cheapside, London. At this meeting reference was made by the DKB team to a merger based on an exchange of shares, which, it was understood by Foulston, would effectively give the BRDC majority control over the combined group. Hesketh would be chairman and Foulston would have operational control, appointments that were not proposed but inferred as being politically necessary if the deal was to work. Foulston, who had said little over her cup of tea with Hesketh, was now extremely direct – under no circumstances, she told them, would the BRDC get its hands on any Brands Hatch shares. Doubtless satisfied that they had done their homework and that the aggressively ambitious Foulston would respond favourably to the proposal, the bankers must have been left somewhat nonplussed by her response. Even her own bankers had been pressuring her into issuing shares to do a deal with Silverstone. But such an obvious move was not part of Foulston's personal plan.

With the review of options completed, on 23 April 1999, at the BRDC's annual general meeting, members were asked to give in-principle approval to the board of directors' recommendation that would bring about a restructuring of its assets and operations, which would be divided between the BRDC and a new company, Silverstone Circuits Group, in which members would receive 100 per cent of the issued shares, to run Silverstone Circuits Ltd and Silverstone Estates Ltd. The proposal, in effect, was intended to ring-fence the BRDC's key assets, including the Silverstone freehold, and at the same time restructure an out-of-date management in preparation for a sale or future flotation. In either event, with the Number One Silverstone contract in her briefcase, it would put Foulston in prime position. Brands Hatch Leisure supporters within the membership were urged to back the proposal, but, at the death, failed to do so, because, it was believed, they were uncomfortable with the complexity of the issue. The members voted two to one in favour, but short of the 75 per cent required under BRDC rules for the matter to go any further.

Undaunted, Foulston decided to go for her only option. If she couldn't get Silverstone, then she wanted the next best thing: the British Grand Prix contract. In early May she returned to Ecclestone to state her case. Once again she found that Ecclestone, long scornful of the Formula One facilities at Silverstone and its management, was ready to respond positively. Out of those talks came a second contract, known as the Brands Hatch Grand Prix contract: if the BRDC did not sell to Foulston, the British Grand Prix would be transferred to Brands Hatch in 2002 for six years with an option for a further five years. It would be worth $11 million a year to Ecclestone, the additional $1 million to cover the risk should Foulston need to switch the Grand Prix to Brands Hatch. This contract was intended, of course, to put greater pressure on the BRDC to sell to Foulston. The loss of the British Grand Prix would, at a stroke, cause the value of Silverstone to plummet. Who would want to buy Silverstone without its crown jewel?

Before the contract was signed, on 14 May 2000, and before the discussions from which it emerged had taken place with Foulston, Tommy Sopwith, the then chairman of the BRDC and Silverstone Circuits Ltd, and Denys Rohan, had gone to see Ecclestone in London to discuss the price he wanted for the race to remain at Silverstone. Ecclestone claims he made every effort to help them to retain the British Grand Prix. 'What I said to them was, "Next door [in an adjoining office] we keep all the contracts for all the circuits. Look at all the contracts and you can have the cheapest of any European circuit, whatever it is. Rub out the name on the contract and put your name in, and it's for the same price." He [Sopwith] said, "No, we can't do that. You'll have to take less." Then Nicola came along on the scene and made an offer even I couldn't refuse.'

The offer she put on the table was, said Sopwith, 'too rich for us'. He was adamantly opposed to selling Silverstone to Foulston, whom he saw as a ruthless, profit-driven entrepreneur. While discussing the future of Silverstone, he said: 'If she was listening to this conversation, she would tell me that I was a silly, blue-blazered old fart who didn't know what he was talking about.' Although some believed that Silverstone could have matched Foulston's offer by adopting a sharper commercial attitude, the annual compound percentage increase, at more than twice the rate of inflation, was seen as a risk too far. A downturn in Formula One's fortunes could, it was feared, put Silverstone in a significant negative position with a long-term contract round its neck.

Foulston's delight at getting the British Grand Prix was followed by the stark reality that Brands Hatch hadn't hosted a Formula Once race for 13 years, during which time circuit standards and spectator facilities had advanced enormously. She now had to set about raising the capital to fund a major redevelopment programme. The early cost, and this figure would escalate considerably, was estimated at £30 million, which the Royal Bank of Scotland agreed in a package deal. Foulston's plans included the remodelling of the Grand Prix and Indy circuits, new pits, a media complex, helipads and a 15,000-seat, 18-tier grandstand, together with landscaping, roadworks and parking.

Banging the publicity drum, Foulston was soon announcing the news that the FIA had approved the provisional design plans. With Ecclestone on her side, the FIA's blessing was never likely to prove a difficulty. Getting the necessary planning permission through in time posed the real problem. She had considerably less than two years in which to get the show up and running. Ecclestone, anticipating the problems she might face, included a standard penalty clause in the contract – if Brands Hatch was not ready in time, she would pay him a sum of $11 million, one year's fee. But, unbeknown to Ecclestone, none of this mattered to Foulston.

From the day she had begun talking to Rohan about a takeover of Silverstone some 12 months earlier, her central aim had been to get control of the British Grand Prix. It had never been part of her plan to deliver a Grand Prix at Brands Hatch, any more than if she had been successful in acquiring Silverstone, which she wanted purely for the market valuation of the Grand Prix, on which she planned to raise sufficient debt to modernise Brands Hatch and then sell the two circuits at a figure she had already calculated would enable her to retire and live in high style for the rest of her life.

She had seen what the stresses and strains of big business had done to her father, how all he had achieved had been wiped out by his early death. At the age of 20, even before she was appointed commercial director of Brands Hatch Leisure, Foulston had vowed to make her pile and retire by the age of 40, the age her father was when killed at Silverstone. She was determined to enjoy a better-quality life. It was for this reason that she had rejected the idea of what would have been in effect a reverse takeover, with BRDC members becoming shareholders: she would have needed their approval in order to sell. Only two trusted colleagues within Brands Hatch Leisure Plc knew of her real agenda in going for Silverstone and then the Grand Prix contract.

In June 1999, just one month after Ecclestone announced that Brands Hatch had been awarded the contract, Foulston was formally and secretly talking to Les Delano, a director of Octagon, the sports marketing and entertainment division of the New York-based InterPublic Group (IPG), one of the world's largest advertising and marketing communications groups, with an annual revenue that year of $4.56 billion. She had, in fact, started informal talks with Delano even while bids were being made for Silverstone at the beginning of the year. Octagon was an obvious first call. A positive relationship through the Octagon-owned Flammini World Superbike Championship, a round of which was staged at Brands Hatch, had already been established.

To Foulston's advantage, Delano – he took part in the Le Mans 24-Hour race in 1986–7 – was also a keen fan of motor sport, as were Frank Lowe, the founder of Octagon and shortly to be appointed its chairman and chief executive, and Phil Geier, the chairman of IPG. Selling Brands Hatch, which now offered the critical allure of the British Grand Prix, wouldn't prove to be the toughest sales pitch Foulston had ever made. The talks with Delano, after he had consulted with the IPG board, proved positive and, by September, the due diligence process began, with Brands Hatch Leisure making disclosures of all its operational activities, including all Formula One contracts, and the far from certain position of planning permission, without which the contract with Ecclestone would have been made null and void. This was the big obstacle Foulston had to overcome.

Exuding confidence, she insisted that the proposed redevelopment meant little more than a formality – an extension to existing planning permission, rather than a change of use. Her confidence was based on a local-plan designation called WK2, which encircles the boundary of Brands Hatch and associated buildings. Within that area, the planning authority of the local Sevenoaks District Council accepted and allowed motor sport, recreation and leisure activities, but subject to certain criteria governing noise, visual intrusion, Green Belt violation and vehicular access. In fact, Foulston's proposed plans fell foul of all of these conditions. Area Planning Officer, Mr Colin Smith, said a few months later: 'Brands Hatch's view is that they have WK2 designation and that means they can do anything associated with motor racing. Our view is that they can do anything related to motor racing but subject to all the controls that are in place through the local-plan policies. That is where the arguments will occur.' Due to the impact on the environment, and possible conflict with national planning policies, Smith believed it was highly likely that the Government would take the matter out of the hands of the council by calling it in for judgement, which would mean a public inquiry. 'Even with the best scenario,' added Smith, 'I think it will prove a very tight schedule for the work to be completed in time for a Grand Prix in 2002.'

However, in her talks with IPG, Foulston's precarious position was strengthened by a report issued by planning consultants engaged by Brands Hatch Leisure which stated that, in their opinion, planning permission would be eventually granted. In September, Brands Hatch Leisure submitted an application for outline planning permission to the local planning authority, which was done principally to demonstrate to IPG, who, somewhat naïvely, had accepted without question or analysis of the planning consultants' report, the extent of Brands Hatch Leisure's confidence in its success and its determined commitment to meet the deadline for the 2002 Grand Prix.

By 9 November the legal and technical process had been completed. By then Foulston had also taken care of another very important matter. The previous month she had gone to see Ecclestone once more, to avoid making the same calamitous mistake that the BRDC had made. Rather than risk his wrath by his finding out through a leak, she told him that she was selling Brands Hatch Leisure to Octagon. When he asked why, she explained that she needed the money to finance the hugely expensive modernisation of the circuit. Ecclestone accepted her explanation, unaware, like others, of her real agenda. With the legal and technical process complete, Foulston began to turn the screws to complete the deal within 30 days of the year end. It was for this reason that she had particularly targeted an American company, because of US business regulations which govern the acquisition of UK companies. They allow, for example, an initial 21-day deadline for the completion of an open offer for the acquisition of 90 per cent of the issued share capital, which suited Foulston's strategy perfectly.

Her determination to close the sale of Brands Hatch within 30 days of the year end was based on no more than an intuitive fear that the beginning of 2000 would see the start of a global economic downturn that would badly hit the share value of a small company like Brands Hatch Leisure and from which it would take months, if not years, to recover. On 10 November an offer to buy was issued, with closure to take place at 3 pm on 30 November. IPG in New York became focused on the legal and technical process, assuming that the commercial realities of the deal – not least the uncertainty of the planning permission – had been satisfactorily dealt with elsewhere within the company. When a lone voice raised certain doubts, Foulston threatened to pull out.

While these backstage negotiations had been going on, Foulston had been wearing another hat, publicly declaring that everything was on schedule for a British Grand Prix at Brands Hatch in 2002. 'It would be a first for me to sign a contract I couldn't deliver on,' she said. And of comments that the huge financial burden she was taking on would cripple the Brands Hatch Leisure Group with no guarantee of where the British Grand Prix would be staged after 2006, she said: 'People who hold that view tend not to be financial entrepreneurs. If anyone can source a lot of money, spend a lot of money, and make a lot of money, it is Brands Hatch Leisure.' But by early December 1999 it was no longer Foulston's problem. Octagon bought Brands Hatch Leisure for £120 million – at £5.46 a share based on net earnings forecast at £5.4 million before tax. It was an extremely good price, as it was based on the historic earnings of a Grand Prix whose future at Brands Hatch was far from certain. The takeover enriched Foulston by almost £50 million.

A month later she resigned for 'personal reasons' as chief executive, to be replaced by Rob Bain, formerly with Ernst & Young, who had joined Brands Hatch Leisure as financial director in 1998, two years after advising Foulston on its successful stock-market flotation. Foulston was able to walk away from the company because it seems that IPG had failed to notice that her contract allowed her to parachute in the event of a change of control. Her managing director, Richard Green, had a similar contract. He walked away with £1 million.

It wasn't until June 2000 – 13 months after Ecclestone had awarded Foulston the British Grand Prix contract and she had long gone – that Brands Hatch Leisure was finally in a position to submit a planning application for its redevelopment programme to Sevenoaks District Council, which went before its planning committee without the recommendation of the council's planning officers. Nevertheless, on 26 June, the committee voted 12–6 in favour. But by then the feared intervention of the Government, with all the time-consuming bureaucracy it would inevitably involve, took place. Three days earlier, on 23 June, the Department of Environment, Transport and Regions (DETR) had issued an Article 14 Directive, which removed the responsibility for the decision from the district council. The directive didn't necessarily mean that the Government would call the application in for judgement – Bain was confident it wouldn't – but that is precisely what happened two months later.

The sheer scale of the proposed development programme and its impact on the environment led to Secretary of State John Prescott deciding to call in the application on 8 September for a public inquiry, thanks in no small part, it was suspected, to an effective lobbying campaign by the BRDC – it allegedly included organising a protest petition to Sevenoaks District Council – whose directors were well aware it would scupper any hopes Brands Hatch Leisure realistically had of getting its circuit ready in time for 2002. Its last start date was, in fact, that December. Following pressure from Brands Hatch Leisure, it was agreed to fast-track the inquiry, set for 9 January 2001 and due to last three weeks. The DETR's decision was anticipated to be announced by the end of May at the earliest, a time when ministers were expected to be otherwise occupied in campaigning for a second term of government for the Labour Party. Assuming that timetable, it left Brands Hatch Leisure with little more than about 12 months to complete what they initially assessed would take two years – a build time it was claimed, with hopeless optimism, that could still be achieved by substantially increasing the labour force.

Observing Brands Hatch Leisure's acute discomfort from the sidelines, no doubt with a sense of some *schadenfreude*, were certain senior members of

Top: Ecclestone poses with his partner, Frederick Compton, and Compton's pre-war Studebaker.

Middle: Ecclestone begins to make his mark. He rented the forecourt, to the right, from Compton for his fledgling motorcycle business.

Left: The Compton & Ecclestone mobile workshop – one of the first of its kind.

Top: Ecclestone wearing the winner's laurels at Crystal Palace in 1949 or 1950, where he notched up one of his rare wins.

Bottom: A classic photo of Ecclestone burning up the track at Brands Hatch in 1951.

Top: Ready for the off. Notice the corrosive effect of the methanol-based fuel in the fuel tank.

Bottom left: Being shielded from the rain – a far cry from the umbrella-carrying models of later years – at Brands Hatch in 1952.

Bottom right: In his white leather cap, Ecclestone, in a Cooper, is ready to thrill the crowds at Brands Hatch in 1952.

Top left: Ecclestone in playful mood with Jennifer, Frederick Compton's daughter, and son Douglas (*top right*) on the bank of the River Cherwell, Oxford.

Bottom: The damaged chassis of Ecclestone's car following a collision with Bill Whitehouse at Brands Hatch in 1953.

ɔp: A Christmas motor sport function. (*Left to right*) Ivy and Bernie, Jimmy Oliver, ck Brabham and his wife Betty, and Frederick Compton and his wife Jean, in the id-fifties.

ɔttom: Ecclestone with Max Mosley at Kylami for the South African rand Prix in 1976.

Top: With adversary Jean-Marie Balestre, former President of FISA and the FIA.

Bottom: Max Mosley entertains Tony Blair, the future Prime Minister, at the British Grand Prix at Silverstone in 1996.

op: Ecclestone with his second wife, Slavica, and their daughters Tamara and Petra.

ottom: Max Mosley at the Monaco Grand Prix in Monte Carlo, May 2008, shortly efore winning a vote of confidence from the FIA.

Bernie Ecclestone at the Belgian Grand Prix in 1999.

Silverstone's BRDC. The tide of events was turning most favourably in their direction. It confirmed the opinion of those within the BRDC who had believed from the beginning that Foulston had been chasing an impossible deadline – one which, in line with her plans, had never existed – and that sooner or later Brands Hatch Leisure would be forced to try to strike a deal to stage the Grand Prix at Silverstone. Prior to Octagon's arrival on the scene, it had been Tommy Sopwith's opinion, though, that BRDC members were unlikely to agree. He said: 'It would be much more economic [for Brands Hatch Leisure] regardless of the rent ... but I would be surprised if our members would say yes.'

At that time he favoured a return to the negotiating table with Ecclestone to secure the Grand Prix at Silverstone. 'It would be, as our American cousins say, a whole new ball game [but] I would not underestimate the little man [Ecclestone]. We have a long way to go before we come out of the end of this one.' He believed that, as with everything else in Formula One, in the end it would all come down to money. He said: 'I think Bernie only wants one thing. Bernie wants to be richer than he is. I can't imagine anyone being richer than he is, but Bernie can.'

But the deadline was not actually as critical as the BRDC and others had thought. Ecclestone was so keen to help Foulston stage the British Grand Prix at Brands Hatch that he was prepared to postpone the contract a year, to 2003, a concession that would, in fact, prove unnecessary with Octagon's takeover of Brands Hatch Leisure and the arrival of Martin Brundle as Sopwith's successor as chairman of the BRDC and Jackie Stewart as its president. There emerged a fresh dynamic to find a way of resolving the situation to their mutual advantage.

In December 2000, a year after Octagon had purchased Brands Hatch Leisure, IPG's chairman and chief executive, Frank Lowe, Brundle and TAG McLaren boss Ron Dennis met for discussions that led to a solution that went far beyond merely leasing Silverstone once a year for the British Grand Prix: the BRDC would grant Octagon a lease to manage the Silverstone circuit for 15 years. Such an arrangement was made possible by the intervention of Ecclestone, who had entered the arena to broker the talks between the two parties. He had taken a risk in backing Foulston and he didn't want to lose face by it appearing that a deal with Silverstone had come about by chance. He agreed to triple the five-year Grand Prix agreement to justify the massive investment that Octagon proposed to make in Silverstone, including the construction of a new pits complex, improving spectator facilities and major improvements to access roads, as a core part of a lease contract.

An essential element of the contract was Ecclestone's insistence that IPG underwrote the massive costs involved. It was rapidly conveyed to Phil Geier, the chairman of InterPublic, in New York, who agreed that IPG would carry the risk. Les Delano flew to London from New York with Geier's guarantee. Octagon's estimated expenditure, in addition to increased development costs estimated at that time at more than $20 million, included an annual lease payment to the BRDC of £5 million, and an annual fee to Ecclestone of $10 million. To facilitate the deal, both the BRDC and Ecclestone agreed to receive staggered payments for the first five years.

To claw back its costs – at one stage Octagon wanted a 25-year lease to improve the level of projected returns – it was speculatively claimed that it planned to stage high-profile events from conferences to pop concerts. But a spokeswoman in New York insisted that only motor sport events would take place at Silverstone. She said: 'The purpose of this transaction from the Octagon standpoint was to be able to combine all commercial activities of Silverstone with those of the BHL group, not simply to promote the British Grand Prix. The combination of BHL and Silverstone professional management, and the marketing power of Octagon as well as the resulting synergy benefits, make this an attractive prospect for Octagon. We have no plans to extend operations beyond motor sports-related activities.'

There was some doubt, though, that, given the aggregate costs it faced, Octagon was likely to show a profit on such events alone. 'Even when we were paying Ecclestone £4 million for the Grand Prix we weren't covering our costs,' said a senior BRDC member, although that, it was countered, was because some of its management was less than efficient. More credibly, it was believed that the company got itself into an inevitably high-spending situation because it had relied on Nicola Foulston's reassurances. 'It took her word at face value over the development costs and the ease with which it would get the necessary planning permission,' said the BRDC member. 'Once it got in so deep, there was no turning back.' The Octagon spokeswoman declined to respond to questions on this claim.

Certainly the new regime, which took over Silverstone Circuits Ltd as part of the lease deal, introduced a new and profitable commercial phase for the BRDC as property landlords. It agreed a deal with Ford to develop 4000 square feet of its new technology park to accommodate the transfer of its Jaguar team from Milton Keynes and its Cosworth operation from Northampton, in a multi-million-pound development to include a full-sized wind tunnel, a turn of considerable good fortune for Silverstone, which ironically came about through Foulston's personal ambitions.

It concluded a remarkable episode in British motor sport, a win-win situation for Silverstone – which will continue to stage the British Grand Prix thanks to a 'blue-chip' tenant who will finance its transformation into one of the best circuits in Europe – and Nicola Foulston, who disappeared into the sunset with a king's ransom to finance her lifelong departure from the corporate rat race. And, at the age of 33, seven years ahead of her 'retirement' deadline.

The extraordinary degree to which organisers and circuit owners feared Ecclestone, and which exists in more moderate form to this day, is indicated by an incident involving his helicopter at Silverstone in the mid-eighties. With his pilot at the controls, it landed in a prohibited area and demolished a number of marquees, causing damage to cars, as well as slight injuries, it was claimed, to a number of people.

Circuit manager Chris Kelf arrived on the scene and 'created merry hell'. Ecclestone was unapologetic. 'His attitude was: "I'm Bernie Ecclestone, I'll put my helicopter down where I want to,"' said Kelf. The incident was reported to the UK's Civil Aviation Authority, responsible for investigating such incidents and their prosecution, by air-traffic controllers who were on duty at Silverstone to supervise the landing of light aircraft. To Kelf's relief – 'it was all brushed over because it was Bernie' – there was no official inquiry. It would have almost certainly attracted the interest of the media and caused embarrassment to Ecclestone, which, as Kelf quickly discovered, was the last thing that the Silverstone management wanted.

In fact, because of their concern over the harm it might cause to their relationship with Ecclestone, it was Kelf who found himself in trouble – 'the management had a go at me' – for daring to rebuke Ecclestone. As for the damage to the cars and the injuries to the members of the public – 'it was nothing dramatic' – it was 'all quietly sorted out'.

According to Ecclestone, it was his chequebook that sorted it out after the helicopter hire company refused to pay for the damage caused to cars by wheels sent spinning from a display overturned by the helicopter's downdraught. Max Mosley, who was also on board the helicopter, said: 'The wheels were rolling everywhere. A canopy was also blown over, but no people were injured.' Ecclestone insisted that he was suitably apologetic. 'I said at the time, "I am terribly sorry [but] I am not the pilot. You should speak to the pilot." I said to the pilot, "Go and sort this out with him [Kelf]."' He agreed to pay the bill to prove that he was not the kind of person who believed that he could do what he liked. 'That is not my style.'

11

THE BEGINNING OF BERNIE'S TELEVISION RIGHTS STRANGLEHOLD

The commercialisation of Formula One began the day when Jim Clark's Lotus 49 competed in a race in the red, white and gold livery colours of a cigarette brand, Gold Leaf, with a sailor's head logo on its sides. The date was 20 January 1968, and the event was the Lady Wigram Trophy race, the third round of the New Zealand/Australia Tasman series, at Wigram, New Zealand. The eyebrow-raising arrival of Clark's car in the paddock was the result of months of secret negotiations with tobacco manufacturers Imperial Tobacco.

The ever-controversial boss of Team Lotus, Colin Chapman, was aware that the abandonment of the traditional British racing green would incur the singular displeasure of the bewhiskered blazer-and-flannel traditionalists within and without the FIA, who believed it an inviolable, if unspoken, rule that cars ran in their traditional national colours – red for Italy, blue for France and silver for Germany. It was a hallowed custom that Chapman was prepared to sweep aside, happy to risk the opprobrium of the sport's rulers for the comforting compensation of a three-year contract worth £100,000, a significant contribution to annual running costs estimated in those days at about £90,000.

Track officials at Wigram at first refused to allow the Lotus on to the track, relenting only at the last minute when Chapman defiantly stood his ground. The wily team boss had successfully gambled that the more complaisant organisers of a relatively minor series on the other side of the world, unlike their counterparts in Europe, were far less likely to persist to the point of disqualifying such a crowd-pulling entrant from the race, which, incidentally, Clark went on to win. That summer, in England, Chapman tested the water further by entering the same car, this time driven by Graham Hill, in the non-championship Race of Champions at Brands Hatch. On this occasion it provoked a more powerful protest, although not from the sanctioning authority, Britain's Royal Automobile Club, but from a senior executive of ITV, a major British commercial television company. He phoned Chapman during the second practice session to warn him unless the sailor's head logo was covered, the broadcasting of the race would be cancelled. Chapman backed down. He issued instructions for the logo to be taped over, which made little difference anyway. Given the poor quality of television coverage at that time, it could hardly be seen.

But the die had been cast. Formula One's ruling bodies – from the FIA to the national motoring organisations – were being forced to accept that a significant groundshift was taking place, no matter how much it might be seen by some to demean a beloved gentlemanly ethos which abhorred the thought of being corrupted by commercial considerations. By the following March, in the first Grand Prix of the 1969 season, Gold Leaf Team Lotus, with the FIA's approval, officially appeared on the grid at Kyalami, South Africa. In 1970, at the Spanish Grand Prix, another major sponsor arrived on the grid – Yardley, the perfumery division of British American Tobacco, who, in return for painting BRM's cars in its pink livery, agreed to pay the team boss, Louis Stanley, an estimated £50,000 over two years.

For the first time commercial sponsorship started to mean more than Dunlop and Esso meeting the cost of tyres, oil and fuel, or the meagre salaries of the better-known drivers. The days when the manufacturers of spark plugs and brakes supplied their products free of charge and demanded little in return were effectively over. Drivers' overalls, bedecked with advertisers' patches, became such a premium advertising 'billboard' that the ceremony of placing a laurel wreath over a driver's shoulders was stopped because it obscured company logos. The likes of Niki Lauda, whose arrival at Ferrari in 1974 coincided with an explosion in sponsorship budgets, was among the first to enjoy the mega-bucks. In addition to a £163,000 retainer from Ferrari, personal sponsorship deals with ten international companies increased his income by a further £379,000, a colossal sum in those days.

Sponsors' money increasingly influenced which team a top driver would join, and, with it, came hard-nosed bargaining and conflict not seen in the days when a driver was happy to sign for a team that would provide him with little more than the best car it could produce. Even the RAC, by 1973, was willing to take the sponsors' shilling, agreeing to change the name of the British Grand Prix, a title which it owned, to the John Player Grand Prix. The company setting the pace was the American tobacco giant Philip Morris, which, through its Marlboro brand, moved into Formula One in 1972, in a two-year deal with BRM worth in excess of £100,000, plus win bonuses and funding for marketing projects.

To extract maximum publicity, Marlboro flew 100 journalists, all expenses paid, to its European headquarters in Geneva, and then, in a chartered Air France jet, to the Circuit Paul Ricard in southern France – the previous year the company had agreed to fund a new track safety system in return for an exclusive ten-year contract on its advertising panels – for the association to be formally announced. In the centre of the track Englishman Peter Gethin, the winner of the 1971 Grand Prix at Monza, emerged in the new Marlboro-BRM car from a giant mock-up Marlboro cigarette pack. It made the front page of the motoring press throughout Europe.

There were press parties at every Grand Prix; tobacco industry fat cats who were wined and dined on gourmet food before meeting the drivers and touching the cars; tall Scandinavian girls, in skintight suits, travelled with the team to every race; full-sized replicas of the Marlboro-BRM cars were made for display in airports, hotel lobbies and town squares; drivers attired off-track in livery-colour blazers and white turtle-neck jumpers; more than a million stickers featuring the World Championship team logo and the national flag of each Grand Prix event were produced to become collectors' items. When the team, accompanied by a convoy of trucks, passed through towns and cities, it was like a travelling circus. At one Monaco Grand Prix, Marlboro entertained 300 VIP and celebrity guests by hiring a 300-foot yacht, which became so overcrowded that it began to sway on its moorings. Marlboro was 'buying' the Formula One racing scene.

Although the Marlboro promotion was costing $3 million a year by 1973, Philip Morris saw it as a smart investment giving a high-dollar return. Market research was demonstrating that the brand recall of the Marlboro presence was many times that achieved with comparatively larger advertising budgets, and governments with anti-tobacco laws weren't scrutinising too closely large popular events promoting their national heroes. There was one team boss, though, who looked down on it all with the utmost disdain – the legendary Enzo Ferrari.

Senior Marlboro management drove to Ferrari's headquarters at Maranello, Italy, in the hope of securing his signature on a major sponsorship contract. 'Il Commendatore' received them warmly, provided a splendid lunch, followed by a tour of his private racetrack on land opposite the Ferrari factory, and then signalled the end of the meeting by stating that as long as he lived Ferrari would remain the Italian red and not be decorated in the colours of some 'commercial entity'. He believed that sponsorship put the teams under too much pressure to a degree that risked drivers' lives. Later, in 1981, seven years before he died at the age of 90, Ferrari accused constructors of putting 'illegal' pressure on a race starter during the Belgian Grand Prix at Zolder, which allegedly led to a pit-lane accident and the death of a mechanic. It caused a strike by drivers, who ignored team orders to get into their cars. Commented Ferrari: 'If cars were still painted in their national colours instead of the colours of sponsoring companies, then constructors ... would not say: "I have 60 men to employ and major sponsorship to justify." I pay my drivers, they do what I tell them. Racing should never have been allowed to get this far.'[1]

But, of course, it had. Sponsorship, through the newspaper coverage it generated, was succeeding in boosting spectactor figures considerably. By 1977 a record number of 1,435,000 spectators – the average gate figure was 84,411 – were attending Formula One Grands Prix. While the printed media had begun to cover Formula One – in Britain the *Daily Express* was first off the mark in giving fuller coverage of Formula One to be quickly followed in 1973 by the *Daily Mirror*, at that time Britain's biggest-selling daily newspaper – the UK's two television companies, the commercial ITV and the state-subsidised BBC, remained firmly opposed to being used as a free marketing medium. The previous year the BBC took particular exception to stickers promoting condoms on the Surtees cars at the Race of Champions at Brands Hatch. Outraged, the BBC insisted the stickers be removed or coverage of the race would be cancelled. Surtees, supported by the FOCA, stood firm. The BBC cancelled its coverage. In days before the mega-bucks television deals, the teams weren't unduly concerned: the sponsors were bankrolling large chunks of the teams' running costs; the two major television companies weren't paying a penny.

The increase in public interest in Britain had been aroused by the clash between Malboro McLaren's James Hunt and Ferrari's Niki Lauda for the 1976 World Championship title. So much so that the BBC and ITV, who had refused to cover the earlier rounds due to the level of tobacco sponsorship, were forced to review their head-in-the-sand policy. Both agreed to give it some coverage, but even then the best effort was the BBC's 20-minute clip of edited highlights. As it turned out, the race was something of an anticlimax. Lauda, who hadn't long recovered from his near-fatal injuries at the Nurburgring, withdrew after two laps because of a monsoon-like downpour, leaving Hunt to finish fourth and collect four points – giving him 69 to Lauda's 68 – and the World Championship title. However, the interest aroused by the race persuaded the BBC that it should reconsider its policy. In 1977 it began giving live coverage of Formula One races, and the following year the first Grand Prix programme appeared, a pilot that remained on air for 19 years. Formula One, with all its gaudy, vulgar sponsorship, had become mainstream television.

Hunt was a natural for the media. A good-looking, 29-year-old former public schoolboy, whose social life saw him featuring as frequently in the gossip columns as the sports pages, his contest with Lauda had the British newspapers arousing patriotic passions in every reader. Lured from the cash-strapped Hesketh team by the Marlboro chequebook towards the end of the previous season after Emerson Fittipaldi suddenly decided to move to the Brazilian team Copersucar, he was the right driver at the right time. It was something that Ecclestone recognised, too. He offered Hunt $1 million for a one-year contract, at that time the biggest deal ever offered to a world champion. Ecclestone planned to set up a company to promote and market Hunt, which, in his words, would 'turn him into a very big cult figure'.[2]

To Ecclestone's great disappointment – 'he's a very silly boy' – Hunt refused the offer on the advice of his brother, also his accountant and agent, who had successfully negotiated three major advertising contracts. He believed that the figure fell some way short of his younger brother's true earning potential. It would also have fallen foul of his contract with Marlboro McLaren, with whom he went on to win nine of his ten Grands Prix before retiring midway through the 1979 season, after 18 months with the Wolf team. Five years later Ecclestone, still convinced of Hunt's worth to Formula One in the publicity it would generate, offered the former world champion a staggering £2.5 million to make a Grand Prix comeback. Once again Hunt refused, claiming he saw no point in risking his neck for money he didn't need. Whatever his wealth, tragically he would not enjoy it for long. His lifestyle became increasingly intemperate and, in 1993 at the age of 46, he died of a heart attack.

In less than a decade Formula One, in profile, wealth and structure, had undergone enormous changes. With television's door gradually creaking open, Ecclestone, having strong-armed television rights from organisers who, for the most part, had no idea of their potential, while others were glad to give them away simply for the promotional value of television coverage, was ready to storm through it. In October 1977 he described television as 'the big key' to the future of Formula One and has since been credited as the one who had the foresight to see the potential riches that television coverage could offer. But the kudos is misplaced.

As early as 1973 another, no less sharp than Ecclestone, had already spotted the promise of television. He was American sports management agency boss Mark McCormack, then in his early forties, who had been hugely successful in signing up top US golfers – in the same way that Ecclestone would later represent the teams – which enabled him to negotiate highly lucrative deals with commercial television stations. Hoping to establish a similarly enterprise in

Formula One, he made a presentation to senior management at the Lausanne headquarters of Philip Morris, suggesting a forging of resources and expertise. The company turned down McCormack's proposal because it believed it was big enough to go it alone. Later, behind the scenes, senior executives scuppered his approach to the Automobile Club de Monaco, the organisers of the Monaco Grand Prix and the Monte Carlo Rally, whose promotional interests McCormack was keen to handle. Philip Morris blocked the move because it saw the Monaco Grand Prix as a key promotional event – one year it flew the entire US board to the event at a cost of more than $200,000 – and feared that McCormack's control would soon see sponsorship costs rocket. Organisers and promoters in Formula One came to know this same fear.

McCormack, who had represented Graham Hill and Jackie Stewart – his fee to Hill was 50 per cent – had been unsuccessful because, unlike Ecclestone, he had no control over the teams and, consequently, no power to dictate terms to the organisers and the sponsors. But it was McCormack's success in exploiting television coverage of golf in the US, and his efforts to launch a similar promotional strategy in Formula One, that had alerted Marlboro to what television coverage had to offer. McCormack's enterprise had not gone unnoticed by Ecclestone, the opportunist extraordinaire. During the late seventies he took it as his own to begin the creation of his vast riches.

Ecclestone's approach in the early days to the selling of television rights negotiated from organisers was piecemeal. That the commercial potential of television was beginning to emerge in mainland Europe was evidenced by the fact that coverage of the Monaco Grand Prix in 1976, for example, was seriously threatened because the cost per camera had escalated beyond what the French television company believed the race was worth. Due to similar demands elsewhere, Eurovision, the trading arm of the Geneva-based European Broadcasting Union (EBU), which represented the negotiating interests of public-service broadcasters, was said to have discouraged television companies from broadcasting live any of the Grands Prix during the 1979 season.

Ecclestone averted any direct confrontation by joining the club. He commissioned a small television production company to provide video coverage, the rights of which he sold on an ad hoc basis through Eurovision. It was not an ideal arrangement to Ecclestone: profits that he could be enjoying were going elsewhere. He by far preferred the hands-on control of an in-house operation. It led to the formation of his own production company – FOCA TV, which consisted of three cameramen, an editor and their dog. In 1982, a little more than 12 months after the FOCA and the FIA had signed the Concorde Agreement, which granted the constructors the television rights, he signed a three-year contract with the EBU to market coverage of Formula One. (It was, incidentally, an EBU official who alerted Ecclestone to the unsightly display of advertising display panels and signage at Formula One races. He resolved the problem during his negotiations with organisers by claiming the rights, which he passed on to the lucrative benefit of AllSport Management.) In 1982 International Sportsworld Communicators (ISC) was formed by Ecclestone to market the television rights of non-Formula One events. Hired to market these rights, and also appointed as a director of the company, was an Argentinian called Alejandro Ignacio Deffis-Whittaker, who had been in charge of Marlboro's television activities. He had moved from the advertising industry in his home country to work with Marlboro in Spain and London, where, as part of the international sports promotion group, he specialised in organising the strategic positioning of racetrack banners and negotiating with television crews to ensure maximum coverage.

According to his successor, Deffis-Whittaker 'did a pretty good job at raising the profile and revenue'. It seems he did too well. On a small salary but with a big commission on sales, he enjoyed success that was said to have led to a dispute with Ecclestone over money allegedly due to him, and, finally, his departure. His successor was Phil Lines, who had been head of group marketing at a leading television news agency, later acquired by Reuters. He had also played an executive role at an international sports marketing agency selling commercial and television rights to the World Cup and Olympics. But when he arrived for his first day at his new employer's offices in Knightsbridge, Lines realised that he was on a new learning curve.

'I remember walking into Princes Gate at about 9.25 am, with Bernie standing there with his watch, saying: "It's a 9 o'clock start." From that moment on, I knew this was not like anywhere else, where you basically were judged on your results and what you achieved. It was very obvious that everything revolved around Bernie and evolved from Bernie. He had a group of rather sycophantic people who had been there for a number of years who didn't move without Bernie saying move. Unfortunately, that for me created problems, in that everything went through Bernie and, of course, it was far too much, far too much, for any one person to be able to handle. In a normal company you would have a structure with 'this would be your responsibility, this would be your responsibility', [but] with ISC everything went through to Bernie and sat on his desk, and unless you got a decision out of Bernie you were stuck. I found that very frustrating. If you wanted to do a deal whereby you wanted to sell some Formula One archive film to one of the Formula One sponsors, you could negotiate a price and it could be agreed, but it would have to go to Bernie for his approval. You constantly had people who wanted to do deals but you couldn't [complete them].'

Eight months later an exasperated Lines decided to quit. 'I went to see Bernie and said that it was not the way I could work. He said goodbye. I was Bernie's adviser on a day-to-day basis on television matters, stretching from some production-related issues through to commercial sales, including marshalling and keeping out renegade cameramen. In terms of man management, Bernie is not the sort who sits down with you and says, "How do you feel, how's it all going?" You would sometimes be invited down to his favourite pub, but you would always be part of the entourage. The pub was round the back of Princes Gate. You would always end up listening to Bernie. It's his show. The only people who were there by the time I left were accountants and lawyers.'

Lines worked for a brief spell as an independent consultant before rejoining his former company. In the meantime, though, he did some work for Ecclestone, which remained unpaid. It was settled after he received a phone call from his former boss, who wanted to know whether his new job came with a company car. Told that it did, Ecclestone enquired about his wife's mode of transport, explaining: 'I've got this Alfa Romeo sitting outside. Come and get it, it's yours.' Said Lines: 'It was instead of paying my fee, which was about £2000. The Alfa Romeo was certainly worth a good deal more.'

By 1985 FOCA TV had expanded considerably, in size and revenue. It now had a full-blown production team broadcasting Formula One, through the EBU, to an audience of more than one billion in 95 countries, according to a statement issued by the FOCA. Television was, said Ecclestone, 'a vital element of the continued commercial success of the sport'. That year he renewed the contract with the EBU for a further five years, which would gross a total of 11.2 million Swiss francs (£3.55 million) in the 32 countries in which the EBU had territorial rights, although in 1990 the total television rights revenue was about $3.3 million. But that was small beer compared with the riches to come, thanks to the emergence of privately owned commercial television stations, and two events that took place in 1987.

The first, in February, was his appointment as vice-president of the FIA's promotional affairs. It was made by Balestre, whose authority had been made complete the previous year by his appointment as president of the FIA, an office he now held in addition to the presidency of the FISA. The newly created title was assigned to Ecclestone to mark the FIA's gratitude for the money his marketing efforts were adding to its financial well-being. That, at least, was the official version. The reality was that by bringing Ecclestone into the establishment Balestre hoped to neutralise him.

The person who put the thought in Balestre's head was Max Mosley, who had recently been appointed president of the FIA's Manufacturers' Commission, responsible for technical, sporting and off-road sub-commissions.

The circumstances came about after he had succeeded, against all the odds, in persuading the Commission to support Balestre in his decision to ban a Peugeot group B rally car, which led to the company suing Balestre for tens of millions of francs, an action which it eventually lost on appeal. This news, delivered personally to Balestre in the offices of the French motor sport organisation, the Fédération Française du Sport Automobile, in Rue du Longchamps, Paris, where he had been waiting on tenterhooks, was received with unbridled joy expressed in a full Gallic embrace.

In this cordial atmosphere Balestre began to confide in Mosley about the 'worries' that he had about Ecclestone. The principal cause of his anxiety was the fear that Ecclestone and the teams might break away from the FIA to set up a rival series. There existed no contract between the FIA and the FOCA to legally prohibit such a split. Balestre, knowing Mosley's closeness to Ecclestone, sought his advice. Mosley suggested that he might copy the practice deployed by the English establishment down the ages when it wanted to quieten a revolutionary – make him a member of the establishment. The idea clearly attracted Balestre. Thus, it wasn't long before a beaming Balestre announced the appointment of a new FIA establishment figure to look after its promotional affairs – the ultimate poacher turned gamekeeper. But there were many who were far from pleased by the news. They feared that too much power was being put into Ecclestone's hands. His new role gave him executive authority not only in Formula One but in all motor sports authorised by the FIA, which, in the latter, would be exercised by ISC to their considerable financial detriment.

The second event took place in September – Ecclestone's recruitment of a 35-year-old Swiss, Christian Vogt, a highly experienced media consultant, who had been handling the TV rights outside of Europe for the Union of European Football Associations (UEFA), the Fédération Internationale de Football Association (FIFA) and the International Amateur Athletics Association (IAAF). Ecclestone phoned Vogt to arrange a breakfast meeting at the Sheraton Park Tower Hotel, near his luxurious offices in Knightsbridge. With a considerably expanded portfolio of television rights to market thanks to his new appointment, Ecclestone was very much in need of someone of Vogt's skills. By their last cup of coffee the terms of Vogt's employment had been agreed. Vogt was under no illusions about working for Ecclestone. He knew of his reputation as a ruthless taskmaster but he was ambitious for the challenge and financial rewards that his new boss had put before him.

While he also oversaw the marketing of non-Formula One events through ISC, Vogt was responsible for increasing the earnings potential of Formula One television rights. It was the emergence of privately owned commercial television companies in the mid-eighties that caught his imagination, which inspired a radical change in the television marketing of Formula One. He suggested to Ecclestone a new route. Instead of going through the one-shop market of the EBU, which set broadcasting fees, he proposed that Ecclestone, in negotiating terms with a host broadcaster, should also acquire the exclusive rights to sell its coverage to commercial broadcasters in other countries. At first, said Vogt, Ecclestone was sceptical. 'It took quite a while to convince Bernie to do that, because it was a high risk.'

He added: 'First of all, going country by country meant a lot of hard work, and nobody was doing it in those days. Nobody could do any TV sports deal without going through the EBU. If it had failed, sure, we could have gone back to the EBU, but they would have had us by the curlies [in future negotiations].' But it turned out to be the right idea at the right time. Vogt set up a round of secret discussions, first with Canale 5 in Italy, which was then owned by Silvio Berlusconi, followed by TF1 in France and the biggest independent television company in Germany, RTL.

'It was very attractive for them to have Formula One, but the risk was that we were going with people who didn't necessarily have the exposure or geographical coverage that was needed in these territories. The advantage was that as we were all starting together, so to speak, they did a proper job. Even so, it was a big gamble. For many people it was a stupid thing to do: why spend two years working on all these countries individually, when you could do one contract [with the EBU] and be happy?' The answer, of course, lay in the vastly more profitable deals that could be negotiated free of the EBU's constraints. Berlusconi, for example, paid an estimated $1 million a race, according to a senior EBU official.

The freedom of negotiation also enabled Vogt to shrewdly insist on two contractual clauses that were essential in ensuring the most effective coverage: television companies not only had to take an entire season's races but broadcast them live. 'That was a key issue. The other one was that they had to do live qualifying and post-race reports. If you look at the old EBU deals, there was absolutely no commitment. The public-service broadcasters went on air when they felt like it. They would stage Monza live but not put on the next Grand Prix. It didn't do a thing for Formula One. It was a joke to come in whenever they wanted to. My idea was to squeeze the lemon as much as it could be squeezed, that they can't just put the races on when it suited them, that they had to do it live, that they had to have pre-race programmes and all that.'

When word reached the EBU, it was believed the breakaway was doomed to fail, that Ecclestone could not succeed against the collective marketing power it represented. Press spokesman Jean-Pierre Julien said: 'At that time we didn't believe it would work. Of course, since then we have seen that it was possible.' In fact, its success was said to have been the commercial turning point for Berlusconi's Canale 5, which was given the exclusive contract to screen the Italian Grands Prix at both Monza and Imola. Public-service broadcasters, aware that their bargaining strength no longer lay in membership of the EBU, began negotiating with FOCA TV.

The EBU's monopoly on the TV rights marketing of Formula One was over, and, in Europe alone, opened up a potential audience of nearly 400 million to Ecclestone. The air-time of Formula One, estimated Vogt, was doubled. Multiplied by the number of viewers, it meant that Ecclestone was able to increase by 'about tenfold' the sum he had been receiving through the EBU. 'We weren't in a hurry,' he said. 'The deals were done in a top-secret way... I mean, it was very competitive ... we made it competitive, because we played one off against the other.' The annual accumulative global television viewing figures increased from 17 billion under the EBU to 26 billion.

Vogt remained with Ecclestone for five years. The split was principally caused, of course, by money – or, as Vogt diplomatically put it, 'different interpretations of our contract'. Nevertheless, Vogt, who later became involved with Milan-based Media Partners International to launch a breakaway European football Super League, enjoyed his time with Ecclestone. 'It was very enriching. It was a very busy time. It was like a war.' He also learned to close his ears to much of his employer's dealings, which he declined to discuss. 'Even if you listen, you forget about it. You don't ask too many questions of yourself inside, either.'

Ecclestone's appointment as the FIA's vice-president of promotional affairs was received with some trepidation by the organisers of non-Formula One events. To give him their commercial rights, they complained, was effectively to surrender their roles as organisers. Ecclestone was characteristically contemptuous of their criticism, brushing it aside as coming from 'lots of people... frightened that they will lose power they think they have but probably don't have, anyway'.

His comment was, in particular, a pointed reference to the Automobile Club de l'Ouest (ACO), the organisers of the Le Mans 24-Hour race, who since 1982 had owned the trademark of the high-profile race, and had enjoyed considerable financial benefits gained from sponsorship and television rights, as well as the not insignificant track signage and off-track trade, all of which, by courtesy of Balestre's authority, had now been assigned to the control of Ecclestone. When the news of his appointment was announced, the ACO issued a statement in which it refused to surrender its television rights to the FISA's 'chosen one'. It added: 'To accept such a situation would be tantamount to the ACO resigning its role as organiser.'[3]

Over the next three years an acrimonious battle ensued between the FISA and the ACO, with the Le Mans race under almost constant threat. French politicians came to the defence of the ACO's stand but to no avail. The club finally capitulated and rescinded its claims to television rights in 1990, but, as part of a bitterly fought agreement, was guaranteed the World Championship status of Le Mans for the following five years. Two years later, however, in October 1992, the ACO was back in court, claiming breach of contract. The FISA, it claimed, had failed to field a minimum of 50 cars – it had fallen as low as 28 – and had not provided, as their contract stipulated, TV coverage at least equal to that which had been achieved by the organisers. From being covered by 41 channels in 26 countries, which had generated an income of £600,000, coverage had dropped to four countries, with no fixed contracts, and no live coverage at all in France, claimed the organisers.

A court in Paris agreed that the FISA had not met its contractual obligations in respect of television coverage and awarded the ACO a payment of damages and interest totalling 1.65 million francs for loss of television rights revenue. Both the ACO and the FIA appealed against the judgement, the former arguing that the damages weren't enough and the latter against the judgement itself. In November 1993 a court in Paris ruled in favour of the ACO, almost doubling the earlier award to three million francs. In February 1996 the FIA lodged a final, and unsuccessful, appeal. It brought to an end, at least locally, a conflict that confirmed in many people's minds the view that Ecclestone was using his new authority to ensure that air-time scheduled for motor sport by television programme planners was reduced to the benefit of Formula One. It was a charge, of course, that Ecclestone vehemently denied. So did Vogt, adding that his best efforts failed to attract the interests of television to these championships due to a lack of public interest.

All the same, Ecclestone's efforts in promoting other formulae seemed to enjoy a singular lack of success. It was with Formula One in mind that experienced Bernie-watchers believed that, shortly after his appointment as vice-president of promotional affairs, he attempted to launch a new series, the Production Car World Championship. It had, of course, the support of the accommodating Balestre, who, at an FISA plenary conference in October 1987, promised the series would be as spectacular as NASCAR-style stockcar racing. It was supported with equal enthusiasm by Ecclestone's other principal ally, Max Mosley, a gesture which now had particular significance.

Eleven months earlier Mosley had been elected in rather undemocratic circumstances to the presidency of the FIA's influential Manufacturers' Commission, which transparently demonstrates the autocracy of Balestre and his alliance with Ecclestone, to succeed Frenchman Philippe Schmitz. Mosley, in fact, had been out of motor sport since the end of 1982 to try his hand at politics. During 1983–4 he had worked assiduously for the Conservative

Party, particularly in the Westminster North constituency, with the aim of being adopted as a Conservative candidate. He abandoned his political aspirations after claiming to be totally unimpressed by the calibre of senior party officials. He also became convinced that the legacy of his father's name would be seen by selection committees as too great a handicap, despite an opinion to the contrary of former Prime Minister Harold Macmillan, given during a late-night conversation at Chatsworth, the Derbyshire country home of Mosley's uncle and aunt, the Duke and Duchess of Devonshire, a few years before his death in 1986.

All the while, Mosley had maintained contact with Ecclestone and, by 1986, decided to return to the Formula One fold. As Ecclestone appreciated, Mosley's skills were in the politics of persuasion, and that it was within the FIA that they could be most effectively exercised. He approached Balestre, who agreed that the Manufacturers' Commission, with Schmitz's three-year term about to come to an end, provided as good an opening as any. The votes of the Commission members were cast overwhelmingly in favour of Schmitz being re-elected, with Mosley coming last out of the nominations. Totally ignoring the wishes of the manufacturers, Balestre proposed at a meeting of the World Motor Sport Council, responsible for approving the Commission's vote, that it should be rejected in favour of Mosley. The council's compliant delegates obligingly concurred. But the manufacturers had yet to swallow a further humiliation.

In agreeing to stand for the position, Mosley made it clear that he would require a 'very substantial salary'. That, replied Balestre, would not be a problem. He would simply get each of the manufacturers to pay a fee. It was something, he said, he was willing to do as long as the money went into the FIA, which would retain half of it. It was a move that was met with some resistance by the manufacturers, until Mosley managed to persuade them that, with him at the helm, the Commission would be much more effective. As the official link between the FISA and the manufacturers, Mosley was now in a perfect position to enlist their goodwill, which was vital if Ecclestone's plan was to succeed.

Ecclestone claimed that Procar, as it came to be known, a series for unsponsored silhouette saloons scheduled to start in 1989, was just what the manufacturers needed to test new technology. It would, he said, be structured around strong manufacturer involvement featuring top drivers in 50-minute race slots in between Grand Prix weekends. It would be blitzed by television and newspaper coverage. But manufacturers' suspicions were raised by the proposed rules. Cars had to be based on Group A shapes, weigh 750 kilograms and be powered by 3.5-litre Formula One engines or 2.8-litre turbo engines. The regulations would generally follow Formula One with a similar governing protocol. Tailor-made, in fact, for Formula One racing at a time when the manufacturers' engines were much needed. Renault had withdrawn from Formula One at the end of 1986, albeit temporarily, followed a year later by the more long-term exit of BMW, which had supplied Ecclestone's Brabham team.

At a press conference poorly attended by the media, Mosley claimed that 12 manufacturers had agreed to take part, although, when asked to name them, he declined, claiming they wanted to make their own announcements.[4] The announcements never came. In fact, according to Ecclestone, six out of seven manufacturers had given verbal support at a meeting in the Hôtel Crillon in Paris. In the event, only Alfa Romeo, for whom the Brabham team at that time was building the Alfa 164 Procar, and who in the same year – 1988 – had bought Ecclestone's Motor Racing Developments factory at Chessington, seemed to share the enthusiasm of the FIA's vice-president for promotional affairs for a new series.

The manufacturers overwhelmingly rejected it, claiming that the cost of building the cars would be too expensive. Ecclestone put the snub down to the rationale of a manufacturer like Mercedes facing the prospect of being beaten by a car produced by Alfa or Peugeot. 'That's the one thing they can't stand.' He also believed that some of the manufacturers thought they did not have the 'right model in the range that [could] follow the regulations correctly and be competitive. It's all about being competitive.'[5] Others believed the manufacturers' reluctance had more to do with concerns over Ecclestone's motive. Said a senior FIA delegate: 'They suspected that Ecclestone's hidden agenda was to use Procar to shepherd them into Formula One.'

Ecclestone and Mosley continue to believe it was a great opportunity missed. The Alfa 164 proved 'spectacular' on a demonstration run at Monza. 'When it came down the main straight, the entire grandstand stood up,' said Mosley. Ecclestone recalled that its lap time was faster than a Formula One car. He said: 'Since then they have spent fortunes to achieve two per cent [of television coverage] compared to what they would have got [with Procar].'

With a Procar series yesterday's business, Ecclestone now turned his attention to a motor sport that was indeed keenly supported by the manufacturers – the Sports-Prototype World Championship, which had existed under different names since 1953. The FIA's newly formed World Motor Sport Council, which had now replaced the FISA's executive committee, announced in October 1988 that it would be relaunched as the Sportscar World Championship. To oversee the series Balestre announced the formation of a Permanent Bureau, of which he, Ecclestone and Mosley would prove its most influential members, and a Sportscar Commission representing the FISA, the manufacturers and four participating countries. Three months later the Permanent Bureau abolished the position of championship co-ordinator, who, among other duties, was responsible for negotiating with the manufacturers and promoters, a role that Ecclestone and Mosley would now assume.

With the kind of ballyhoo that had accompanied the launch announcement of Procar, Balestre confidently declared that the Sportscar World Championship would come to equal the worldwide status of Formula One. A two-year transitional period would allow a new class of Formula One 3.5-litre car which, although less powerful than the manufacturers' turbocharged cars, would have a 150-kilogram weight advantage – 900 kilograms compared with 750 kilograms – and no fuel restriction. From 1991 the 3.5-litre engines would be compulsory, with ten years' stability of the engine rules. It once again raised suspicions over the motive behind the new series: was this yet another attempt to lure the manufacturers into Formula One? Over the next 18 months a number of changes to the rules, regulations and calendar by the FISA, proposed and supported by either Balestre, Ecclestone and Mosley, or all three, left the manufacturers – Daimler-Benz, Nissan, Alfa Romeo, Peugeot, Mercedes, Jaguar and Toyota – in a state of nervousness, uncertain of the series' stability, or the return on the tens of millions of dollars they were investing in the series.

Their anxiety was reflected in the number of cars registered to take part in the 1991 launch: just 17, compared with more than 30 predicted by Balestre. The all-important media coverage was poor, spectator figures down and further confusion caused by tinkering with the calendar and the last-minute cancellation of the event in Jerez, Spain. All in all, it proved a disastrous re-packaging of the successful Sports-Prototype World Championship. Rather than its rebirth, it turned out to be its burial. By November 1991 a sport that had rivalled Formula One during the sixties and had enthralled the crowds for nearly 40 years, was in its death throes through lack of entries for the following season.

Mercedes and Jaguar, disappointed by the size of the field, declined to commit themselves, and were later followed by Nissan. Peugeot and Toyota, plus a number of privateers who, after investing heavily in 3.5-litre technology, were left stranded. The decision to recommend cancellation of the series was taken at a meeting of the Sportscar Commission in a hotel at Heathrow Airport following a vote on its future. Only Peugeot, BRM, Toyota and privateer Euro Racing were prepared to make a firm commitment. A request by Mosley for a show of hands had three, including Ecclestone and himself, voting in favour of its cancellation, Toyota and Peugeot voting against, and four, including Mercedes, Jaguar and Nissan, abstaining.

Over the next 12 months Peugeot, Toyota and Mazda tried to revive the series with a shortened eight-race calendar. But there was no improvement in media coverage – the lifeblood of any sport and essential to the manufacturers – and, subsequently, spectator figures. Twenty-six cars were committed to compete, but many of the private teams who had pledged to support the series failed to do so, and some of those who did faded away after the early races, leaving a field of fewer than a dozen cars. The series was finally laid to rest in October 1992.

Ecclestone refuted criticism that, through International Sportsworld Communicators, he had failed to ensure that the series had received the same degree of commitment to media exposure that he gave to Formula One. Their frustration was shared by the private teams. Privateer Tom Walkinshaw, the boss of Tom Walkinshaw Racing (TWR), commented: 'People have spent millions of dollars and it's been flushed away. The manufacturers have supported it [but] the other side of the package never came – the media side.'[6] He also believed that it had been a mistake for Balestre and others to claim that the series would equal the status of Formula One. It raised expectations that couldn't be achieved.

Even before the launch of the series, teams were unhappy at the lack of promotion, for which, as the FIA's vice-president of promotional affairs, Ecclestone was responsible. He passed the ball back to the teams and manufacturers. 'We've done a lot more than what they've been doing. It's their championship, and they've done nothing, and we've done a helluva lot to try and promote it. A promoter doesn't want to put a race on when only 3–4000 go to the race. In the end, the promoter says, "What do I need this race for?" And the minute there's no people sitting there, the television companies look at it and say, "If there's no interest for the public to go and sit down, there can't be any more interest for us to put it on TV." So we, as I said, have to make sure that people go to the races. And the only way that will happen is if the promoter gets enough support to promote the racing.' Ecclestone claimed that he had been supporting the promoters – with a limited amount of money available to him. Yet he had rejected the idea of a promotional fund to which the manufacturers would contribute. That was not, he insisted, the 'way to go'.[7]

At the same time, he blamed the manufacturers for not doing enough. 'They should be asking us what we would like them to do.' Which was? 'Generally assist. They've got vast networks everywhere, and they could be running all sorts of competitions. If they just got on with their own thing properly, it would be good. The only people getting anything out of the sports car championship are, in fact, the manufacturers. Nobody else. The promoters are losing money, the FIA are having a lot of work and expense ... but the people that really, really need the championship, wanted the championship, are doing nothing to support it.'

Ecclestone, supported by Max Mosley, claims today that, far from discouraging manufacturers from contributing to a promotional fund, that was precisely what he had tried to establish. Said Mosley: 'The thing about the sports cars was that we wanted the manufacturers to all chip in so we could get the thing going, but they wouldn't. We said to them, for example, if your programme costs $10 million, spend another $500,000 each and we can have sensible television.'

However, it seems it was not the lack of media coverage or promotion alone that threatened the series. Ecclestone's financial demands were proving so crippling that a round scheduled for the Nurburgring in August 1991 was in grave danger until, at the eleventh hour, it was rescued by the personal intervention of Otto Flimm, the FIA's deputy president of touring and automobile, and president of Germany's biggest motoring organisation, the Allgemeiner Deutscher Automobil-Club. Flimm, a friend of Ecclestone, was able to work out an agreement to ensure it was staged at the circuit, even if it was for the last time.

The manufacturers were now left with nowhere to go – except, of course, into Formula One, which, some respected commentators believed, as with the aborted Procar series, had been Ecclestone's intention all along. And that was where Mercedes and Peugeot ended up in 1994 and 1995 respectively, supplying engines for Jordan and Sauber. As for Ecclestone's motive, Balestre confirmed, in a telling comment, the suspicions of those who believed that it had been twofold: to kill off the potential television threat of the Sportscar World Championship to Formula One and, at the same time, entice manufacturers into Formula One. Responding to criticism of the problems that had befallen the series and of its future, Balestre said at a press conference: 'Mr Ecclestone has his own ideas – he prefers Formula One, which is his God-given right. He ran into difficulties setting up the new championship.'[8] The enigmatic Balestre had made a similarly puzzling statement in March 1988, when, at the end of a Manufacturers' Commission press briefing on the launch of the ill-fated proposed Procar series, he said: 'Please remember that this is an FISA idea that has now been ratified democratically by executive committee. You mustn't blame it all on Bernie Ecclestone and try to say that he wants to compete against other championships and kill them off.'[9]

Ecclestone was also able to exercise his 'God-given right' in his marketing support of the World Rally Championship series, the fortunes of which, in his hands, fared little better. His control of the promotion of the World Rally Championship series had been in effect since 1993, when ISC was appointed by Mosley to market its commercial interests. Until then the four main teams – Ford, Mitsubishi, Subaru (Prodrive) and Toyota – had been happy with the way media coverage had been handled, with the host national broadcasters being allowed to film and screen the 14-series event free of charge. The film was also distributed overseas to maximise coverage. It was a relationship that worked to everyone's advantage. But with the arrival of ISC, as with other series, things quickly changed for the worse.

The company demanded that the teams signed an Event Accreditation Agreement acknowledging that the global commercial rights belonged to the FIA. But the teams, angry at the way in which they saw the series being hijacked for Ecclestone's financial benefit, refused to comply. The FIA came to ISC's aid by announcing a new rule, Article 28, which without warning was imposed on the teams during the 1994 Monte Carlo Rally. It vested in the FIA all film and picture rights and authorised ISC to claim them on its behalf. The manufacturers faced the choice: either sign the agreement or lose FIA authorisation and World Championship status. They signed.

Under the agreement's terms, no longer would host broadcasters be allowed to show the series free of charge. Instead, the World Rally Teams Association (WRTA), which until its demise in 1999 represented the manufacturers, became formally responsible for commissioning television coverage of the series for distribution to broadcasters worldwide, while ISC would negotiate the all-important financial terms. The contract for providing coverage was won by BBC Worldwide Ltd, an independent television production company whose predecessor, BBC Enterprises Ltd, was set up in 1979 to develop a co-ordinated approach to the BBC's commercial activities. ISC decreed that the manufacturers would pick up BBC Worldwide's production costs – thought to be in excess of £2 million a year, a figure which, on the grounds of contractual confidentiality, the WRTA refused to confirm. ISC's marketing operation then moved in to sell the film to national and international broadcasters at considerable profit.

However, ISC discovered another way of making money out of the manufacturers: if a manufacturer wanted to use film from an event as part of, say, a marketing campaign, ISC insisted on the full market fee, even though, of course, it was the manufacturers' chequebooks which made the series possible in the first place. The same applied if a manufacturer wanted to hire a film crew to shoot one of its own cars for a special marketing promotion. The company had to negotiate a contract with ISC and pay a top-dollar rate. 'Whatever happens, the money always flowed into Mr Ecclestone's pockets,' said an independent producer.

While manufacturers conceded that the involvement of ISC led to an increase in the quality of coverage of the World Rally Championship series, they added that its benefit was greatly diminished by a marked drop in television viewing figures, a costly predicament well known to the organisers of other events subjected to ISC's marketing strategy. It proved a major disappointment in a motor sport that, according to Mitsubishi Ralliart and Toyota Motorsport, the sporting divisions of the two manufacturers, had 'probably' attracted the largest spectator audiences of any sport in the world.

The fall in television coverage had, they claimed, caused greater difficulty in attracting sponsors, who had gravitated towards Formula One.

Not for the first time, ISC's claims in respect of the television coverage it had achieved led to an interesting conflict of statistics. The company reported that in 1997 it had succeeded in achieving 18 hours and 37 minutes of coverage in France, 25 hours and 26 minutes in Germany and 17 hours and 55 minutes in the UK. However, according to figures supplied by Sri International, a Brussels-based independent television monitoring research company, to the European Commission, its data for the same period told a very different story: 5 hours and 37 minutes in France, 21 hours and 3 minutes in Germany and 9 hours and 29 minutes in the UK.

Ecclestone claims that he tried to increase the appeal of the series by proposing at that time that it did away with reconnaissance, which was considered a crucial part of the pre-event preparation to note the route hazards. Instead, he said, competitors should drive 'blind'. It had, he added, the extra advantage of reducing the competitors' workload. Perhaps, but it provoked a wave of criticism and was condemned by drivers as 'ridiculous' and 'too dangerous'.

Ecclestone, once again supported by Mosley, argues today, as they did then, that it was quite the reverse – knowing the hazards ahead through reconnaissance tempted drivers to push their skills, and luck, to the limit, which increased the possibility of accidents. For years, said Mosley, competitors in the RAC rally relied on standard pace notes until the rally establishment successfully lobbied for the introduction of reconnaissance. 'They spent a fortune doing these three-week "recces" and the accident rate actually went up.' All the same, it seemed a curious viewpoint from someone who had consistently supported the appeal of more dramatic television.

He subsequently lost all interest in rallying, which, coincidentally, suffered a downward spiral in television coverage, failing to recapture the popularity of earlier years. Predictably, Ecclestone sees the results achieved by ISC in quite a different light. 'Before we took the TV rights, [the coverage] was much worse. We improved them a lot, and [it] is not much better now, except it costs the guy that's running it quite a lot more than it cost us.'

A clue to its lack of success can perhaps be found in a comment he later made about rallying: 'It's like watching the Olympics and then a load of amateurs. It's not a spectator sport, it's for competitors; people don't want to watch it.' Certainly Ecclestone wasn't keen to do so as a spectator. Although they were in the company of a world champion driver and navigator, he and Mosley got lost on their way to the only rally that he has ever attended. 'Bernie took one look at the mud,' said Mosley, 'one look at his shoes, and said, "I'm not going out there," closed the door and drove off.'

Ecclestone's criticism of rally driving was in marked contrast to an opinion he expressed on his appointment as vice-president of promotional affairs, when he declared that rallying was one of three events that would form the 'basic structure' of motor sport of the future. The other two, he said, would be Formula One and Procar. He expressed a grand vision to see motor sport fans turning on their television sets every Saturday afternoon in every country in the world, when they would be able to watch some form of the sport, including motorcycle racing. He said: 'The only obstacle to getting it right is people.'[10] It was the opinion of many in motor sport that he had had no intention of getting it right if it in any way threatened Formula One and, thus, his financial interests.

A former employee of Ecclestone's confirmed what many had long suspected – that once he had become involved in the promotion of a motor sport that might threaten Formula One's television dominance, it was gradually starved of the lifeline of promotion and publicity. It was, he believed, Ecclestone's deliberate policy to kill off the competition to keep Formula One at the top of television's motor sport schedules. 'If you look at the history of motor sport outside Formula One, Bernie has dipped in and out of motorbikes, sports cars, rally cars, and the people who were running these motor sports were always in the shadow of Formula One and they were torn between going hell-for-leather against Formula One, or being tempted by Bernie saying, "Come into the family, I'll build it up, I'll make it another Formula One."

'But what Bernie tended to do was to just get hold of it and then just kill it. And they've [the organisers] signed a contract for three years before they could think of getting out of it. From a long way back, Bernie saw Formula One as the only product and he would do whatever he needed to do to ensure that Formula One stayed on that pedestal. There have been many times when Formula One has been extremely boring ... when I think broadcasters were questioning why they were paying such large sums of money. And there were some attractive alternatives [such as] motorcycle racing, Group C sports cars and touring cars [which] could all have presented a serious threat to Formula One. If you look at the essence of why Bernie is so successful, I think a very key part of it has been his ability to keep, one way or another, Formula One up there, head and shoulders above everything else, with the exception of the US, and to keep everybody else down.'

Ecclestone concedes that such comments reflect 'what lots of people said, but it's not true. We spent a lot of money trying to improve [television coverage of other championship series] ... we got better television coverage than what they had before, and it is certainly better than what is being done now. So anyone who says we tried to kill it off is just talking rubbish.'

12

THE RISE OF PRESIDENT MAX, HOW THE FIA LOST MILLIONS, AND THE SHOWDOWN IN BRUSSELS

The ascent to power of Bernie Ecclestone was paralleled by the fortunes of his friend and confidant Max Mosley, who, by the end of the eighties, had risen from the role of the constructors' legal adviser in the days of the protracted FOCA–FISA war of attrition to being a member of the executive committee of the FISA by virtue of his appointment as president of the Manufacturers' Commission. Now, as the nineties beckoned, the suave 51-year-old would shortly be preparing to reach the pinnacle of motor sport – the presidency of the FISA itself.

Given Ecclestone's multi-functional roles, Mosley's reason for standing had more than a touch of irony. He believed that Balestre, as president of the FIA, the FISA and France's national sporting authority, the Fédération Française du Sport Automobile (FFSA), was guilty of an 'overwhelming conflict of interest'. He asserted that the 'President of the FISA should have no other job in motor sport'. There was certainly good reason to believe that the weight of Balestre's different hats was proving overly stressful: in November 1986 he suffered a heart attack, which surprised few who had witnessed over the years his hot-tempered and highly excitable manner. It provided an opportunity for a touch of high drama, which his Gallic temperament adored. Accompanied somewhat dramatically by a doctor and nurse a few weeks later, he arrived at a meeting of the FIA's executive committee to announce that he intended to retire, fuller details of which he would make known once he had fully recuperated. In the new year, at a special meeting of the executive committee, he confirmed his intention to retire at the next meeting of the General Assembly in October.

But in June he did a U-turn and informed the executive committee that he intended to run for the vacancy. When a delegate later reminded him that he had said he was going to retire, he replied: 'Yes, but I didn't say I wouldn't stand as a candidate.' It was a flippancy that caused him to make a serious miscalculation, and which would contribute significantly to events that would bring about his fall from office. For although he was re-elected, in October 1987, he believed that it was for a full four-year term, taking him to 1991, whereas delegates believed they had voted him back in office to complete his previous unfilled term of two years, taking him to 1989, when the president, as was the tradition, was due to stand for re-election, along with the vice-presidents and World Motor Sport Council (WMSC) delegates.

Balestre's insistence that it was for a four-year term put him out of synchronisation with the general elections and caused him, in 1991, to overlook the fact that he was due to stand that October. It wasn't until August of that year that his misinterpretation was corrected by Marco Piccinini during a visit to Balestre's holiday home in Opio, near Grasse, in the south of France. As the two men enjoyed the cool water of the swimming pool, Piccinini casually enquired what his host was planning to do about his forthcoming election. 'Election?' replied Balestre. 'What election?' The realisation of his error, and the embarrassment of its implications, pulled him up with a dreadful start.

At a dinner for motor sport journalists a day or two later, he seized the opportunity to calmly announce that, as of that moment, his campaign for re-election was underway. He put on a confident and self-assured front, but privately he remained highly discomfited by the mistake and furious with the FISA's general secretary, Yvon Léon, whom he unfairly blamed. Léon, he insisted, should have reminded him, though there is no reason why he should have known that Balestre needed 'reminding'. However, if Balestre had been caught napping, Mosley hadn't.

Like others, he had been aware of Balestre's gaffe and found that it offered him the perfect opportunity to set about his political ambitions within the FIA. Indeed, for at least three months he had been busy on the hustings, quietly lobbying the support of the more influential delegates. It proved not to be a difficult mission, due in no small part to an invulnerability that Balestre may have believed his alliance with Ecclestone had given him. He had come to believe that he no longer needed to maintain the support or goodwill of the delegates because, in the words of a senior member of the World Motor Sport Council, he felt that he 'no longer had to rely on anybody. He knew that if he had Bernie [on his side], he didn't need to ask anybody what to do, because everybody was either fearful of him or Bernie. But it isolated him from the people whose support he now needed.'

An apparent tendency to look for problems where none existed added to his notoriety. 'He could never operate unless he had an opponent out there,' added the senior member of the WMSC. 'When he didn't have an adversary he created one.' It was an egocentric imperiousness that also earned Balestre the scorn of the media through a tendency to make inflammatory accusations which, ruing their repercussions, he would then deny having made. Now 70, he was seen as an unpopular despot who was ready for toppling. It was a mood that the charming and energetic Mosley was most willing and able to exploit.

He concentrated his early efforts in countries he considered less likely to be in thrall to Balestre. One of his first, and most important, stops was America, where he sought the support of the national sporting authority, the Automobile Competition Committee for the United States (ACCUS), whose members voted overwhelmingly in favour of backing him. There were just two dissenters – senior figures in motor sport, who believed that Mosley would not succeed unless he was able to enlist the support of Ecclestone, a view expressed to him at a private meeting. Ecclestone, it was suggested, should be persuaded to indicate to the more vulnerable Grand Prix countries, such as Brazil, Mexico, Portugal, Spain, Australia and Japan, that they would lose their Grand Prix unless Mosley received their support.

Ecclestone himself was apparently not at all convinced that Mosley would win. In a subsequent phone conversation with one of the two senior motor sport figures, he expressed the view that Mosley 'didn't have much of a chance'. A senior FIA delegate believed that Ecclestone decided against adding his weight to Mosley's cause. 'I think he [Ecclestone] played it right down the middle. It was a smart move. He was solid with Balestre, and he knew he had Max, anyway. He put himself in a position where he couldn't lose.' It is a view that, up to a point, Mosley shares, although he believed that, due to a common language, he was Ecclestone's preferred choice. 'I think Bernie Ecclestone would have been quite happy with me or Balestre. He was on good terms with both. However, as he doesn't speak French and Balestre speaks little English, he probably finds it easier to communicate with me.'

Another early stop for Mosley was Japan. As president of the Manufacturers' Commission, he had used his position effectively to establish cordial relationships with companies such as Toyota, then the world's second-biggest car manufacturer, and which had considerable influence with the national sporting authority, the Japanese Automobile Federation (JAF). But even without Toyota's influence, Mosley was in already in a favourable position due to Balestre's behaviour two years earlier at the 1989 Japanese Grand Prix at Suzuka.

He found himself controversially involved in a highly public row after Ayrton Senna collided with Alain Prost in the forty-sixth lap, taking his arch-rival out of a race that was crucial to his World Championship hopes. Historical accounts accuse Balestre of insisting that Senna, who went on to cross the line, should be disqualified for 'dangerous manoeuvres'. Senna himself charged Balestre with attempting to manipulate the race in favour of his countryman, which attracted wide media coverage. But on this occasion at least, Balestre, who was not unknown to use his authority to influence FIA inquiries, was not guilty. He had made the mistake of entering the stewards' room as they were still studying reports and videos. It was misconstrued that he had joined the stewards with one intent – to ensure they came down on Prost's side. 'But that wasn't the case,' said one of the stewards, who was present in the room. 'All he said was, "I am glad that I do not have to make that decision."'

The decision to disqualify Senna, who came second to Prost for the World Championship title, was based on the fact that Senna had restarted his car and rejoined the race, not at the point of exit but after cutting across an entire chicane. The decision later caused McLaren boss Ron Dennis to threaten legal action against the FISA, which fuelled even further negative publicity for Balestre. It had all been very embarrassing for his proud Japanese hosts, but it was a minor incident compared to the offence caused by Balestre's decision not to attend a dinner in honour of Crown Prince Takamatsu earlier in the week. It was made in petulant mood following an incident during a qualifying session, when Nigel Mansell suddenly stopped his car. Thirty seconds earlier the race director had left the control room at the request of an official of the JAF, who was concerned that the FIA delegation should be ready on time to be bussed to the dinner in Nagoya, Japan's third-largest city, in the Chubu region, and some distance from the circuit. While the official was being reassured, the race director turned to see through the control room's glass window that his colleagues were all staring intently at the television screen. Concerned, he returned to see on the screen Mansell standing by his car. He immediately called for a red flag.

At that moment Balestre stormed in to the control room, demanding to know why the qualifying session hadn't been stopped. It seemed that one of the teams, who had seen the incident on their own television screen, had complained to Balestre standing nearby. Heated words followed, with the race director, an FIA vice-president, insisting that he had stopped the race and that if Balestre didn't leave the room, then he would and Balestre could take over. His pride affronted, Balestre left the room as he had entered – in a state of high dudgeon. By the time he, as head of the FIA delegation, was due to join his colleagues for the dinner, his sulky mood had not abated. He declined to go.

His absence was seen by the Japanese as an unpardonable public insult which they would not quickly forget.

Thus it was, when Mosley arrived in Japan to seek the JAF's support, he was pushing at an open door. Like the Americans, they willingly lobbied other countries on his behalf. Shrewdly, Mosley concentrated his efforts on the smaller countries, to whom he promised to balance more fairly their interests against those of the more politically powerful European bloc. By the time he announced that he was throwing his silk top hat into the ring and standing against Balestre – a month before the election was due to be held – he believed he had the support of about 49 of the 72 member countries. He had also diplomatically overcome some concern from the traditionalist camp that he was too thick with Ecclestone by pledging to resign 12 months later if they had any cause to be dissatisfied.

In Balestre's camp, Yvon Léon and senior FIA officials, although obliged by the rules of office to remain strictly impartial, began working energetically, albeit belatedly, to whip up support for their leader. Their reports back to Balestre must have buoyed him considerably. They suggested that he had the overwhelming support of member countries. Less than a week before the election Balestre was sufficiently gung-ho to announce that he did 'not expect a strong challenge from Mr Max Mosley, who has not yet personally informed me of his candidature'. For mischievous measure, he added: 'I find this disloyal from someone whom I introduced into the FISA, and the information reaching me from all sides proves that he is indulging in a campaign aimed at destabilising the FISA and brainwashing the member countries with false truths.'[1] On the night before the election Balestre was confidently putting the final touches to his victory speech. An analysis of a complete list of countries' voting intentions in his possession assured him that he could count on the support of every country bar four – two who intended to vote for Mosley and two who might. But he was in for a major shock.

Ecclestone, who by now had revised his opinion on Mosley's chances, thought so, too. On the morning of the election he went to Balestre and suggested that he should offer a power-sharing deal to Mosley in return for standing down. Balestre instantly dismissed the suggestion, such was his certainty of victory. Mosley had been unaware of Ecclestone's approach, but, reflecting years later, he believed that he would have been in a very difficult position if it had been made. 'I hope I would have had the courage to have said no,' he said, 'but I was by no means sure that I was going to win. It was absolutely in the laps of the gods.'

On 9 October 1991, at the FISA's plenary conference in Paris, Mosley was elected the ninth president of the FIA's sporting division by 43 votes to 29, six votes less than his straw poll had indicated he could count on. After 13 years as the president of the FISA, Balestre nobly announced his own defeat in the grand conference room of the Automobile Club de France, which was bedecked with flags of the FISA nations. A former associate described Balestre as being 'terribly upset by the result. He didn't expect Max to topple him. He didn't think it would happen.' Few did. He had become an iconic figure within motor sport, considered by some to be simply too powerful to be brought down.

Defeat for the proud Frenchman, who tried, unsuccessfully, to force an election rerun, would have been all the more painful because of the way in which so many countries had misleadingly concealed their true voting intentions. For all the criticism of Balestre, he was described by a former FIA official as 'a sincere man [who] always thought he was doing right. He made a lot of mistakes, but not with malice. He just wanted to get his point over and get it through. But he was not pursuing any personal wealth. He did not make money out of the FIA.' In accordance with his electioneering pledge, the new president's first official act was to hand in his resignation to Yvon Léon, to take effect at the following year's plenary conference. If he failed to live up to expectations, he was ready to be voted out, a shrewd move that helped to sway a number of crucial votes. The following year, 1992, he was duly re-elected with ease.

In December 1990, some 11 months before he was elected president of the FISA, Mosley had decided to end his commercial interests in motor sport. He resigned as the sole director of a company called Tamastar Ltd, which he had formed in June 1976, around the time he became the FOCA's legal adviser following his departure from the March team, to offer a motor-racing consultancy service. His wife, Jean, was listed as his partner. He described himself as 'a professional adviser to the motor-racing industry', but it seemed few sought his advice. Minimal activity passed through the books of the Oxford-based company until the mid-eighties, when Ecclestone became a director in 1986, a position from which he resigned a year later. They had in mind a joint venture outside of motor sport. To that end they set up a subsidiary building company called Logicgap Ltd, but the project proceeded no further. Mosley described the venture as 'moderately successful', yet, two years later, the company was dissolved without trading.

Between 1987 and 1989 Tamastar's turnover increased dramatically to £246,000, £283,000 and £1,293,000. Mosley's salary, including dividends, during this period was £98,000, £435,000 and £416,000. In 1989 the company also paid out £652,000 in consultant's expenses, Mosley being the consultant. This turn of good fortune was due solely to his work as president of the Manufacturer's Commission, for which, of course, Balestre had arranged for the manufacturers to provide a salary. He insisted that there had been no conflict of interest between his ownership of Tamastar and his role as president of the Manufacturers' Commission. 'Everyone concerned knew who did what and for whom. The presidency of the Manufacturers' Commission was never a full-time job.'

Mosley's role within Tamastar was filled by his 49-year-old wife, Jean, who had been involved in the company since its formation and was its only other member. The company was soon in financial difficulties, running up losses of £113,000 by 1992. It arranged a loan of £75,000 from its pension fund, which was repaid by Mosley as part of an interest-free loan of £90,000. It did nothing to turn the business round, which was now specialising in boat hire. In 1993, although the company had ceased to operate as a motor-racing consultancy, Mosley, now the president of the FISA and shortly to become the president of the FIA itself, engaged the services of Tamastar at a cost of £20,000, the company's sole source of revenue for that year. The payment, said Mosley, was for consultancy services that he personally required and for which he paid.

Whatever her skills and expertise, Mrs Mosley, the sole member of the company, was certainly not qualified to act as a motor-racing consultant. Her services were effectively non-existent, although Mosley produced an interesting explanation of her role to justify the payment. 'As I was married to her before I even saw a motor race, she is probably the one person I talk to about all these things and I can completely trust in a very difficult world. The fact is that we talk about what is going on, and who is up to what, and how it is all happening, probably most days ... not to her great pleasure because she is not that interested ... but it is perfectly legitimate for me to say that I consulted her. Who else do I consult? Particularly if I am not happy about something going on with Bernie. There is nobody else I can talk to. So I think it is a little unfair to say that her services were non-existent.'

One of Tamastar's few clients was Simtek Research, which Mosley had set up with 23-year-old Nick Wirth, a college friend of the son of Robin Herd, a co-founder, with Mosley and others, of the March team. After graduating with a first-class honours degree in mechanical engineering and naval architecture from University College London and winning the Institute of Mechanical Engineering's prize for the best final-year thesis, Wirth spent a brief spell with March before setting up Simtek Research with Mosley in 1989 to provide research and development services to motor manufacturers.

Its start was promising, with an annual turnover of £1.76 million and pre-tax profits of £867,000 in 1990. But, despite obtaining development and design work from BMW AG, BMW Motor Sport, Ligier and the French Government, it was short-lived, incurring losses until 1993, when it effectively ceased trading. From 1991 it had one other important customer – the FISA, of which Mosley had just been elected president. The company, which specialised in simulation and wind-tunnel experiments, carried out a variety of confidential work, which included analysing the safety aspects of various categories of cars. The work, said Mosley, was confidential because: 'I didn't want anybody to know the outcome. It is one thing to know something and it's another to be able to do anything about it.' The work had been obtained for Simtek Research through the efforts of Mosley, who, despite being president of the FISA, did not resign as a director of the company until December 1992. Tamastar also benefited through his association with Simtek. During 1990 and 1991 it was paid a total of £35,000 for its consultancy services. As Mosley had resigned from Tamastar in December 1990, the consultancy work in 1991 must have been undertaken by the inexperienced Mrs Mosley. Mosley insisted that there had been no conflict of interest.

Ambitiously, Wirth decided to move into Formula One in 1994 with his own racing team – Simtek Grand Prix Ltd. Unfortunately for Wirth, a personable and engaging character but without the ruthless business skills to survive in Formula One, he fared no better here. By the Monaco Grand Prix in 1995, his company was in dire financial difficulties, despite loans of at least $3 million earlier that year. Less than two months later the assets of both Simtek Research and Simtek Grand Prix Ltd, with combined debts totalling almost £6 million, went under the auctioneer's hammer.

Mosley declines to discuss his personal wealth, which appears to be based on money that 'finally percolated down' through his family, proceeds from the sale of the March team, and 'business with Bernie outside of Formula One – in property mainly', despite Logicgap Ltd effectively being a dormant company. Nevertheless, even though his position with the FIA is non-salaried, he enjoys the prestige and luxury of a mews home in a fashionable part of central London and a most comfortable lifestyle.

Following his re-election to the presidential office of the FISA in October, 1992, two months later Mosley moved to ring-fence the power source of his position by creating an FISA Financial Council, of which Ecclestone was appointed a member, on the shrewd principle that when you take over a business the first thing you do is grab the chequebook. He was firmly of the opinion that Balestre, who had taken his defeat badly, was quite capable of attempting to leave him isolated and powerless by ensuring that his cronies on the FIA's Finance Committee, which controlled the FISA's budget, outvoted him – he was now a member of the committee by virtue of his office – whenever it suited his book.

The Financial Council, though, never met. It was made redundant by an improvement in the relationship between the two men and the threat that Mosley had perceived gradually lost its force. Balestre, who had been dissuaded from attempting to recapture the FISA presidency by standing against Mosley in the 1992 election, had become a dispirited figure with failing health. The fighting disposition of the once fearsome and belligerent Frenchman, now past 70, had become diminished over the years and his sense of invincibility damaged by his defeat.

Mosley recognised the time was right to move for the ultimate seat of authority within motor sport – the presidency of the FIA itself. Over the next few months, as the relationship between the two men continued to improve, Mosley proposed that, if Balestre should agree not to stand for re-election, which fell due in June 1993, he would be assured of an authoritative and prestigious position within the FIA. That position would be as president of the Senate, a powerful body Mosley planned to introduce if elected, as part of a major restructuring of the FIA hierarchy. It was a proposal designed to appeal to the pride and pomp of a conceited man. Balestre agreed.

Mosley was thus left with the formality of announcing his intention to stand in a contest that appeared to be very much a one-horse race – until, that is, a month before the election, when the distinguished figure of Jeffrey Rose, an FIA vice-president and chairman of Britain's Royal Automobile Club, put forward his name. His decision to do so was first prompted by what happened at a breakfast meeting some weeks earlier with Mosley and Ecclestone at the RAC's Clubhouse, its London headquarters, which lasted from 8.30 to about 10 am, and which had been requested with some urgency by Ecclestone. He informed Rose that Mosley was going to be the next president of the FIA. Could Mosley count on the RAC's support?

Rose, somewhat startled by the news, declined to pledge the RAC's vote without first consulting his colleagues. But even at that moment he thought it unlikely. As a founding member of the FIA, which was established as a federation of motoring clubs and associations, he couldn't see how the RAC could support someone who represented neither. There was also some concern within the RAC that Mosley was too close to Ecclestone and his commercial interests, particularly in Formula One. The RAC decided it was unable to give Mosley its support. Instead, it was agreed by his colleagues that Rose himself should stand, on the motoring club platform: here was someone, a leading figure in a leading motoring club, who could be sure to represent the interests of all motoring organisations and associations worldwide.

Now it was Rose's turn to go to Mosley. If he would withdraw his candidature and pledge his support, he would be given control of motor sport, while he, Rose, concentrated on road-car issues. Mosley declined for two reasons. He couldn't be sure that his authority would be unfettered, but, more importantly, Mosley himself wanted to get more involved in promoting road safety and environmental legislation and political activities in Brussels. 'That is what really interested me,' said Mosley. 'It is satisfying because you can work like hell in Formula One and you maybe save one life every five years, whereas road safety really is very, very significant. You are talking about thousands of lives over a reasonable period. That's what turns me on, in the same way that money turns Bernie on.'

With Mosley's response went Rose's main hope. A quintessential establishment figure who remained chairman of the RAC until 1998, 63-year-old Rose soon discovered that other and no less influential clubs had already lined up behind Mosley, with the active support of Ecclestone, and that the smaller clubs were bound to follow this lead. The election of Balestre's successor, Rose concluded, had already been decided. On the day of the election, 10 June 1993, he addressed the FIA assembly, explained the RAC's position and withdrew his name, leaving Mosley to be elected unopposed. That October, when Balestre formally stood down, Mosley, as head of an organisation representing some 150 national motoring organisations on five continents, became president of the FIA, and one of the most influential political figures in the motoring world. He was now uniquely placed to work more effectively and efficiently with the vice-president of promotional affairs.

One of Balestre's final duties as president of the FISA was to negotiate in 1990 the share of the television revenue the FIA would receive for the duration of the next Concorde Agreement, to run from 1992 to 1997. As coverage of Formula One continued in popularity during the eighties, its television rights had become increasingly important to a governing body whose principal source of income had once come from homologation fees. In 1987, the year when Ecclestone was appointed the FIA's vice-president of promotional affairs, the FIA, coincidentally, was for the first time to enjoy a 30 per cent share of its commercial rights.

However, over the next couple of years Balestre was said to have been disappointed to find that the anticipated increase of riches had failed to occur. In fact, in 1990, its percentage share revenue produced a return of no more than $1 million. According to Mosley, Balestre 'had every reason to fear for future TV rights' because he had seen the collapse of Canal 5, the French television company owned by his friend Robert Hersant, and, as a result, the loss of a lucrative television contract. He was also concerned, added Mosley, about 'currency risk', preferring a fixed sum in francs, the currency of the FIA's expenditure, rather than an uncertain percentage in US dollars.

It was for these reasons that Balestre decided to listen to a proposal from a company called Allsopp, Parker & Marsh Ltd (APM), whose activities included advertising, promotion and the marketing of motor-racing events, and of which Patrick 'Paddy' McNally, the long-standing friend and close business associate of Ecclestone, was co-owner. The company claimed to have a solution to Balestre's anxiety. It would, he was assured, eliminate all risk to the FIA: in return for its 30 per cent share of television revenue, APM would guarantee a fixed annual royalty payment of at least $3 million. Although Balestre knew little of McNally's company, he nevertheless agreed to its proposal. It was not long before he came to believe that he had made the right decision.

In 1992 the FIA's first payment from APM was $5.6 million. By 1994 it had reached $7 million, and $9 million by 1996, the final year of the contract. The FIA, it seemed, had been smiling all the way to the bank, with Balestre the toast of Place de la Concorde for his shrewd judgement. But, based on figures supplied by a Formula One team boss and documents leaked from within the FIA and the French tax investigation authority, the Paris-based Direction Nationale des Vérifications de Situations Fiscales, which began an inquiry in 1994, the FIA should have done a good deal better. Far from the uncertain revenue flow that Balestre believed was likely to be generated, television revenues, thanks to Ecclestone's efforts, soared. As McNally put it: 'No one had taken into consideration the negotiating abilities of BCE [Ecclestone].' Between 1992 and 1996 they totalled an estimated $341 million, of which $102 million – 30 per cent – went to APM. The FIA's share, under the terms of the fixed royalty deal, came to no more than $37 million. The FIA had ended up $65 million the poorer. And that figure did not include loss of television revenue from non-Formula One championships or other commercial activities.

Mosley, who states that he was unaware of the details of the APM agreement until after he was elected president of the FISA in October 1991, was reported in the London *Financial Times*[2] as claiming that senior officials of the FIA had been unhappy with the deal, and that he suspected that the full membership of the FIA never knew about the huge sums of money negotiated away by Balestre, comments which he later denied making. He claimed, however, that 'Balestre had up-to-date information from Ecclestone, who advised him against the APM deal'. Balestre and the FIA Finance Committee, he added, 'formed their own view, as they were entitled to do'.

It seems then that Balestre had made a major mistake in declining to take the advice of his vice-president of promotional affairs. Yet one is left to wonder how frank Ecclestone had been in giving Balestre the full benefit of his counsel. For while Ecclestone was fully aware of Balestre's alleged misgivings over the future level of television revenue following the financial problems that had befallen Canal 5, he kept from Balestre information that might have encouraged him to reconsider signing away the FIA's 30 per cent. Said Ecclestone: 'As it happened, what he [Balestre] didn't know was that already at that time I had thought this Channel 5 [Canal 5] was going to get into problems ... and I got another deal [with another television company].' It was an extraordinary admission for Ecclestone to make. As vice-president of the FIA's promotional affairs, he was surely obliged to put such information before Balestre. It suggests that, for whatever reason, he used his position as president of the FOCA, in which role he negotiated television deals, to abuse his position within the FIA by failing to inform Balestre of the new contract.

Certainly at the time in 1990, when Balestre and APM were negotiating the terms of the fixed royalty deal, Ecclestone had great confidence in the future of television revenues. He was so confident, in fact, that it was at that time he decided not to renew the FOCA's contract with the European Broadcasting Union, which expired that year, in order to pursue highly profitable single-country deals, which, as Christian Vogt has revealed, increased 'about tenfold' the money Ecclestone had been receiving through the EBU and elsewhere. Ecclestone's confidence in the future might also have been boosted by the profits of his International Sportsworld Communicators (ISC), which marketed the FIA's substantially less lucrative non-Formula One television rights, but which increased from £2.2 million in 1989 to £3.4 million in 1990 and £4.87 million in 1992. Indeed, ISC continued to do so well that Ecclestone was able to pay himself a dividend of £4.1 million in 1995, which was transferred to an offshore company in Jersey called Microner Investments Ltd.

Given the importance of television revenue to the FIA's prosperity, it could also be argued that Balestre was negligent in observing prudent business practice by failing to seek security from APM in default of payment, or, at least, in authorising due diligence on the company to ensure its financial stability. If so, he would surely have been alarmed by the secrecy surrounding its activities. While the company, which was formed in November 1983 with McNally, Luc Jean Argand, a senior partner in a Geneva-based law firm which represents the legal interests in Switzerland of the FIA, and Beat Corpataux, a Swiss accountant, as its directors, did very well between 1985 and 1988, with profits of $33.44 million against a turnover of $45 million, the company ceased to trade in 1988, with losses of £485,000, after changes in British tax laws brought an end to its tax exemption due to non-resident status.

In commenting on the value of due diligence, considered a fundamental precaution in such financial arrangements, Mosley justified its absence on the basis that McNally, because of the 'almost total' dependence of his Paddock Club on the goodwill of Balestre and the FIA, wouldn't have dared risk losing it by failing to have delivered the agreed payments. Said Mosley: 'Balestre could have turned to this [the importance of McNally's 'goodwill' with Balestre and the FIA] in the event of default. Much better than "due diligence".' An unusual comment in that Mosley, of all people, would have known that the existence of the Paddock Club depended not on Balestre, or the FIA, but Ecclestone.

In September of that year a company called Allsopp, Parker & Marsh

(APM) was formed in the Republic of Ireland, where it fulfilled certain conditions to register as non-resident for tax purposes – neither its directors nor legal owners were resident in Ireland. The company included in its constitution a provision that enabled it to claim exemption from filing annual returns. In this way it was able to keep its finances from public scrutiny. But it was a malpractice: the exemption is granted to companies who do not trade for profit, a claim that APM was not entitled to make.

Documentary evidence proves that the two companies were one and the same, but a question mark remains over their ownership. In the instance of the company registered in England there were 12 £1 nominal shares issued: McNally and Argand had one share each, with the rest in the names of nominee directors. In respect of the company registered in Ireland, two nominal shares were issued: Argand had had one share since 1989, and a member of his office owned the other. One would imagine that Ecclestone, as the FIA's vice-president of promotional affairs, would have been meticulous in knowing who owned the company and to whom, as the person responsible for the distribution of the television revenue, he was paying such large sums of money. It seems not. In reply to a question about the ownership of APM, he said that he had 'always understood' McNally to be the owner. The answer to the identity of the beneficial, as opposed to legal, owner lies in a trust in Guernsey, where the ten remaining shares eventually ended up.

There is some interesting evidence linking Ecclestone to APM. Argand, a director of the company, was a trustee of Orion, a Swiss-based trust set up by Ecclestone to safeguard his fabulous family wealth. A legal adviser to the trust was tax expert Stephen Mullens, who, as secretary of a company bought off the shelf for the setting up of APM, was involved in its initial regulatory filings to Companies House, London, where the incorporation and annual returns of UK companies are recorded for public inspection. Mullens – he had been introduced to Ecclestone by Argand, who has been involved in the legal affairs of drivers for many years, including the drawing up of the business contract between Ecclestone and Jochen Rindt in January 1970 – later became a partner of solicitors Marriott Harrison, who acted as Ecclestone's legal advisers in a subsequent $1.4-billion Eurobond sale, and whose London offices, from December 1990 until early 1993, were given as the registered address of APM.

Both Argand and Mullens also became directors of Excelis, a Paris-based company specialising, among other activities, in the organising and promoting of sporting events, including managing the Paul Ricard circuit purchased by Ecclestone, along with the local airport and hotel, for £11.5 million in 1999. It was neither McNally nor Argand, incidentally, who first devised the option of an index-linked annual fixed royalty payment. That device was the inspiration of Ecclestone, who came up with it three years earlier when FOCA members, in signing the 1987 Concorde Agreement, agreed to an identical deal.

An interesting footnote to this affair is the fact that Balestre, in believing they would prove more profitable than the television revenue, agreed that APM could sell on its behalf the merchandising rights to certain FIA events. APM proceeded to seek the assistance of another company whose expertise was well known to the FIA – Ecclestone's International Sportsworld Communicators (ISC). Even then, the realisation of their anticipated value failed to meet the FIA's expectations. APM did little better in marketing the broadcasting rights of non-Formula One championships, which had also been assigned to them. Once again it sought the assistance of ISC, which, in August 1996, acquired the rights from the FIA for itself.

McNally, invited to comment on the activities of Allsopp, Parker & Marsh, declined to do so unless he was first sent a copy of the entire manuscript. 'Without it, I cannot see how we can properly consider your request,' he replied in a letter from the office of AllSport Management in Geneva. He has steadfastly refused over the years to be interviewed about either his personal or business life. The idle days of gossip-column celebrity gave way long ago to the more serious pursuit of making a substantial fortune, which has created a deep aversion to the publicity he once enjoyed. It seems to take an intervention from Ecclestone, whose patronage has been largely responsible for McNally's riches, to persuade him to face questions from the media.

When McNally was approached during the German Grand Prix at the Nurburgring by investigative reporter Mark Killick as part of an investigation by BBC TV's *Panorama* into the financing of Formula One, for a programme to be broadcast in November 1998, he firmly refused to be interviewed. Killick, trying to establish the beneficial owners of the company and the Paddock Club, went to Ecclestone for his assistance. Ecclestone told him he would fix it. A week or two later Killick received a phone call from McNally. He would be happy to meet at the Berkeley Hotel, in London, for breakfast. It turned out to be not so much an interview as a presentation of a four-page statement typed by McNally himself.

The 'old' company of APM, he said in the statement, had begun in the early eighties – 'I still have the three-line letter from BCE [Ecclestone] wishing APM good luck' – with the acquisition from Ecclestone of the advertising rights to the Grands Prix of France, Austria, Belgium and Holland. McNally described these events as the 'lame ducks' of the Formula One calendar, where 'the promoters wanted a race, but did not have the necessary funds and passed on all their commercial rights'. The relationship with Ecclestone was the key to the ensuing success of APM, including the setting up of AllSport Management, which it licensed to provide on-track retail concessions and trade displays, and not least the management of the highly profitable Paddock Club. Said McNally in his statement: 'The early relationship with BCE has stood APM in good stead – opening doors and giving the company credibility in the marketplace.'

APM went on to negotiate advertising and marketing contracts – 'to market on an international basis, ensure uniformity in advertising ... provide consistency in service and standards in keeping with the high standards of Formula One generally' – with circuit owners at the majority of Formula One events, adding Monza and Imola in 1998. 'APM wasn't particularly keen [on] the Italian races ... but CBE insisted that the Italian tracks had a face-lift.' Soon afterwards APM became promoter of the Austrian Grand Prix and had the contract for the Chinese Grand Prix, due to take place in Zhuhai, 36 miles from Hong Kong, in 1998, but a few months later this was cancelled due to infrastructural problems. APM also became adviser to the owners of the state-of-the-art Formula One stadium in Sepang, where the Malaysian Grand Prix was launched in 1999, an arrangement that would have been directly due to Ecclestone's influence.

McNally's statement went on to indicate that the activities of APM were directly linked to Ecclestone's interests: 'APM's involvement is not so much conditional as logical considering each race is part of the same World Championship.' In the circumstances of this 'logical' business relationship between the two men, Ecclestone imposed upon circuit owners and promoters the condition that APM's services be engaged. In return, APM worked with owners and promoters to occasionally subsidise fees demanded by Formula One Administration (FOA), Ecclestone's company, on behalf of the teams. It also made payments direct to FOA, details of which, added McNally in his statement, were covered by a commercial confidentiality clause. McNally insisted to Killick that Ecclestone had no part in the beneficial ownership of APM.

Balestre commented on the FIA deal with Allsopp, Parker & Marsh through the Fédération Française du Sport Automobile, of which he remained honorary president. But, oddly, he insisted that the deal he agreed was not with Allsopp, Parker & Marsh but with the FOCA, which would have been negotiated and signed by Ecclestone. In a brief statement, accompanied by three pages listing his titles and achievements in motor sport, he confirmed Mosley's explanation that, nervous about future television revenue, he had agreed to an annual fixed royalty deal paid in French francs because of the unstable US dollar and because of the decision by television companies not to renew their Formula One contracts. A request for confirmation brought the following response from Balestre, this time through the FIA: 'The 1990 agreement concerning television rights ... was signed by the FIA and the FOCA, following the unanimous decision taken by the FIA General Assembly.'

Ecclestone had earlier declined to comment, referring all questions to Mosley.

In the light of the tens of millions of pounds of television revenue lost to the FIA as a result of the fixed annual royalty deal with Allsopp, Parker & Marsh, one might imagine that Mosley, as Balestre's successor, would have immediately rejected any thought of committing the FIA to a similar agreement. After all, he had the benefit of knowing that television revenues had increased substantially and were likely to continue to do so. Nevertheless, when the time came to negotiate with Ecclestone the FIA's share of television revenue, he locked the FIA into a very similar deal. Not for five years, though, but for 15 years. And not this time with Allsopp, Parker & Marsh, but with Ecclestone. Once again, the FIA would receive an index-linked annual fixed royalty for the duration of the contract, which, known as the Formula One Agreement – quite separate from the Concorde Agreement – was agreed by the Senate in February 1995 and signed the following December to have effect from 1 January 1996 through to 31 December 2010. And, once again, it seems likely that the FIA will end up much the poorer.

Including an estimated sum of $225 million for 1997, figures prepared by Formula One Administration show that it is contracted to receive from broadcasting companies worldwide between 1998 and 2004 a gross revenue totalling $1.555 billion. On the evidence of the FIA's share of $38 million in 1999 out of a revenue of $£241 million, its royalty payment represented a percentage figure in the region of 15 per cent. By the end of 2004 it will receive, therefore, a total sum of $232.5 million, as opposed to $465 million – the 30 per cent that Mosley surrendered. These figures, of course, make no account for revenue the FIA will lose during the remaining six years of the 15-year contract, from 2005 to 2010. The teams and Ecclestone, on the other hand, will fare considerably better. The 11 Formula One teams, who receive 47 per cent of television revenues, will split between them an estimated total of $730.85 million, with Ecclestone pocketing the balance of $590 million. For the record, the gross revenue for the same period of all of Formula One Administration's commercial contracts, from television and radio broadcasts to title sponsorship, video production and Grand Prix promotions, will total approximately $2.313 billion. Mosley claims that he had little choice but to remain with a fixed royalty deal in order to protect the long-term interests of the FIA. For a start, he insists, there was no way that the teams, or Ecclestone, would have agreed to continue with the 30 per cent signed away by Balestre. It would have left Ecclestone with just 23 per cent of television rights revenue, not nearly enough to fund his huge investment in the digital technology of pay-TV, which, at that time, promised enormous global returns. 'My negotiating position was nil,' said Mosley. 'All right, I could have gone to some of the teams like Ferrari and said, "Hang on a minute, Ecclestone's copping at the moment 53 per cent of the business. We can do this differently. The FIA wants only 20 per cent, 15 per cent, whatever... You can have all the rest. Cut Ecclestone out." And what would Bernie do? To use that old nuclear phrase, it would have been mutually assured destruction.'

It was the bedazzling potential of pay-TV that prompted Mosley to suggest to Ecclestone in early 1994 a 15-year agreement, on the same fixed royalty terms agreed with APM, on condition that, at the end it, all the commercial rights were signed over to the FIA. 'It was rather like a 99-year freehold lease – you get small returns in the beginning, but somebody else takes the risk and you get everything back at the end. That was the key to it – if we didn't get all those rights back and completely under FIA control, we would lose control of the World Championship because Bernie was building the whole thing up.' Mosley viewed Ecclestone's growing control with concern for a particular reason – the FIA had no direct contract with him. Its contract was with the FOCA, who then assigned the commercial rights to Ecclestone, leaving him unencumbered by any contract with the FIA.

So Mosley proposed a different contractual structure: the FIA signed a contract with Ecclestone as well as with the FOCA in leasing the rights, while he did a deal with the FOCA, continuing to pay the teams their share. 'I said to him that, instead of a five-year deal with the teams, he would have a 15-year deal with us, which was much more bankable. It would enable him to raise additional finance for pay-TV, which otherwise would have been quite difficult to do.' In February 1995 Mosley went to the Senate for its approval, and then he and Ecclestone spent the next ten months hammering out the finer details of the 15-year agreement.

One of the more important details for Ecclestone, in order to protect his pay-TV interests, was that he acquired beyond dispute legal ownership of the commercial rights of the Formula One World Championship, which he and others had claimed, and which Mosley did not now dispute – 'ownership of the rights in the Formula One World Championship was not as simple as was assumed in the early Concorde Agreements' – generally belonged to the organisers or promoters, the party that took the commercial risk, although this could vary from country to country. In England, for example, ownership depends on who owns the land (and can grant or refuse access), while in France and Brazil, certain intellectual property rights belong to the relevant sports federation by law. In yet other countries the performers have an interest.

Ecclestone's lawyers proceeded to negotiate at least 14 different legal systems worldwide to secure the rights from every conceivable holder in each country so that, no matter who owned what rights in which country, they were secure everywhere. These commercial rights were added to those already in Ecclestone's rights portfolio, acquired by Formula One Administration Ltd by virtue of its business of running the commercial side of the championship. As part of the deal, the FIA agreed to hand over its few commercial rights – 'Whatever they were, he [Ecclestone] was better off with them than without them,' said Mosley.

He was confident that he had secured an 'outstanding' deal. 'My belief is that I got a better deal than anyone else could have because it was more difficult for Ecclestone to take a hard line with me as we had worked together for so long. A major dispute would have threatened to destroy the entire structure, whereas now we are looking at a very bright future.' That future, however, no longer looks so rosy. While in 1997 pay-TV accounted for nearly half of television income, its worldwide popularity by 2002 was very much on the wane. At the wedding in Madrid on 6 September 2002 of the daughter of the Spanish Prime Minister, José María Aznar, one of the principal guests, Rupert Murdoch, told fellow guest Flavio Briatore, Managing Director of Renault F1 UK, that he was offering broadcasters 50 per cent less for television sports rights due a protracted downturn in advertising revenue. The days of mega-fees were finished, he added, with television fees being halved over the next couple of years. The effect on the pay-TV coverage of Formula One could be devastating – a close associate of Ecclestone's believed that a sustained drop in income below his 53 per cent share was likely to see him close the entire operation down.

Mosley was unperturbed by the possible collapse of pay-TV revenue: 'I thought it would become a massively valuable asset. I was wrong. But then so were a lot of people about dotcom companies. Had it been a massively valuable asset, it would have all come to the FIA, all established and working, on a plate, in 2010. But don't forget, in the end, the FIA has risked nothing.' One thing is certain, and that is that the special relationship between Ecclestone and Mosley has proved to their mutual benefit in oiling the political and commercial wheels of Formula One. 'I'm very aware that if someone other than Bernie were running the commercial side of things, life might be very much more difficult for me. And I like to think he realises that if someone other than me were running the sporting side, life might be more difficult for him.' A former FIA official put it another way: 'They are wedded together. They cannot split, because they need each other.'

Mosley's election as president of the FIA brought with it sweeping reorganisation that did much to reduce a committee-bound bureaucracy, including the abolition of the FISA, which was replaced as motor sport's governing body by the World Motor Sport Council, comprising 19 motor sport delegates and the presidents of the Fédération Mondiale du Karting, the Manufacturers' Commission and Ecclestone's company Formula One Administration. Ecclestone's rise in authority was further marked by his appointment to the Senate, a body of which Balestre was appointed president in return for letting Mosley stand unopposed in the FIA presidency election, and which was established by Mosley to take any decisions 'required by the current management of the FIA and deal with urgent matters'.

The Senate was actually proposed by Ecclestone and its members represented the powerful European forces: Otto Flimm, president of Germany's Allgemeiner Deutscher Automobil-Club, the biggest motoring organisation in Europe; Marco Piccinini, a director of the Ferrari board who would later play a corporate role in Ecclestone's disastrous flotation bid; Rosario Alessi, president of the Automobile Club d'Italia; Alfredo Cesar Torres, president of the Automóvel Club de Portugal; Michel Boeri, president of the Automobile Club de Monaco; and the only non-European representative, Paul R. Verkuil, president of the American Automobile Association.

Meeting quarterly, the Senate also took on the duties of the FIA's Finance Committee, responsible for approving all significant financial deals, in particular those agreed between Mosley and Ecclestone, before they went to the annual meeting of the General Assembly for approval. Criticisms that the Senate became a mere rubber-stamping process for decisions made by the two men were firmly rebuffed by Mosley, who added that only someone 'very naïve' would see its members, three of whom were qualified lawyers, as 'rubber-stampers'.

It was the Senate who approved the purchase from Ecclestone of an executive jet to ease Mosley's busy travel schedule. It took place soon after his election, when it was suggested to Ecclestone that the new president ought to receive an honorarium in return for his services. Ecclestone was said to be of the opinion that Mosley didn't need to be paid, but that a private executive plane for his use would make his job much easier. It so happened that he had a Falcon jet for sale, which was duly purchased for about $2.5 million. Mosley used it for several years before it was sold, to be replaced by a Learjet 31 hired from Ecclestone, an arrangement that was superseded by the purchase in 2002 of a Learjet 60, again purchased from Ecclestone.

The streamlined hierarchy introduced by Mosley allowed more efficient control of the FIA generally and the World Motor Sport Council in particular. It also put Ecclestone in an extremely powerful position, politically and commercially. In addition to being president of the Formula One Constructors' Association and president of the FIA's promotional affairs, he was now, as the man with his hands firmly on the Formula One purse strings, one of the most important members of both the inner sanctum, the Senate, and the World Motor Sport Council. Ecclestone and Mosley, who little more than a decade earlier had been arch-opponents of the FIA, were now effectively running it.

It was in this politically benevolent atmosphere that the World Motor Sport

Council and the General Assembly, the FIA's law-making body, approved Mosley's decision to award Ecclestone the Formula One television rights in December 1995. But in the same year, at a meeting in October, the General Assembly went a step further. It unanimously approved a proposal of the World Motor Sport Council, tabled at a meeting the previous March, which claimed the television rights of all FIA Championships, Cups and Challenges. It came into effect in June 1996, when the World Motor Sport Council extended the rule to include all events that took place in more than one country, such as the Paris–Dakar Rally. Two months later, in August, the television rights of 19 FIA championship events were awarded to Ecclestone's International Sportsworld Communicators (ISC) for a 15-year period. Ecclestone now had control over the marketing of every major motor sport on every FIA calendar.

The motor sport championships were: World Rally Championship, World Grand Touring Car Championship, Formula 3 Intercontinental Championship, European Rally Championship, International Touringcar Championship, Asia-Pacific Rally Championship, African Continent Rally Championship, Middle East Rally Championship, Karting World Championship, Formula 3000 International Championship, World Cup for Cross Country Rallies, European Truck Racing Cup, European Championship for Rallycross Drivers, European Drag Racing Championship, FIA Cup for Electro-Solar, European Championship for Autocross Drivers, European Hill Climbing Championship, Historic Grand Touring Cars, and Thoroughbred Grand Prix Cars.

Ecclestone justified the length of the contract by claiming that such a period of time was necessary in order to recoup losses as a result of the 'large resources' invested in the filming of non-Formula One events and their marketing to television broadcasters. However, this claim was in direct contradiction to a letter from ISC to a third party, which stated that 'ISC does not itself engage directly in the activity of filming motor sport events (it does not, for example, employ any technicians or cameramen). ISC invariably engages or licenses third party production companies ... to produce footage of events for which the FIA has transferred the television rights to ISC.'

With control of the television marketing of all other motor sports, Ecclestone was now in a perfect position to ensure that no other event could threaten the dominance of Formula One as the number-one motor sport and, therefore, its television revenue. There had been legal clashes in earlier years over the television rights of non-Formula One events, as seen with the Automobile Club de Monaco and the Automobile Club de l'Ouest over, respectively, the Monte Carlo Rally and the Le Mans 24-Hour race, but that, as much as anything else, had been a political issue of the FIA being seen to assert its authority. This was a very different ball game.

Ever since the breakaway from the European Broadcasting Union, Ecclestone had been pumping huge sums of money into his television production company to boast the latest state-of-the-art digital technology. The General Assembly, unwittingly or otherwise, had now ensured, through the 15-year agreement awarding him the FIA's Formula One television rights and the granting of all non-Formula One television rights to ISC, that Ecclestone's massive investment had the best possible protection the FIA could offer. But it was highly probable that, legally, the FIA was in no position to award the non-Formula One rights to Ecclestone. As Mosley conceded, ownership of the rights was not as simple as had been assumed in the early Concorde Agreements, a discovery that would have surely applied with equal force to all motor sports.

Mosley was scornful of any suggestion that the rules had been introduced to restrict television coverage of 'lesser' motor sports to the benefit of Formula One. The vast majority of the General Assembly's 120 delegates, he insisted, would hardly have agreed to such a move when only 14 of them hosted the Formula One races; the remaining delegates would have refused to allow television coverage of their own national motor sport events to be systematically suppressed. To agree with that assertion would be to fail to understand the control that Ecclestone and Mosley wielded over the General Assembly. There were few delegates with an eye to their future who would have dared oppose either man within or without the assembly's august gathering.

In an attempt to allay the mounting disquiet of organisers and promoters affected by the new rules, Mosley sent an open letter to the presidents of the FIA's national sporting authorities in April 1996. He justified them by arguing that 'with the expansion of international television and the vast number of channels (both satellite and free-to-air) which will shortly be available, any other course would involve substantial risks. For example, individual teams and sponsors making programmes that are just advertising disguised as sport; many organisations competing for air time and offering inducements to television channels to show programmes; all sorts of companies springing up from outside motor sport, offering television facilities, and so forth. The results would be chaos, reduced overall coverage and damage to the image of international motor sport.'

The letter did nothing to mollify the organisers. While whatever some organisers and promoters of non-Formula One motor sport earned from television coverage was little enough, it was nevertheless a crucial source of revenue. That they were allowed to retain television rights in their own country was, in practice, of very little worth indeed. For if organisers or promoters wanted their event to be marketed in other countries, where the potential financial returns lay, they were compelled, of course, to go through ISC. And organisers first had to make heavy financial investment in television equipment and expertise to produce a quality considered suitable by ISC. A senior executive of an event in the FIA World Cup for Cross Country Rallies, which he requested not to be identified for fear of 'rocking the boat', explained: 'It was completely at our expense with zero return for us. It is nonsense to say we had rights in our country. It didn't mean anything at all. We had to give ISC our video material free of charge and they, supposedly, would market it on our behalf. Frankly, we didn't put huge resources into it because we knew that ISC had absolutely no interest in distributing our product round the world. They never showed us any evidence that they had actively promoted our sport ... throughout the rest of the world.'

The impact of the agreement with ISC had a devastating effect even on major manufacturers such as Opel, Alfa Romeo and Mercedes. In the light of the disasters of Procar and the Sportscar World Championship, Alfa Romeo and Mercedes in particular were looking to the German-based national touring car championship, the Deutsche Tourenwagen Meisterschaft (DTM), to provide a major international showcase. However, since its launch in 1986 operating budgets and vehicle costs had grown to such an extent that the manufacturers were having difficulty justifying its cost as a national championship. They successfully applied to the FIA for the series to have international status, which would give much wider television exposure and the opportunity to recoup some of their costs through host countries. The FIA, which largely meant Mosley and Ecclestone, agreed, and in 1995 the DTM became the International Touringcar Championship (ITC). That was when their troubles started.

By the end of the 1996 season, serious concerns were being expressed by the manufacturers about the level of television coverage the series was getting through the efforts of ISC. The following March the championship suffered a major blow in Germany, the heartland of the series, with the loss of television coverage when the independent German television network, RTL, which also, incidentally, broadcasts Formula One, was unable to agree terms with International Touringcar Racing, the organisation which ran the series for the FIA, and which was promoted by ISC. It was suspected that the popularity of the ITC series was proving too much of a threat in Germany for the liking of Ecclestone. Trying to pre-empt such speculation, he issued a statement before the breakdown in talks between RTL and International Touringcar Racing in which he claimed that 'if ITC is better than Formula One, then so be it. Formula One had better get its act together and do a better job, because we are not interested in protecting anything.'[3] It was a statement that did more to confirm than deny that very aim.

The likes of Opel executive director Jürgen Stockmar and Hans Wilhelm Gäb, General Motors' European vice-president of public affairs, felt in no way reassured. They were experiencing at first hand the damage that was being done by ISC to the ITC series. In a letter to Ecclestone dated 19 June 1996 they were highly critical of the level of media coverage achieved by ISC, including restrictions imposed by the company that year on the general sports media at the first four rounds of the championship at Hockenheim, the Nurburgring, Estoril and Helsinki. They complained that television coverage, both in Germany and overseas, had been 'a fraction of previous years' viewing figures'; spectator attendance at the two German tracks had also been 'significantly below' that of previous years; and the control by ISC of cameras had been so tight that even the manufacturers had been prohibited from shooting video footage of their own cars.

In a five-point action list, whose implementation was necessary to 'justify the high financial and technical commitment required', Stockmar and Gäb wanted ISC to make television and video material freely available without restriction to all interested TV stations and to make available detailed information of international television coverage achieved by ISC. Ecclestone claimed in reply that he had personally made efforts to see 'greatly improved television coverage that has been enjoyed in the past ... and this has been achieved'. Despite contractual agreements he had inherited, he added that he had also 'managed to expand the coverage' in Germany. The FIA attempted to confirm Ecclestone's 'achievement' in a press briefing in June 1997, when it claimed that, as a result of centralised marketing through ISC, television coverage of the ITC had been 'a major success', exceeding the international coverage of its parent series, the DTM.

But such claims were not borne out by the experiences of organisers, manufacturers and competitors. Nor by the Institut für Medienanalysen, a research company which analysed viewing statistics provided by the Gesellschaft für Sozial- und Konsumforschung, an official monitoring agency set up by German broadcasters. Coverage of the ITC series on free-to-air, satellite and cable television in 1996, compared with the previous year, had dropped by 22.98 per cent, with audience viewing figures down from 237.1 million to 146.12 million, a decrease of 38.37 per cent.

Criticism of ISC was also made by Alfa Romeo, which three months later followed Opel in withdrawing from the ITC. Due to a lack of television and media coverage, the company was no longer able to justify the high cost of competing in the series. The decision by Opel and Alfa Romeo to pull out at the end of the 1996 season left Mercedes as the sole manufacturer. Unable to continue alone, it was forced to withdraw, finally killing a motor sport which had enjoyed huge popularity in Germany for ten years and at one time had been as successful as Formula One. Mosley responded to the manufacturers' withdrawal by claiming that it had nothing to do with lack of television coverage, but with the 'very high cost of running cars suitable for the event'. Another factor, he added, was the lack of interest outside of Germany in a series consisting mainly of cars and drivers 'who were German or mainly known in Germany'. Proof that the FIA was not to blame (as a result of awarding the television rights to ISC), was, he added, the fact that neither Opel nor Alfa Romeo had refused to each pay $2.66 million compensation 'due to the FIA by each of them under the terms of the guarantees that they offered in return for the FIA's endorsement'.

The guarantees were actually covered by Ecclestone as an essential feature of an unusual arrangement that enriched the FIA by £5.3 million. It came about through a deadlock between the manufacturers and the FIA, who had insisted that, if they wanted the Deutsche Tourenwagen Meisterschaft to become an international FIA championship, they would have to undertake, jointly and severally, to provide a field of 24 cars, a stipulation they were not prepared to meet. At a World Motor Sport Council meeting on 30 March 1995, Ecclestone, after talks with the three manufacturers, offered to guarantee that they would take part; if any one of them failed to do so, he would pay the FIA $8 million. In that event, under the terms of an agreement with the three manufacturers, he would seek recovery of his money from them. When Opel and Alfa Romeo withdrew, blaming poor media coverage by ISC, Ecclestone promptly paid the FIA a total of $5.32 million, which he then claimed from the two companies. Mercedes, for their part, successfully argued that as they were prepared to continue, they ought not to be penalised. The FIA agreed and decided not to demand the full $8 million from Ecclestone, a gracious consideration that, in a reversal of similar circumstances, it is unlikely he would have granted them.

One of the ways in which ISC caused fatal harm to the coverage of the ITC series was illustrated by the experience of three Japanese television stations. Although no Japanese driver or car took part, they were nevertheless happy to screen highlights because Bridgestone, a Japanese company, supplied the tyres. Traditionally, they received the highlights free of charge with the blessing of the organisers and the manufacturers, who were delighted to get the exposure. This was particularly so for Mercedes, which had a major market in Japan. As the independent television production company was paid by the manufacturers for covering and distributing the film footage, it was a win-win situation for everyone. However, once ISC became involved, relationships with the Japanese television companies rapidly soured. When one of them contacted a German television production company requesting material of a championship round, they were referred, as the FIA had insisted, to ISC. The Japanese television company was told that film would no longer be supplied free of charge. Instead, it would have to pay $15,000 per race. It was the beginning of the end of television coverage of the series in Japan.

Another popular motor sport to suffer from the marketing monopoly of ISC was European Truck Racing, which had enjoyed the enthusiastic and generous patronage of truck manufacturers such as MAN, Daimler-Benz and DAF. Figures supplied by the Institut für Medienanalysen showed that the aggregate viewing audience of European Truck Racing in Germany in 1997 compared with the previous year had dropped from 540,000 to 370,000, with rally coverage, incidentally, down from 980,000 to 420,000. For the same period the coverage and viewing figures of Formula One showed a marked increase: the number of free-to-air, satellite and cable broadcasters increased from 41 to 51, news items from 790 to 1614 and the number of viewers from 481.56 million to 811.32 million. 'The compulsory assignment of rights pushed through by the FIA,' said MAN, 'has the result that the organisers and manufacturers bear all economic risks and Mr Ecclestone receives all marketing profits'. Daimler-Benz claimed that when ISC was made responsible for the marketing of television rights, all those active in motor sport became dependent on one person and his companies.

ISC's control of non-Formula One motor sport also produced another casualty. This was the small independent television companies whose principal business came from covering the more popular championship and international series. Such a company was AE TV Cooperation, based in Heidelberg, Germany, and owned by Wolfgang Eisele, an intense, quietly spoken German, who set up his small motor sport television production company in 1983. Over the next few years the business prospered and expanded to cover rallying, rallycross driving and drag racing for the international television market. Eisele, in conjunction with a sister company, also had spent ten years building up the international television market for the International Touringcar Championship. By 1995 the future for Eisele was looking good. At the age of 40, with no particular empire-building aspirations, he had reached a point where he was content with the size of his company and its turnover of 1.8 million Deutschmarks (about £760,000).

But the effect of ISC's marketing stranglehold was so debilitating that he was eventually forced to reduce his staff from 12 to two. Suddenly the company he had worked so hard to build up was in dire trouble. He decided he had two choices: either roll over and die, or fight back. 'What Ecclestone was doing was so wrong,' said Eisele. 'It was like me setting up the World Federation of Ball Sports and claiming the rights to every sport from football to lacrosse.' He decided to catch a plane to London.

On a dull November day in 1996, Eisele sat in Ecclestone's expansive, immaculately furnished Knightsbridge office opposite Hyde Park to plead his case. He knew well Ecclestone's reputation and expected little, but he held on to the hope that Ecclestone might throw him a bone and at least let him continue to cover European Truck Racing, one of the more popular international series on the FIA calendar, with races in France, Italy, Spain, Germany, Finland, Great Britain, Czechoslovakia and Belgium. The event had been a major source of income for Eisele, and now, as he sat before the poker-faced Ecclestone, he attempted to persuade the Formula One boss to relent. His best efforts were in vain. As he reflected later: 'It was as if we were on different planets. It was as if he was up there and I was down here; we couldn't connect.'

At the end of the two-hour meeting, the German, despondent and fearful for the fate of his business, left Ecclestone's office for his return flight to Frankfurt. He now believed he had nothing to lose by playing his only card – a complaint to the European Commission in Brussels that Ecclestone's relationship with the teams, the FIA, the organisers and television broadcasters amounted to a flagrant breach of competition law. A motor sport contact advised him to see a young German lawyer, Dr Wolfgang Deselaers, a specialist in European competition law and a partner in Oppenhoff & Rädler, a German law company with offices in Brussels, where Deselaers was based. Deselaers had his doubts about taking Eisele as a client. His initial reaction was that Eisele was way out of his league, lacking both the cash and political clout to take on the combined forces of Ecclestone and Mosley. At the same time, in this classic David-and-Goliath conflict, he was attracted by Eisele's determination to fight back.

His new client's improbable situation caused Deselaers to advise a cautious approach to save costs, with, first, legal action in a civil court to clarify whether the FIA's centralised television marketing of all international championships contravened European cartel law. Deselaers proposed to argue that television rights should belong to the parties who took the financial risks. On 10 and 27 February 1997 he filed complaints at districts courts in Frankfurt and Cologne respectively against the FIA to freeze their claim to the ownership of all television rights and against Ecclestone and ISC to restrain implementation of that claim. On 27 May he moved on to the second stage: a formal complaint to the European Commission in Brussels against the FIA and ISC, alleging they had infringed European Community competition laws under Articles 85 and 86 of the EC Treaty, which prohibit cartels and abuse of a dominant position. Deselaers believed that Ecclestone's various commercial interests and executive roles within the FIA constituted a clear conflict of interest by allowing him to regulate the market activities of Formula One's competitors.

The complaint by Eisele was filed at the office of the European

Commission's Directorate-General for Competition, whose Commissioner was a 55-year-old Belgian, Karel van Miert, a former vice-chairman of the European Community's Confederation of Socialist Parties and a Socialist Member of the European Parliament, who became the European Commissioner in charge of competition policy in 1993. It marked the beginning of a highly bitter and personal battle between Max Mosley and van Miert that would last for three years, and which would prove a major obstacle in Ecclestone's ambitious plans for Formula One, and the furtherance of his wealth.

13

THE SINKING OF BERNIE'S $2.5 BILLION FLOTATION PLANS

Bernie Ecclestone was gambling big on his digital television plans. He had begun exploring its commercial potential as early as 1992 and three years later, at the Belgian Grand Prix, was so enthused by the results of experimental tests by his FOCA TV that the following year he invested £36 million of his own money in the company's further development, which was responsible for reducing his salary in 1996 from £29 million to a mere bagatelle of £600,000. But Ecclestone believed it was a salary cut worth taking when compared with the revenue he believed that digital television coverage of Formula One would generate within the next few years. Such was his confidence in its long-term financial returns that he predicted that it would one day make Formula One independent of sponsors, who at that time were contributing about £135 million a year.

He believed a major draw would be a multi-feed broadcast – actually his concept – to persuade the more enthusiastic Formula One fan to pay at least $20 (about £12.50) in return for 'directing' his own race. At the press of a button he would be able to select any one of several options: general coverage, the contest between the leading cars, the competition between other cars, pit-lane activities featuring interviews with drivers and team managers, a channel giving real-time lap and general statistics, or, and tipped as the biggest attraction of all, on-board cameras enabling the fan to switch from cockpit to cockpit. At the 1996 German Grand Prix at Hockenheim he predicted that all Grand Prix races would eventually be pay-per-view, although he declined to forecast the year. The early signs certainly looked encouraging.

In April 1996, at the European Grand Prix at the Nurburgring, he announced a £50-million deal with the KirchGruppe, a major German television company owned by media magnate Leo Kirch, who in 2001 was co-ranked the sixth richest man in Europe, with an estimated personal fortune of £7.6 billion, to broadcast pay-TV coverage of Formula One through one of his channels, DF1, in a pilot scheme scheduled to be aired in Germany, Austria and Switzerland that July. Four months later Ecclestone announced a similar deal with Paris-based Canal+ to broadcast in France and Italy. It would be available in Britain, he forecast, by 2002. He also had contracts with RTL Plus in Germany and public-service broadcaster RAI in Italy.

FOCA TV, which became F1 Communications, was based at Biggin Hill, Kent, the former RAF wartime airfield, which Ecclestone would buy in 1997 and where he hangar'd his two Learjets. It would soon, and rapidly, expand to become a 300-tonne mobile television production facility spread over 1400 square metres, complete with its own electricity generators and satellite communications equipment. Manned by a staff of 280 – three-quarters of the people in Ecclestone's employ – it would require three 747 jumbo jets to transport the equipment to races outside Europe and 28 purpose-built articulated lorries within Europe. Key production staff would be flown to every race in an Ecclestone-owned BAE 146 jet, decked out in Formula One livery, air hostesses and napkins included. It was, it should be noted, against the backcloth of this degree of investment and potential returns that Ecclestone wanted to make sure that his plans could in no way be threatened by non-Formula One motor sport, which the FIA's General Assembly guaranteed when Mosley awarded their television rights to Ecclestone's International Sportsworld Communicators.

By the middle of 1996 Ecclestone, at a personal cost of many tens of millions of pounds, had developed and established a company at the forefront of digital broadcasting technology. He believed he was now in a position to capitalise his huge investment and make himself fabulously rich by pursuing a suggestion from his close friend Marco Piccinini, a former boss of the Ferrari team and a member of the influential Formula One Commission and who two years later would become the FIA's deputy president of motor sport. Piccinini suggested to Ecclestone that he should float Formula One Administration (FOA) on the stock market. While Ecclestone was attracted by the capital he confidently expected it to raise, there was another, more pragmatic, reason that persuaded him to investigate the suggestion further, and it marked an awareness of his mortality: how would his wife, Slavica, in whose name his shares in FOA were held, cope with the running of Formula One's complex commercial interests on his death? A successful flotation would ensure an experienced management structure to safeguard its future.

By September 1996 Ecclestone was having secret talks with American investment bankers Salomon Brothers to discuss the flotation of Formula One Administration, whose principal assets could be stored in a briefcase – a portfolio of 66 contracts with free-to-air and pay-TV companies. The length of the free-to-air contracts ranged from five to ten years while the pay-TV contracts, which covered 94 countries, were for up to 11 years. The television contracts included a five-year agreement with ITV signed ten months earlier and worth £60 million, nearly ten times the figure the BBC had been paying. The offer had been on a take-it-or-leave-it basis, without the BBC having the chance to bid. Ecclestone decided to take it. Senior BBC executives, who claimed the BBC had nurtured and promoted Formula One for 20 years, were furious when the news was suddenly announced by ITV. But its manner was in keeping with Ecclestone's business code. He will, he insists, always accept a 'sensible' offer and never go to another party and play one off against the other to raise the bid.

Leading the Salomon Brothers team was 32-year-old Cambridge and Harvard graduate, Christian Purslow, the company's high-flying director of media investment banking, who was formerly with Crédit Suisse First Boston, where he made his name handling Virgin's bid for MGM cinemas. Purslow also had meetings with Mosley to confirm that a flotation would have the full support of the FIA. Mosley assured him that it would – he had negotiated with Ecclestone a ten per cent stake for the FIA in the flotation, optimistically estimated at the time to be worth $300 million, in return for agreeing a ten-year extension to the 15-year contract due to expire in 2010, but which, as its length fell foul of European Union anti-trust rules, would not take effect.

As an indication of the FIA's support, that September, at the Italian Grand Prix at Monza, Mosley enthusiastically flagged the prospect of a flotation 'within the next five years'. Ecclestone, he said, had done a 'brilliant' job in turning the sport into a multi-million-dollar business, adding that 'the entrepreneurial phase is now almost finished. The final stage is the development of pay-TV and digital transmission. There will then be a phase where the business needs to be managed, at which point Bernie may decide to go public. The FIA would welcome that because it would mean that every detail of F1 finances would be out in the open.'

The date agreed for the launch of one of the biggest share flotations in sporting history was 13 July 1997, to coincide with the British Grand Prix, a date selected by Purslow, whose team was hired by Ecclestone as his exclusive financial advisers for the next ten months. The company to be floated was to be called Formula One Holdings (FOH), which was incorporated in December 1996, and, promoted as 'sexy' media stock to hype up its market appeal, was expected to be valued as high as £2–2.5 billion.

FOH became a wholly owned subsidiary of SLEC Holdings, a family trust registered in Jersey in the name of Ecclestone's wife, Slavica, in May 1997. In October 1997 SLEC Holdings, as part of an elaborate tax-avoidance scheme, became a subsidiary of Bambino Holdings Ltd, which is owned by Orion, the trust set up in Switzerland to protect the family wealth. Ecclestone's decision to sign away his fortune to his wife was met with universal scepticism. What was his angle? There wasn't one, says Ecclestone. 'No one in the world believes that I would have given all that I had to my wife, but that is actually what I did. I wanted to make sure that she and the children were well looked after if anything happened to me.' The money went into a trust to avoid Slavica, a non-domicile, paying 40 per cent in inheritance tax to the UK government in the event of Ecclestone's death. The decision to move the shares into a trust proved all the more percipient when, in June 1999, at the age of 68, Ecclestone underwent a triple-bypass heart operation, the success of which was by no means assured.

The two principal companies within FOH were Formula One Administration Ltd and Formula One Management Ltd, a subsidiary of Petara Ltd, a trust set up in Jersey in July 1994. Two other companies, Formula One Productions Ltd and Formula One World Travel Ltd, were respectively subsidiaries of Formula One Management Ltd and Petara Ltd. It was this complex cat's-cradle of companies that the bankers had to sell to potential investors wary of Formula One's highly individualistic boss. If all went to plan, it was estimated that the Ecclestones would be at least £700 million the richer, with a 40 per cent shareholding being retained in Slavica's name. With an estimated wealth at that time of about £750 million, the family fortune would soar to almost £1.5 billion.

Salomon Brothers lined up an impressive 18-strong syndicate of blue-chip investment banks to take the flotation to the market, including Deutsche Morgan Grenfell, Merrill Lynch, SBC Warburg, BZW, Morgan Stanley Dean Witter, Nikko and NatWest Markets. Ecclestone, as chief executive, had assembled his board-in-waiting: Marco Piccinini was appointed deputy chief executive; Helmut Werner, former chief executive of Mercedes, was appointed non-executive chairman; and David Wilson, a former Ladbroke Group financial executive, finance director. Everything seemed in place. But if everyone appeared in unison on the surface, there existed considerable acrimony behind the scenes between Ecclestone and three leading team bosses, McLaren's Ron Dennis, Frank Williams and Ken Tyrrell, which seriously threatened a smooth, trouble-free launch. The three team bosses were ready to exploit that threat to the full.

They claimed to have had no knowledge of the Formula One Agreement agreed between Ecclestone and Max Mosley prior to its signing in December 1995, which granted him the television rights for 15 years until 2010. They felt that in failing to consult them he had acted unfairly and improperly. In the 1992 Concorde Agreement FOCA members had agreed to transfer management of its commercial rights to one of Ecclestone's companies, Formula One Promotions and Administration, in return for annual royalty payments, similar to those agreed between Balestre and Allsopp, Parker & Marsh. They saw Ecclestone's 'secret' agreement as a betrayal of their relationship. Also unbeknown to the teams, the name of FOCA Administration Ltd, which represented the teams and to whom the rights had been previously leased for Ecclestone to market, was changed to Formula One Administration, of which he was sole director, and which took effect from February 1997, as details of the flotation launch were being finalised.

The three team bosses had long maintained that the FIA had had no right to assume ownership of the rights. This conflict with Ecclestone – and Mosley – was something of a running sore, a continuation of an earlier dispute over the future ownership of Formula One's commercial rights in the event of Ecclestone's death. As early as 1993, Dennis, Williams and Tyrrell, the sole survivors of the first Concorde Agreement of 1981, began discussions with Ecclestone to acquire through a trading vehicle called Newco an option to purchase Formula One Administration Ltd on his retirement or death. At one stage Ecclestone was thought to be open to a deal, which the three men wanted to see concluded in time for inclusion in the 1997 Concorde Agreement. With the support of Luca Montezemolo, the Ferrari team boss, Dennis and Williams – Tyrrell didn't want the cost – brought in their lawyers to draw up a draft agreement. In January 1995 what became macabrely dubbed the Dying Agreement was circulated to the teams, stating, in effect, that, on Ecclestone's death, Formula One Administration would be bought from his heirs for its market value less 30 per cent by a company formed by the teams, the size of whose shareholdings would be largely based on seniority. It got no further than Ecclestone's paper shredder.

He claimed that it would give 51 per cent control of the company to Dennis, Williams and Tyrrell, a counter-argument they firmly denied – 'it was totally democratic with no one team having control,' said Tyrrell. But Ecclestone had another reason to reject the bid – by now he was talking to Mosley about the 15-year deal with the FIA to help raise the necessary finance to fund the expansion of his burgeoning pay-TV business. (Mosley, incidentally, claims that it took him about 18 months to overcome Ecclestone's resistance, due, he believed, to a sense of loyalty to the teams.) From that point, the Dying

Agreement, and team bosses' ambitions with it, died on its feet. Said Ecclestone: 'If all the teams owned it, they'd destroy it. They can't agree on anything, not even on how to share their money out. They think they can run the business – I know they can't.'[1]

During July and August 1996 a frosty exchange of letters passed between Tyrrell, who believed that the interests of the teams had been subjugated in favour of Ecclestone's and the FIA's, and Mosley, who believed that the constructors could have negotiated directly with the FIA 'but they chose not to'. To which Tyrrell replied: 'The greatest shock from your letter was the revelation that you believe we, the FOCA, should have been negotiating directly with the FIA for our own future, because Bernie was negotiating for his future and not ours. Were we not entitled to expect the FOCA president would represent our interests above his own?'

In his correspondence with Mosley, Tyrrell's contentions were based on four claims: Ecclestone should have at all times acted solely for the FOCA and should not have negotiated any arrangements on his own behalf – as president of the FOCA, this raised a clear conflict of interest; ownership of the rights belonged to the teams due to their importance over the years to Formula One; that the teams were receiving an inadequate share of Formula One's commercial revenue; and that Mosley had taken Ecclestone's side rather than that of the teams.

Mosley's reply was that Ecclestone had 'for at least 15 years' run his own Formula One business with his position as FOCA president. 'It is difficult for me to understand how anyone can claim this was a situation of conflict of interest, when it was precisely the arrangement that some of the teams hoped to take over for their own benefit later on, by purchasing the business from Bernie or his estate'; that the teams' claim of ownership of the commercial rights, which they had agreed to the contrary in successive Concorde Agreements, had no basis 'in law, in custom or in fact'; that the signatories to the Concorde Agreement were not prohibited from collective bargaining (with Ecclestone) within the agreement to secure a share of other commercial revenues – 'I do not believe the FIA should interfere in such negotiations'; that the FIA was 'strictly neutral' in the commercial arrangements between race promoters and the teams, including Ecclestone in his 'race-promoter' capacity.

'If anything, the FIA has favoured the teams, because we at no time asked them to give up any part of the television income in return for the very big investments Bernie was making in digital TV, time-keeping, circuit hardware, etc, which were for their benefit and as well as his and, ultimately, the FIA's. It was the FIA which made these investments feasible, even if risky, by swapping its percentage for a fixed fee. In one respect, however, the FIA does prefer Bernie: he has never claimed (as have some of the teams) that the rights in the

FIA World Championship belong to anyone other than the FIA. With Bernie, the FIA knows that it will get back its rights intact after the contract period without any disputes.' Later that month Mosley attempted to isolate Dennis, Williams and Tyrrell by sending copies of his letters to Tyrrell to the teams. In one, he warned that the confrontation had serious implications for the future of Formula One and 'will almost certainly result in the loss of major sponsors and engine suppliers'.

Such was the degree of anger within the FOCA that some team owners, believing that Ecclestone had breached his legal obligations as president of the FOCA, began discussing a plan to remove him from office. Ecclestone, it was argued, had had no right to negotiate the purchase, for his own interests, commercial rights which, under the terms of the Concorde Agreement, had been assigned to the FOCA for him to market. The proposal to unseat Ecclestone got no further for lack of the necessary support, and, to thwart any future attempt to remove him, Mosley agreed that a new clause would be inserted in the 1997 Concorde Agreement which gave the FIA the right to veto his successor to the presidency of the FOCA.

Due to the long-standing and unresolved tension between them and Ecclestone and Mosley, Dennis, Williams and Tyrrell now refused to add their signatures to the new Concorde Agreement due to take effect from January 1997, and which the rest of the teams had signed the previous March. In return for the loss of 'their' television rights, they were insisting on a substantial increase in the teams' share of television revenue, as well as a wedge of the huge revenues generated by advertising and corporate hospitality – estimated at more than £90 million a year – and fees paid by organisers and promoters, said to total an estimated £80 million a year.

Ecclestone refused to yield, claiming that no team, or teams, was bigger than Formula One. The three rebel team bosses, for their part, continued to claim that it was the likes of McLaren, Williams, Tyrrell and Ferrari who attracted the crowds, the media interest and the sponsors. Without them, Formula One would be like the Premier League without Manchester United, Liverpool, Arsenal and Tottenham Hotspur. Ecclestone set out to bring the three rebel teams to heel by the simple expedient of divide and rule, with money as the lever, guaranteed to succeed in Formula One like nothing else can. Purposefully excluding invitations to Dennis, Williams and Tyrrell, he called a meeting of team bosses at the Excelsior Hotel at Heathrow Airport on 7 August 1996, where he received their immediate and total support by offering them their rebel colleagues' shares of the 50 per cent of the television revenue allocated to the FOCA and distributed equally between Concorde Agreement signatories.

Whether it was the loss of their share of television revenue or a decision to keep their powder dry until Ecclestone's flotation put him in a more vulnerable position – more probably the latter as events would indicate – a few weeks later Williams indicated to Mosley that he might be prepared to sign the Concorde Agreement on equal terms to the other teams. It was also hinted that Dennis and Tyrrell might agree to do likewise. In early September, at Ferrari's headquarters in Maranello, the teams met to discuss the change of heart. It was welcomed with unanimous approval – but only to a point. They weren't prepared to welcome the three back into the fold if it meant returning their colleagues' shares. The meeting was adjourned for three months, until January 1997, when a compromise solution was put on the table. However, it essentially excluded the three teams from the new financial arrangement for 12 months, which was rejected out of hand by Dennis, Williams and Tyrrell, who had now engaged their own lawyers. Their reply was to issue an ultimatum to Ecclestone – either allow them back in on equal terms by 26 March or face a complaint to Brussels under the European Commission's competition rules.

All three men were willing to go to the edge with Ecclestone. Williams and Tyrrell, in particular, were seasoned stalwarts of the FOCA and had stood alongside Ecclestone in the front line of battle against Balestre and the FIA during the stormy seventies. None of them was a mug punter in his thrall. And, although not in his financial league, they had the money to go more than a few bloody rounds. Dennis, a former mechanic with Cooper and Brabham – he quit some time before Ecclestone bought the team – took over McLaren Racing in 1982, which by 1995 was, after Ferrari, the second richest team in Formula One, with an annual turnover of £48.5 million. He and Williams were attributed with personal fortunes of £150 million and £97 million respectively. Tyrrell's wealth did not put him in the rich list but he was scarcely in need of an Oxfam food parcel. In 1997, at 72, and after more than 30 years in Formula One, he sold the Tyrrell Racing Organisation he had launched in 1968 to British American Racing for £18 million. (Tragically, he didn't live long enough to enjoy the money. Five years later, on 25 August 2001, one of the more honest and charismatic figures in Formula One died of cancer.)

In threatening to take Ecclestone to Brussels, the three men knew they were touching something of a raw nerve. By now the German independent television production company boss, Wolfgang Eisele, and his lawyer, Dr Wolfgang Deselaers, were getting ready to go through the German courts for a legal ruling on Ecclestone's control of Formula One and file a complaint to the European Commission. Although Ecclestone had yet to come toe-to-toe with the bureaucrats of Brussels, the mere mention of their name even then was, said a Formula One insider, 'like the sight of holy water to a vampire'. With the proposed flotation soon to be announced, the very last thing Ecclestone wanted was a protracted and highly public dispute in Brussels with the three stars of his show as witnesses for the prosecution. Over the next few weeks he came up with a fresh set of proposals in the hope of ending the dispute once and for all. Although its terms were kept confidential, it effectively meant a redrafting of the Concorde Agreement which reinstated the three teams to full parity, their respective shares of television revenue to be restored the following season – a total of £70 million – and full involvement in what was described as 'a multi-million-pound incentive plan'. It seemed that peace had finally been restored. Unhappily for Ecclestone's flotation plans, it would prove an all too brief respite.

As someone with an obsessive need to be in control, the way in which news of the proposed launch reached the public domain put Ecclestone in a high state of lather. There it was, splashed across the pages of two Sunday broadsheets in March, at least a week ahead of the scheduled date. There had been a leak. Ecclestone was incensed. The Grand Prix teams had known nothing of the planned flotation. He had been caught off-balance. It was not the most propitious of beginnings in a relationship that, given Ecclestone's visceral mistrust of the City, was never likely to be smooth and cordial.

Such an unpromising start was followed by a typically indiscreet statement from Ecclestone in which he professed his complete disinterest in a flotation, as well as a considerable lack of confidence in his financial advisers. 'My feeling is to wait and see. Whatever we put on the market will be valued at that figure, so I may as well wait for the revenue stream from pay-TV, which will bring in enormous profit and give Formula One its full worth. Salomon Brothers is telling me this is a stupid attitude, and the market is good at the moment. The more they talk the less interested I am.'[2] It was believed that the leak seriously impaired their relationship, which over the weeks ahead was not improved by the difficulties Salomon Brothers encountered in persuading Ecclestone to be more open with his books.

Commenting on Ecclestone's unorthodox practice of keeping his financial affairs well hidden, Formula One Holdings' finance director, David Wilson, said: 'Bernie has always kept a tight rein on all financial information to protect his position in negotiations with broadcasters, teams and promoters. Now the company is going public that has to be balanced against the need to be more transparent.'[3] It soon became clear that the flotation was going to take a lot longer to organise than Salomon Brothers had envisaged. Essentially, they were having considerable difficulty in pulling together a satisfactory five-year trading history for a draft prospectus that had to go before the Stock Exchange for approval before it could be distributed to potential investors. There were, it was understood, inadequate explanations of where the television revenues had gone in previous years, why some had ended up in Geneva and some in

London. Ecclestone, it was said, was feeling uncomfortable at the degree of business detail the prospectus would have to reveal. It became increasingly clear to Salomon Brothers that a July launch was going to prove a difficult target to meet. Not for nothing was Ecclestone described by a London investment banker as 'the client from hell'.[4]

As rumours abounded in the City of an increasingly tense relationship between Ecclestone and Salomon Brothers, doubts were being cast on a price tag of £2–2.5 billion on a company whose market worth was being calculated on nothing more tangible than television contracts, with assets valued at about £8 million. Television rights sales the previous year had been no higher than £220 million with profits at £85 million. In the view of John Stittle, senior lecturer in accounting and finance at Anglia University, even a £2-billion valuation meant valuing the company at a multiple of 20 times its earnings level, 'which demonstrated a quantum leap of faith in the size of future revenues. And even that valuation assumed the most optimistic discounted projected earnings at typical media sector estimates and included extremely optimistic forecasts of pay-for-view television revenues.' Stittle agreed with investment fund managers and financial experts who believed that a more realistic basis of valuation would have been between £1 billion and £1.5 billion.

Some analysts suggested that the anticipated revenues accounted for as much as a third of the company's expected price, a calculation that apparently did not stand up well against audience figures in Germany, where Ecclestone had signed the £50 million deal with the KirchGruppe. The figure had fallen far short of the 700,000 subscribers that were expected by the end of 1997. Similarly, in France and Italy, where it was estimated 15 per cent of viewers would buy into the digital satellite service, only 30,000 of the channel's 500,000 subscribers had signed up for the $130-a-year package by September 1997. An industry analyst claimed senior executives at Canal+ were 'very mad' at the poor level of consumer interest. He added that the five-year deal between Ecclestone and company chairman Pierre Lescure was in danger of not being renewed 'if they do not find a solution, because it is a total disaster in terms of financial returns. The same thing has happened in Germany.'

It seemed that fans were sufficiently satisfied with the quality of free-to-air coverage to be disinclined to dip into their pockets for the additional cost. Earlier in the year, shortly after the news of the planned flotation was made public, there was speculation at the Brazilian Grand Prix that Ecclestone was planning to limit free-to-air coverage to encourage fans to subscribe to his digital television channel – a tactic not dissimilar to that deployed to promote Formula One to the cost of other motor sports. The dilemma for Ecclestone was that while the potential of digital television was enormous, he was aware that he needed the wider and more popular shop window of free-to-air coverage to keep sponsors happy.

The quality of free-to-air coverage, with just four on-car cameras, continued to prove so attractive, to the detriment of Ecclestone's pay-per-view revenue, that two years later, in April 1999, faced with complaints from digital television companies who were getting little in return for paying vast sums for a multi-feed service, he threatened once again to reduce the amount of on-board camera coverage to free-to-air television companies to make pay-per-view more attractive. He began to insist that if they wanted to continue to offer multi-feed coverage, they should help compensate the digital companies. The dispute led to the UK television network company, ITV, abandoning coverage of the qualifying session of the 1999 French Grand Prix.

By the end of 2000 – four years after its introduction – only seven countries had taken Ecclestone's pay-TV deal, leaving him out of pocket each year by many millions of pounds. Its lack of success, he insisted in a Formula One magazine, was due to broadcasters who had 'failed to get behind it like they should'. Hinting, for the first time, that perhaps he had got it wrong, he added: 'It's difficult to know whether pay-per-view is really what people want or not.'

While in early May Christian Purslow and his colleagues were still struggling to get a draft prospectus together for the approval of the Stock Exchange, 450 miles away in Frankfurt a district court was about to add to their woes. Independent television producer Wolfgang Eisele, who eight months earlier had pleaded in vain with Ecclestone to allow him to continue to cover European Truck Racing, was having his day in court, the first of many.

His lawyer, Dr Wolfgang Deselaers, asked the court to rule that the central marketing by the FIA of the television rights to European Truck Racing was a violation of European competition law. The court agreed, and on 4 June it issued an interim judgement which returned the rights to the organisers of the series throughout Europe. It was a significant ruling that challenged the FIA's claim to the television rights of the 18 other FIA international series and 17 FIA-authorised international series. (Mosley has subsequently insisted that the FIA had never claimed the television rights of the authorised series.) It threatened far-reaching implications for all sports in which pan-European or global television rights were controlled by one organisation. It also threatened Ecclestone's flotation: if legal ownership of the television rights was in doubt, what was Formula One Holdings putting up for sale? The court's decision plunged the flotation plans into even greater disarray. Salomon Brothers needed this legal broadside like Custer needed Indians.

Ecclestone and Mosley's response was swift and harsh – if the FIA didn't have the television rights to European Truck Racing, it would kill the series. A statement was authorised by Max Mosley announcing that the 1997 FIA European Truck Racing Cup would be cancelled. Two days later the response of the Frankfurt district court judges, following a complaint by Deselaers, was equally uncompromising: they warned that if the FIA proceeded to do so, its president, Max Mosley, would be liable to imprisonment and/or a maximum fine of 500,000 Deutschmarks. The FIA backed down, but with little grace. That same day Joachim Mann, sports director of the Allgemeiner Deutschland Automobil-Club, and president of the FIA's Truck Racing Commission, sent a fax to truck-race organisers informing them of the court's decision and that they were advised not to conclude contracts for television rights with Ecclestone's International Sportsworld Communicators. Mosley interpreted Mann's actions as deliberate interference in the issue of television rights; moreover, in running with the hares and running with the hounds, he had been 'incredibly disloyal'. He was called to appear before the FIA's World Motor Sport Council and invited to resign, which he did.

For Mann, who also had to resign his role as Formula One clerk of the course at the Nurburgring, it was an ignoble and humiliating end to more than 20 years of unstinting service to motor sport. (Mosley, incidentally, was not one to have the authority of the FIA easily challenged. At a more mundane level, when Britain's *Motoring News* dared to criticise the FIA for unfairly imposing a 12-month ban on Toyota Team Europe for using illegal turbo charges in the World Rally Championship, he telephoned the editor to say that he was withdrawing the FIA's co-operation with the paper until its standard of accuracy had improved.) The interim judgement, and media speculation about its implications for Formula One television rights, greatly irritated Ecclestone and Mosley.

Two days later Mosley issued a statement to clarify 'a significant lack of understanding of television in motor sport'. The lengthy statement went on to warn that if the European Commission decided the central marketing of Formula One was illegal, it 'would not change Formula One. The central marketing operation would simply move outside the European Union and continue as before. If the organisers in the European Union were then prevented from disposing of their rights to Formula One or were forced to allow all sorts of television producers to film at their event, the number of Formula One races in the European Union would decrease from the present ten to perhaps two or three, or even fewer. This would have a major effect on certain local economies, but would not damage Formula One itself, except in the short term. It must never be forgotten that of the FIA's 113 countries, only 15 are in the European Union. The other 98 are unaffected by the European Union's decisions. Of the global television audience for Formula One, less than 20 per cent is in the European Union. The relative importance of the

European Union audience is forecast to decrease steadily as world audiences continue to grow.'

It was an aggressive exhibition of sabre-rattling that few outside of the FIA took seriously: to kill Formula One in Europe, where at that time seven of the 17 events on the Formula One calendar were staged, would have inflicted devastating damage in loss of prestige and sponsor interest. It would also be inconceivable that Ferrari, Mercedes-Benz and Peugeot would agree to a move that would bring an end to an Italian, German or French Grand Prix. Ecclestone himself later acknowledged its implausibility, when he said: 'We would never move out of Europe ... the cost of moving all the races out of Europe, with all the transport fees, would be enormous.'

Just when Purslow and his team were probably thinking that things couldn't get any worse, they did. For while Ron Dennis, Frank Williams and Ken Tyrrell had agreed in May to sign the 1997 Concorde Agreement, the result of 22 drafts, they had yet to add their signatures – and refused to do so unless they had a stake in the flotation. A series of meetings was held in early June, which resulted in Ecclestone proposing either an increase in the teams' shares of television revenue or a ten per cent shareholding in the new company. To the team bosses it wasn't enough; they wanted both: a 20 per cent shareholding and an improved television rights cut. At a meeting on 6 June, Ecclestone stormed out, insisting the flotation would go ahead without them. Dennis, Williams and Tyrrell believed that they were now in the driving seat. It was thought that their delay in adding their signatures to the new agreement had been a deliberate ploy in order to apply maximum pressure on Ecclestone at a crucial stage of the flotation.

Ecclestone acknowledged that the latest dispute would hardly encourage the confidence of fund managers, but saw it all as a matter of perception. 'We have seen many teams come and go. We've seen Lotus and Brabham disappear and others take their place. Everyone said Formula One was finished when Ayrton Senna died. Most of the teams are happy in any event, and I don't foresee a problem.' However, there were now noises of discontent coming from the teams who had already signed the redrafted Concorde Agreement. They hadn't realised, they said, that, in doing so, they had waived their rights to any claim in the shareholding.

For the time being, Ecclestone remained adamant that there would be no free equity. 'The teams can go to hell. Some of them think they have me by the balls but their hands aren't big enough. Under no circumstances will they get any free equity or a position on the board. I don't blame them for wanting it but Formula One is bigger than the teams and it could float without them.' Whether it could or not, by now the question, at least for the time being, had become academic. The problems that Salomon Brothers had encountered had made a July launch an impossible deadline to meet. Ecclestone now billed it for September.

In addition to the intense hassle he was getting from Frankfurt and the teams, his relationship with Salomon Brothers was reaching a pretty low point. Soon after Ecclestone announced the postponement of the flotation, Max Mosley came up with another plan – that the FIA should float Formula One rather than Ecclestone. His reasoning was that the FIA could make a better claim to the title to the championship. It inaugurated the series in 1950, owned the trademarks and, with Ecclestone continuing to market the commercial interests, it would, thought Mosley, prove more attractive to investment institutions. And with Ecclestone one stage removed, it might stand a better chance of succeeding. Confidential talks were held with SBC Warburg, a member of the syndicate of investment banks selling the flotation. SBC agreed it made sense – but Ecclestone didn't. He believed it conflicted with his claim to ownership of the television rights. It went no further. Around the same time, BZW, Barclays' investment banking arm, proposed a deal to bring British Sky Broadcasting (BSkyB), Rupert Murdoch's satellite television channel, into Formula One by acquiring a stake in Formula One Holdings. Such was Ecclestone's frustration at what was going on around him that he had seriously considered calling the float off. 'All these people want to do is have bloody meetings with everybody,' he said.

Investor interest had reached such a depressing level that it was generally considered unlikely that the flotation would even take place in September, if at all. In an effort to fire up a somewhat indifferent market, Salomon Brothers heroically suggested to Ecclestone that he went off on a three-month international marketing trip. But the 'client from hell', who cared nothing for his reputation, would have none of it. 'I'll be damned if I'm going to do their job for them when they are being paid to market the company. I'm busy running this year's competition and after that I will be busy setting up next year's. I'm in no hurry and it [the flotation] will happen when I'm ready.' As anticipated, September came and went without the launch taking place. Ecclestone fixed another new date: early 1998. However, as he well knew, there were two serious impediments: the conflict with Brussels – and that included the sub-drama with Wolfgang Eisele – and the teams.

Mosley attempted to assist in the former by writing to the European Commission for Competition seeking a 'comfort letter' from its Commissioner, Karel van Miert, to the effect that his department had no concerns about the management of Formula One, something, he later claimed, he had been endeavouring to obtain from van Miert for three years, ever since he had become aware of a potential conflict. Mosley, who requested the letter within two weeks, spelt out once again the consequences to Europe if it was refused. One option, he said, would be to 're-locate both the FIA and Mr Ecclestone's company outside of the EU and severely limit the number of F1 races in Europe'. Van Miert, clearly resenting Mosley's threatening tone, replied that 'threats against me will not prevent an assessment of all the relevant issues in the proper manner'.

Happily for Ecclestone, the conflict with the teams finally proved somewhat easier to resolve. In October, a month after the second postponement, he returned to the negotiating table with a compromise. He offered the teams a ten per cent equity in trust, with the right to dividends but not share ownership, and a 50 per cent cut of the television income. He also agreed that the teams could have a presence on the board, although, to ensure no one team was more powerful than another, it would be rotated annually. The offer was also contingent upon the teams committing themselves to the Concorde Agreement for ten years, rather than five, a lengthy contractual arrangement to help woo the fund managers, but which would also arouse the concerns of van Miert.

The teams' ten per cent was due to come out of Ecclestone's shareholding in Formula One Holdings, reducing it to 30 per cent, with 50 per cent on offer to the public and ten per cent to the FIA. 'The teams have stopped squeezing my balls and all the commercial aspects have been resolved,' said Ecclestone optimistically. The Concorde Agreement, after more than 50 drafts, was finally signed by all the teams – McLaren, Williams, Tyrrell, Ferrari, Prost, Jordan, Sauber, Benetton, Minardi, Arrows and Stewart – in May 1998 in the presence of Prince Albert of Monaco at the principality's Grand Prix. At least one problem was out of the way.

There still remained the gadfly Eisele, an irritant that Ecclestone attempted to dispose of in a manner not unsurprising in someone who believes that the solution to every problem can be found in his wallet. His plan was to buy Eisele off, although, more subtly at first, through a business partnership. The ground was laid by Eisele's fellow countryman, Hans Gunther Schmidt, the boss of the former Formula One team ATS, and a friend of Ecclestone. It led to a meeting at Speyer, near Hockenheim, in mid-July 1997 – two months after Eisele had lodged his complaint to the European Commission – at which Ecclestone proposed a three-way partnership between the two men and Christian Vogt, Ecclestone's former employee, who had played a central role in setting up exclusive Formula One contracts with independent television companies in the late eighties.

They would take equal stakes, proposed Ecclestone, in a deal being negotiated with the French television station Canal+, to produce an international pay-for-view channel called MotorMania, which would cover every form of motor sport. Canal+ would be putting up 50 per cent of the funding capital, explained Ecclestone. The rest would be covered between the three of them. It was a golden opportunity for Eisele, whose once thriving business was now barely covering the cost of the office rent. But there was a condition attached to the partnership. Eisele would have to withdraw his legal actions and the complaint to Brussels. It was a condition he was not prepared to accept and the meeting came to an early end.

Undaunted, a month later Ecclestone invited Eisele to another meeting. This time, said Eisele, a payment of $5 million was discussed. This meeting was held at the Olden, a 15-bedroom hotel built in 1899 in the main street of the fashionable Swiss ski resort of Gstaad, which Ecclestone had bought two months earlier for £4 million and on which he reportedly planned to spend a further £17 million on expansion and refurbishment. Gstaad became a popular retreat for Ecclestone's associates. On the day of his meeting with Ecclestone, Eisele saw that Marco Piccinini, the FIA's deputy president of motor sport, a former boss of the Ferrari race team and now a non-executive director of Ecclestone's company, Formula One Holdings, was among those enjoying its comforts. Also at the hotel – not far from Ecclestone's luxurious chalet situated near the five-star turreted Palace hotel, the fabulously expensive eyrie of the world's beautiful people – was Vogt.

That the sum of $5 million was on the table is not in dispute, but whether Ecclestone offered it or Eisele demanded it, and in return for what, remains uncertain. Ecclestone claimed it was the price Eisele wanted in return for withdrawing his European Commission complaint and court actions. As a down payment, he said, he transferred $500,000 to Eisele's bank account. 'He told me he wanted a few quid for just trust, so asked if I would send half a million dollars on account. We were going to sort the details out later. I would give him another $2 million and the balance of $2.5 million when the Commission gave us the clearance, which he said he could engineer for us. Then he gave me his bank account number and we just transferred the money to him.'

Eisele denied that he had requested a payment of $5 million as an out-of-court settlement, adding that their discussions went no further after Ecclestone imposed an unacceptable condition. 'In withdrawing my complaint to the Commission, he also wanted me to give him [the names of] all my informants and paperwork [in support of the complaint], which I refused. He also wanted me to influence my lawyer to lose the court cases, which again I refused.' Eisele admitted that he did receive $500,000 from Ecclestone, which, he claimed, was for agreeing to withdraw the part of his complaint critical of Ecclestone's various conflicting roles within the FIA. It was not, he said, an upfront payment for any further co-operation. 'I did not ask for $500,000. He just did it. He said he wanted to send me a clear signal. "Please give me your bank account [details]," he said. They were his words. Before I did it, I spoke to my lawyer. He [Ecclestone] just wanted to buy me off.' Four days later, said Eisele, the money was in his account. Ecclestone later attempted to recover the money through a court in Heidelberg but was unsuccessful, said Eisele, due to lack of documentary evidence. It was an odd statement to make because documentary evidence does exist, and it suggests that it was Eisele who had made the running. In a letter to Ecclestone dated 27 May 1998 he confirmed his proposal for a 'settlement agreement', which had been verbally made in January. It stated that in return for his company withdrawing its complaints against the FIA and Ecclestone's companies – International Sportsworld Communicators and Formula One Administration – to the European Commission, and its legal actions in courts in Cologne and Frankfurt, Eisele would receive, in addition to the $500,000 already paid, a payment of $2 million once all actions had been withdrawn, a further $500,000 from International Sportsworld Communicators, and a final payment of $2 million from Ecclestone on the flotation of Formula One Holdings.

Ecclestone's lawyers were unhappy with the sum requested by Eisele. In a confidential memo to Ecclestone dated 5 November 1999 a payment of $5 million was deemed 'disproportionate to any damages he could have suffered ... wielding the threat that the interests of the Formula One Group [a reference to the proposed flotation] could be seriously damaged without his co-operation.' Ecclestone denied that he had made any suggestion to Eisele that he should 'influence' his lawyer to lose the legal actions – 'that is rubbish; all Eisele had to do was drop them' – but conceded that he had wanted the names of the parties who had supported or assisted him. For Ecclestone suspected, while Mosley at that time was convinced, that Mercedes-Benz, the principal participant in the truck series, wanted to see Eisele win the day to maintain the status quo. 'It was all part of a huge movement to have a go at us,' said Mosley. His concerns were hardened by a meeting called by Eisele and held in a Frankfurt hotel on 23 March 1997, which, along with representatives from two other motor sports, was attended by Wolfgang Deselaers and a representative from Mercedes. A main item on the agenda was a discussion on 'solidarity process'.

That July Mercedes acted as an intermediary, unsuccessfully as it turned out, to bring Eisele and Ecclestone together to discuss their differences. Ecclestone became so concerned that the car manufacturer appeared to be backing Eisele that he approached Jürgen E. Schrempp, the chairman of DaimlerChrysler, the parent company of Mercedes-Benz. 'I have a close friendship with the number-one guy there. I asked him face to face, and he denied that Mercedes was involved. I would have been super upset [if they had been].' Ecclestone accepted Schrempp's denial but Mosley remains doubtful to this day. 'There were all sorts of reasons for believing that they had been quietly making trouble. It is a big company and [people] lower [than Schrempp] have a lot of power.'

Back in the courtroom, Eisele and Deselaers proceeded to apply even more pressure on Ecclestone and the FIA. Two months later, on 15 October 1997, they extended the court action to also include the television rights to three other championship series – the European Rally, European Drag Racing and European Rallycross, which AE TV Cooperation had also once successfully covered and distributed for the organisers.

As the powers of the European Commission and its potential threat to Ecclestone's flotation plans became more ominously apparent, it was decided by Mosley to strengthen the FIA's political clout by becoming part of a recognised international federation within the Olympic Charter of the International Olympic Committee (IOC), which was giving its support to sports federations lobbying the Commission for a more flexible attitude in applying its competition rules, if not a complete exemption through a modification of the European Union Treaty. According to Eisele, Ecclestone believed that an alliance between the FIA and the IOC would create sufficient political power to see off the European Commission. Eisele claimed Ecclestone told him: 'Do you think you're going to win against me? We're going to fund the organisation and get involved with the IOC, and we'll see whether the European Commission can fight this.' On 19 September 1998, some 14 months after this exchange, Mosley was in Frankfurt 'in order to strengthen its [the FIA's] position towards the European Union [and its competition rules]', reported the German daily newspaper the *Frankfurter Allgemeine*.

In a press release to the German news agency, Deutsche Presse-Agentur, Mosley announced that the FIA had joined a working group of the International Olympic Committee. It would work, added the press release, under the leadership of the IOC president, Juan-Antonio Samaranch, and comprise Primo Nebiolo, president of the Olympic Summer Sports Association; Marc Hodler, president of the Winter Sports Association; Jacques Rogge, the president of the European Olympic Committee; François Carrard, the IOC's General Secretary; Gerhard Aigner, General Secretary of the European Football Union; and Mosley. In the event that the FIA was unable to reach an agreement with the European Commision, Mosley was reported as saying, it was possible that the FIA would file a complaint with the European Court of Justice. The FIA had reason to expect the full support of the IOC. Samaranch was also president of the Royal Automobile Club of Cataluña, organisers of the Spanish Grand Prix and the World Championship rally series in Spain.

It was agreed that members of the working group would call on European leaders to promote the case for the European Union to ease its competition rules. A meeting with Tony Blair at Downing Street went smoothly enough, until Chris Smith, the then Minister for Culture, Media and Sport, asked of Samaranch: 'Why is that the UK is such a sporting country and yet doesn't have a single person at the top of any of the big sports federations?' Mosley joined in the laughter while straight-faced Smith, bemused, looked on.

14

BERNIE'S ANNUS HORRIBILIS

Nineteen ninety-seven was Bernie Ecclestone's *annus horribilis*. The deal-maker extraordinaire had stepped outside of the world of Formula One, which he manipulated with ruthless ease, to discover that his power and authority held little sway in a City suspicious of his somewhat opaque business dealings. In deciding to float Formula One's assets, he found that its success was dependent on forces outside of his control, a state of being which was deeply at odds with an obsession to control his own path. So it was with the European Commission, which he saw as a body of time-serving bureaucrats. He was highly mistrustful of both, believing that, in their different parasitical ways, they lived off the hard graft of others. Yet the predicament in which he found himself was largely of his own making.

The labyrinthine structure of his companies and overseas bank accounts apart, he made a serious miscalculation in not resolving the television revenue dispute with Ron Dennis, Frank Williams and Ken Tyrrell before he was ready to go public. It simply added to the City's sense of uncertainty about the man and his business. In the same vein, he made a considerable gaffe in failing to seek the guidance of the European Commission to establish that his television contracts and agreements with the FIA, broadcasters and promoters, the very basis of the assets he was proposing to float, were compatible with the European Commission's competition laws or merited exemption under Clause

3 of Article 85 of the Treaty of Rome, which, simply put, allows restrictive agreements, if they are beneficial to an EC member country's economy, and whether such contracts and agreements were indispensable to achieve these benefits. These were errors of arrogance of a man who, over many years and in every area of his personal and business life, had been used to having his way. Why should it prove otherwise with the City's faceless suits or the paper-shufflers of Brussels?

On 5 September 1997 – about six months after the news of the launch was made public, and which was now about to be postponed for the second time, until early 1998 – the Commission's Directorate-General for Competition, received an application from Ecclestone in which he sought exemption from the competition rules. And in doing so, he handed on a plate everything that van Miert and his colleagues needed to know about his myriad business activities. For in making the application, it was necessary to supply copies of the amended 1997 Concorde Agreement between the FIA and the FOCA; the Formula One Agreement between Formula One Administration and the FIA, which gave Ecclestone the 15-year television rights; the Broadcasting Agreement between Formula One Administration and television companies; and copies of the contracts between Formula One Administration and promoters.

According to a Brussels lawyer, Ecclestone had been advised that clearance would prove little more than a formality. Instead, it provided the Commission with much of the proof it needed to establish a case against Ecclestone and the FIA. For while Wolfgang Eisele and others had been able to supply evidence of their own dealings with Ecclestone and the FIA, here, in one delivery, was a detailed account of every area of his worldwide operations and of his commercial relationship with the FIA and related parties. As a direct result, the Directorate-General for Competition was able to identify several serious breaches of EU competition rules.

Apart from a number of more minor infringements and the more obvious conflicts caused by Ecclestone's various roles within motor sport and the FIA, all contracts of more than five years attracted the concerns of the European Commission, which included the ten-year contracts with the teams and several free-to-air broadcasters of the same duration, contracts with a number of pay-television companies of up to 11 years, and, notably, the 15-year contract with the FIA, this last being crucial to Ecclestone's digital television plans. The European Commission is firmly opposed to a contract longer than five years, unless it involves, for example, a massive joint investment by two companies combining resources to produce a new product or service, and even then for a period of no longer than 15 years. Ecclestone's business enterprise fell far short of this consideration.

Evidence of monopolistic practice was plentiful: some of the television contracts offered a 33–50 per cent discount to broadcasters who agreed to show only Formula One, which confirmed the long-held suspicions of those who believed Ecclestone had deliberately suppressed other motor sports to benefit Formula One; the 20 promoters – national sporting authorities or circuit owners – with whom Ecclestone had contracts had to give an undertaking that no form of open-wheel single-seat car races other than Formula One and Formula 3000 would take place on their circuits; restrictive working conditions were imposed by International Sportsworld Communicators on non-FOCA TV film crews; the company also had a non-negotiable right to impose a FOCA TV film crew at a circuit without notice; and there was the FIA ultimatum that an organiser or promoter would not be allowed to stage a Formula One race or championship, international series or motor sport event which took place in more than one country, unless television rights had been assigned to either Formula One Administration or International Sportsworld Communicators.

Following a preliminary examination of the documents, the Directorate-General for Competition found that the business practices of Formula One Administration, the FIA and International Sportsworld Communicators were not compatible with competition rules. It consequently found to Ecclestone's dismay, that Formula One Administration did not qualify for exemption under Clause 3 of Article 85 of the Treaty of Rome. In December 1997 the European Commissioner for competition, Karel van Miert, authorised warning letters to be sent to Formula One Administration, International Sportsworld Communicators and the FIA in which it was stated that it was believed that the terms of the Concorde Agreement created 'a serious restriction of competition' and that the duration of the exclusivity of the 15-year contract between the two parties was 'excessive'. Mosley dismissed the letter, claiming it contained so many errors of fact that the FIA spent many months encouraging the Commission to make inquiries 'to get the facts right, because once we've got the facts right we can have a sensible discussion. In a nutshell, I think that letter was hastily conceived and contained numerous inaccuracies.'

The response from Brussels proved the final nail in the coffin for Ecclestone's plan to turn Formula One into a public company. Within days the substance of van Miert's letters had been leaked and the flotation was dead in the water. Automotive industry and technology corporate financier Nicky Samengo-Turner, of London-based investment bank Vision Capital, said: 'Everything that could go wrong with that flotation did go wrong. There seems to have been a serious lack of communication on every front, not least between the various investment banks within the syndicate and the ultimate investment institutions involved in the issue: the teams' commercial sponsors, who really provide the majority of their income, and therefore working capital. They claimed that they were never consulted for their views on the flotation.' The bruising experience, though, did no harm to Christian Purslow's career. He was later appointed managing director of Salomon Brothers – renamed Salomon Smith Barney in December 1997 – to become head of the company's media and investment banking in Europe.

On 4 February 1998 Karel van Miert, whose relationship with Mosley seemed to take on a personal dimension, followed up his warning letters to Ecclestone and Mosley by taking a sideswipe at the FIA in the legally privileged assembly of the Belgian Parliament. 'The FIA,' he said, 'is a powerful body which does not hesitate to use all means possible to strengthen its position. But, in contrast to what has happened at national level, the European Commission will resist these methods.'[1] This reference by van Miert to national events was in respect of a dispute between the French-speaking Walloon regional government of Belgium, in whose territory the Grand Prix at Spa-Francorchamps is held, and the federal government, which announced in December 1997 a ban on all tobacco advertising and sponsorship by 1 January 1999.

The instant response from Ecclestone was to announce the cancellation of the 1998 Belgian Grand Prix unless the ban was lifted on Formula One. The local business populace, alarmed at the loss of the estimated 1.2 billion francs the Grand Prix attracts, feared the impact on the local economy and urged the federal government to reconsider its decision. Spa-Francorchamps, incidentally, is owned by the local authority and its officials are willing to grant all and any concession to keep the Formula One circus returning year after year for the benefit of the money and prestige it attracts. It is promoted through Spa Activities, formerly Racing Francorchamps Promotion SPRL, in which Ecclestone has a principal interest. In addition to the obligatory television rights, it reportedly pocketed the receipts from the gate – and the public toilets. According to a Brussels lawyer, Spa Activities is also provided by the state with accommodation near the circuit for media facilities. Astonishingly, the company then receives a further payment from the state – for allowing the media to use it. The Belgian Green Party claimed that local politicians were prepared to agree to such a one-sided deal because, economically, the Walloon region was 'a banana republic. They are afraid to lose the Grand Prix.'

In reply to the federal government, the Walloon government insisted that any decision to ban tobacco advertising was one that came within its constitutional authority and went on to declare its support for the race with tobacco advertising and sponsorship. Ecclestone immediately announced the reinstatement of the Belgian Grand Prix. In December 1998, while the Belgian Parliament voted to refer the dispute to the country's independent judiciary, a decision that led to the Walloons winning the day following a ruling by the judiciary that a tobacco ban should not be imposed in advance of a directive being considered by the European Commission.

Following his criticism of the FIA in the Belgian Parliament, van Miert turned the screws further by giving an interview to the *Wall Street Journal* in which he repeated a claim that he had rarely seen a case where there had been so many breaches of competition rules. With his flotation plans at that stage teetering on the edge – and the FIA's ten per cent stake perilously poised with them – van Miert's warning letter and public criticisms were seen by Ecclestone and Mosley as both unjustified and inaccurate. It was enough to compel Mosley, said to be a more zealous litigant than Ecclestone, to pursue legal action against van Miert.

At the Court of First Instance in Luxembourg in May 1998, the FIA alleged that the warning letters sent to Formula One Administration, International Sportsworld Communicators and the FIA had been issued to journalists and thereby constituted an unlawful release of confidential documents. It was made worse, in Mosley's words, by 'the outrageous statements he himself [van Miert] made to the press [the *Wall Street Journal*]'. In October 1999, following an internal inquiry that attributed the release of the letters to an allegedly inexperienced staff member unaware of their confidentiality, the Commission issued the apology Mosley had sought. But Mosley refutes the inference that it had been an accident. Copies of the letters had been issued, he claims, by an experienced presswoman seconded from the office of former British Labour Party leader Neil Kinnock, now an EU Commissioner, who was acting on the instructions of van Miert's office. She was left to carry the can and 'shoved off to an obscure corner of the administration'.

In addition to the apology, the Commission also paid the FIA's legal costs. 'Our lawyers tells me this is the first time this has ever happened,' said Mosley. The issue of the FIA's costs was certainly one that had occupied the court's lengthy deliberations. But his claim was not the whole truth. While the FIA was awarded costs of 40,000 euros, it was a mere tenth of the sum it had sought – 400,000 euros, which, in fact, was in excess of the FIA's actual costs. 'It was a real smack in the eye for the Commissioners,' said Mosley. 'It was seen in legal circles as a tremendous victory for us, and that really pissed van Miert off.'

Said a senior Commission official: 'We saw no reason whatsoever why we should pay the FIA's costs. The FIA had repeatedly not attended the hearings that the court called. The general impression in these quarters was that the FIA desperately wanted to keep this case going to be able to say that they have a court case going on against the Commission [to deflect criticism of the commercial relationship between Ecclestone and the FIA].' Van Miert claimed the Commission's actions were justified. He commented: 'Their bill was extremely high. We said no way. The problem of the warning letters was caused by a simple mistake, for which we apologised. As for my comments, I felt I was entitled to make them because they had tried to minimise things all the time. They were not being truthful.'

Mosley believed that the difficulties Ecclestone and the FIA were encountering with the European Commission had been caused not by any infringement of competition rules, but the political division in Belgium over tobacco sponsorship. The political force behind the tobacco ban, he explained, was the Flemish Socialist Party, of which van Miert was a strong supporter. The dispute that followed caused 'a constitutional crisis', which 'gravely embarrassed the Flemish Socialist Party and associates of Karel van Miert in the party'. Van Miert laid the blame for the 'crisis' at Mosley's door because it had been provoked by the threat to the Belgian Grand Prix. He then succumbed to hard lobbying by his socialist colleagues to declare the FIA's contracts anti-competitive. Overnight, according to Mosley, a once friendly van Miert became hostile, and Formula One's problems with Brussels began. The basis of Mosley's account was disputed by a spokeswoman for the Belgian Embassy in London, who said: 'The issue provoked constitutional interpretation, yes. But a constitutional crisis, never.'

Mosley presented his analysis in the January 1999 issue of *Business Age*, as part of a highly flattering article spread over 15 pages, plus a front cover proclaiming: 'Why Europe Has to Accept Sport's New Order' – namely Ecclestone and Mosley. Its publication was a consequence of a feature on Ecclestone by its editor, Tom Rubython, which had been published by the magazine six months earlier. This one was highly critical of Ecclestone, running under the headline 'Can You Trust This Man to Run a Public Company?'. Its allegations led to legal action – and, by way of an apology to mollify Ecclestone, the fawning article, which gave Mosley a platform to criticise van Miert. It was one of the last issues of *Business Age* to appear, and the magazine, already in a financial crisis, ceased publication in April 1999.

From its ashes two months later emerged *EuroBusiness*, of which Rubython was the editor and Ecclestone the bankroller, reputedly investing £4 million in the new venture – £1.5 million in capital and the rest in promoting the magazine at Grand Prix meetings. In July the magazine devoted its front cover and a four-page article, under the headline 'Europe's Most Powerful Man', to another flattering profile – but this time on van Miert, whose report on Formula One Administration and the FIA had yet, of course, to be published. And, in its April 2000 issue, *EuroBusiness* once again turned its searing spotlight on Ecclestone and Mosley – devoting no fewer than 55 pages in resounding praise of their management of Formula One.

But Ecclestone's involvement with the magazine threatened to cause him some embarrassment. On 22 September 1999 its finance director, Jeanette Hunt, walked out of her office, at the insistence of her husband, PR consultant James Hunt, after alleging that she'd been asked to prepare false management accounts in order to extract more funding from Ecclestone, whose company, Eurobusiness Publications Ltd, had a majority shareholding in the magazine's publishing company, European Business Press Ltd. She subsequently further alleged that, unbeknown to Ecclestone, a series of fraudulent activities had taken place, claims that she repeated to Ecclestone at a meeting on 30 September. She was, she said, prepared to return to work if a management restructuring took place. Hunt left Ecclestone's office confident it would take place. When it did not, she wrote a stinging letter to Ecclestone on 29 December railing at the 'appalling treatment' she had received. On 21 January she received, and accepted, an offer of £8000 from Mukesh Adani, a director of European Business Press Ltd and one of Ecclestone's trusted lieutenants, in full settlement of any claim against the company.

However, Hunt decided to pursue her grievance with the Industrial Tribunal and filed a complaint on 4 March 2000. An article indicating that she would blow the lid off Ecclestone's business empire at the tribunal hearing was published a short while later in *Punch*, the monthly magazine, whose ongoing financial losses forced its owner, Harrods boss Mohamed Al Fayed, to bring an end in May 2002 to its 161-year history. Clearly based on detailed information that could only have come from within the company, the piece was evidently designed to bring pressure on Ecclestone. Hunt was, it said, 'determined to expose his business methods and commercial secrets'. To Ecclestone, such a threat would have been brushed aside: whatever they were, it is certain that Hunt had no knowledge of them.

Following a provisional hearing on 15 December 2000, the Industrial Tribunal resumed at Stratford, east London, on 11 June for a two-day hearing, which found in favour of the respondents, European Business Press Ltd (and also its predecessor, Business Age Magazine Ltd), and Eurobusiness Publications Ltd. Other factors aside, not least that Hunt had effectively dismissed herself, the application was dismissed as out of time – it had not been filed within a period of three months as required by UK employment law. Silverman Sherliker, solicitors for Hunt, argued unsuccessfully that her 'negotiations' with Ecclestone and others had not made it 'reasonably practical' for her application to be submitted any earlier, grounds which allow an extension of the three-month time limit.

This episode finally came to a peculiar close more than two years later when Hunt wrote to Mukesh Adani, sending similar letters to Rubython and Ecclestone, apologising profusely for allegations 'which were in fact made up. I very much regret having accepted a settlement from you of £8000 that I then sued the company for unfair dismissal and only succeeded in wasting everybody's time. Please accept my sincere apologies for conduct I now realise was wholly unsatisfactory.'

Through their solicitor, Nicholas Lakeland, the Hunts declined to comment further.

Although it had come too late to make any difference to the fate of the flotation, Wolfgang Eisele and his lawyer, Dr Wolfgang Deselaers, suffered a considerable set-back in the Frankfurt district court on 18 March 1998 when, contrary to their confident expectations, judgement in the legal action against Ecclestone's company, International Sportsworld Communicators (ISC), over the television rights to European Truck Racing went against them. The three judges decided that if there had been a violation of the television rights or European competition law, it could only be contested by the organisers who were directly affected, rather than a television company such as AE TV Cooperation, whom the court considered to be a third party. Eisele and Deselaers were stunned by the decision. Nine months earlier – on 4 June 1997 – the very same court had agreed, on Deselaers' application, to issue an interim judgement preventing the FIA, and, consequently Ecclestone, from marketing the European Truck Racing Cup which Eisele's company, AE TV Cooperation, had once successfully covered and distributed for the organisers. The legal validity of Deselaers' application had in no way been questioned. He lodged an immediate appeal.

On the same day the judgement was announced, Mosley – with Ecclestone's endorsement – made a political gesture considered to be a peace offering to Brussels. He issued a statement relinquishing the FIA's claim to the television rights of all motor sports other than Formula One, the World Rally Championship, the World Grand Touring Car Championship and the Formula 3000 International Championship, subject to clarification by the European Commission. However this gesture might have been perceived politically in Brussels, little was being surrendered financially. The television rights to these four championship series accounted for more than 90 per cent of television revenues.

The way in which the news was communicated by ISC to the organisers provides another example of the degree of power that Ecclestone wielded within the FIA. For the letter sent to the organisers of the European Rally Championship, European Championship for Rallycross Drivers and the Electro Solar Cup was dated 13 March – five days before the World Motor Sport

Council had met to discuss and approve the decision to return the television rights. Ecclestone's sphere of influence within the FIA was such that he could confidently send out such a letter without fear of error or contradiction.

Further evidence of Ecclestone's control of motor sport in general, again ably assisted by Mosley, is offered by the way in which the World Grand Touring Car Championship came into existence. As with other series, that control was made possible through the FIA introducing in October 1995 a rule which gave Ecclestone the marketing rights of all non-Formula One events through ISC. It was used on this occasion to bring about the downfall of a successful series known as the BPR Global Endurance GT Cup, and replaced by the World Grand Touring Car Championship, the creation of Ecclestone and Mosley.

The BPR GT series was the brainchild of French businessman and motor sport enthusiast Patrick Peter and two associates – fellow countryman Stéphane Ratel, who was then Competition Director for Venturi Competition, a small French car manufacturer, and who, in 1996, launched the Lamborghini Supertrophy, and Jürgen Barth, head of Porsche's customer relations. The three men came together in 1993 and founded a company called the BPR Organisation to stage endurance races for GT cars, the first of which was held at the Paul Ricard circuit in January 1994. In 1995, at the request of Peter and his associates, the series was accredited as an FIA international series, and by 1996 its 12-race calendar had become sufficiently popular throughout Europe and Japan to attract television coverage by Eurosport, the largest pan-European television network. However, its increasing success was soon to be cut short.

In September 1996, hour-long television coverage of a round of the series at Brands Hatch, which received second billing to the Portuguese Grand Prix, was followed by a fax from Ecclestone to Barth stating that unless the television rights to the series were assigned to ISC, it would be contravening the FIA's new international sporting code law which granted the television rights of all motor sports to ISC. As television revenue at that stage was non-existent – the series was surviving principally on sponsorship money and a modest contribution from Eurosport to help cover the costs of television production costs – Ecclestone's demand presented no financial threat at that stage of its development. But Peter, Ratel and Barth wanted to retain control of television rights to protect the series' independence, which meant the right at some future date to exploit its television coverage potential. Two meetings followed – in Paris and London – between Ecclestone and the three men but without resolution. Ecclestone refused to brook any other solution: no television rights, no GT series.

Consequently, on 11 November, the FIA announced the creation of its own

GT series – the World Grand Touring Car Championship. According to Peter, Ecclestone was willing to allow the BPR Organisation to organise the new series, but he would handle all negotiations with sponsors and circuits while his company, ISC, would handle the television rights. BPR, for its part, would concentrate on its relationship with competitors. Its income would come from competitors' entry fees and ticket receipts. However, a contract to that effect failed to materialise following disagreement between the two parties on its length of duration: BPR wanted a long-term contract, which the FIA and Ecclestone opposed until the series had first established its potential success, a factor Peter believed had already been proven and which was further confirmed by the FIA's plan to stage its own GT series.

A month before the FIA announced its intention to launch its own series, the BPR Organisation had verbally agreed a renewal of contract with a sponsor and, in order for it to be validated, Peter requested, with somewhat ludicrous optimism in the circumstances, that the FIA renew its registration of the BPR GT series for the 1997 season. Inevitably, the application was rejected, thereby officially erasing the BPR Organisation's series from the FIA's international calendar. Over the next couple of months Peter, Barth and Ratel conferred to consider what was now seen as their only recourse – legal action against Ecclestone. It would, in reality, be never more than a threat in order, as Ratel put it, to 'optimise our negotiations'. At a meeting in February 1997 it was agreed that the BPR Organisation would engage the services of a Paris-based lawyer, Christian Lamonin. However, it was an offensive that did not for long have Ratel's support, due, he claimed, to an autonomous decision by Peter to actually proceed with legal action against ISC and the FIA.

At this time, Ratel added, he was in London about to finalise negotiations with Ecclestone on behalf of the BPR Organisation. His response to Peter, in writing, was to refuse to give his support, adding that from that moment he no longer wished to be 'linked' to his actions. The decision to go to law, said Ratel, was based on Peter's conviction that there was a strong case building up against Ecclestone in Brussels. '[It] was motivated by a meeting he had in Brussels with some people involved with the [European] Commission ... who gave him the assurance that Ecclestone's position was to be challenged at a very high level, and that he had more to gain by fighting him than working with him.'

Following an approach from Max Mosley, Ratel accepted an offer to organise the FIA's series. It was, he said, a 'fantastic opportunity to work in conjunction with the FIA and Bernie Ecclestone, because more than anyone he has proved himself successful in racing'. Ratel, who went on to run his own successful company, the Stéphane Ratel Organisation, with offices in Paris and London, added: 'It was a unique opportunity to run a World Championship, which I thought would increase our business tenfold. It was Mr Peter's view that we could succeed without that and we shouldn't accept any agreement with the FIA.'

A few days later Peter found himself in splendid isolation. For Barth accepted an offer from Mosley to join Ratel. He denied an allegation that he had been pressured by his employers, Porsche, to accept the offer because they did not want to be seen to be connected in any way to the threat of a legal action against Ecclestone. 'No pressure was put on me at all,' he said. 'It was simply a good offer, and one that I decided to accept.'

Max Mosley roundly refuted Peter's account of events. He blamed the collapse of the BPR series on a partnership dispute between Ratel, Barth and Peter over whether the series should be converted into an FIA championship. Another major factor – although this contradicts the claim of Ratel and others over the difficulties in agreeing a mutually acceptable contract – was 'a culture clash' between Peter, who had wanted a contract clearly setting out the terms of agreement between BPR and ISC, and Ecclestone, 'who has always operated on an informal handshake basis'. It appears therefore the dispute was not over the length of a contract, or a contract at all, but Ecclestone's willingness to sign one.

Peter acquired total ownership of the BPR Organisation and proceeded, in June 1997, with a legal action against Ecclestone and ISC, claiming damages of nearly £14 million for 'illegal dismissal of contractual relationships, customer misappropriation and unfair competition'. In November Peter formally lodged a complaint against Formula One Administration, International Sportsworld Communicators and the FIA, alleging a breach of the European Commission's competition rules, and requested interim measures to prevent Ecclestone, his companies or the FIA from obstructing the running of an international GT series.

According to Ecclestone's lawyers, there followed a series of rulings issued by the Directorate-General for Competition, which, it is suggested, clearly indicated its willing support of Peter's complaint. Within days of it being lodged, for example, senior officials made it clear that if the FIA's World Motor Sport Council did not allow Peter to stage an international series in 1998, then his application for interim measures would 'become more serious'. And when Formula One Management requested a short extension of time to present its submission to Peter's complaints, it was told, claim Ecclestone's lawyers, that it would be conditional upon receiving reassurances that 'nobody was in a position to obstruct Mr Peter's plans to organise his series in 1998', irrespective of safety measures and other factors which might not necessarily comply with the FIA's rules and regulations.

In January 1998 Peter further alleged to the Commission, quite falsely, according to Ecclestone and his lawyers, that Ecclestone had been responsible for orchestrating a refusal by the Allgemeiner Deutscher Automobil-Club, the organisers of the Nurburgring, and the Royal Automobile Club de Belgique, the organisers of Spa-Francorchamps, to allow his GT series to book their circuits. Due to the apparent desire by senior Commission officials to see Peter satisfied, Ecclestone readily agreed to a meeting with him, which took place over dinner in Gstaad in late January and was also attended by Peter's wife.

Peter made it clear, claims Ecclestone, that he had influence in the Commission and offered several times to become his representative in resolving the complaints against him, his companies and the FIA – once they had arrived at a financial agreement to compensate him for his alleged losses. That meeting was soon followed by another, this time at the Hôtel Crillon, where, in the presence of Ecclestone's external lawyers, Peter revealed how much he wanted – a total of $15 million, with $10 million for him and $5 million for Lamonin. Ecclestone refused point blank, and negotiated him down to $2 million. Then Peter suggested, it is alleged, that the money should be paid in a way that concealed it from the French tax authorities. He wanted $1 million as the agreed payment and the other $1 million paid 'under the table'. When Ecclestone's lawyers refused to agree, he proposed that $1 million should be paid into a Swiss bank account to the benefit of a company called Larmoran Participation Inc. Again Ecclestone's lawyers declined to become involved in 'any dishonest representations to the tax authorities'. On 26 May 1998 the sum of $2 million was paid by International Sportsworld Communicators to Peter's GTR Organisation.

With that business out of the way, Peter once again boasted of his influence and contacts within the Commission, which he was prepared to put to Ecclestone's service for a financial consideration. In a letter dated 25 June he stated that, 'thanks to the experience I gained about the Community practices during the past months together with my knowledge of your file', he was 'convinced' that he could help remove 'some obstacles' that Ecclestone and the FIA faced with the Commission. As a 'goodwill officer', he sought a payment of $2.5 million, plus 'a monthly allowance' of $50,000, excluding expenses 'and taxes'.

The payment, which would also include the services of his lawyer, Lamonin, would be paid to Peter & Associés, his communications and advertising company. It was, he stressed, important that the money was not paid to him or to his GTR Organisation: 'The more independent I will remain from yourself and the companies of your group, the best chance this mission will have of becoming successful.' The proposal went no further after Peter failed to respond to a fax dated 16 March 1999 from Ecclestone's lawyer querying the efficacy of such an arrangement, the apparent conflict of interest that Lamonin's role would create – he also represented the Association de Défense Internationale du Sport Automobile, which had been highly critical of both Ecclestone and Mosley – and the nature of the payments he was seeking.

Mosley offered to produce documentary evidence that senior staff within the Directorate-General for Competition had 'repeatedly encouraged' Ecclestone to make a substantial payment to Peter. It did not, though, materialise. He insisted, nonetheless, that John Temple Lang, a Director of the Directorate-General for Competition, had telephoned Ecclestone to persuade him to settle the grievance with Peter. Ecclestone confirmed the call. 'I can't remember whether he called me or I called him, but he said it would be nice if we could sort out the Patrick Peter business.'

Temple Lang claims that he had 'very few direct contacts' with Ecclestone, 'apart from the couple of times when he came to see us. He telephoned me, I believe, once or possibly twice. I am sure I never took the initiative to contact him by letter or phone. My contacts were with his solicitors.' But did he in any way, directly or otherwise, encourage Ecclestone to reach an accommodation with Peter in order that he might withdraw his complaint? 'Without consulting my notes, which, of course, are in the Commission, I cannot be certain that I never said anything "directly or otherwise" which might have been on the lines you suggest. But I am sure that I never actively encouraged Mr Ecclestone to reach a settlement or to get Mr Peter to withdraw his complaint.'

All the same, Ecclestone might have saved his money. Although on 3 June 1998 Peter formally withdrew his complaints, after agreeing a financial settlement with Ecclestone, the Commission decided to continue to investigate his allegations because of the 'strong evidence' they offered of 'a very serious infringement' of competition rules.

Over the following months Ecclestone continued his efforts to make peace with Brussels. He agreed to modify certain clauses within contracts to bring them into line with European competition rules. They were contained in an amended Concorde Agreement sent to Karel van Miert's office on 27 August 1998. Ecclestone agreed to end the practice of offering massive discounts to television companies to broadcast only Formula One, and to withdraw the undertaking demanded of promoters that they held only Formula One and Formula 3000 races at their circuits. However, in characteristic style, he insisted that his agreement was conditional on other undisclosed breaches being resolved in a manner satisfactory to him. He defended the exclusivity of contracts with television companies by claiming it related to certain rights only and did not preclude other broadcasters from broadcasting in that country, a claim that was somewhat misleading. It certainly covered the all-important Formula One series to the exclusion of all other races, and, in respect of other motor sports, they could only be sold through Ecclestone's much-criticised company, International Sportsworld Communicators.

His desire for a speedy accommodation with Brussels was given fresh impetus by a new device to capitalise on Formula One's assets, an alternative route to a stock-market flotation which had been proposed to Ecclestone during the early summer of 1998. It was a $2-billion issue of Eurobonds, which are debt securities issued by companies and governments worldwide and marketed internationally, mainly to institutional investors. They guarantee a fixed rate of return over a set period of time against future cashflows – in this case revenue from television contracts – and are considered, as a short-term investment, to be less risky than equity, whose return is dependent on the economic fluctuations of the market. Ecclestone's financial advisers – not Salomon Brothers – believed fund managers, merchant banks and potential investors would find the asset-backed bond bankable on the strength of the predicted gross television revenues of the television contracts in Ecclestone's briefcase.

To Ecclestone, there were to be two distinct advantages to this route: a Eurobonds issue does not require the same degree of financial disclosure as a flotation, and its anticipated success was seen as a means of generating market confidence in the financial accountability of Formula One Administration, which would hopefully create investor awareness of Formula One and its economic potential in advance of a future flotation bid. Ecclestone's advisers for this venture were Morgan Stanley Dean Witter, a US investment bank which had been part of the original 18-strong syndicate in the failed flotation. The FIA was once again in full support by modifying its commercial rights contract with Ecclestone, this time in return for $60 million – Mosley had tried to get £100 million – which was increased from $50 million after Mosley explained to Ecclestone that he needed the extra $10 million to purchase number 4 Place de la Concorde, an imposing building on the corner of Rue Royale, near the FIA's headquarters at number 8, which he wanted to leave as his 'legacy' to the FIA, but which was thwarted by another interested party. Instead, the money went on purchasing an office building in Trafalgar Square for the offices of the FIA Foundation, founded to promote road safety improvements and legislation.

At 3 pm on 28 September 1998, before 200 hand-picked investors in the ritzy surroundings of London's Grosvenor Hotel, Morgan Stanley managing director Karl Essig announced the launch of the $2-billion Eurobond offering by Formula One Finance, which was anticipated to be rated single-A with an expected term of five years. Essig gave a 15-minute delivery on its details before introducing Ecclestone, who was flanked by one of his former arch-opponents to the Concorde Agreement, Ron Dennis, the boss of McLaren, the World Championship team, and Luca di Montezemolo, the president of Ferrari, the World Championship runners-up team. Representing Formula One Holdings, apart from Ecclestone and legal adviser Stephen Mullens, was Marco Piccinini, its deputy chief executive and a former boss of the Ferrari team.

Dennis and di Montezemolo were there to field any questions about the relationship between Ecclestone and the teams. Ecclestone opined that having the two men there was 'a bit of risk ... because they are very much their own men [and] I am never sure of what they might say'. It was pure marketing spiel. They were there, with well-rehearsed scripts – Dennis, who not long before was ready to see Ecclestone in court, described the bond issue as 'super-sound' – to demonstrate that the disunity between the teams and Ecclestone which had caused so much damage to the failed flotation was a thing of the best-forgotten past. Predictably, the public noises from Ecclestone and his associates exuded supreme confidence. But Ecclestone's financial advisers may even then have been having their doubts.

Just four days before the launch was announced at the Grosvenor Hotel, two Morgan Stanley bankers went to Brussels in an attempt to obtain information on the likely outcome, negative or positive, of the Commission's investigation into the activities of Formula One Management, International Sportsworld Communicators and the FIA. They met with John Temple Lang who informed them that, due to the complexity of the case, which involved not only an analysis of Formula One but also an analysis of international motor sport and the role of the FIA, it would be several more weeks before an indication of the Commission's stand could be given. It was impossible to communicate in writing, even provisionally, what that stand might be. This information was also given to Alison Finlaye-Browne, who headed Ecclestone's legal department. The next day Ecclestone himself contacted Temple Lang to find out for himself what he had told Morgan Stanley. He was now in no doubt about the Commission's position.

Nevertheless, he was sufficiently confident in his belief that all would turn out well to state in a press release issued on the day of the Eurobond launch that 'all the concerns raised by the Commission have now been, or can be, dealt with'. Stephen Mullens, legal adviser to Formula One Holdings and Ecclestone's family, was also quoted in the *Financial Times* the next day as saying that there were 'just a few minor issues to resolve' with the European Commission. The press release was faxed to van Miert's office on the day of the launch by Marriot Harrison, solicitors acting on Ecclestone's behalf. Van Miert responded swiftly: such statements, he insisted, did not accord with the facts. It was followed by a letter from van Miert to Ecclestone stating that he was unwilling to confirm the claims made in the press release and those by Mullens in the *Financial Times*.

Charges in the media that the press release was guilty of misleading the market were quite wrong, insists Ecclestone. He knew the objections the Commission 'had at that time and we knew they could be resolved and we did resolve them. All we were commenting on was what they did say, not what they might say. Now things maybe subsequent to that might have come out that we didn't know about, so we couldn't know whether they could be solved. How would we know?' For the FIA, Mosley saw the press release as a statement of opinion sincerely and truthfully expressed, and therefore it could not be said to have been issued with the intention to mislead.

On 8 October, ten days after the launch, Ecclestone, at the request of Morgan Stanley, wrote to Temple Lang asking him to confirm that what he had told his financial advisers of his dealings with Brussels was 'a truthful representation'. The detailed response was a four-page letter dated 19 October which did not confirm the accuracy of all of Ecclestone's assertions. Temple Lang's letter repeated that the European Commission's investigation was far from complete and was looking at the overall way in which international motor sport, including Formula One, was organised and at the commercialisation of television rights to these races. Despite the points made in this letter, it failed to dissuade Ecclestone from issuing an open circular to prospective investors on 17 November in which he continued to insist that all the EC's 'concerns ... have been, or can be, dealt with'.

The presentation at the Grosvenor Hotel was the first of a series of roadshows to be held in Europe and, importantly, Asia, where Ecclestone had dedicated considerable time and effort to developing a major Formula One arena in the twenty-first century. But the timing of the launch, when markets were suffering a worldwide backwash from a dramatic downturn in the Asian economy, was considered by City bankers to be not the most helpful. Only the most highly rated bond issue, it was believed, had a favourable chance of success. The market was described as 'a tough one', particularly for a bond rated single-A. Many issues had been postponed because of poor market conditions. Morgan Stanley claimed to be unconcerned. It agreed that a 'plain vanilla' bond tapping generalist investors would have been too risky, but the bond was aimed at the more sophisticated investor, who, it was believed, would see through the volatility of the market and recognise the opportunity of a unique investment. The nature of the bond would not be affected by the state of the global markets. That, at least, was the theory. In practice, it turned out somewhat differently.

Normally, before a bond is issued, an application for a listing is submitted to the Stock Exchange which enables buyers to trade it on the stock market.

The listing becomes effective once all the bonds have been fully subscribed and delivered to the investors. The time period between the launch of the issue and day of completion varies between three and six weeks. However, three months after the launch date, the application to the Stock Exchange by Morgan Stanley had still to be approved. A delay in such circumstances is invariably caused by an application failing to meet the Stock Exchange's principal requirements relating to a company's financial history or trading status. It raised once again questions about the complexity of Ecclestone's financial dealings. Said a merchant banker: 'It was a reflection of the fact that, as everybody knew, it hadn't been that easy to put this thing together, either from the point of view of finding buyers for it, or from the point of view of getting the agreement of the Stock Exchange on what needed to be disclosed in order to get a listing.'

While Ecclestone's Eurobond sale in 1998 proved no more successful than his aborted flotation, he might have taken some comfort from the legal difficulties that were besetting the man principally responsible for the European Commission investigation – independent television producer Wolfgang Eisele. On 3 November 1998 Eisele appeared before an oral hearing at the Court of Appeal in Frankfurt, where his lawyer, Dr Wolfgang Deselaers, was attempting to overturn the judgement of Frankfurt District Court in March, which, against all expectations, had decreed that any violation of television rights could only be contested by those parties directly affected. In the court's opinion, Eisele's company, AE TV Cooperation, was not so affected, although for several years it had covered and successfully marketed European Truck Racing, European Rally, European Drag Racing and European Rallycross on behalf of the organisers. Deselaers believed that the oral hearing had gone well.

The comments of the three judges, said Deselaers, had explicitly indicated that their decision would go in the plaintiff's favour. At the beginning of the hearing the presiding judge explained in detail why the court considered the marketing practices of the FIA and Ecclestone infringed European Commission competition rules. 'Moreover,' said Deselaers, 'the court explicitly said that AE TV would seem to be entitled to challenge these infringements in court. If they had had any intention of rejecting the appeal, there would have been a proper legal procedure asking us to comment on their concerns.' But, to the astonishment of Deselaers and the FIA's lawyers, that is precisely what the court did do. Seven weeks later, on 15 December, the same three judges, in announcing their decision, dismissed the appeal by AE TV Cooperation and agreed with the lower court's judgement of the previous March.

'It was a major shock,' said Deselaers. 'It was a complete U-turn. I cannot offer any reasonable explanation. At the oral hearing in November it was clearly stated that Mr Eisele could challenge this unfair competition. To my knowledge, it is almost without precedent in German litigation that a higher court declares explicitly, yes, we intend to give the rights to the plaintiff, without expressing any doubts as to whether AE TV Cooperation would be entitled to challenge the infringement of competition rules, and then render a judgement which is in complete contradiction of that declaration. We couldn't believe the judgement. Nobody could believe it. Even the FIA lawyers had thought they had lost the case.'

Eisele proceeded to lodge a final appeal to Germany's Federal Court of Justice in Karlsruhe. 'What else can I do?' he said. 'I have been fighting this for more than two years. I will continue to fight until the end.'

15

BRUSSELS DELIVERS ITS VERDICT – AND BERNIE MAKES ANOTHER BILLION

By March 1999 Morgan Stanley had made little headway in the Eurobond sale. They had, in the words of a merchant banker, 'run into a wall'. The collision was put on course by the ratings agencies concerned over the quality of the bond declining to give it a single-A rating. It led to the issue being scaled down from Morgan Stanley's valuation of $2 billion to $1.4 billion, a figure which had been offered by Westdeutsche Landesbank (WestLB), a small regional German bank, the previous December. Contrary to the expectations of Morgan Stanley, Ecclestone appointed WestLB as joint lead managers.

Leading its team was a 37-year-old American, Robin Saunders, the head of its asset securitisation and principal finance group, who had joined WestLB less than 12 months earlier from Deutsche Bank. She was the principal architect of a plan to rescue the sale through the two banks underwriting the issue, with WestLB taking two-thirds and Morgan Stanley the rest. Guaranteeing interest payments was a strategic risk aimed at creating in the market the confidence it lacked in the future of Ecclestone's television contracts, against whose revenue the bonds were being issued. To safeguard its interests, WestLB wanted a closer involvement with Formula One Administration and, as part of the deal, Ecclestone agreed to the appointment of Saunders, whose drive and shrewdness he had come to respect, to its board, where she took on an increasingly influential role. For someone from the City, his admiration for her was a notable first: 'She does what she says she'll do, and that is unique.' [set as superscript] 1

Saunders had been chiefly responsible for structuring the terms of the deal, which stipulated Ecclestone put up a total of $400 million as security against television revenues failing to cover interest payments. The figure broke down into two parts. In the first retention, $100 million was secured to cover two years' interest in the event of a shortfall, and, in the second, $300 million worth of assets was put up as collateral which could be pulled in to pay off the bonds if necessary. This was seen as a safeguard against the possibility of the result of the European Commission's investigations adversely affecting future television revenues.

Although it prompted cynical comment from some financial commentators – 'WestLB's decision to take up so much of the Formula One bond emphasises that other potential investors see no reason to buy what Ecclestone is so anxious to sell' – Ecclestone's advisers believed it would help gain the confidence of investors as a prelude to a fully fledged flotation, which he was rather optimistically forecasting could take place as early as 2000 – a clause in the sale guaranteed increased payments of interest if it did not take place within five years. The timing of the Eurobond rescue was considered significant. Ecclestone and Saunders would have been aware that the publication of the European Commission's long-awaited report – and any critical comments – was imminent. They wanted a head start on any potentially negative publicity anticipated to flow from the conflict of opinion that might inevitably follow.

On 30 June 1999, a month after the completion of the bond rescue was announced, the European Commission's Directorate-General for Competition issued a 185-page report on its investigation, which had begun two years and one month earlier. Known as a Statement of Objections, this alleged that under Articles 85 and 86 of the EC Treaty, the FIA and Ecclestone's companies Formula One Administration (FOA) and International Sportsworld Communicators (ISC) had been accused of abusing their 'dominant position' to restrict competition. It stated: 'We have found evidence of serious infringements of EU competition rules, which could result in substantial fines.' The report listed four areas of competition abuse.

Firstly, FIA regulations prohibited participation in non-FIA authorised motor sport, which meant that the FIA had the power to block series competing with its own events, as everyone involved in motor sport, from drivers and track-owners to promoters, car manufacturers and organisers, had to be licensed by the FIA. Failure to comply with the prohibition meant the removal of the FIA's licence or permit. 'It is therefore unlikely that a participant will choose to enter an event which is not authorised by the FIA. This also makes it extremely improbable that an organiser would agree to organise an event that is not authorised by the FIA.' Licensees and authorised organisers having to accept the prohibition was an abuse of its dominant position.

Moreover, added the report, it represented a very substantial obstacle for any organiser wishing to organise international series which could compete with FIA series. This was significant because of the FIA's commercial interests in the success of FIA series, particularly Formula One. 'This prohibition is designed to, and has the effect of, increasing the difficulties which already exist for undertakings wishing to organise or promote a motor sport series which would potentially challenge the dominance of the FIA in the organisation and the dominance of FIA/FOA and ISC in the promotion of international series within the EU. This FIA abusive conduct weakens the competition in both markets.'

Secondly, the introduction in 1995 of the broadcasting rules empowering the FIA to acquire the television rights of all the motor sports it authorised, which it then transferred to International Sportsworld Communicators – the regulations which had triggered, through the complaints of Wolfgang Eisele and, latterly, Patrick Peter, the Commission's investigation. Although the FIA had greatly reduced its claim on television rights, as a result of Eisele's legal action, the Commission claimed it had continued to abuse by claiming the rights of championship series incorporating the FIA name. While the rules on television rights introduced in 1995 were not directly applicable to Formula One, the Commission claimed that the FIA's tactics had much the same effect on that sport: under the terms of the Concorde Agreement the FIA was able to compel participating teams to transfer to the FIA any rights they may have had in the broadcasting of Formula One, which were then transferred to Ecclestone's Formula One Administration. There was also a separate agreement between Formula One Administration and the promoters of Grand Prix events which gave Ecclestone any broadcasting rights the promoters might have possessed. The company was also invested by the FIA with the power to determine who could or could not promote a Grand Prix.

The Commission also stated that the FIA could not claim exclusive television rights. It was one of a number of claimants, along with the organisers, the promoters, the track owners and the teams, all of whom could reasonably claim shares. 'The Commission takes the view that the FIA's argument based on the protection of its intellectual property rights [its organisational and regulatory activities] cannot justify the FIA's abusive conduct in acquiring for itself other media rights which belong in the first instance to other participants.' Claims to sole ownership of these rights were an abuse of its dominant position.

Further, the Commission alleged that, owing to the various links between the FIA and FOA, Ecclestone was in a position of dominance with regard to Formula One, especially as, under the Concorde Agreement, FOA was granted the right to draw up the Formula One calendar, a power previously exercised by the FIA. It gave Ecclestone the right to decide whether a promoter would run a Grand Prix. FOA was able to abuse its dominant position because the FIA made its approval dependent on the promoter accepting FOA's 'abusive terms' (a willingness to hand over all commercial rights). Furthermore, the FIA stood to gain financially since it received a share of the value of the promoter's broadcasting rights through its commercial arrangements with FOA.

Thirdly, the FIA had used its power to set up a rival series in order to force an event out of the market. It cited as an example the fate of Patrick Peter's BPR series, which was stripped of its FIA authorisation to be replaced by an identical series, the FIA GT championship. The FIA's handling of the series and its promoters/organisers, said the Commission, constituted exclusionary behaviour, which had the object or effect of eliminating a rival promoter/organiser competing with FIA championships, as, for instance, Formula One, for television time and sponsorship. 'The BPR case is a clear example of how the FIA has used its certification/authorisation system in order to eliminate an independent international series organised and promoted by BPR, which had managed to attract a lot of interest from broadcasting and thus to sell the TV rights of its series. The BPR was developing an effective source of competition to the FIA's championships and to their commercial exploitation by one of the vice-presidents of the FIA, Mr Ecclestone.'

The Commission's fourth and final concern was the way in which Ecclestone had protected Formula One with three devices which effectively eliminated rival championships: the contracts between Formula One Administration and the promoters which prohibited circuits staging any motor sport that could compete with Formula One; the Concorde Agreement, negotiated by Ecclestone in October 1997 to get the teams' support for the flotation, which locked them into ten-year contracts, rather than the usual five; and the contracts with television broadcasters which imposed a massive financial penalty of 33 to 50 per cent if they televised a motor sport event considered by FOA to be a competitive threat to Formula One.

But one of the report's more damning allegations challenged the very enforceability of the television contracts between Ecclestone and broadcasters. 'The Commission takes the view that as the FIA abusively acquired the broadcasting rights to international motor sports events it could not validly assign these rights to Formula One Administration and International Sportsworld Communicators. Consequently, Formula One Administration and International Sportsworld Communicators were not in a position to conclude legally enforceable contracts with broadcasters giving them all the rights which the FIA claimed to have.'

In summarising the Commission's allegations, the report said that one of its most significant conclusions was that many of the contracts, particularly those involving broadcasters, were concluded on the basis of a situation unlawful under European Union competition law. They would need to be renegotiated, it added, if the Commission's allegations were ultimately upheld by the European Commission.

Mosley's response was issued on 31 January 2000, five months after the procedural deadline, owing to a delay by the European Commission in submitting all its files of evidence to the FIA – an indication, he offered, of its incompetence. But that was a mild reproach compared with the stinging criticism he saved for the FIA's 107-page response, which was reinforced by a personal letter to Italian academic Mario Monti, a member of the European Commission since 1995, who had been appointed to succeed Karel van Miert as Commissioner for Competition following a corruption scandal in Brussels shortly after the Statement of Objections was issued. (Although van Miert and the majority of his colleagues were not in anyway implicated, it led nevertheless to the departure of Commissioners en masse.) Mosley claimed the Commission had made 'a hopeless muddle of the facts and [is] completely confused about the regulations and general functioning of motor sport'. He insisted that the Statement of Objections was 'hopelessly flawed'.

Beyond the Statement, he also accused the Commission at a press conference of acting improperly, alleging that its Director-General, Dr Alexander Schaub, had colluded with Patrick Peter in an attempt to force Ecclestone to surrender the television rights to the FIA World Rally Championship, which Peter would then take over. In a letter in November 1999 to rally organisers worldwide, Peter claimed, alleged Mosley, that the Directorate-General for Competition 'had already approved his plans to take over "all the [organisers'] rights, starting with television rights"'. Mosley added that, despite official denials by Schaub's department that there was any plan to force Ecclestone to give up the rally television rights, four weeks later he wrote to Ecclestone to suggest that if he gave up the television rights to the FIA World Rally Championship it would make the 'problems' concerning Formula One 'less acute and much easier to deal with'. Mosley's letter to Monti continued: 'Any disinterested reader of the Statement of Objections and the FIA's response will conclude that in the course of these proceedings, the services of the competition department have broken the laws of the EU, behaved grossly improperly and displayed incompetence amounting to abuse.'

However, Mosley was unable to produce the letter Schaub had allegedly written to Ecclestone asking him to give up the rally television rights, or the one dated November 1999 allegedly sent by Peter to rally organisers stating that Schaub had approved his plans to take over the organisers' rights. Peter's lawyer, Christian Lamonin, produced a copy of a two-page letter dated December 1999, which, he claimed, his client had sent to rally organisers. But it refers to managing the television rights in association with Ecclestone. It reads: 'Our plan is to find very quickly an agreement with Mr Ecclestone in order to manage for you all your rights, starting with the TV rights.' It was this letter that Mosley had, in fact, been referring to, but it seems that, unwittingly, he had taken it out of context. Neither did it state that the Directorate-General for Competition 'had already approved his [Peter's] plans to take over the organisers' television rights'.

Mosley was highly critical of John Temple Lang at the press conference. By the time the Statement of Objections had been issued, the relationship between the two men, for Mosley at least, had long been strained. Mosley believed he had been 'very much prejudiced' towards the FIA and Ecclestone's companies. Temple Lang, a professor in European community law at Trinity College, Dublin, and visiting senior research fellow in the Law Faculty at Oxford University, strongly refuted Mosley's allegation. In May 2000 he was appointed Hearing Officer by Mario Monti in response to complaints from competition lawyers over many years that their clients' arguments were neglected by Commission officials. Temple Lang argues that this was not a post to which he would have been appointed if guilty of Mosley's charge. Further evidence of his impartiality, he added, was his decision four months later to resign on the grounds that he believed the Commission's anti-trust department did not have the will to introduce reforms that would ensure companies were given a fairer hearing.

There was certainly a touch of irony about Temple Lang's resignation in that it has been Mosley's consistent claim that at the heart of the FIA's problems with the European Commission had been an unwillingness to listen to a reasoned and cogent argument. Despite the circumstances of Temple Lang's departure from Brussels, Mosley felt disposed to claim the credit. His criticism of him had 'been the beginning of the end. If you talk in the legal circles in Brussels, the general consensus is that we got him fired. And I think it is quite right that he was. He was not an independent, disinterested public servant.' Commented Temple Lang: 'Mr Mosley's statement is, of course, entirely untrue. My resignation from the position of Hearing Officer had nothing to do with my contacts with Mr Mosley or his colleagues.'

That the Commission had, in fact, got as far as issuing a Statement of Objections surprised those who had believed that Ecclestone, keen to remove the uncertainty hanging over the future of television revenues and its impact on his flotation plans, would do whatever was necessary to resolve by compromise his differences with the Commission. That, said a senior Morgan Stanley executive at the time of the Eurobond launch, had been 'the way things have gone until now and I don't expect them to be any different in the future'. Brussels-based lawyer Jean-Paul Hordies, a specialist in EU broadcasting and media rights, had believed it would be inconceivable that Ecclestone would not do all that he could to quietly resolve his differences with the Commission. 'I cannot imagine that he would let them adopt a formal Statement of Objections,' he said. 'It would result in a public confrontation, which would be very messy and expensive for Mr Ecclestone, and sooner or later he would have to agree to the required modifications anyway.'

Certainly the FIA, according to Mosley, had made every effort to satisfy the European Commission's concerns. Time and again, he said, the FIA had offered to amend rules considered by the Commission to be anti-competitive; but these offers, and proposed meetings to discuss them, were repeatedly ignored. He continued to believe that van Miert had pursued the investigation in an attempt to avenge the success of the FIA's legal action against the European Commission over the leaking of the warning letters to the FIA, FOA and ISC in December 1997, and for prejudicial interviews he had given to the media.

'In the absence of any other explanation for the Commission's unusual tenacity in pursuing such a weakly presented and argued case, the FIA's victory over the Commission ... may provide some pointers. The Commission will not have welcomed being forced to apologise publicly for its wrongdoing and to pay what, by reference to past practice, is a high sum by way of costs. However, a body which is supposed to exercise a quasi-judicial function should not allow any disappointment at such an embarrassment to cloud its judgement on the substantive case. It seems probable, however, that the former Commissioner's determination to pursue the FIA at all costs and to ignore the rules of natural justice, which was manifest in the leak and prejudicial statements, is equally manifest in the Statement of Objections.'

In rejecting the Commission's Statement of Objections, the FIA gave notice that it requested an oral hearing to challenge its conclusions, the next stage in the European Commission's judicial process and attended by the anti-trust authorities of all EU member states. The FIA anticipated that it would run for three days, during which it proposed to call team managers, sponsors, advertisers, circuit owners, broadcasters 'and other expert witnesses'.

The FIA also made it clear in its response that, should the oral hearing confirm the Statement of Objections, it would proceed to challenge the decision before the Court of First Instance in Luxembourg. Potentially, it was an extremely costly road to go down. If the oral hearing went against the FIA, it would be liable from that point to annual fines of up to 10 per cent of its turnover. A European Commission spokesman said at the time: 'Theoretically, it could go on for at least a couple of years.'

While Mosley was fulminating, Ecclestone was keeping a low profile. By the end of 1999 his response to the Commission's Statement of Objections had still to be made known. A spokeswoman said at the time that the Commission was not allowed to confirm whether or not a party had responded to a Statement of Objections, and Ecclestone's office, through his lawyers, declined a request for clarification. But Ecclestone had, in fact, opted for an oral hearing. The date of 10 May 2000 was set aside by the European Commission for the beginning of a three-day hearing. This promised to be the scene of a revealing and highly public confrontation: the last thing that Ecclestone, unable to control the run of events and what he might be compelled to disclose, was likely to want.

Similarly unenthusiastic, although for quite different reasons, was the new Commissioner for Competition, Mario Monti. He did not want his staff and budget stretched to breaking point over the next couple of years trying to nail down a can of worms opened by his predecessor, Karel van Miert. Aware that between them Mosley and Ecclestone had the financial and political means to battle to the death, he had little political kudos to gain from the blood, sweat and tears that a protracted legal battle would inevitably bring. It was, in fact, a public hearing that none of the parties involved wanted, a consensus that led to a quiet diplomatic exchange and a far less bloody and less public process of resolution.

On 26 April, with the hearing only two weeks away, Mosley wrote to Monti with a set of 'concrete proposals', which the Commissioner, in his reply of 2 May, described as 'innovative and constructive'. However, added Monti, they could not be discussed until after the hearing. It presented Mosley and Ecclestone, as had doubtless been pre-arranged, with the grounds for requesting that the oral hearing be postponed. On receiving the request Monti issued instructions to his department that 'settlement discussions' should take place with the FIA immediately. Over the next few weeks a series of hurried meetings took place in Brussels and London, in time for an extraordinary meeting of the FIA's General Assembly in Paris on 28 June. What was agreed at these meetings formed the basis of a framework of action unanimously approved by its 143 worldwide delegates: that the FIA would amend the Sporting Regulations denounced in the Commission's Statement of Objections as abuses of competition law.

Among other things, it meant, in effect, that Ecclestone's involvement and influence would be restricted to the commercial activities of Formula One. To this end Ecclestone had already acted to remove one major obstacle to a peaceful agreement with the Commission – his ownership of International

Sportsworld Communicators. Its sale, concluded in early April, had been in the spirit of the 'innovative and constructive' proposals laid out in Mosley's letter to Monti. The buyer was David Richards, the chairman of Prodrive, the company which ran Subaru's rally team, who paid an undisclosed sum described by the new owner as 'colossal' – believed to be £30 million.

In order that Ecclestone could protect his huge financial investment in his digital television interests beyond the expiry in 2010 of the agreement between SLEC Holdings and the FIA, a new, stunning and ground-breaking agreement came into being, because of Mosley's ingenuity. In late 1999 he suggested to Ecclestone that the 15-year contract be extended by no less than 100 years, until 31 December 2110. It followed an unsuccessful attempt by Mosley to persuade the World Motor Sport Council to satisfy the European Commission's concerns by agreeing to sell to Ecclestone its ownership of the Formula One trademarks, with the World Motor Sport Council remaining solely as the regulator. Ecclestone agreed to pay the FIA $400 million in cash with a payment of a further $100 million in the event of a successful flotation. The majority of the council members voted against the proposal, believing that it would leave Ecclestone free to sideline the FIA as the regulator. 'They didn't really care whether it was $300 or $500 million,' said one of Mosley's associates. 'They were terrified that they might lose their stewards' armbands and all that nonsense.'

Mosley then suggested to the FIA's lawyers the more radical solution of copying the UK property practice of selling the leasehold, but for so far into the future that it was as good as selling the freehold. As far as European competition law was concerned, Mosley believed a 100-year deal was as good as the FIA disposing of all its commercial interests, which would ensure that it could have no incentive to favour Formula One in the event of the emergence of a rival series, which was one of the Commission's principal concerns. The lawyers were deeply sceptical, but it worked, after Mosley was able to persuade Mario Monti to give his approval to the new concept.

At this stage Mosley removed himself from any further formal discussions with Ecclestone. Because of media comment and, in particular, BBC TV's *Panorama* was highly critical of the 15-year commercial rights deal he had done with Ecclestone – 'I wanted to sue, but Bernie said it wasn't worth it' – Mosley claims he did not want to be seen to be compromising the FIA's negotiating position. At the FIA General Assembly on 8 October 1999, a four-man negotiating team including three members of the Senate – Rosario Alessi, president of the Automobile Club d'Italia; Michel Boeri, president of the Automobile Club de Monaco; Otto Flimm, president of the Allgemeiner Deutscher Automobil-Club; and John Large, honorary president of the Confederation of Australian Motor Sport – were appointed to represent the FIA.

After a series of meetings with Ecclestone over several weeks, Alessi, Boeri, Flimm and Large were united in agreeing a deal which left Mosley somewhat stunned. In return for signing away its commercial interests for the next 100 years, the FIA would receive a payment of $300 million – at the end of seven years. How could they be sure? Well, they reported to Mosley, Leo Kirch, the owner of the KirchGruppe, who at that time was negotiating with Ecclestone a $550-million purchase of half of SLEC Holdings, with an option to purchase a further 25 per cent for $1 billion, would sign a promissory note. It was a remarkably naïve deal. But one that was made possible by Mosley not only giving the four men carte blanche to avoid any media criticism of himself, but also the power to close the deal with the full authority of the FIA.

During their talks with Ecclestone, Mosley says, he was urging Alessi, Boeri, Flimm and Large to 'go for more, go for more'. And he certainly had every good reason to do so. At one stage, he was informed by Ecclestone that he was 'going to talk them into $200 million'. Locked into the deal, Mosley believed there was no way that he could persuade Ecclestone to renegotiate. But, in an attempt to improve the FIA's position, he offered Ecclestone a 6 per cent discount for early payment in the present and in cash – which, said Mosley, was calculated, based on an assumed compound interest rate of 6 per cent over seven years, to be worth $309 million. Ecclestone agreed.

However, out of that $309 million would come the $60 million which Ecclestone had promised the FIA for modifying their commercial rights contract to enable the launch of his $1.4-billion Eurobond sale in September 1998. It reduced the actual figure that the FIA would receive in return for locking away its commercial rights for 100 years to $249 million, but which, again at an assumed compound interest rate over seven years, was calculated, says Mosley, to be worth £309 million. He believed it was the best deal he could cut and, in early June 2000, it went before the Senate and the World Motor Sport Council, before being approved at an extraordinary meeting of the FIA's General Assembly on 28 June. It was a most excellent deal for Ecclestone. By way of comparison, the KirchGruppe paid £600 million to FIFA for the 2002 World Cup rights; Sky paid £1.1 billion for the English Premiership football rights; and ITV paid £120 million for three years of television highlights.

With the background political moves and pressures to conform with the European Commission's Statement of Objections, and the apparent lack of firm interest by any other party, it may well have been thought that the General Assembly had had little alternative but to vote in favour of Ecclestone's proposal. Not so. Another influential and powerful party was indeed interested, and one which was in a financial position to better Ecclestone's offer. Its members were major manufacturers Fiat, Ford, BMW,

DaimlerChrysler and Renault, who in recent years have together come to control more than half of the Formula One teams. Their interest in countering Ecclestone's bid was born in the main of increasing discontentment caused by the fortunes being raked in by others – and principally Ecclestone – thanks to the tens of millions of dollars they were pumping into the sport each year as the team owners and engine suppliers.

In April, about ten weeks before the General Assembly was due to meet to vote on Ecclestone's offer, Mosley had contacted Paolo Cantarella, the chief executive of Fiat and president of the Brussels-based Association des Constructeurs Européens d'Automobiles (ACEA), a lobbying group formed in 1991 to represent the interests of European car manufacturers – though the events that followed were an initiative of the Formula One manufacturers alone – to invite an alternative offer. At a meeting with Cantarella in Turin in early June, Mosley confirmed the FIA's enthusiasm to discuss the sale of the 100-year rights, adding that it would be 'very glad' of an offer.

Cantarella, aware that the General Assembly was due to meet at the end of the month to vote on Ecclestone's offer, fired off a letter to the FIA several days later requesting that any decision should be deferred until the manufacturers had had time to consider their counter-bid. Mosley's response was to insist that the manufacturers' offer, if it was to be considered, had to be ready for the meeting of the World Motor Sport Council, which was due to take place about a week later, and the General Assembly on the 28th. Given such an impossible time constraint, the manufacturers, unable to formulate in less than three weeks what had taken Ecclestone, a four-man negotiating team and Mosley some eight months to finally conclude, were unable to proceed any further.

With Ecclestone's offer the only one on the table, the World Motor Sport Council and the General Assembly decided to accept it on 'a bird-in-the-hand basis', as Mosley put it. All the same, he added, the manufacturers could have still made a bid. Although Ecclestone's offer had been accepted by the General Assembly, it 'remained on the table' for ten months. 'Mr Cantarella ... could have made a firm offer at any moment during that period,' he said. That apparent opportunity came about, in fact, because the FIA was still awaiting payment of the $60 million for the Eurobond deal, which had been due in July. It caused the behind-the-scenes relationship between Ecclestone and Mosley to become somewhat strained. Ecclestone maintained that his family trust, SLEC Holdings, in whose name the 100-year commercial rights were being acquired, had not failed to comply with the agreement. The full payment had been put in escrow before the deal had been agreed.

However, he argued that the agreement could not be finalised until Mario Monti had signed a final settlement which allowed the existing commercial rights deal between SLEC and the FIA to 2010, along with the 100-year rights, as a one-off 'leasehold' sale. It was strongly suspected that Ecclestone had another reason for holding back. He was playing for time until he had concluded negotiations with Leo Kirch, which finally took place in February 2001. He wanted to use Kirch's money to fund most of the deal with the FIA and he wanted to make quite sure Kirch was on board before he released the $60 million in escrow.

In January 2001 Mosley flew to Turin for a meeting with Cantarella. Ostensibly, its purpose was to encourage the manufacturers to proceed with an offer. It could also have been a ploy to exert pressure on Ecclestone to hand over the money. The manufacturers, suspecting that they were being sucked into a political dog-fight, decided to keep their chequebooks closed. Although Mosley was aware that there would be no offer forthcoming, the FIA nevertheless announced the following month that it was preparing to sell its rights to the manufacturers. The news, which was designed to give Ecclestone something to think about, coincided with a public ultimatum from the FIA that he had to settle the payment by 22 March, when an extraordinary meeting of the General Assembly was due to be held. The assembly agreed at its meeting to a proposal by the Senate that Ecclestone be given a final opportunity to complete, which he duly did on 24 April.

The FIA also was paid $4.6 million in compensation, the sum Mosley had estimated it had lost in interest because of the delay. But the money didn't come from Ecclestone, although it was to him that Mosley took his case. Ecclestone instantly rejected Mosley's petition, and then phoned Marco Piccinini, Mosley's deputy president, to tell him of the call from his president. Piccinini, greatly fearing that the entire deal was in danger of going under, phoned Mosley to implore him to drop his demand. Mosley agreed – but then phoned Ecclestone to pursue the payment. Ecclestone, in turn, called Kirch. Mosley, a touch mischievously, then called Piccinini to tell him what he had done. 'Oh, my God, oh, my God,' Piccinini exclaimed fearfully. Kirch, whose company would be liable for 75 per cent of the sum, agreed to pay, with Ecclestone covering the remaining 25 per cent.

The dispute between Ecclestone and Mosley was interesting not only for the detail of its public airing and its tone – on 2 February Mosley issued a statement denying that there was any 'question of extorting money from Mr Ecclestone' – but in that it had reached the public arena at all. Gone was the time when the thought of either man, bound in word and deed for 30 years, becoming embroiled in such controversy could be dismissed as unimaginable. At the height of the confrontation Mosley had seriously considered putting pressure on Ecclestone to pay up by going to court to argue that the FIA owned the trademarks of Formula One, Formula One World Championship and the Formula One Grand Prix. He went so far as to seek the advice of leading counsel and a leading trademark junior, but was persuaded that the complexities and costs of a hearing would probably prove pyrrhic.

Incidentally, whenever the ownership of Formula One arose in conversation with Ecclestone, Mosley would vary slightly an analogy he had used in disputing the claims of Dennis, Williams and Tyrrell. He likened Formula One to a restaurant owned by the FIA. Ecclestone, as the chef – the teams were the customers – had done a marvellous job and made it enormously successful. But the fact remained that he was the chef, not the owner. The FIA was. It was an analogy that Ecclestone forcefully rejected – he owned Formula One. Full stop.

On 26 January 2001, nine months after the settlement talks between the European Commission, Formula One Administration and the FIA had begun, Mario Monti formally announced the details of the 'peace deal'. They confirmed what had been unofficially known for some months: that Ecclestone would no longer continue as the FIA's vice-president of promotional affairs; that the FIA would end all involvement in the commercial activities of Formula One, thereby restricting itself solely to the function of regulatory authority; and that, in addition to the removal of the penalty clause punishing broadcasters who wanted to broadcast other motor sports, the duration of free-to-air television contracts would be limited to five years in the case of host broadcasters and three years with others.

Monti said in a statement that 'substantial modifications' had been made to the FIA's rules and commercial arrangements, as a result of which 'the Commission is satisfied that the FIA's role in future will be limited to that of impartial motor sports regulator'. Referring to the sale of International Sportsworld Communicators, Monti noted that Formula One Administration had sold its interests in rallying and all motor sports other than Formula One, and 'had agreed to make a number of changes to the current arrangements relating to the marketing and broadcasting of Formula One races'. The main elements of change listed in the statement were in verbatim:

- FIA has amended its regulations to strengthen the rights of motor sport organisers, circuit owners and participants, and to make it clear that FIA will act impartially as between all forms of motor sport of which it is the regulator.
- FIA will no longer have commercial interest in the success of Formula One and the new rules will remove any obstacle to other motor sport series competing with Formula One.
- FIA will retain its rights over its championships and the use of the 'FIA' name and Trade Marks but has removed from its rules any claim over

the broadcasting rights to events that it authorises and has agreed to waive any claim to broadcasting rights under the relevant clauses in the Formula One Agreement ['Concorde Agreement'].

• FIA has made it clear that its decisions will always be reasoned, and that those decisions may be challenged before national courts.

• The FOA group of companies has sold its interests in all forms of motor sport including Rallying and will therefore only have an interest in Formula One (Mr Ecclestone will no longer handle FIA's promotional affairs and will also reduce his role in FIA in other ways).

• FOA has agreed to limit the duration of its free-to-air broadcasting contracts (to five years in the case of host broadcasters and three years in other cases) and has removed provisions which penalise broadcasters which wanted to broadcast other forms of open wheeler racing.

Said Monti in the statement: 'The changes already adopted, together with those agreed in principle, will benefit all citizens interested in motor sport, as well as the sport's participants. The continued role of FIA as the regulatory authority will ensure that the existing high standards for participants and spectators will be maintained. At the same time, the changes allowing the introduction of new and competing forms of motor sport and creating new possibilities for circuits and broadcasters will bring more choice to consumers both as spectators and as television viewers.' The Commission, said Monti, was now in a position to give its preliminary approval to the new rules and arrangements, once third parties had had the opportunity to comment following their publication in the Official Journal of the European Communities.

While all seemed neatly resolved, there remained one awkward question: was Monti's agreement to a 100-year-old contract in violation of the Commission's own competition rules? Monti thought not. It appears he sanctioned it on the grounds that 'a longer duration of exclusive arrangements can prove to be justified, particularly when an operator wishes to enter a new market with an innovative service or to introduce a new technology requiring very high risk and heavy investment'. This was a reference to Ecclestone's massive financial investment in digital technology, but legal opinion doubted whether it legitimately fell within this consideration.

Jean-Paul Hordies, the Brussels-based lawyer who specialises in European media and broadcasting laws, believes that it did not. 'There is absolutely no reason for an exemption on these grounds. The only situation under which the Commission [can] grant an exemption would be where there is massive investment in a joint venture over a considerable period of time. If you take two major companies investing together to do something completely new, which needs such joint forces, the Commission may accept that. A good example would be, say, Renault and Fiat working together in order to produce an electric car on a global basis. That would be grounds for an exemption.' Nevertheless, Monti was prepared to accept Ecclestone's digital television company, founded ten years earlier and well established, as 'a new technology requiring very high risk and heavy investment'. Mosley continued to insist that the essential difference was the extreme duration of the contract, that it was as good as an outright sale of the FIA's commercial rights, which therefore put the agreement outside of the Commission's jurisdiction. Neither, he added, did the contract create a new market.

There remained one other apparently contradictory issue: the question of the actual ownership of the television contracts, which, on the evidence of the Commission's own investigation, challenged the validity of the FIA's right to assign them to Ecclestone. The Commission's Statement of Objections had concluded – and it was one of its 'most significant conclusions' – that, as the FIA had abusively acquired the broadcasting rights, it could not validly assign them to Ecclestone. His companies, therefore, had not been in a position to conclude legally enforceable contracts with broadcasters. They would, said the Statement of Objections, have to be renegotiated. Yet that relationship, with Monti's approval, was being allowed to continue unremedied.

Here, Mosley claims, without any doubt the FIA would have won the argument in the Court of First Instance on the grounds that, while a promoter may be owner of the commercial rights to an event, the FIA owned the commercial rights to the championship series. The value of the commercial rights were greatly enhanced by the inclusion of an event in an FIA championship series, in return for which those rights were assigned to the FIA and then granted to Ecclestone for marketing. 'It is certainly right and proper that a promoter may not wish to assign his commercial rights to the FIA. It is also perfectly right and proper that the FIA may not, in that case, wish to include the event in a championship series, unless he agrees to do so. That is the thing that they [the Commission] resolutely refused to understand or accept.'

Legal opinion in Brussels did not share his confidence: 'This was not the point of the Statement of Objections, which was that the FIA had allegedly acquired them on the basis of saying to organisers or promoters that unless they assigned them to the FIA they would not be allowed to take part in an FIA series. That would certainly appear to be abusive. A claim that the value of commercial rights might well be increased by inclusion of a circuit in an FIA series is no doubt a valid one, but it seems to me to be a quite separate issue.'

Before the settlement terms were agreed, Dr Wolfgang Deselaers, the lawyer who represented Wolfgang Eisele in his legal actions against Ecclestone, commented: 'As a result of the Statement of Objections, which will undoubtedly be confirmed by the European Commission, the Commission can order the FIA to put all [television] contracts out to tender. The teams, the organisers, the promoters, the television broadcasters may get a better deal elsewhere. Maybe so, maybe not. Who with, and how? That is not what it is about. It is now all about free competition, and that would seriously endanger the economic viability of Formula One Administration.' Yet, as Monti's approval of the FIA's 100-year television contract ensured, freedom of competition would not be the victor. The Directorate-General for Competition declined to comment.

At the end of it all, more than three years after the European Commission had begun its investigation, after all the endless meetings and planning and plotting and legal sideshows, threatened and actual, what had been achieved? Certainly little to diminish Ecclestone's power or fortunes. His severance from the FIA was of little account to him. He had exploited it well and it was no longer of any political benefit, a spent force to his ambitions and future plans. Similarly, the disposal of International Sportsworld Communicators was no great loss. It had served its purpose in the suppression of certain motor sports to the immense commercial advantage of Formula One and Ecclestone's personal enrichment, increased even more by its sale. In reality, Ecclestone had lost very little, but had gained much in return. He secured what he had fought tooth and nail to protect – the television rights to Formula One, and now for 100 years, no less. As for the apparently sweeping modifications to the FIA's rules and regulations, as well as commercial arrangements, to confine it to the role of an 'impartial motor sports regulator' and thus open the way for the introduction of 'new and competing' forms of motor sport, they had come far too late. The FIA was agreeing to open up a field that would attract few, if any, new runners. The proverbial horse – with Ecclestone and his moneybags on its back – had already bolted.

And the spoils of the hugely expensive battle pitted by the combined forces of Ecclestone and the FIA against the European Commission were, in the end, decided by compromise and political expediency orchestrated by Brussels itself.

16

GOODBYE KAREL ... HELLO LEO

Seven months after his departure from the European Commission, Karel van Miert, in an article published in the German magazine *Focus*, claimed, among other comments, claimed that 'certain people' had spent 'a great deal of money' trying to 'destroy' him. It had been even more stressful than an investigation into the activities of a Belgian steelworks, which led to its closure and the need for him to have police protection from the threats of angry steelworkers. In October 2000 Mosley sued for libel, an action he lost not because the claims were true, but because the High Court ruled that there was no reasonable prospect of a jury deciding that he could be identified by the article. A year later Appeal Court judges upheld the ruling.

This bizarre episode finally closed the book on his career in Brussels. He went on to become president of the Netherlands Business School, near Amsterdam – and lecturer in European competition policy.

And what of the fate of Wolfgang Eisele, whose complaint set the European Commission off on the trail of Ecclestone and the FIA? In July 2000, six months before Mario Monti announced the settlement with Ecclestone and Mosley, Eisele, attempting to overturn a court judgement that any violation of television rights could only be contested by those parties directly affected, agreed to withdraw his final appeal to Germany's Federal Court of Justice in Karlsruhe in return for a substantial payment from Ecclestone, the details of which, as usual, were covered by a confidentiality clause.

Dr Wolfgang Deselaers, Eisele's lawyer, suspected that Ecclestone had agreed to a settlement after he was given to understand that it would be easier to settle his differences with the European Commission if Eisele was removed. 'I think the Commission made it clear to them [Ecclestone's lawyers] that it [would be] much easier for them [the Commission], politically, to settle with Ecclestone in respect of Formula One if there was nobody around saying it was a scandal.'

The discussions which led to the pay-off had taken place over many months. It had taken so long because 'maybe it wasn't too clear to him [Ecclestone] that the small Mr Eisele could really endanger the flotation of Formula One, that this small case which became bigger and bigger could really be a hindrance to his Formula One plans'. As far as Eisele's actions against Ecclestone and the FIA were concerned, their objective, he said, had largely been achieved through the suspension of the FIA's Article 27 in February 1998, which returned the marketing, including the crucial television rights, of all non-Formula One championships to the organisers. Of the settlement with Ecclestone, he said: 'It was the right time to find a solution, rather than to fight the next ten years in court.'

Such settlements are not an uncommon strategy in Ecclestone's defence of his interests. Eisele and Patrick Peter are two notable examples. Another less publicised one is businesswoman Nicky Morris, who in 1998 set up a website called Formula1.com, which two years later was reaching 750,000 viewers a month and, encouragingly, managing to break even from its revenue of advertising, Grand Prix ticket sales, merchandise sales and the syndication of content. That is, until its existence was drawn to Ecclestone's attention, along with the fact that Morris had registered the 'F1.com' domain name. His first move was a complaint in March 2000 to the World Intellectual Property Organisation in Geneva (WIPO), claiming that the name 'F1' and the domain name were the property of Formula One Management and therefore an infringement of trademark rules. WIPO found against Ecclestone after Morris, who argued the name was generic, demonstrated that many businesses unrelated to Ecclestone's commercial activities use 'Formula 1' or its abbreviation in their names.

Pressure on Morris was stepped up by the FIA posting notices at the Malaysian Grand Prix in 2000 warning that photographers who abused their press accreditation would have it removed. As a result, two leading photo agencies were compelled to cease supplying Morris with picture coverage. Around the same time, Ecclestone issued a court action against Morris in San Francisco, claiming trademark infringement. Morris retaliated by bringing an anti-trust lawsuit, which, unsuccessfully, Ecclestone attempted to block by applying to have it dismissed. The date for the hearing was set for February 2002. But, a month before legal battle was due to commence, a confidential settlement offer was made to buy Morris's dotcom company, which she accepted.

Before the success of the Formula1.com website, Ecclestone was said to have been relatively unmoved by the Internet as a medium to promote Formula One, although, with broadband capability giving access to high-quality video pictures, it was being increasingly seen as providing a strong promotional platform. Consequently, he was, it was reported, ready to invest £30 million in an official site. Now he had Morris's. The power of his money had won the day yet again. Following the publication of the Commission's Statement of Objections in June 1999, Ecclestone was approached by various companies who, now aware of the details of the Commission's findings, were looking for a stake in Formula One. They included Rupert Murdoch's BSkyB, the American venture capital firm KKR, and Nomura, as well as one from a consortium which would have given a substantial stake to the Formula One teams. Their approaches, inevitably, reached the ears of Robin Saunders, the head of Westdeutsche Landesbank's asset securitisation and principal finance group, who had structured the $1.4-million Eurobond rescue operation. Given her favourable relationship with Ecclestone, she was in pole position to move quickly to pull off a prestigious coup.

Capitalising on her inside knowledge and relationship with Deutsche Bank, whom she had left to join WestLB, and which, through Morgan Grenfell Private Equity, its capital venture arm, already had a 45 per cent shareholding in the Arrows team, she approached Ecclestone, who introduced her to Stephen Mullens, lawyer for the Orion trust, which safeguards the Ecclestone family wealth and owns the shares in SLEC Holdings. He, in turn, introduced Saunders to Luc Jean Argand, one of the trustees, which led to a series of meetings between Argand, his fellow trustees – whose number included a banker – and her former employers, which, by mid-September 1999, resulted in the agreed sale of up to 50 per cent of SLEC Holdings Ltd, the Formula One holding company, in a $1.3-billion deal. Morgan Grenfell agreed to pay $325 million for a 12.5 per cent stake, with an option to take up a further 37.5 per cent valued at $975 million. Saunders, who, combined with the Eurobond sale, had in the space of four months put a total of $2.4 billion in Ecclestone's family trust, was thought to have done well in getting what was generally seen to be a high price, particularly as there was considerable pressure on Morgan Grenfell to either take up the option or sell it on by a deadline of 1 February 2000. Despite a frantic series of meetings with potentially interested bidders, including media and television companies, sports management groups and venture capitalists, the deadline passed with Morgan Grenfell unable to meet either option.

(Ecclestone was actually not best pleased by the trustees' decision to sell the shares. But, following his heart operation and given his advanced years, they believed that, in the event of his death, their value would drop dramatically. He later acknowledged the wisdom of their prudence. 'Think about this for two minutes: I'm gone, Slavica marries a strapping young guy who can do all the things I can no longer do ... he comes along and says, "Darling, what's happened with this. It's completely mad. You should sue them." And if she's passionately in love, and it's no aggravation to her, he would go to a lawyer and they'd sue the trust. They are obliged to act in the best interests of the trust. They were absolutely correct.')

Standing in the wings, however, was San Francisco-based American private equity firm Hellman & Friedman, who had already come to an agreement with Ecclestone to take up the option if Morgan Grenfell failed to do so. A principal figure was Melbourne businessman Ron Walker, who had been responsible, on behalf of Victorian government premier Jeff Kennett, for securing the controversial Grand Prix in Melbourne's Albert Park in 1996. He was now the go-between for Ecclestone and another Australian, Brian Powers, a managing director of Hellman & Friedman and chairman of John Fairfax Holdings, Australia's leading newspaper and magazine publisher. Walker knew Powers, a former executive in Kerry Packer's media empire, through their association of mutual friends and business interests.

The day after Morgan Grenfell's option deadline expired, Hellman & Friedman moved to take it up. Fourteen days later, on 16 February, the deal was closed in London, with Hellman & Friedman paying $712 million for the 37.5 per cent stake. In a fanfare of bullish hope, it was announced that Formula One was expected to be floated within 12 months, with Powers leading the roadshows in both Europe and America. Amid the standard razzmatazz, Hellman & Friedman's chairman, Warren Hellman, declared his company was 'thrilled' to be making its largest investment to date. It soon had good reason.

One month later Hellman & Friedman and Morgan Grenfell agreed to sell their shareholdings to German media company EM.TV & Merchandising AG. With Walker once again playing a pivotal role, the Munich-based company agreed to pay $1.65 billion in cash and equities for the shareholdings of a 50 per cent stake in Formula One. In little more than a month Hellman & Friedman had made profits of more than $247 million. The precise figure earned by Walker was kept confidential, but it is understood that his activities earned him fees totalling $93 million.

The EM.TV deal included a compulsory 25 per cent share option to be taken up within 12 months, which some observers mistakenly interpreted as a sign that perhaps Ecclestone was beginning to relax his grip on Formula

One. It was an interpretation he was quick to nail, insisting that whatever the extent of EM.TV's shareholding, he would remain in absolute control of the reins. To him, their 50 per cent gave them no more control than owning 5 per cent. EM.TV, he proclaimed, had control of nothing. Control of all commercial activities, through Formula One Administration, of which Ecclestone was chief executive, lay with the Ecclestone family trust, which, as it was in the name of his wife, Slavica, meant that he remained very much at the helm.

EM.TV's plans to increase its shareholding received a crippling setback by October when an accountancy error, said to have occurred during the $680-million acquisition the previous March of the Jim Henson Company, maker of *The Muppets* TV show, forced the company to correct its half-year figures, which led to a drop of 30 per cent in share value and wiped about $2.7 billion off its market capitalisation. Far from thinking of taking up the 25 per cent option, the company declared that it was prepared to consider selling part of its 50 per cent stake in order to ease regulatory concerns over the control of Formula One, although, more accurately, it was in order to halt the falling share price.

All the while, Formula One manufacturers had looked on from the sidelines in a state of consternation. Concerned that half of Formula One could once again end up in the hands of a media 'outsider', Paolo Cantarella, Fiat chief executive and president of the Association des Constructeurs Européens d'Automobiles, the European manufacturers' association, had, within the week, approached Ecclestone on behalf of certain manufacturers to express their interest in taking up all of EM.TV's stake, plus a further 10 per cent. The proposal had an obvious appeal to Ecclestone.

Based on the $1.65 billion paid by EM.TV, which put a capitalisation value of $3.3 billion on Formula One, the sale of a 60 per cent shareholding would generate a further $1.3 billion for his family trust. Having the manufacturers as stakeholders in Formula One was attractive to Ecclestone for one other significant reason. Given that they were frustrated as key players by their impotence in a sport they largely subsidised, it would end their threat to set up, as had been speculated more than once, a rival motor-racing series, now made more feasible by the commercial freedoms established by the settlement of the European Commission's Statement of Objections. Indeed, Ecclestone's one criticism of the trustees' decision to sell the SLEC Holdings shares was the resultant hassle it would cause him with the manufacturers.

By late 2000, while a due diligence was being carried out on SLEC Holdings by TAG McLaren Holdings, discussions were taking place for a preferential three-tier shareholding structure, with A, B and C shares being made available respectively to team-owning manufacturers; the manufacturers who supply the engines; and independent team owners. In the opinion of Dr Mark Jenkins, senior lecturer in strategic management at the UK's Cranfield School of Management, who spent two years studying the commercial structure of Formula One, it was only a matter of time before the manufacturers began to play an increasingly influential role in Formula One. Back in July 1999 he gave three reasons.

Firstly, a continuing global concentration of the motor industry suggested that in a few years' time there would be six car manufacturers – two in the US, two in Europe and two in Asia – and with manufacturing capacity and technology on equal par, brand-enhancing involvement in motor sport, which promotes the right kind of sexy, dynamic image, would become all the more crucial. Secondly, the dependence of the teams for works engines would lead to a more committed relationship with the manufacturers, and, thirdly, the end of tobacco sponsorship in 2006 would lead to the constructors becoming even more dependent on the manufacturers. 'Consequently, the manufacturers will want to play a greater role in the ways in which motor sports in general, and Formula One in particular, are marketed and run,' said Jenkins.

But the manufacturers, whose sidelining in the bidding for the 100-year television rights contract with the FIA just seven months earlier was still a recent memory, were once again to be frustrated. A few months later, in February 2001, it was announced that Ecclestone had agreed a deal with the KirchGruppe. It bought half of EM.TV's 50 per cent stake for $550 million and paid close to a further $1 billion for the compulsory 25 per cent option, giving Kirch and EM.TV a 75 per cent controlling interest. The news provoked an immediate response from the manufacturers concerned that the KirchGruppe, with vested interests in its own struggling pay-TV company, would combine resources with Ecclestone's considerable digital television interests to reduce free-to-air coverage of Formula One in order to give a much-needed boost to subscriber audience figures. By 2000 a predicted audience figure of 2.9 million had barely exceeded two million, and that at an estimated cost of $3 billion.

In an effort to mollify the manufacturers, both Ecclestone and Kirch issued statements of reassurance that the future of free-to-air coverage was safe. But the manufacturers remained unconvinced, preferring to believe that the Ecclestone–Kirch alliance posed too big a threat to their lifeblood of global publicity. This, in addition to getting what they saw as less than an equitable return on their massive bankrolling of Formula One, prompted them to a new level of action. They were now ready to set up their own World Championship series.

In April 2001, when the KirchGruppe and EM.TV held a 75 per cent controlling interest in SLEC Holdings, the Ecclestone family trust which owns the 100-year television rights, he announced that he would stay at the helm of Formula One until at least the end of the Concorde Agreement which was to expire at the end of 2007. The statement was intended to make clear that his grip on Formula One remained as strong as ever, hinting even that it might remain so beyond that agreement. A precondition of his remaining in charge of daily operational control, the statement continued, had been a guarantee that his policy of worldwide, live free-to-air television coverage remained unchanged.

This was for the benefit of the Formula One manufacturers – Fiat, Ford, BMW, DaimlerChrysler and Renault – who believed that the deal with the KirchGruppe was a deal too far for their interests. Leo Kirch attempted to strengthen the guarantee given to Ecclestone by offering the manufacturers the right of veto if any move was made to take Formula One away from free-to-air television. Kirch's chief executive officer, Dieter Hahn, flew to Italy in an effort to reassure Paulo Cantarella, Fiat chief executive and the then president of the Association des Constructeurs Européens d'Automobiles, that the interests of their Formula One members would not be harmed. The trip proved a damp squib. The two men failed to agree, and Hahn departed leaving Cantarella unconvinced. He preferred to suspect that the pay-TV interests of Kirch and Ecclestone, which were failing to live up to profitable expectations, would sooner or later diminish free-to-air coverage, which would reduce even further what they saw as poor returns on team budgets costing on average more than $100 million a year, most of it funding new engine and design technology. (Mercedes-Benz was said to have spent more than $240 million on the 2003 season.)

The ACEA sent a warning shot across the bows through a press release declaring that the manufacturers 'do not accept that Formula One can be directly or indirectly controlled or exploited by just one television broadcaster, with the risk of limiting the viewing to the sole subscribers to pay-TV'. If the deal went ahead, 'the manufacturers, which ... are the principal players in Formula One, will consider alternative solutions'. These included, the ACEA warned, terminating the current Concorde Agreement and the setting up of an alternative World Championship series. Once the deal between Ecclestone and Kirch was signed, the manufacturers began to make good their threat. A press release issued 4 May 2001 stated that the manufacturers had signed an agreement to form a company to set up an 'open-wheel, single-seat motor-racing series' by 1 January 2008.

Over the next few months, the structure of a joint company called GPWC Holdings BV, registered in Holland, was put in place. Cantarella was elected chairman, a position to be rotated annually between members of the board, which comprised vice-chairman Professor Jürgen Hubbert, management board member, DaimlerChrysler; Patrick Faure, executive vice-president, Renault; Dr Burkhard Goeschel, director of research and development, BMW; and Dr Wolfgang Reitzle, premier automotive group vice-president, Ford.

On 27 November 2001 the board members met with Formula One team bosses to invite them to participate in the proposed new World Championship series. A press release stated that it would 'channel all Grand Prix-generated incomes such as that from TV rights, promotion of races, hospitality activities, track advertising, merchandising, internet opportunities and the like, through their joint organisation, with the aim of substantially improving the financial benefits of all participating teams and ensuring full economic transparency'.

Such a breakaway series threatened to have a devastating impact on the future of Formula One. The withdrawal of the top-of-the-bill teams – Ferrari (90 per cent owned by Fiat), TAG McLaren (40 per cent owned by DaimlerChrysler, with Ron Dennis owning 30 per cent), Benetton (owned by Renault), Jaguar (owned by Ford) and Williams (engines supplied by BMW) – would certainly undermine, if not destroy, the universal appeal of Formula One. It would also, if successful, seriously threaten the value of the 100-year television rights, a principal asset of SLEC Holdings. There was perhaps a further factor for Ecclestone to consider: by then he would no longer be able to count on the support of Mosley, who down the years has played a key role in the rise of Ecclestone's political and financial fortunes. On 5 October 2001, at the age of 61, Mosley was re-elected President of the FIA for a third four-year term at the FIA's annual General Assembly in Cologne; he later declared his intention not to stand again.

Someone who would certainly play no part in future proceedings was Leo Kirch, who had paid Ecclestone $1.55 billion for a 50 per cent stake in SLEC Holdings. In May 2002, less than five months after the manufacturers had invited the rest of the teams to join forces, severe cashflow problems and an unmanageable debt-load forced his pay-TV operation, KirchPayTV, to file for insolvency after shareholders and creditor banks Commerzbank and DZ Bank were unable to agree a $132-million bridging loan. A month earlier he had resigned as chairman of the KirchGruppe; his departure was accompanied by that of chief executive Dieter Hahn.

In late 2001 KirchPayTV was under considerable pressure to achieve a series of undisclosed financial targets linked to financial backing provided by Rupert Murdoch's BSkyB Group, which had a 22 per cent shareholding interest and had an option to call in the loans if the targets weren't reached. It had been this kind of straitjacket pressure that had helped to convince the manufacturers that Kirch's interest in SLEC Holdings was solely in the pay-TV potential of Formula One's global television audience, to the detriment of the much wider audience of free-to-air broadcasting. Although Kirch's departure removed the manufacturers' anxiety about Formula One television coverage going pay-per-view, it did nothing to stay their demand for a bigger share of commercial revenues in return for their investment dollar.

In proposals drawn up by bankers Goldman Sachs on behalf of GPWC, the manufacturers guaranteed to increase the teams' income by 60 per cent in 2008, and nearly treble it by 2010. They planned to achieve it by substantially increasing the teams' share of the television rights, from 47 per cent of the gross to 75 per cent of the net, plus a substantial stake in other Formula One-related revenue, from track signage, retail merchandise and Paddock Club hospitality, all of which would be increased by shrewder negotiations.

These were clearly nervous times for the manufacturers. Prior to a meeting with teams at a Munich hotel on 10 April 2003, their spokesman at Mercedes-Benz refused to confirm its purpose or that it was even due to take place. In an attempt to thwart any unauthorised leaks, the teams were compelled to sign confidentiality agreements covering the details of the GPWC proposals drafted by Goldman Sachs. Ironically, this showdown between Ecclestone and the manufacturers was a rerun of the days when, a little more than 20 years earlier, as the confrontational president of FOCA supported by a group of insurgent constructors, he had unsuccessfully tried, with Mosley's counsel and collaboration, to wrest control of Formula One from his adversary, Jean-Marie Balestre, the president of FISA, and the continental manufacturers by setting up a breakaway world championship series. Now it was the manufacturers who were the rebels taking on an 'establishment' created by Ecclestone and Mosley.

Whatever Ecclestone's private concerns, his response to the manufacturers' threat was, typically, one of deadpan indifference. With about five years of the Concorde Agreement still to run, he believed he had time on his side, that he could afford to sit it out. To Ecclestone it was business as usual. As far as he was concerned the pressure was on the manufacturers to unite the teams – no easy task, as he more than anyone knew – and then produce a proposal acceptable not only to him, but also to a consortium of banks: Bayerische Landesbank, Lehman Brothers and JP Morgan, major creditors of Leo Kirch's fallen media empire, and to whom its 75 per cent shareholding had reverted.

First, the manufacturers had a number of obstacles to surmount, not least that of gaining the confidence of the rest of the teams – especially that of the smaller, less wealthy privateers such as Jordan, Minardi and Sauber – that a breakaway rival series would be underpinned by the contractual guarantee of a long-term commitment to Formula One. Both Mercedes-Benz and Renault have over the years dipped in and out of Formula One whenever it has suited their economic fortunes.

The contract in existence between Ecclestone and the teams was to run for ten years. It was thought most unlikely that the teams – and this included BAR and Toyota in addition to the privateers – would agree to less than five years, if not seven. The question was whether or not the manufacturers could persuade their respective boards to approve such a commitment. It would mean in effect a contingent liability – a commitment to expenditure against anticipated revenues – of billions of dollars in uncertain future trading conditions. It was considered improbable that the likes of Jürgen E. Schremp, the cautious chief executive officer of DaimlerChrysler, the parent company of Mercedes-Benz, and his main board of directors would approve a liability that could threaten its core business.

It was also believed that the manufacturers faced a major marketing problem in that a rival series would not be able to use the title of Formula One, the copyright of which is owned by Ecclestone. Its appeal would therefore be greatly diminished in the eyes of the all-important broadcasters, who would not be keen to pay top dollar for an event lacking the global brand of the Formula One World Championship series. Like sponsors, they crave stability. If they had to push the button, they would, it was thought, stay with Ecclestone on the basis that it was better the devil they knew. They would also be concerned about the manufacturers' decision to exclude the FIA from their plans, which stipulated an alternative regulatory body. The decision to do so was made on the probable, and understandable, grounds that Mosley was so close to Ecclestone. But, politically, it was not perhaps the most tactically prudent of moves. Mosley, believing that the exclusion of the FIA was an attack on its primary business, made calls to the ACEA and to certain chairmen of the manufacturers. The response from both parties was implicitly critical of any move to exclude the FIA.

Both were aware of the lobbying power that the FIA wields in Brussels, which is such that it can significantly influence European Commission legislation on a range of issues from car emissions to safety features. A movement of the FIA's stance, which is generally finely balanced between the manufacturers and the safety tsars, could cost the manufacturers dear in production costs. But instead of seeking a form of alliance with Mosley, the snub to the FIA ensured that he and Ecclestone were brought closer together in standing against a breakaway series.

When the FIA agreed to sell to Ecclestone its commercial rights for 100 years, its lawyers insisted on the inclusion of a clause giving the FIA the right to veto any sale of shareholding which could constitute change of control, which was what would take place if the manufacturers were successful in achieving their intended aim of acquiring the 75 per cent stake of the three banks. As things stood at that time, Mosley was not in the mood to give it his blessing.

Finally, the manufacturers had one other problem to resolve – that they could guarantee the teams a calendar of 16 Grands Prix. It was thought improbable that they could, as Ecclestone had the promoters' contracts in his bottom drawer, along with the television contracts, most of which extended well beyond 2008, the start season of the proposed rival series. It could be said the manufacturers were all dressed up with nowhere to go.

The obvious threat to Ecclestone's hand was the loss of the star performers. Would Formula One be the same without Ferrari, McLaren, Williams and Benetton? Ecclestone was convinced it would. He would cite the departure of the classic names of Brabham and Lotus as evidence that Formula One is bigger than any team. How it might survive a haemorrhage caused by the departure of the principal members of the cast in one swoop, though, would certainly test that theory to its absolute limit.

But Mosley believed that Ecclestone was right. He was of the opinion that it would be perfectly feasible to run Formula 3000 cars, just ten seconds slower per lap than Formula One cars, without lessening the spectacle for spectators or television audiences. With engines lasting a season rather than a race, they would also be considerably cheaper for the teams to run. Further, and crucially, its credibility could be greatly enhanced by Ecclestone using his ample wallet to lure three or four of the leading drivers to compete in the FIA-backed world championship. In those circumstances, it was thought that Ferrari, the one irreplaceable team and, historically, ever ready to use its unique marque to its best advantage, would not be long in following suit, which would mean the beginning of the end of the manufacturers' rival series.

But all the speculation, predictably, came to nothing. As with the historic battles between the FOCA and the FISA of previous years, both sides knew they had too much to lose by fighting to the death. As then, peace was restored through the art of compromise. Negotiations between Ecclestone, the banks and the manufacturers dragged on for almost two years before a provisional settlement was reached. On 4 December 2003 a secret meeting was held in Geneva between representatives of GPWC; the three banks, as the shareholders of SLEC; Bambino Holdings Ltd, of which SLEC is a subsidiary; and Ecclestone, as the chief executive officer of Formula One Administration. A statement was issued by Dr Gerhard Gribkowsky, chief risk officer of Bayerische Landesbank; Prof Jürgen Hubbert, the DaimlerChrysler board member responsible for Mercedes-Benz, and chairman of GPWC; and Ecclestone, which declared that they were 'very happy' to have 'reached a breakthrough in our negotiations about the future of Formula One. The outcome is in the best interests of Formula One and the millions of its fans around the world'.

It was agreed that a Memorandum of Understanding would be prepared by the end of the month detailing the 'future structure' of Formula One. It was understood at the time that Ecclestone had agreed to a 'significant' increase in the teams' share of all Formula One-related income, while, in return, the teams agreed to a lengthy extension of the Concorde Agreement due to expire at the end of 2007. It would, however, be another 18 months before a Memorandum of Understanding was finally signed.

Progress was interrupted by the interest of CVC Capital Partners, a Luxembourg-based global private equity and investment advisory firm, in acquiring Bayerische Landesbank's 48 per cent shareholding, which, after prolonged negotiations, finally took place in November 2005. At the same time, CVC acquired Ecclestone's 25 per cent shares in SLEC Holdings, the proceeds of which he invested in Alpha Prema, a subsidiary of venture capital firm Alpha D2 in which CVC has a majority stake. The following month Alpha Prema acquired JP Morgan's stake, while in March 2006 CVC bought Lehman Brothers' 14.1 per cent shareholding.

The manufacturers now found themselves at the negotiating table with a different animal indeed. In addition to a more equitable share of Formula One revenues, the manufacturers wanted Formula One to be self-sustaining, with the remainder of the profits being reinvested in the sport to cover the cost, for example, of track maintenance and the setting up of independent funds to assist smaller teams through temporary financial difficulties. But these proposals got short shrift from CVC. A spokesman for one of the manufacturers said: 'They had a much more aggressive approach as to what to do with the business. It became very clear to us that we had no chance whatsoever of stopping them taking money out of the sport.'

The manufacturers also had two other issues on their agenda. They wanted to be involved in structuring the race calendar and, more importantly, to have a principal role in naming a successor to the ageing Ecclestone. They were fearful of a destabilising power battle in the absence of an heir apparent capable of matching Ecclestone's skills and expertise. Said the manufacturers' spokesman: 'There was a zero long-term strategy. Any other company that generates the kind of turnover that F1 generates has some sort of succession back-up plan. Bernie didn't. He didn't even have a chief executive officer at the time.'

Neither CVC nor Ecclestone was moved by the manufacturers' arguments. But they did succeed in persuading Ecclestone and CVC to agree to a 50-50 split in Formula One revenues, a ground-breaking agreement that was formalised in a Memorandum of Understanding at the Barcelona Grand Prix in 2006. It was signed by the manufacturers – BMW, Daimler, Honda, Renault and Toyota – on one side and, on the other, by Ecclestone and Donald Mackenzie, head of CVC's London operations. 'We didn't get all that we wanted,' commented the spokesman, 'but an equal division of the revenues was a very big improvement compared to what it used to be.'

All in all, just another another day and another deal in Formula One wonderland.

17

THE CASH-FOR-ASH AFFAIR

Until November 1997 the name of Bernie Ecclestone would have meant little to people outside of Formula One. Then, literally overnight, to his immense anger and great embarrassment, it all changed. He became a front-page figure at the centre of a sleaze scandal that rocked the six-month-old New Labour government of Prime Minister Tony Blair. Another colourful incident was about to be added to his chequered CV. And a new phrase to describe a million pounds – a 'Bernie'. That was how much he had paid, it was whispered behind cupped hands, to bring about a change in government policy exempting Formula One from a ban on tobacco sponsorship and advertising, which were worth a combined estimate of $250–300 million a year to the teams.

It was a sensational affair which began innocently enough in October 1995 with an invitation to Blair, then Labour Party leader, to visit a British Grand Prix. It ended in a political storm which raged for months, and with Blair being the first Prime Minister to be rebuked for breaching House of Commons rules on disclosure of gifts and hospitality. Allegations of impropriety were also levelled against one of his senior ministers and the credibility of a close adviser was seriously damaged, while an apologetic and chastened Blair, who had delighted in mocking the previous Conservative government for a series of tacky kiss-and-tell exposés involving its MPs, was compelled to go on television to try to persuade a sceptical British public that, in his own words, he was 'a pretty straight kind of guy'.

The invitation had come from Max Mosley during a visit to Blair's home in Islington, north London, where, over a cup of coffee made by the Labour Party leader himself, Mosley promoted the FIA's road safety and environmental work. Tobacco sponsorship and advertising were not discussed. The meeting had been arranged at Mosley's request by David Ward, who had worked as head of policy for John Smith, the previous Labour leader, until his death in 1994, shortly after which he joined the FIA as director general of its European Bureau in Brussels, and went on to become director general of the FIA Foundation. Following his appointment as president of the FIA in 1993, Mosley had tried unsuccessfully to headhunt Ward, with whom had had developed a friendship through his interest in motor sport. In the mid-1970s, as a student, Ward had been a keen go-kart racer; he later took part in amateur sports car events and is a former winner of the Lords versus Commons charity race at Brands Hatch. Their friendship enabled Mosley to be persuaded to donate several thousand pounds to Smith's Industrial Research Organisation, which, among things, financed his office.

When Mosley expressed his interest in meeting Blair, Ward was in a position to pull the right strings. And Blair was happy to respond – his close advisers had been made aware of the donors to Smith's organisation, and, further, Ward believed that Mosley's contacts in motor sport and the automobile industry could prove invaluable in boosting the Labour Party's war chest for the government elections that were just 18 months away. Some four months later, in February 1996, Ward received a phone call from Jonathan Powell, Blair's chief of staff, and a former first secretary at the British Embassy in Washington, where he had learnt much about successful fund-raising from closely monitoring Bill Clinton's election campaign. Powell wanted to know one thing: did Ward think that Bernie Ecclestone might make a donation to the Labour Party? Ward, aware of Mosley's invitation to the British Grand Prix, suggested that Blair follow it up. He would then have the opportunity to meet Ecclestone, who had just been named in the press as Britain's highest-paid businessman, with a salary that year of £54.9 million, which would lay the ground for an approach at a later date. Powell thought it a good idea. Arrangements were made for Blair to attend, with his family, the 1996 British Grand Prix.

Other distinguished guests were three leading Tory Government figures – Kenneth Clarke, the Chancellor of the Exchequer, Ian Lang, the Trade and Industry Secretary, and Peter Lilley, the Social Security Secretary – who had been invited by the organisers, Britain's Royal Automobile Club. They received none of the red-carpet treatment laid out for the Blairs, which included Cherie Blair being introduced to the top Formula One drivers and given a chauffeur-driven ride around the circuit by Damon Hill, before meeting Ecclestone in the opulent seclusion of his expansive, black motor home, whose tinted windows and video cameras to screen visitors caused it to be dubbed 'the Lubianka' by the media. Also present were Mosley and Ward. The four men engaged in lightweight conversation for about 20 minutes, during which time Ecclestone enthusiastically demonstrated the white-hot technology of his bank of digital television monitors, before being joined by the chairman of BMW, Bernd Pischetsrieder. Again no mention was made of tobacco sponsorship. It proved a successful flesh-pressing exercise. Ecclestone was impressed by the energetic young Labour leader. In a letter to *The Times* he later described Blair, by now Prime Minister, as 'a person of exceptional ability who ... would do an outstanding job for our country'.

That autumn, with the election less than seven months away and fund-raising efforts being stepped up, it was decided at the Labour Party's new headquarters in Walworth Road, south London, to make an approach to Ecclestone. Among the key figures kept informed of earlier events were the party's general secretary, Tom Sawyer, spin doctor-in-chief Peter Mandelson, Blair's press spokesman, Alastair Campbell, and former pop music promoter Lord (Michael) Levy, a tennis partner of Blair's whose fund-raising skills have raised millions of pounds for the Labour Party's electioneering war chest. Powell was no longer involved in fund-raising strategy. It was decided that the approach would be made by Levy through Mosley. The decision to approach Ecclestone was a difficult one to make: while the Labour Party desperately needed the kind of donation that Ecclestone could make from his small change, it could not afford to be seen to be benefiting, no matter how indirectly, from tobacco company sponsors who were putting tens of millions of pounds a year into Formula One. Its election manifesto included a promise to ban all sports-related tobacco advertising or promotion.

In January 1997 Mosley, who believed a generous donation from Ecclestone would do no harm to his connections in Brussels, raised the matter with Ecclestone. It was an opportune time to do so. Blair had just overruled a proposal by Gordon Brown, the shadow Chancellor of the Exchequer, to raise the top level of income tax from 40 per cent to 50 per cent if the Labour Party was elected. Mosley pointed out to Ecclestone that Blair's action had saved him millions of pounds. It was a point not lost on Ecclestone, who that year had paid a personal tax bill of £27 million. He agreed with Mosley's suggestion – and issued an instruction to his accountant to draw up a company cheque for £1 million against his director's loan account and for it to be sent to the Labour Party. (Brown's intention to raise the top level of income tax was seen by some as not so much a threat as a vote-catching ruse to attract the support of the dynamic entrepreneurs and businessmen that Blair was so keen to court as part of his business-friendly strategy.)

Within days of its landslide triumph on 1 May, the Labour Government, determined to show the country that it had elected a Government of action who would keep its manifesto promises, began to beat the anti-smoking drum. Tessa Jowell, the public health minister, who made her reputation on the back benches as a determined anti-smoking campaigner with a Bill to ban smoking in public places, seized the enthusiasm of the day to repeat the Government's election manifesto pledge to ban tobacco advertising. Two weeks later, on 15 May, during a House of Commons debate on the Queen's Speech, Frank Dobson, the Secretary of State for Health, went a stage further and announced that the ban would also include all sport sponsorship.

But, rather than do it through domestic legislation, with all the political flak it might attract, it was thought to be more politically expedient to pass the buck to the European Union and a regenerated directive banning sport sponsorship and advertising, which had been first proposed in 1982 and was now back on the agenda in Brussels. Fourteen days later Dobson sent a memo to Blair's office seeking a clear understanding of the government's negotiating position on the directive. It was a shift of tactic that alarmed Ecclestone and Mosley. As tobacco sponsorship at the British Grand Prix had been voluntarily banned since 1984, domestic legislation would have zero effect. But support of a ban throughout Europe threatened, they feared, a serious conflict, not least because it would prove ineffective.

Ecclestone's response to Dobson's House of Commons statement was a threat to reduce the number of Grands Prix in Europe – and the first casualty, he warned, would be the British Grand Prix at Silverstone. Only the Grands Prix in Italy, Germany, Monaco and Portugal – the first two countries were too important to drop and the last two were opposed to any ban on tobacco sponsorship – would survive. 'All our contracts with promoters and organisers worldwide state that if any country brings in legislation that in any way affects any of the teams' sponsors – not just tobacco, whatever it might be – then we have a right to not be in that country,' he said. It was claimed that contingency plans had already been set up in readiness for a Europe-wide ban. 'It would be sad to lose traditional circuits like Silverstone but the World Championship is the most important thing.' The axed European Grands Prix could easily be replaced, he added, by staging races in Morocco, Croatia, Dubai, Abu Dhabi, Malaysia, Korea and China, where there were no problems with tobacco sponsorship or advertising.

(It was, at best, a bluff. The loss of Grands Prix in Britain, France, Spain, Belgium, Austria and Luxembourg would have created enormous problems for Ecclestone, not only for his flotation plans, which had been announced that March, but also in retaining the support of sponsors who would not wish to be seen to be associated with a manoeuvre to sidestep European law. As for the replacement Middle and Far East venues, at that time discussions with Malaysia, South Korea and China were still taking place – Malaysia was finally added to the Formula One World Championship for 1999, with China a reserve event – but the other countries were considered unsuitable candidates for political and economic reasons. Ecclestone himself would later admit that moving out of Europe was never a realistic option.)

Ecclestone and Mosley argued that a Europe-wide ban would be pointless. Television coverage of races outside of Europe would ensure that tobacco sponsorship and advertising would be broadcast throughout member states. The obvious logic of this argument had been amply demonstrated by a legal dispute in 1992, when a court in the French town of Quimper imposed a £4.2-million fine on the Williams-Renault team for showing the Camel cigarettes logo during the Australian and Japanese Grands Prix. By being broadcast on French television, it was held to violate France's anti-smoking laws. Team boss Frank Williams refused to pay the fine, and the court warned that it would impound the team's equipment at the 1993 French Grand Prix. Ecclestone, as president of the FOCA, immediately announced the withdrawal of the teams from the event, and Mosley went a step further by cancelling it.

Following urgent discussions at senior political level, legislation was hurried through by the French Government to amend the law banning television advertising and thereby permit the broadcasting of motor sport events promoting tobacco outside of France. When the news was announced, the French Grand Prix was promptly restored. This court case exposed the obvious flaw of a Europe-only directive – unless a ban on tobacco sponsorship could be enforced worldwide, in almost 200 countries where Formula One was broadcast in one form or another, it would prove unworkable. It was an overwhelming argument, combined with the massive lobbying power of the tobacco industry and, more quietly, expressed by Ecclestone and Mosley, that had succeeded in causing the previous Conservative Government to join Germany, Denmark, Holland and Greece in vetoing the European Union's proposed directive.

Ecclestone and Mosley tried to strengthen opposition in the UK by claiming that a loss of Grands Prix in Europe would risk losing Britain the kudos and benefits of being the centre of the Formula One industry, as well as an estimated 50,000 jobs. Both points were something of an exaggeration. The number of jobs quoted included the entire motor sport industry, right down to the production of specialist flameproof overalls. The figure for Formula One was actually nearer 8000. Moreover, the UK would not suffer mortal damage if Formula One were to quit Europe completely. Business between the British motor-racing industry, long renowned for its advanced technical skills and expertise, and overseas companies would continue largely unaffected.

As part of an intensive lobbying campaign, Mosley, accompanied by Frank Williams, the boss of the Williams team, and Ron Dennis of McLaren, went to Westminster to present Formula One's case to a meeting of peers at the invitation of Lord Astor of Hever, an enthusiastic motor sport fan – Ecclestone refused to go: 'I wouldn't waste my time with them' – while David Ward and senior FIA colleagues were getting ready to embark on a hectic round of lobbying calls on key political figures in Brussels and European countries on the Formula One calendar. Both Jowell, who was put in charge of a policy review, and Dobson, very much aware of the Formula One lobbying campaign, were becoming increasingly concerned that the proposed sponsorship ban could turn into a major headache for a government that in opposition had been so implacable in its denunciation of tobacco advertising.

On 5 June Jowell attended a meeting of the European Union health council to assure delegates that the British Government was likely to support a Europe-wide ban on tobacco advertising and promotion, but, at the same time, indicated that there could be problems with sport sponsorship. Dobson reinforced the point by sending a memo to Blair 12 days later recommending that the government kept its options open on a sponsorship ban.

In a letter to Jowell dated 12 July, Mosley once again explained the futility of a Europe-only ban, and also attempted to press home the logic of a worldwide ban but through a phased reduction in tobacco sponsorship to avoid 'de-stabilising teams and events. If an agreed policy can be secured in Europe, then it would be possible for the FIA to apply the same agreement to all rounds of the Formula One World Championship throughout the world.' The phased reduction would bring an end to tobacco sponsorship on drivers' overalls, then trackside hoardings and, finally, the cars. Mosley followed up the letter with a request to meet Jowell to discuss a worldwide phased reduction linked to the EU directive. It took place on 23 September, when Mosley and Ward called at her Whitehall office. Also present was sports minister Tony Banks. Mosley went through the familiar arguments – the pointlessness of imposing a Europe-only ban, the potential loss of jobs and prestige to Britain if the Formula One industry was diminished in Europe – during an amiable meeting, but one which he found frustrating. He was not at all sure that they appreciated the full implications of the proposed directive. In the words of Ward, their 'whole attitude was negative'. Nevertheless, Mosley agreed to send Jowell a written submission of Formula One's case.

Mosley gave a full account of the meeting to Ecclestone, who had been busy elsewhere seeking the support of some high-powered friends in several European governments. They included Helmut Kohl, the then German Chancellor, and Professor Romano Prodi, the then Prime Minister of Italy, whom Mosley went to see. Prodi allowed Mosley to labour through their hour-long meeting in his pidgin Italian, only to subsequently learn that Prodi, who had taught at the London School of Economics for several years, spoke fluent English. Kohl, apparently, was particularly supportive of Ecclestone and Mosley's mission. A long-standing friend of Ecclestone's, he was concerned about the effect of a sponsorship ban on the huge tobacco industry in Germany. Ecclestone made arrangements for Mosley and he to have a meeting with Kohl in Bonn on 28 September. It was fortuitous timing. The following month Kohl was scheduled to meet Blair at Chequers. At the meeting in Bonn Kohl reassured Ecclestone and Mosley of his support and agreed to take up Formula One's case with the British prime minister.

In Frank Dobson's view, it was becoming clear that some sort of compromise would have to be reached. On 14 October he sent Blair a detailed report of the political implications of any European Union directive that did not permit at least a lengthy transitional period for Formula One. The likely backwash, in Dobson's assessment, could cause unnecessary damage to the Government's popularity. The report had been requested by Blair's office in advance of a meeting due to take place two days later with three men Blair had last met 16 months earlier at the British Grand Prix at Silverstone – Ecclestone, Mosley and Ward. The meeting had been requested by Mosley, who believed the FIA was making little progress with Dobson or Jowell. In Ward's words, they had become exasperated by 'the serious stupidities of the Department of Health, in that they did not take seriously what we were suggesting'. He added: 'I think they found us a nuisance, mistakenly believing that we were acting on behalf of the tobacco industry, and trying to destabilise their plans, although we pointed out bluntly that we had nothing to do with the tobacco industry.' Both Dobson and Jowell, he said, seemed indifferent towards discussing the FIA's phased reduction strategy.

There can be little doubt that by this stage Blair had been made aware of Ecclestone's £1-million donation, and that, indeed, since the general election there had been discussions of another contribution by Ecclestone – said to be for £500,000 – to the Labour Party, which, after campaign expenditure of more than £20 million, was £4.5 million in the red. With Blair was his private secretary, who was there to take notes, and Jonathan Powell. The meeting lasted for about 20 minutes, the notes of which, most unusually, were made public during the height of the ensuing storm in an attempt to clear Blair of having made any unfortunate comments or promises in support of Formula One's position. According to the notes, Blair said he did not 'need persuading about the basic case in favour of Formula One' but added that he was 'also in favour of a ban on tobacco ads'. Mosley emphasised the point that a move out of Europe to the Far East, where there would be no tobacco sponsorship restrictions, would lead to more, not less, tobacco advertising being broadcast on British television. The notes attributed Ecclestone with saying that he had put 'a lot of effort' into digital television and that it 'would go with the races' (out of Europe), with all the commercial loss it implied for Britain. At the close of the meeting Blair promised he would 'think about' what they had said.

What the notes did not record, and which Mosley insists was made clear by both he and Ward, was that the EU's proposed directive was almost certainly illegal under EU law and that the Government should stay with domestic legislation. This opinion was based on the work of Ward, who, some weeks before the meeting, examined EU laws to discover that the harmonisation of laws to improve public health is expressly excluded by its own Treaty. Mosley claims he explained this point, which had been submitted in writing in advance of the meeting, and which 'Blair, being a lawyer, immediately understood'. He further explained that, in the event of its failure, the Government, in introducing domestic legislation, would be able to congratulate itself on being seen to have done exactly what it pledged in its pre-election manifesto. However, it seems that Blair preferred the advice of Dobson and Jowell, who reassured him that, in their opinion, the proposed directive would go through without difficulty.

Over the next 24 hours Blair, without reference to Cabinet ministers, sent a note to Dobson agreeing that Formula One should be treated as a special case on the basis that it would not be realistic to assume that the teams could replace the scale of their sponsorship investment in the timescale that could be reasonably expected of other sports. True to his assurances to Ecclestone and Mosley, Helmut Kohl promoted Formula One's case at his meeting with Blair at Chequers three days later, on 20 October, where he was said to have 'exerted heavy pressure'. It was understood to have been a quid pro quo situation – Blair at that time was seeking Kohl's support for a future place on a proposed European Union central bank.

On 24 October Jowell sent a memo to Blair, with copies to the Foreign Office, Chris Smith's Department of Culture, Media and Sport, the Cabinet Office and UK representatives in Brussels, informing them that the British Government proposed granting Formula One a lengthy period of exemption from any tobacco sponsorship ban. By the end of the month a draft letter had been sent by Jowell to European Union countries setting out the British Government's position, and on 4 November they were formally notified.

The announcement, seen as a major policy U-turn by the Government, was received with a wave of criticism. By then Jowell had already phoned Mosley to pass on the news. She thought he would be well pleased. He was not, and told her so. He pointed out that it would not be applauded by the seven countries within the EU who did not host Formula One, nor would it be popular with other sports dependent on tobacco sponsorship. It was, he thought, politically maladroit. Jowell's announcement was also seen by some inside the Labour Party as a betrayal of its manifesto pledge. And one person, aware of Ecclestone's donation of £1 million, decided to pick up a phone and call a national daily newspaper.

Two days later, on Thursday 6 November, a journalist on the London-based broadsheet, the *Daily Telegraph*, phoned David Hill, the Labour Party's chief press spokesman, at its headquarters in south London to ask whether Ecclestone had ever given money to the Labour Party. Hill said he had no idea. He called the newspaper back a short while later to say that he had been unable to check it out because the position of treasurer had been vacated and his replacement had yet to take up office. By then Downing Street had been alerted and a hurried closed session of Blair and his closest advisers agreed in principle that Tom Sawyer, the Labour Party's general secretary, should seek the guidance of Sir Patrick Neill QC, chairman of the independent Whitehall watchdog, the Committee on Standards in Public Life. The next day other newspapers had picked up the story but, as the Labour Party headquarters became almost paralysed by a general state of panic, they, too, were stonewalled. Downing Street decided to proceed to seek Neill's guidance.

That Friday night Sawyer faxed a letter to Neill for his 'clear guidance'. But although it referred to 'a substantial personal donation' from Ecclestone towards its general election campaign expenses, its emphasis was on whether or not the Labour Party should accept a second donation (the £500,000) which, stated the letter, had been discussed with Ecclestone since the election – 'where an appearance of a conflict of interest might be thought to arise'. It added: 'The Prime Minister has decided that in the light of our approach to the Directive [in proposing an exemption for Formula One] and to avoid any possible appearance of a conflict of interest, we should consult you on whether it may be properly accepted.'

Over that weekend the storm clouds were beginning to gather. Reports in several Sunday papers carried speculative and damaging stories about a financial link between Ecclestone and the Labour Party, while its media machine continued to insist it was all mischievous fiction. By mid-day the following Monday, Sawyer had received the benefit of Neill's guidance. While he believed criticism of the £1-million donation to be 'wrong and unfair', in the interests of 'openness and transparency' the Labour Party should decline the proposed second donation and return the first. That evening, in the House of Commons's lower reporters' press gallery, David Hill held a briefing which acknowledged for the first time that Ecclestone was on a list of donors who had given more than £5000. When the news reached Ecclestone, he was incandescent with anger.

He had been given no warning of Hill's announcement. Suddenly he was isolated, uncertain of what was going on. Just hours before Hill's press briefing, his solicitors, Herbert Smith, the law firm which represented Ecclestone and the FIA in their competition law dispute with the European Commission, repeated a statement they had issued over the weekend on their client's instructions – that he had not made any donation to the Labour Party. However, a couple of hours later, he was made to appear a liar. As a result of Hill's briefing, he was forced to admit that, in fact, he had.

Ecclestone was confronted by the media pack as he left, with Max Mosley, an FIA disciplinary hearing at the RAC's Motor Sports Association's premises in Colnbrook, Berkshire, where Michael Schumacher had his second listing in the 1997 World Championship removed for his part in a controversial accident involving Jacques Villeneuve at the Spanish Grand Prix in Jerez. Ecclestone was in a corner. When asked to comment on what was now being said by Downing Street, he replied between gritted teeth: 'Well, if Mr Blair said that, he wouldn't lie, would he?'

The clumsy way in which it had all been handled – 'If they [the Labour Party] dealt with this in that way, one wonders how they deal with other things you don't hear about' – caused Ecclestone to believe, not without good reason, that he was being set up as the villain of the piece. He was particularly concerned about how it might appear overseas, where he conducts 90 per cent of his business. 'Blair dropped me in it. It was very embarrassing. I was suddenly the bad guy. People thought I was trying to bribe the government, when it was a donation to the Labour Party before they were elected. I like to think I can walk into the offices of people without that sort of thing hanging over me. I don't need it.' He said he would have been ready to respond to the media when, as part of the Labour Party's anti-sleaze initiative to show greater accountability of financial sources, the names of donors who contributed more than £5000 were to be published in its annual report the following October. 'It would have been all right if they had done what they said they were going to do. We could have all said the same thing.'

He also believed that a decision by Blair to set up a wide-ranging inquiry headed by Neill to look at the whole issue of party funding also reflected badly on him. 'They only did that to cover themselves,' he said. 'But it made it worse for me... I was suddenly put over again as the one behind it all.' He refused an invitation to appear before the Neill inquiry the following April – the only witness to do so – to answer questions about what he expected in return for his million pounds. After the contemptuous way in which he believed he had been treated by Blair, he was unwilling to be questioned, suspecting a political agenda behind the invitation: 'If you appear, you get yourself involved.' He believed he had also been portrayed in no less a bad light by the alleged second donation, which, in his letter to Neill, Tom Sawyer stated Ecclestone had offered.

Contrary to what had been claimed, he had made no such offer, he insisted. As an affirmation of his innocence, he swore the truth of his denial on the lives of his two daughters, Tamara and Petra, which to Ecclestone is a deadly serious oath. Indeed, he hadn't made a second offer – at least, technically. He was aware that discussions were going on between David Ward and Millbank but they got no further before the balloon went up. At that stage no firm figure had been mentioned to Ecclestone or agreed by him. 'I didn't play a part in any of that. At that stage it was all talk.' Ecclestone believes he had every reason to have felt much maligned on two fundamental counts. On the first count, he insists, the £1 million donation had had nothing to do with the tobacco issue but his tax affairs. And on the second, he and Mosley hadn't sought an exemption for Formula One but a period of phased reduction. Blair had granted them something that they had never wanted.

The Government faced fresh round of criticism when it became known that Tessa Jowell's husband, David Mills, was a legal adviser and non-executive director of the company which ran the Formula One team Benetton until his resignation the previous May, when the new Government took office. Mills had been a close associate of its former managing director, the flamboyant Italian, Flavio Briatore, who boasted of his close friendship with Ecclestone. Their business association was renewed in 1998 when Mills joined a London-based sports management and venture capital company which assisted in the administration of a company based in Holland supplying Mecachrome engines to Formula One teams and run by Briatore. Jowell dismissed scathing innuendo from political opponents as a vile and politically motivated slur campaign.

She and her husband, she added, had acted with absolutely integrity throughout to avoid a conflict of interest. Because of his former connection with Benetton, she had sought clearance to handle the policy review from Dobson and Sir Graham Hart, permanent secretary at the Health Department, as well as notifying the office of Lord Nolan, the former chairman of the Committee on Standards in Public Life. The long-running affair had become so damaging to the squeaky-clean image of the New Labour Government that Blair felt it necessary to go on television on 17 November to apologise for the way the story had been handled and to deliver his you-can-trust-me-I'm-the-Prime-Minister message. But 11 days later, just as the heat was beginning to cool down, two Labour-dominated Commons select committees put the episode back on the front pages when it roundly rejected the Government's intention to exempt Formula One.

The day after Jowell appeared before the Select Committee on Health to defend the Government's decision, it issued a report stating that Formula One should be placed under the same pressure as any other tobacco-sponsored sport. The committee recommended that the Government should reconsider its position. Its chairman, Labour MP David Hinchliffe, said: 'I think the Government have had the wool pulled over their eyes by Formula One. It is a case that could have been made similarly by other sports but they had the integrity not to make that case.' The Government's proposal was received with equal hostility by the Commons committee which scrutinises European legislation. It believed it could wreck the European Union's directive and that it was unfair to other sports, and warned that it might breach European anti-discrimination rules.

But the Government's embarrassment was not over even then. Three months later, following a complaint lodged by Tory MP Andrew Robathan, Blair came in for personal criticism from the Committee on Standards and Privileges over the visit with his wife, Cherie, and three children to the British Grand Prix. It was estimated that the cost of the hospitality was £300 per head – £75 more than the figure allowed for MPs or their spouses before it needed to be registered under the Commons rules. Sir Gordon Downey, the Commissioner for Standards, rejected an explanation by Blair that it had been an official duty undertaken as leader of the Opposition. Conceding that there was undoubtedly some confusion over the rules governing official visits, he nevertheless noted that six other Members of Parliament who were also at the Grand Prix had registered their attendance. Downey's judgement put Blair in the history books as the first Prime Minister to be rebuked for breaching the Commons rules on disclosures of gifts and hospitality.

The credibility of Jonathan Powell, Blair's chief of staff, was also seriously damaged. He had played a pivotal role in securing the donation from Ecclestone, and had failed to advise Blair against meeting Ecclestone in Downing Street, a high-profile event that naturally attracted the attention of the media. It would seem astonishingly naïve of him not to have realised the vulnerable position in which he was placing Blair, and that, in his world of mischievous leaks and spin, the worst possible interpretation would be placed on Ecclestone's £1 million donation and the Formula One exemption.

On 22 June 1998 the European Union adopted the directive banning all forms of tobacco advertising and sponsorship, although, in line with the argument put forward by Mosley and Ward, it would be short-lived. In the meantime, it decreed that tobacco sponsorship of sports in Europe would end by 30 July 2003 – except for certain global sporting events such as Formula One which depend on a high level of tobacco sponsorship. They would be given a three-year extension, until 1 October 2006, to find other sponsors, provided there were reductions in both the sums involved and visible advertising. In March, Mosley, at least publicly, appear to welcome the proposed directive and reciprocated by announcing that it would act immediately to eliminate tobacco advertising and sponsorship from Formula One 'if presented with evidence of a direct link between tobacco advertising/sponsorship and smoking'[1], indicating that it could mean a worldwide ban at Formula One events as early as 2002, a decision that could be included in the 1998 Concorde Agreement, which was shortly to be signed.

The FIA said the proposed directive 'provides the sport with the flexibility and time it needs to take decisive action in this area. The FIA therefore intends to study evidence produced by the British Government, among others, and is discussing the issue with the World Health Organisation.' However, while evidence was available to show a direct link between smoking and sport sponsorship, it wanted proof that tobacco sponsorship was a direct cause of young people taking up smoking, rather than encouraging smokers merely to switch brands, as the manufacturers claimed. It then moved the goalposts by redefining the grounds on which it would agree to an early ban. In December 1998 it announced that it required 'evidence of anyone taking up smoking as a result of tobacco sponsorship in Formula One who would not otherwise have smoked ... in particular young people taking up smoking'.

With research by health authorities and anti-tobacco campaigners focused exclusively on the connection between tobacco and sports sponsorship in general, the evidence for a much narrower causal connection to any particular sport simply didn't – and doesn't – exist, as Mosley might well have suspected. In the absence of such evidence – 'at the same time we received wheelbarrow loads of documents from the tobacco industry purporting to show no link' – the 1998 Concorde Agreement was signed two months later at the Monaco Grand Prix. In a terse statement Mosley said: 'The 2002 date has slipped with the signing of the 1998 Concorde Agreement, which prevents us from introducing such a ban before 2006.'

But it seems that Mosley was in no position to hold out the hope of an early ban anyway. He later admitted that 'it would quite obviously have been an untenable position for the FIA to refuse to sign the 1998 Concorde Agreement unless the teams agreed to give up tobacco sponsorship in 2002'. He added: 'As I said to Padraig Flynn [the EU's Commissioner for Employment, Industrial Relations and Social Affairs] in private, "It's difficult to go in front of the teams and say to them, 'You've got to give up $200–300 million worth of income without any evidence that you are doing any harm at all.'"' Yet as Mosley would have been aware of the teams' position from the beginning, why did he hold out hope of an early self-imposed ban? It was suspected that he did so in an attempt to scupper the EU directive itself.

His offer in March came at a time when the more progressive members, particularly the Nordic countries, were furious by what they saw as the UK's back-pedalling on the agreed directive to ban all sports-related tobacco sponsorship from 2003. It raised the obvious question: why was the British Government seeking a three-year exemption for Formula One when Mosley himself was now indicating it could, in fact, be achieved by 2002, a year ahead of the deadline? Clive Bates, director of Action on Smoking and Health (ASH), a British lobbying group actively involved, along with the Department of Health and the World Health Organisation, in supplying the earlier evidence required by Mosley, believes it was done to encourage opposing countries to reject Britain's compromise amendment to the directive, which, without a qualified majority agreement – enough supporting member states weighted by size – would have seriously threatened its further progress. The balance of voting was very fine. Germany and Austria opposed the directive and Spain abstained. The switch of any other member state would have broken the qualified majority in favour of the ban.

'Germany and the tobacco companies were pressing for voluntary action rather than legislation,' said Bates, 'and we believed the FIA's offer was intended to support that initiative. Of course, once the legislative threat had subsided the voluntary ban would have been quietly forgotten. It was skulduggery and mischief designed to wreck the EU directive.' Not so, Mosley insisted. As he was fully confident that the proposed directive was contrary to EU Treaty law and would, if passed, lose on appeal, there was no need to do so.

The 'cash-for-ash scandal', as it became known, continued to haunt Blair. Three years later, newspapers were full of allegations that he and Chancellor Gordon Brown, who had claimed to have had no prior knowledge of Ecclestone's donation, had lied. The allegations were referred to the Committee on Standards in Public Life, but went no further. In October 2000 the committee decided that it was not within its remit to investigate specific complaints. That same month, though, Liberal Democrat European Member of Parliament Chris Davies tabled a question in Brussels asking the Council of Ministers to hold an investigation to establish whether any of Ecclestone's companies had made 'tobacco-related' donations to political parties in Europe. It was aimed, by innuendo, at Ecclestone's friend Helmut Kohl, who had been forced to resign as honorary chairman of Germany's Christian Democratic Party after he refused to name the sources of illegal cash donations.

However, Davies, as he readily conceded, had no evidence to support such an investigation. He agreed to table the question following a call from a *Sunday Express* journalist trying to stand up a line implying that Ecclestone's financial influence in promoting the interests of Formula One reached beyond the shores of Britain. It was a kite-flying bit of nonsense about Ecclestone that ended up as a two-page spread in the newspaper under the headline: 'Is this man the most powerful tycoon in Europe?'[2]

If the affair was continuing to haunt Blair, so it was for Ecclestone, who, of all the cast of characters involved, was, for once, an innocent party, as Mosley and Ward readily concede. He had been persuaded, if not manipulated, to make the donation, which had nothing to do with the tobacco-sponsorship interests of Formula One. Even a letter to *The Times*, published in his name shortly after the storm clouds broke, in which he explained that the £1 million donation was a no-strings-attached gift to help Tony Blair keep the country 'free from the old-fashioned interests', a reference to trade unions' influence on the Labour Party, was actually suggested and written by Mosley in a skewed effort to put the record straight.

In fact, it served only to raise suspicions. To the many who knew Ecclestone, within and without the media, it stretched credulity beyond reason to accept that someone who was politically slightly to the right of Genghis Khan was in any way concerned by the influence the trade unions might have had within the Labour Party. Ecclestone isn't a political animal outside of Formula One. As long as he has the freedom and independence to run Formula One, it is the only governance he is interested in. In any event, at the time of his donation in January 1997 the introduction of the one member-one vote rule in 1993 and the modernising Clause 4 in 1996 to the Labour Party's constitution had already substantially removed the unions' influence; their financial support over the years also had substantially diminished, which was why, ironically, Labour Party fund-raisers had found it necessary to cultivate a new source of cash, namely donors such as Ecclestone.

A more successful effort to set the record straight occurred in April 2002 when Ward contacted Philip Webster, political editor of *The Times*. It resulted in a lengthy feature explaining at length that Ecclestone's donation had been motivated by personal tax benefits alone and not in return for an exemption for Formula One from the proposed European directive. But why had it taken more than four years to set the record straight? Because, explained Mosley, Downing Street refused to do so despite repeated reassurances. In the meantime, over the next two or three years, when the Government became mired in further cash-for-favours allegations, the media would invariably refer to Ecclestone's £1 million donation, tainting him each time by association. He became incensed each time his name was linked to another headline on political corruption. That he and Ward would go to the newspapers if Downing Street did not absolve Ecclestone was made clear to Alastair Campbell, Jonathan Powell and Peter Mandelson. An intermediary, added Mosley, even went to see Blair 'and we got the same response: "I think it's monstrous what happened to Bernie. He shouldn't have got the blame for this. It wasn't his fault ... he didn't bribe anybody." But they never actually went out of their way to put it right.' It was finally decided, 'fairly reluctantly', to follow through with their threat.

Former Conservative Chancellor Kenneth Clarke, a genuine Formula One fan who became chairman of British American Racing, described Ecclestone as 'a fun, exciting, unpredictable pocket dynamo', and this long-running drama was not the first time Ecclestone had been associated with the financial fortunes of a political party. In October 2000 a leak from a senior source within the Conservative Party claimed that he had helped to raise a total of between £600,000 and £700,000 for the party's 1997 pre-election war chest through personal donations from him and business contacts.

Whatever Ecclestone's relationship with the then Prime Minister John Major, whose party was ousted from power by Blair and his New Labour Party, Ecclestone enjoyed the social favour of Margaret Thatcher, a woman whose no-nonsense chatelaine style he would have found much more appealing. He was among five motor sport figures invited to a gathering of the great and the good at Downing Street on the night before Mark Thatcher's wedding on 14 February 1987. In addition to Ecclestone, they included well-connected Formula Three driver Charlie Crichton-Stewart, the then Brands Hatch boss John Webb, and Michael Tee, chairman of CSS International, a sports promotion company which was handling Mark Thatcher's short-lived career in motor sport. During the course of the evening Ecclestone was seen in deep conversation with two other distinguished guests, Lord Hanson and the late Lord White, partners in a business empire ranging from tobacco and chemicals to energy and coal and worth nearly £11 billion. Led by Maggie Thatcher, the three disappeared with her into a side room, to emerge about ten minutes later and rejoin the other guests.

Thatcher was not known for her love or support of Formula One, but, nevertheless, she was prepared to give it her invaluable endorsement by attending an ultra-extravagant bash staged at London's Albert Hall in February 1981 by the Monaco-based Essex Overseas Petroleum Corporation, the sponsors of the Lotus team, to unveil the new Essex Lotus 86. It was a £1.1-million affair for 900 guests, including many senior figures in the oil industry. According to one of the organisers, Thatcher used the occasion for a discreet meeting with two 'ultra-rich' businessmen. 'There were two oilmen she wanted to meet and who wanted to meet her, and it couldn't be done openly,' says the organiser. 'There were wheels within wheels. Even though I was running the party I had no idea what was going on.' Before she left, Thatcher apparently took the opportunity to express her admiration of Ecclestone's shrewdness.

Brabham team manager Herbie Blash, one of a number introduced to her, said: 'Bernie's name came up and she said to a colleague she was very pleased that Bernie was not involved in politics.'

Nearly two-and-a-half years after the European Union directive banning tobacco advertising and sponsorship was introduced, after all the enormous costs politically and commercially involved, it was ruled to be contrary, as Mosley and Ward had claimed, to one of its own laws. In October 2000, following a legal challenge by Germany and cigarette manufacturers, the European Court of Justice overturned the directive on the grounds that it was unlawful: the harmonisation of laws to improve public health is expressly excluded by the European Union Treaty. In response, the European Union's Health Commissioner, David Byrne, announced that Brussels would introduce new measures to prohibit 'pernicious' tobacco advertising and sponsorship. The European Court of Justice added that its ruling did not prohibit individual member states from introducing their own legislation, a move which the British Government said, through public health minister, Yvette Cooper, it intended to pursue.

In December 2000 the Government published a bill to ban tobacco advertising and promotion, but got no further for lack of parliamentary time. In July 2001 an identical Private Member's Bill, tabled by a Liberal Democrat peer, Lord Clement Jones, was introduced in the House of Lords and subsequently supported and adopted by the Government. It was expected to become law in October 2002. It was precisely, claimed Mosley, what he had petitioned in the first place. News of the Private Member's Bill prompted him to pen a letter to Health Secretary Alan Milburn giving the FIA's support – and impishly wishing the government 'third time lucky'.

David Ward believed the Government's central mistake was not merely in the handling of Ecclestone's £1 million donation but, more seriously, in 'its ineptness and naïvety in failing to understand the issues. They not only caused themselves enormous embarrassment, but also blew up their own policy [domestic tobacco legislation]. It was all so crazy and so wholly avoidable.'

18

MARRIAGE, MONEY AND BLACKMAIL

Bernie Ecclestone's marriage to a beautiful model 28 years his junior attracted the inevitable cynical comments. No, he responds with his usual candour, she did not marry him for his money. What is more, he insists, when they met she did not even know how much he was worth. Slavica, with similar candour, admits she had been interested in older men, caused, she believed, by the emotional trauma of her father abandoning her family when she was seven years old. She had, she supposed, been looking for a father figure. Certainly, as part of the chemistry of their mutual attraction, what they had in common were childhoods that, while culturally poles apart, were not so different economically. Indeed, Slavica's early years were profoundly more desperate than her husband's.

She was born Slavica Radic on 25 May 1958 in a sparsely furnished cellar apartment of a house in the old part of the Croatian port town of Rijeka on the Adriatic coast, a squalid low-life area characterised by poverty, violence, drunkenness and prostitution. The departure of her dock-worker father, Jovan, in the early sixties led to divorce, after which Slavica's mother, Ljubica, took her and her three brothers (Slavica was the second-eldest child) to live on the outskirts of the town. So impoverished were they, Slavica claimed, that she was ten years old before she was bought her first pair of shoes. From such surroundings emerged a wilful and troubled personality who consistently truanted and, at the age of 14, frequented the bar of one of the town's seedier hotels.

Caught, with two friends, stealing a pair of sandals from a shop, Slavica was considered by a court to be beyond her mother's control and sent to an institution for problem girls. She was released shortly before her 18th birthday, when she was encouraged to pursue a modelling career by signing up with a local model agency. This led to little, if any, work other than a series of nude photographs which were published in a *Playboy*-style magazine called *Start*.

It wasn't until she decided to move to Milan in 1981 that Slavica's fortunes began to change. She joined the fashion house Armani and dived into the social life she craved. On one notable occasion this led her to the paddock of the Monza Grand Prix, where, by way of introduction, Ecclestone is said to have offered her a Coca-Cola.

Nowadays, with magnificent family homes in Corsica, Gstaad and the French Riviera readily accessible in one of her husband's two private jets hangared at the airfield he owns in Biggin Hill, Kent, and a £20-million yacht in which to reflect on the days of her childhood, the least of Slavica's worries is where her next pair of shoes will be coming from. She wears the kind of baubles that in July 1996 attracted the interest of muggers who pulled a £600,000 diamond ring from her finger shortly after the couple stepped out of their Bentley outside their home in Chelsea. Ecclestone, who suffered a broken nose, was kicked while on the ground. 'My wife thought I was dead. It was all so unnecessary. I was not putting up a fight.'[1]

Much of Ecclestone's serious wealth, through his television interests and Formula One-related companies, of which he was sole director, began in the late eighties. Between 1989 and 1997 he earned at least £190 million in salaries. That, of course, was from known emoluments. In 1996 he became the highest-paid businessman in Britain, with a salary of £54.9 million. The extent of his wealth was publicly acknowledged for the first time in 1995, when he featured in the *Sunday Times* Rich List with a personal wealth rating of £30 million. By 1997 that figure had increased to £275 million, making him the 58th richest man in the country. Within three years, through the Eurobond sale and 50 per cent sale of SLEC Holdings, it had increased to £2.7 billion. It elevated him and Slavica, in whose name the family trust which owned SLEC Holdings was held and who was now the richest woman in Britain, to equal sixth position. By 2001 they occupied third position in the Rich List with a joint fortune of £3 billion; a year later they had dropped to fifth position but with an estimated pile of £4 billion. How much they are really worth would probably take a team of investigators and forensic accountants with access to the world's offshore banks a year or two to accurately evaluate.

As news of Ecclestone's wealth was published in newspapers in various parts of the world, it brought with it the inevitable risk of attracting unwanted attention. It prompted a 48-year-old Croatian, Momir Blagojevic, to attempt, rather recklessly, to relieve him of £1 million in a crude blackmail plot. Its genesis began in 1997 – the year, ironically, when Ecclestone's donation of a similar sum to the Labour Party was very much in the news – following the publication in a Croatian tabloid, *Imperijal*, of a series of sensational allegations involving his wife. Across a four-page spread, illustrated by nude photographs taken during Slavica's late teens, Blagojevic, who claimed to have known her more than 20 years earlier as his confidante and lover, alleged that she had worked as a honey-trap spy to procure information from the rich and the powerful for communist Yugoslavia's secret police, the UDBA. Blagojevic stated in the article that he intended to reveal even more details of her past in a book.

The piece was published shortly before Slavica arrived in Croatia on a family visit. She phoned her husband to tell him herself about it, admitting that she had once known Blagojevic, who had befriended her in Rijeka. But the allegations, she insisted, were completely untrue, a reassurance Ecclestone accepted without question. Within a week a criminal libel suit was filed on Slavica's behalf against Blagojevic and the 21-year-old reporter Roko Vuletic, who wrote the article. At the same time, a civil libel suit was issued against the newspaper for damages of £30,000.

Soon after the trial had begun, Blagojevic made his second mistake: he contacted Ecclestone's lawyer in Zagreb to put a proposal to him – he would withdraw all the allegations in return for $1 million. The lawyer reported Blagojevic's blackmail attempt to Ecclestone. Clearly, Blagojevic had no understanding of whom he was dealing with. To demand money from Ecclestone would be a foolhardy exercise. To do it through blackmail bordered on the insane. Ecclestone, playing for time, agreed to a meeting. He wanted to do nothing to discourage Blagojevic in the optimistic belief that he would soon be a millionaire. Instead, the meeting Ecclestone was busy planning was intended to incriminate Blagojevic, and, in so doing, clear his wife's name as well as provide evidence in support of the legal action against the Croatian.

He rang a British Sunday tabloid, the *Sunday Mirror*, to speak to a features writer who had written an article about his wife, ostensibly to express a mild complaint. His real purpose, though, was to suggest that there was a much better story to be had. A reporter and a photographer, posing as his negotiators, should attend a meeting with Blagojevic, who could be expected to repeat his blackmail threat for the benefit of a hidden tape recorder. The paper's editor, sensing a sensational front-page splash, happily agreed. The meeting took place at a pizzeria in Slavica's home town of Rijeka on 26 March 1998.

True to script, Blagojevic reassured the journalists that, in return for $1 million, he would retract his allegations, claiming they had been fabricated out of a desire for revenge because Slavica had turned her back on their former friendship and had refused to help him financially. He obligingly made all the right threats – his book was 'an exploding bomb' ... 'it would break her' ... 'it's very dangerous for Formula One' ... 'if I make a deal we are on the same side' – and the *Sunday Mirror* had its front-page story, plus, as part of the deal, an interview with Slavica, who told of the deep distress the lies had caused her family. In the circumstances, the evidence of the tape proved unnecessary. Blagojevic and Vuletic made a public apology, followed by the newspaper, which led to Slavica proceeding no further with the respective legal actions.

Ecclestone became convinced that the real motive behind the allegations was a cheap political tactic to cause him deep embarrassment at a time when he was having discussions to stage a Grand Prix in Croatia. The allegations were made in the Croatian tabloid just a month before Ecclestone and Slavica were scheduled to meet the country's Prime Minister, Zlatko Maltese, and President Franjo Tudjman, who were keen for the newly independent state to enjoy the international prestige and exposure of a regular Formula One race. The meeting went ahead but Slavica was said to have been 'deeply uncomfortable'. Said Ecclestone: 'The guy who made the allegations, who claimed he'd slept with her, and she had been with the KGB and all that sex stuff, was put up to it. It was all political, and done to discredit me by people who don't want a Grand Prix in Croatia. But it will happen. Those people don't know me.' The public humiliation of his wife, and the anguish it caused their two daughters, then aged nine and 14, angered Ecclestone. A month after the trial he was still seeking retribution. The apology, he said, came too late. 'I am pursuing it – and I will do whatever it takes to nail him [Blagojevic].'

Ecclestone has a ferocious sense of protection towards his family. He gave me a demonstration of this paternalism two days after I had called at the detached home in Chislehurst, Kent, of the daughter of his first marriage, from whom I had hoped to gain a more accurate understanding of the man behind the headlines and rumours. In a brief conversation on her doorstep, Deborah firmly but courteously refused to respond to questions about her father. Similarly, his first wife, Ivy, when contacted through relatives, had also declined to be interviewed. Given the circumstances, the inquiries were cordial and there was no complaint from either woman.

Then came the telephone call: 'Mr Lovell? It's Mr Ecclestone here. I am told you have been aggravating my relatives. If you continue to cause my family aggravation, or publish anything about me, I will cause you aggravation. Don't cause aggravation to my family.' This was Ecclestone at his hard-nut best. The fact that what he had been told was far from the truth was no defence. The fact that someone had dared to approach members of his family was all that mattered, irrespective of the circumstances. It's not the way to do it with Bernie. That kind of thing is outside of his control, and he doesn't like it. If you want to know something about Bernie, ask him and he'll tell you. Of course, his answers might depend on the mood he's in. But that's all right. Bernie has said it, so there's no problem. It's gospel. (Twelve months later Ecclestone called again – this time with an offer to 'buy your book or turn it into an autobiography'. Both offers were declined.)

A firm rebuttal led to a marked change of attitude – and an invitation to call his secretary to arrange an appointment to see him. It took place three months later at the offices of Formula One Administration in Princes Gate, Knightsbridge – a black glass-fronted nine-storey building formerly owned by arms dealer Adnan Khashoggi and for which Ecclestone paid £7 million in 1985, plus a further £2 million in refurbishments two years later, all reportedly in cash – splendidly located opposite Hyde Park. The entrance door opened to a narrow hallway, flanked either side by a row of modern works of art, leading to an expensive-looking reception desk behind which sat a slim and elegant receptionist – Gucci and cool efficiency sprung to mind.

There was ample room for an easy chair or two, but none was provided. It was, I was told, Ecclestone's way of keeping his visitors literally on their toes: let them stand, keep them tense. Fifteen minutes late, disappointing in someone who prides himself on his punctuality, he emerged from a hallway, grim and unsmiling. I was offered a papal handshake – fingers only – without comment, and a nod of the head as a greeting. Easy, lithe movements belied his 70-odd years, as, without further word, he wheeled round to retrace his steps to his office, which was the size of a small drawing room and not dissimilarly furnished. To the left was a large and, surprisingly, untidy desk, and, to the right, the informality of a coffee table, sofa and armchairs. The room, with floor-to-ceiling windows, overlooked a magnificent lawn, fountain and immaculate flower beds.

He settled his slim, slight frame behind his desk to present a gaunt visage of hollow cheeks and stone-dead eyes, sensitive to bright light and protected by faintly tinted glasses, above which hung a fringe of silvery-grey hair. It was a face that matched well the threatening voice on the phone. He began by setting out the rules of engagement, which, at a stroke, seemed to make the interview redundant: nothing biographical should be published about him or his family, with the rider that if anything was published that was untrue he would take action 'without limitation'. As for his past business activities or his work with FOCA, he couldn't remember any of the details. Because of the controversy over the secret £1-million donation to the Labour Party, which at that time had not been long out of the news, he wanted to keep a low profile. He also laid down a time limit of 45 minutes.

He is wary of the media, and probably with good reason. Until the £1-million donation controversy made him front-page news, he was little known outside of Formula One. It was a traumatic affair, isolated as he was between politicians scrambling to cover their backs and journalists scrambling for headlines. Ecclestone puts journalists in the same category as politicians, lawyers and bureaucrats – a breed to be trusted at one's peril. At the same time, the mistrust could be reciprocated. One of the contradictions of the man is that he is honest enough to admit his inclination to dissemble. He will, he has said, be deliberately evasive if it suits him. For this reason it is not always easy, through his public utterances, to understand what makes Bernie run. There are notable examples to be found in interviews he has given to broadsheet newspapers. In one he claimed to have little interest in money, while in another he said it was the yardstick with which he measured his success. In another interview he said he feared nothing, not even death, while in a magazine article he claimed he 'probably' didn't say it. He told one interviewer that as a child he had to fend for himself out of necessity, while he told another that no, he didn't have a tough upbringing.

Some 50 minutes after the interview deadline had passed, we had got through a host of topics, including the very items he had deemed taboo – him, his family, FOCA, and his £1-million donation to the Labour Party – although some questions were parried with vagueness of detail, while others were treated with a refreshing unpretentiousness and politically incorrect candour, creating in that instant a hint of friendliness that would disappear in the next. At the end of the interview he courteously escorted me to the front door of the building, where, as I walked away, he engaged in a quick crack with some pickaxe-wielding labourers carrying out road repairs. It was an interesting study: the matey, working-class Ecclestone who still has time for the lads.

Even now his working-class background continues to fuel his aggression, a legacy of the back streets of his youth, where the law was laid down by whoever could hit the hardest. If you get hurt, you hurt back or lose respect; only a mug stands for it. When I asked him if he really would seek revenge if he were slighted or crossed, he replied: 'I have a long memory ... I have a long memory.' In recounting Ecclestone's determination to avenge a wrongdoing, a team owner said: 'If you fuck him, he will come back at you two years later. He did that to me ten years ago. Recently he said to me, "We understand each other now."'[2]

In a lengthy interview in Britain's *Sunday Telegraph*, when asked about his 'scary reputation', he replied: 'You cross me and sooner or later I'll get you. I may not get you beaten up or chopped up, but one day I'll level the score.' In the same interview, reference was made to a newspaper report in which he said he was 'so angry' at the lack of police success in finding the muggers responsible for the theft of his wife's £600,000 ring outside their Chelsea home, that 'I did some inquiries myself and found out who they were – but they have not been arrested.'[3] The implication was that he judicially resolved the matter himself. He declined to confirm or deny the accuracy of the report, but said in reply: 'I've never killed anybody. You'd hear about it if I had.' Yet in another broadsheet interview, when asked if his reputation for being someone to be frightened of was fair, he replied: 'Probably.' Why cultivate it? 'I don't cultivate it. It's a matter of fact.'

It is this kind of media coverage that has led over the years to a public perception of a dark and menacing character whom it would be best not to cross, an image that Ecclestone has gone out of his way to promote, despite his claims to the contrary. At the same time, although there is something sad and disquieting about a man worth £3 billion and in his seventies continuing to find it necessary to use threats of violence to state his case, Ecclestone is not himself a hard man. Like many of his breed, his courage is in the power of his money and in the intimidation of the revenge he might wreak, an age-old armoury that shields the weaknesses and insecurities that drive him.

It is, again, his upbringing that has led to his Mafioso-like protection of his family. The unwritten rule was to keep the police and the authorities out of it. You sorted it out face to face. But, for all the strength of the bonds with his family, his pursuit of money has inevitably has come at a high price. His life has been a workaholic existence of 16-hour, or even longer, days, seven days a week. It was not uncommon for him to rise at 5.30am to fly to, say, Paris for an 8.30am meeting, returning to his office in London at noon for a round of meetings that would keep him at his desk until late at night, to be interrupted only for a sandwich when he felt hungry.

His only hobby, and one that fitted in with his hectic, jet-hopping business life, has been to amass a world-class collection of Japanese netsuke ivory miniatures, many of which he purchased when time allowed at overseas Grands Prix. The demands of his schedule were such that he tried to spend 'at least half a day' with his family at weekends; and, as for Christmas, he saw it as 'an unnecessary waste of time', while a Grand Prix, he once said, 'was about the nearest I get to having a holiday'.

His relationship with his parents also suffered. He once said: 'I do have parents, contrary to popular belief, but I don't see them much nowadays. I haven't the time. I saw my father a couple of years ago. I suppose I don't have anything in common with them. I don't get involved in normal domestic affairs.' Whatever the relationship between Ecclestone and his parents, or its complexity, he was unable to bring himself to attend the chapel at their funeral services. His father, Sidney, who retired as a car salesman, died from a heart attack shortly before his 87th birthday, at St Albans City Hospital, Hertfordshire, in 1990.

Ecclestone left the funeral arrangements to his younger sister, Marian Tingey, a widowed mother of three who lives a modest life in a Hertfordshire suburb. Although, she said, he was in the grounds of the church, he refused to attend the chapel service. 'He felt he couldn't go in there. I don't know why. I didn't ask him.' Ecclestone also felt unable to attend the chapel service at the funeral of his 89-year-old mother, Bertha, after she died from bronchopneumonia in a private nursing home five years later. Said Marian: 'I think he was very, very upset when they both died. I think he felt he couldn't again attend (the chapel service) because of ... perhaps, he felt his emotions ... he didn't want to show his emotions ... I think perhaps he felt he couldn't cope with it ... I don't know.'

If Ecclestone distanced himself from his parents, his relationship with his sister became no less detached. Apart from the occasions of their parents' funerals, they have rarely met, although he did attend her wedding in 1958. 'I suppose that was something. As a family we were never close, like a lot of families are close,' Marian said, then adding, almost self-consolingly, 'but I know he's there if needed.' Birthday cards and personal seasonal greetings were not exchanged either. 'I get a Christmas card, but I think that is probably because I am on the Christmas card list from the office, as opposed to a personal Christmas card. But then I don't think that's strange. I've been his sister for 59 years and to me that's the way it's always been.'

Marian's relationship with sister-in-law Slavica was also virtually non-existent, unlike the one she had known with her brother's first wife, Ivy, the former GPO telephonist. She was not invited to their wedding. 'Don't be silly... I don't think anyone was invited.' She had, she said, seen little of Slavica over the years, and even of those occasions she was vague on detail. She was not keen to discuss her sister-in-law any further. 'I am not going to say anything that I might regret I've said. I'd rather leave it at that.'

There is a further manifestation of Ecclestone's working-class pedigree in the boast that his word is his bond. Integrity, he has owned, is what he admires most, and it is, he insists, embodied in the shake of his hand. This was the customary way of doing business in Ecclestone's years as a second-hand car dealer, when deals, in cash or kind, and favours proffered or promised, were agreed on a nod of the head. To default was a serious offence, commercially and possibly physically. Yet, as recorded, a close examination of Ecclestone's earlier business activities confirms there is evidence to demonstrate that his reflections of what was the exact nature of his word are not always reliable.

A more recent example provoked the criticism of a High Court judge. It followed an unsuccessful action by a South Korean construction company whose principals went to court to settle a contractual dispute with Ecclestone. The company had started work on a motor-racing circuit in Kunsan City to stage Formula One Grands Prix from 1998 to 2002. Under the terms of a contract signed in April 1996, Sepoong Engineering Construction Co Ltd agreed to pay Ecclestone's company Formula One Administration (FOA) annual payments of $11.75 million to be increased each year by 10 per cent.

Six months later a letter of credit for the first payment was issued to the benefit of FOA. However, a downturn in the South Korean economy caused a delay in the construction work, a situation worsened, claimed Sepoong, by a dispute over broadcasting rights and tobacco advertising. It led to the proposed Korean Grand Prix missing the 1998 calendar. It also led to Ecclestone calling in the letter of credit. In March 2000 Sepoong attempted to recover the sum in a High Court action. Although Justice Longmore found, 'with some regret', in favour of Formula One Administration, he said that Ecclestone had agreed that the letter of credit could be terminated and a new one opened at a later date if a Grand Prix took place. In the meantime, FOA would not enforce the letter of credit. 'In fact,' said the judge, 'FOA was doing exactly that at the same moment Mr Ecclestone was agreeing that it was not. In this respect, I do have to record that Mr Ecclestone has not been a man of his word.'

He also commented on Ecclestone's unusual method of business and its effect on his recall of events. 'He conducts much of his business by way of meetings without making notes and his memory of what occurred at such meetings is somewhat hazy. He did not prepare himself in any detail and, when asked about documents, had to take some time to familiarise himself with them. He thought he knew what he would or would not say or do in various situations and could thus easily convince himself that he did or did not say or do something if it was different from what he now thinks he would have said or done. I have some reservations about any evidence from him that is not supported by other evidence in the case.'

But Ecclestone firmly believes that Judge Longmore's public admonishment was unfair. Part of the dispute related to what – or wasn't - said at a meeting with two executives of the Sepoong Group, of which the Sepoong Engineering Construction Co Ltd was part, and You Jong-keun, the then governor of the North Jeolla province, where the circuit was to be constructed. Ecclestone insists that the three men had lied in their respective accounts, and that You, who gave evidence by video-link, and, whose credibility was enhanced by a distinguished international profile, had been particularly untruthful.

Certainly Judge Longmore might well have seen the testimony of the three men – and that of Ecclestone – in a different light if it had been known at the time that three years earlier, in 1997, You had accepted a $330,000 bribe from the Sepoong Group in return for giving local authority permission to re-zone the land for the construction of a grand prix track. In March 2002 You was arrested and, in the following September, jailed for five years and fined $253,000 by the Seoul District Court. Said Ecclestone: 'I think that says all that needs to be said about my dispute with them. The fact is I was outnumbered in court. If the judge had known what had really been going on between them, I don't think he would have said what he did about me.'

Ecclestone attributes his success to two four-letter words – hard work. Or as he put it: 'Everyone has had exactly the same opportunity to do what I have done. The only reason that they have not done it is probably because they ... have been sitting on their arses.' Possibly. But, in addition to his ruthlessness and punishing, self-driven work schedule, they would have also required, above all, his instinctive sense of opportunism. That, plus being, as he admits, in the right place at the right time. Ecclestone has never been an innovator, a creative person bursting with ideas, able to create the product and the market. Throughout his life his true skill has been in picking low-hanging fruit.

It began way back in the late 1940s, when an arrogant and sharp kid in his late teens walked into Frederick Compton's second-hand car business to take it over. And it continued through the quick-buck property deals that founded his early wealth at a post-war time when such deals were possible and which funded his move into Formula one; the purchase of an ailing Brabham team whose success was due to others, not least Gordon Murray; the control of the constructors, whose power through FOCA he exploited to subdue the national sporting authorities, promoters and circuit owners; and, finally, the FIA establishment, which he and Mosley came to dominate. The commercial promotion of Formula One through sponsorship, which propelled the constructors into a new age, came about through the likes of Colin Chapman, BRM and Philip Morris; it was others who saw the potential of the money-spinning trackside signage, retail concessions and corporate hospitality market; it was Marlborough who turned Formula One into a multi-million-dollar sponsorship industry; it was Mark McCormack who first spotted the potential riches of television, and, even then, it was Christian Vogt who took Ecclestone's television company out of the Eurovision arrangement for the vastly superior country-by-country deals which led to the development of his highly lucrative digital television company; and even the flotation of Formula One, whose assets consisted of little more than contracts with television broadcasters worldwide, was the idea of Marco Piccinini. But it was Ecclestone, in the right place at the right time, who exploited it all so affectively and lucratively.

The attempted flotation of Formula One's commercial assets was the one time when Ecclestone stood alone, unable to enlist the power of FOCA or the FIA to use the terms to his advantage, and it proved a resounding failure. Out of that disaster, and to his rescue, came the $1.4 billion Eurobond sale and the 50 per cent sale of SLEC Holdings to EM.TV for $1.65 billion to make his family trust $2.69 billion the richer, all of which was engineered by merchant banks he was now forced to trust to do it their way. Only by looking behind the eulogising headlines and articles is it possible to strain fact from media myth. As a former team owner and associate put it: 'There is a lot of the King's clothes about what Bernie has done. When you really look at it, when you get all the newspaper crap out of your eyes, it's been the support and hard graft of others who have made it work, from the teams down. What Bernie did was to cash in on it all so ruthlessly.'

Predictably, Max Mosley sees Ecclestone in quite a different light. He is the man who over 30 years transformed 'a niche sporting contest with a world-wide following and virtually no television coverage into a world-famous branded competition with a global following plus a television audience rivalled only by the football World Cup and the Olympic Games. This has been an extraordinary feat, bearing in mind the state of Formula One in 1969 and its lack of importance to, for example, sports car racing, not to mention the very weak position which motor sport held at that time in the general market for international sport. The person mainly responsible for this transformation has been Bernie Ecclestone. His success has made him rich, but his efforts have also enriched the team owners and drivers. There is nothing wrong with that – indeed, it is exactly what should have happened. In my own case, I have played a modest role in this thirty-year process and I, too, have benefited, although in a different way to Bernie. But then I started life with different problems to him.'

Indeed he did, and most notoriously these problems include exposure of Mosley's involvement in an orgy, claimed by British tabloid the *News of the World* to be Nazi themed which led him, at the age of 68, to the verge of disgrace. He was video-filmed in 'a vice dungeon' in London with five prostitutes – one was the wife of an MI5 officer who had secretly filmed their activities with a camera hidden in her bra, the contents of which she later sold to the newspaper – with whom, for a reported fee of £12,500, he allegedly indulged in Nazi role-playing sex sessions.

Over the following days, Mosley ignored mounting criticism of his behaviour from influential motor sport figures and Jewish Holocaust groups, who demanded his resignation, which he refused to tender on the grounds that what he did was legal, harmless and consensual, and did not involve any Nazi theme whatsoever. In a letter to the FIA's 222 world-wide member clubs, the

FIA Senate, the FIA's legislative assembly, and members of the World Motor Sport Council, he claimed that he had been the victim of 'a deliberate and calculated personal attack' as the result of 'a covert investigation' into his private life and background. The letter stated that he had received 'a very large number' of messages of support from people within the FIA and motor sport which 'had underlined that his private life is not relevant to his work and that he should continue in his role as FIA president. I shall now devote some time to those responsible for putting this into the public domain but, above all, I need to repair the damage to my immediate family, who are the innocent and unsuspecting victims of this deliberate and personal attack.' He announced that he had begun legal proceedings against the *News of the World* for invasion of privacy.

When the story broke, Ecclestone, while describing himself as being 'shocked' by the allegations, was sympathetic to Mosley's plight. 'Assuming it's all true,' he said, 'what people do privately is up to them. I don't honestly believe [it] affects the sport in any way. Knowing Max, it might be all a bit of a joke. You know, it's one of those things where he's sort of taking the piss, rather than anything against Jewish people.' It appeared to be a laudable vote of confidence in a friendship stretching back 40 years, until leading F1 manufacturers, much concerned by the world-wide attention that Mosley's involvement in the scandal was receiving, began to put pressure on Ecclestone to distance himself from the furore.

Mosley went on the offensive by announcing that an extraordinary general assembly of the FIA would be held in Paris on 3 June when a vote of confidence by member clubs in his presidency would be held by secret ballot. The announcement gave Ecclestone the opportunity to appease the F1 manufacturers and other key figures in sport who were calling for Mosley to resign. He personally appealed to Mosley to stand down, an invitation that was declined. In a BBC interview Ecclestone said it was 'regretful' that Mosley had decided not to make that decision. 'He should resign out of responsibility for the institution he represents, including F1. Everyone in a position of authority across F1 rings me to say he should leave. He's been a friend for 40 years. I'd hate to see him forced to go [by being voted out], after all, he has done for the sport. The big problem is that he can no longer represent the FIA worldwide because of these incidents. People would no longer be comfortable speaking to him in the same way.'

This was exemplified in a letter from Sheikh Salman bin Hamad Al-Khalifa, the Crown Prince of Bahrain, to Mosley in which he said that it would be 'inappropriate' for him to attend the next Bahrain Grand Prix, a showcase event of the F1 calendar. An invitation to Israel was also rescinded by Ghaleb Majadle, the Israeli Minister for Science, Culture and Sport, who had asked

Mosley to visit Israel to advise on the development of motor sport in the country, believed by the FIA, 'to be a major addition to motor sport in the region.' Furthermore, F1 manufacturers – BMW, Ferrari, Honda, Toyota, Mercedes-Benz and Renault – postponed a meeting with him to discuss engine changes in F1, claiming that they needed more time to discuss the proposals. They requested the meeting be put back by two weeks – after the vote of confidence on 3 June.

Ecclestone stepped up the pressure on Moseley on two fronts: through the FIA and the F1 teams. As a vice-president of the FIA, he wrote to its 222 member clubs critical of the letter sent by Mosley in which he implied that his departure would not be in the best interests of the organization. Ecclestone had publicly described Mosley's letter as 'a silly mistake.' And at the Spanish Grand Prix in April, he said at a meeting of team principals that he would add his name if all present – Ferrari, BMW Sauber, McLaren-Mercedes, Red Bull-Renault, Toyota, Williams-Toyota, Renault, Honda, STR-Ferrari, Force India-Ferrari – agreed to sign a letter calling for Mosley to resign. Only three declined: Ferrari, STR-Ferrari and Williams. The letter was not sent to Mosley, but it indicated the lengths to which Ecclestone was now prepared to go to see his former consigliere removed from the FIA.

By now, it had become a remarkable public row, once utterly unthinkable between the two men who, during the early days of F1, were seemingly joined at the hip and whose credibility and integrity depended on the silence of the other. If they were to turn on each other in public, the effects of the fall-out would be atomic. Mosley survived, with a vote of 103 for and 55 against, seven abstentions and four null papers. The voting represented a 61 per cent majority.

With the controversial FIA vote behind him, Mosley began preparing for a more searching judgment of his sexual predilections – in London's High Court where on 7 July, before Mr Justice Eady, and represented by James Price QC and junior counsel David Sherborne, he sought exemplary punitive damages from the *News of World* for publishing articles which, it was claimed, constituted an invasion of his privacy under Article 8 of the European Convention on Human Rights, which states that every person has a right to privacy in their private and family life, home and correspondence. It was the first time that the European law has been tested in such a sensational and high-profile case.

Mosley did not deny that he took part in a five-hour sado-masochistic session with five dominatrices at a flat in Chelsea, but vehemently denied that any Nazi role-playing took place. Four of the prostitutes supported Mosley's evidence during the five-day hearing, while the fifth, Woman E, who had secretly filmed the session and whose evidence was considered crucial to the *News of the World*'s case, failed to appear because she was 'unwell'.

On Thursday 24 July Justice Eady delivered a verdict in favour of Mosley, before awarding him damages of £60,000 and costs estimated at £700,000. In a judgment comprising more than 200 paragraphs, he commented on the 'reckless' risks to which Mosley sado-masochistic sex sessions exposed him. Said the judge: 'Many would think that if a prominent man puts himself, year after year, into the hands (literally and metaphorically) of prostitutes or even professional dominatrices, he is gambling in placing so much trust in them. There is a risk of exposure or blackmail inherent in such a course. To a casual observer, and especially with the benefit of hindsight, it might seem that [Mr Mosley's] behaviour was reckless and almost self-destructive. This does not excuse the invasion into his privacy.' All involved, he added, were well known to each other and, as part of a sado-masochistic 'scene', were expected to keep their activities secret. Mosley therefore had a 'reasonable expectation of confidentiality.'

A sombre Mosley said after the hearing: 'This judgment has nailed the Nazi lie upon which the *News of the World* sought to justify their disgraceful intrusion into my private life. I hope my case will help deter newspapers in the UK from pursuing this type of invasive and salacious journalism. I have learnt first-hand how devastating an invasion of privacy can be and how readily papers like the *News of the World* will destroy lives in the knowledge that few of their victims will dare sue them. I want to encourage a change in that practice.' Mosley announced that he would be donating the £60,000 damages to the FIA Foundation to further its work for road safety and environment.

But even as he was returning to the tranquil refuge of his luxury apartment in Monaco to recover from the two most gruelling and career-threatening battles of his term as president of the FIA, there were fresh calls from him to stand down from office, which, while they came from old adversaries such as Jackie Stewart, Eddie Jordan and Paul Stoddard, and which Mosley will instantly contemn, nevertheless echo the opinion of other influential and powerful figures within the F1 industry who have longed desired the departure of Mosley.

It is expected that Mosley will now assume a much lower profile until his scheduled retirement in October 2009, leaving the FIA frontline spotlight to the likes of his two most trusted confidants – Keith Woods, the Director of the FIA Foundation, and Alan Donnelly, Leader of the Labour Party in the European Parliament from 1998 to 2000, and a former Chairman of the European Parliament All-Party Committee on Road Safety and Mobility, who is described as Mosley's 'right-hand man'.

And those who know Mosley well – Ecclestone among them – do not expect him to retire in October 2009. While Ecclestone is sustained by the power of money, Mosley is motivated by the power his position in the industry grants him, which gains him access to political players and the contacts in Brussels who enable him to negotiate at a high level, without which his professional life would lose purpose and meaning.

As events in the Place de la Concorde in Paris and the High Court in London demonstrated, Mosley is not one to back down from a fight when under attack – and there are few indeed within the F1 industry with the stomach or cunning to plot his early departure.

19

WHAT A FUNNY OLD GAME

Although Ecclestone will be celebrating his 78th birthday this year, there will be no slow-down for a man, who, at the age of 69, permitted himself no more than two weeks' recuperation after undergoing triple-bypass heart surgery. His arduous daily schedule has diminished little over the years, and while he might find time to blow out a candle, it will be business as usual, with deals to cut, adversaries to outwit and profits to rack up.

In recent years he has given serious attention to the potential returns of investing a bob or two in a sport which certainly matches Formula One in the departments of ego, greed and ruthlessness – the inaptly named 'beautiful game' of football. While Ecclestone might have difficulty in explaining the difference between the off-side rule and an inside leg, his nascent nose for soccer's lucre picked up the fragrance at least a decade ago, when Roman Abramovich, quick off the mark in the post-Gorbachev free-market reforms of the late eighties, was still wheeling and dealing to accumulate his oil-based billions.

In February 1998 Ecclestone met the principal executives of Milan-based Media Partners – its key figures had worked for Silvio Berlusconi's Italian television conglomerate Mediaset – who were attempting to set up a breakaway European Super League of clubs such as Manchester United, Arsenal, Juventus, Barcelona, Real Madrid, Bayern Munich, Inter Milan and AC Milan. Ecclestone, with his expertise in sports marketing, television rights, pay-for-view broadcasting and, not least, his contacts book, was seen as the obvious choice to handle the broadcasting and distribution to pay-per-view subscribers. His talks with Media Partners went on for several weeks, but finally came to nothing when, eight months later, the Union of European Football Associations (UEFA), football's governing body in Europe, came up with an improved financial offer to Europe's top soccer clubs. 'The opportunity will come again, when the teams once again begin to look for more money, and Bernie will become involved,' said a Media Partners associate. 'If there is money to be made, Bernie will always want to be involved.'

Ten years later, in February 2008, Ecclestone was still keen to cash in on the money-spinning concept of an international super league, but this time consisting of the top four English clubs – Manchester United, Arsenal, Chelsea and Liverpool – who would play a six-match series in countries of his choice and with whom he would set up exclusive broadcasting and marketing deals. It was his reply to a proposal announced by Premier League chief executive Richard Scudamore for an 'international' round of up to ten competitive matches by the 20 Premier clubs, with the host cities bidding to stage the matches. But Ecclestone was critical of the proposal, arguing that few countries would be interested in bidding for matches featuring the lesser-known teams.

Ecclestone was linked to a club takeover back in September 1998, when the Manchester United board was fighting off a £623-million bid by Rupert Murdoch's BSkyB. Ecclestone's name was thrown into the media mixing machine and linked to a £700-million bid by an anonymous group. For very good reasons he emphatically denied any interest in the anonymous group, whose alleged bid made no more than headlines after United refused to supply information to an American bank said to be acting for the group.

To take on Murdoch was certainly something that Ecclestone had no desire to do. Earlier that year, in March, on the eve of the Melbourne Grand Prix, he had signed a deal with Murdoch's American television company, Fox Sports Net, to replace ESPN as the official Formula One channel in the USA. It was speculated at the time to be part of an agreement with Murdoch that would see BSkyB, which went digital in Britain in October 1998, broadcast coverage of Formula One on one of its sports channels.

About that time, Ecclestone was also having exploratory talks with Murdoch to launch a dedicated Formula One lifestyle channel to include interviews with top drivers and their families in the surroundings of their luxury homes, as well as behind-the-scenes coverage of the teams. The last thing he wanted was a head-to-head confrontation with Murdoch in pursuit of Manchester United.

Nine years later, in 2007, Ecclestone appeared to be interested in Arsenal following a boardroom bust-up between his friend David Dein, the vice-chairman of the club, and directors over Dein's support for a possible takeover bid by US billionaire real-estate developer Stan Kroenke, who already owned 12.2 per cent of the Gunners. Dein resigned on 18 April 2007 with immediate effect, owing to 'irreconcilable differences' with other members of the board. Ecclestone had got to know Dein through his 30-year-old son, Gavin, who at the time was engaged to Ecclestone's eldest daughter, Tamara, 22, a budding TV presenter and former model, but their relationship came to an end in November 2007. He believed that Dein had been badly treated. 'I obviously talked to David when they chucked him out, which I thought was a bit unnecessary.'

Less than three months after Dein's departure, Ecclestone appeared to express an interest in Arsenal. But one wonders how seriously. He was quoted as saying: 'If somebody offers me something I think is good value, I will have a go. I'm interested in anything if it's cheap enough,' he said. But it was a meaningless, if not slightly mischievous comment to perhaps wind up the Arsenal board. If he had been serious in putting in a bid, he has more than enough savvy to ensure that the media were the last to hear about it until it suited his purpose. More likely, it was a casual, throwaway reply to a reporter looking for a story. Also, by then members of the board had signed a contractual agreement stating they would not sell their shares for a year, which Ecclestone would certainly have been aware of.

But the realisation of his ambition to become financially involved with a football club wasn't far off. But not at the glamorous level to which he aspired. The team was lowly Queens Park Rangers, which for several years had been lurching from one financial crisis to another, and was now in serious danger of relegation from the Coca-Cola Championship. The only major trophy to grace the club's silverware cabinet was the Football League Cup, which captain Mike Keen had held aloft 40 years earlier at Wembley Stadium – the first time the Football League cup final was played there – when QPR, then in the old Division Three, came back from being 2-0 down to beat West Bromwich Albion 3-2.

The 126-year-old club, based at Loftus Road in west London, has certainly had its episodes of glory under managers such as Alec Stock, Dave Sexton and Terry Venables, and with players such as Rodney Marsh, Phil Parkes, Don Givens, Dave Thomas, Stan Bowles and Gerry Francis. But in more recent years QPR has lived in the shadows of success cast by its west London rivals, Fulham. Four years after being bought by the multi-millionaire owner of Harrods, Mohamed Al Fayed, Fulham gained promotion to the Premier League in 2001, though in 2008 it only narrowly escaped relegation. But if there were trophies for boardroom bungling, QPR's silverware cabinet would have required reinforcing in recent years to support the weight.

The future beckoned promisingly for QPR at the start of the 1992–3 season. One of 22 elite clubs that broke away from the Football League's First Division to form the Premier League after BSkyB outbid the BBC and ITV with a £305-million, five-year contract for the live and exclusive football broadcasting rights, it was in line to enjoy a share of those lucrative rights.

Under Gerry Francis, a key player in the QPR side of the 1970s, and who returned to the club as manager in 1991, the team ended the 1992–3 season in fifth position, outperforming every other London club. The highlight of QPR's stunning season was a televised 4-1 win over Manchester United at Old Trafford on New Year's Day, with Dennis Bailey notching up a hat-trick. Francis guided QPR to ninth position the following season before departing to Tottenham Hotspur midway through the 1995–6 season. He was succeeded by another former QPR player, Ray Wilkins, who had left Loftus Road for Crystal Palace but returned as player-manager a few months later to lead QPR to end the season in eighth place.

However, the departure of top goal-scorer Les Ferdinand – he chalked up 90 goals in 183 games during his QPR career – for Newcastle United in July 1995 for £6 million marked the beginning of a rapid downward spiral. This saw QPR relegated at the end of the 1995–6 season to the Championship's Division One; Wilkins's resignation at the start of the next season; and the humiliation of the club's relegation to the Second Division in 2000–1 – its worst League position for more than thirty years – following the disastrous return in 1998 of Gerry Francis, who left QPR, this time for good, in 2001.

But whatever the calamities on the pitch, they were matched in spades in the boardroom under the chairmanship of media tycoon Chris Wright, a self-proclaimed hippy turned businessman, who, after leaving university, co-founded Chrysalis Records in 1969. During the 1980s the label was at the forefront of the British New Romantic movement, with bands such as Ultravox and Spandau Ballet. It also represented arena-fillers such as Billy Idol, Pat Benatar, Blondie and Huey Lewis and the News.

Wright, then a QPR season ticket-holder and a fan for more than 20 years, first heard in the summer of 1996 that the club was up for sale through its chairman at that time, Clive Berlin, a former player's agent. Berlin approached Wright at the suggestion of Nick Blackburn, who was sales and managing director of Ticketmaster, a London-based worldwide ticketing company.

Blackburn had gone to see Berlin about a ticketing proposal for QPR, and when Berlin told him that the owners, the David Thompson family, which had food group and horse-racing interests, were looking for a buyer, Blackburn suggested he should contact Wright. Blackburn and Wright knew each other well. A chartered accountant, Blackburn had been employed by Wright as financial controller of the Chrysalis Group, departing in 1972 to run Decca's A&R department. The two remained in touch.

Wright received Berlin's approach positively. Apart from his long-standing allegiance to QPR, he would have been encouraged to learn that the club's balance sheet for that year showed a profit of £1.7 million as a result of the sale of Ferdinand. But, thanks to his renowned hands-off style, it would be the nearest he would get to seeing QPR in the black. Negotiations with Richard, David Thompson's son, who had been chairman since 1988, continued through the summer, with the deal on and off several times. It was finally concluded just two days before the start of 1996–7 season, with Wright inviting Blackburn to become a club director. 'You know a lot about football,' he said. 'Why don't you join the board?'

Aided by a £4-million loan from Barclays Bank, Wright paid £13 million for QPR. He also bought, in a separate deal, Wasps Rugby Club, for which the trustees were given £3.5 million worth of shares in a new holding company, Loftus Road plc, which had been set up for a Stock Exchange flotation. At a time when clubs – and a new breed of investor – were being dazzled by the millions being poured into the Premier League for the television rights, it was a move that raised £12 million capital. Blackburn had suggested to Wright the idea of Wasps playing at Loftus Road. Wright, backed by his advisers, agreed it would make the flotation more attractive to investors.

The club now flush with cash, £8,000 per month was paid to Wright, who became a part-time non-executive director, while Berlin was rewarded with a £100,000 salary, plus bonuses, benefits and car. A payment of £100,000 in 'success fees' was also made to Harbottle and Lewis, a London-based law firm specialising in media and entertainment, for the role one of its partners, Charles Levison, and also a director of the club, played in the acquisition and flotation. Berlin, who on Wright's arrival stood down from the chairmanship to become chief executive, began to spend with imprudent ease. QPR's long-standing and successful strategy of buying cheap and selling at a profit ended up looking like one of buying expensive and selling at a loss.

Two illuminating examples were strikers John Spencer and Mike Sheron. Spencer, who was bought from Chelsea for £2.5 million in November 1996 on an annual salary of £400,000, was transferred to Everton two seasons later for £1.5 million. QPR paid Stoke £2.75 million for Sheron, who enjoyed an annual salary of £450,000 until he was sold 18 months later to Barnsley for £1.5 million. A more prudent transfer was midfielder Gavin Peacock, who was acquired from Chelsea for just under £1 million, although on an annual salary of £350,000 until his retirement in 2002.

The players' wages bill was a major drain on QPR's finances, and most of them were on five-year deals. It didn't stop there: 15 youth team players were also on full-time salaries, some paid as much as £50–60,000 a year. Four were paid over £100,000 a year and put on long-term contracts. They were selected by Berlin and youth team manager Chris Geiler as the young players most likely to make the first team. Concerned about the 1995 Bosman ruling on the transfer of players, Wright and his board wanted them on long-term contracts to avoid the risk of losing them on free transfers. But not one of them turned out to be good enough for the first team. QPR ended up with 61 full-time professional players and a wage bill a third higher than the club's income.

During these balmy days certain directors' pay rocketed. Whereas on Wright's arrival the highest-paid director had received a mere £4,932, in 1997 ten directors, including Wright, were paid a total of £490,000. Even when there must have been cause for concern the following year over the club's increasing running costs, 11 directors were paid a total of £373,000, and nine were paid a total of £512,000 in 1999. And this was at a time when the club was also being hit hard by the end of 'parachute' money paid to ex-Premier League clubs for two seasons to ease the loss of TV revenue. The one person QPR couldn't put on the transfer list was Berlin himself. He had been given a long-term contract as chairman by Richard Thompson shortly before his departure, which effectively gave him total control. He kept Wright informed of important management decisions by popping round to his nearby office.

There was within the club, said Blackburn, a lack of professionalism in some areas, 'a casual, sloppy nature'. Citing the disappointment of relegation as a possible cause, there was, he added, 'an endemic culture within the club that wasn't very healthy.' By the beginning of 2001 QPR, mostly under the guidance of Berlin, who after his departure in 1998 ended up once again as an agent, had managed to accrue debts totalling nearly £27 million, although some of it was down to Wasps, who were losing £1 million a year.

It was only the sale of the rugby club's former training ground in Sudbury, Middlesex, in 1999 to McAlpine Homes for £11 million that provided the money to keep QPR afloat until the end of the year 2000. The sale of the ground for residential development – it comprised six acres in a prime residential area, and had been the rugby club's home since 1923 – sparked a High Court case which led to its former owners, the trustees of the amateur Wasps Football Club, being awarded £2.4 million damages against property consultants Lambert Smith Hampton for advising the trustees that the ground would never get planning permission.

By late 2000 Wright had invested in loans and gifts a total of £20 million in QPR, which was now bleeding money at a rate of £570,000 per month, and which he was personally funding. Outside of the boardroom, he was also facing financial pressure after a £10-million divorce settlement with his wife,

Chelle, in January 2002, which hit his cash liquidity. His love affair with QPR was also fast heading for the rocks.

He was now paying the price for a management style that was seriously threatening the club's existence. As a public company, its overdue accounts revealed it to be technically insolvent, a fact that the Stock Exchange had to be made aware of. By November 2000 the advice of the accountants was for Loftus Road plc to go into administration, a strategy to keep the creditors from the door and give time for the administrators to find a buyer. Initially Wright was reluctant to agree. 'I didn't want it to go into administration,' he said, 'but there were people on the board who had careers in the city to consider and they were very concerned that everything … had to be absolutely whiter than white. I had to respect the fact that what these other chaps were saying was accurate and that things had to be done correctly and we had to call in the administrators.'

On the terraces, Wright was facing a revolt by the fans who four short years earlier had lauded his arrival. He was booed and jeered when Second Division Colchester United hammered QPR 4-1 at Loftus Road in the first round of the Worthington Cup in September 2000. But it turned violent when the side lost 2-0 at home to Fulham in a midweek match the following January. After QPR had notched up just four wins in 28 League games – and received a 6-0 FA Cup mauling by Arsenal the previous week – angry fans tried to storm the directors' box. Wright was stunned by the level of verbal and physical violence and decided it was time to resign. 'Why would I want to stay after that?' he said. 'It's one thing to be pumping your own money into the club with the supporters behind you, but it's something else when you're doing that and they're trying to lynch you.' Two months later, after announcing the club was going into administration, he resigned as chairman.

Blackburn, formerly Wright's deputy chairman, and who became acting chairman immediately after the Fulham fracas, claims that the media group boss was not 'the right person' for the job. 'Chris didn't like to fail,' he elaborated, 'and was frustrated that he couldn't find answers to bring success to the club. He's also very sensitive to criticism, and a worrier. The lack of success at the club was really getting to him. He's used to winning. But you can't win every football match. You've got to deal with it. You've got to plan. And I think it's just not in his nature to be like that.'

Wright himself was under no illusions about his failure to deliver. He said: 'You need a different kind of person to be chairman of a football club. You need a real, cut-throat businessman who would probably be very good running a used-car lot, that kind of mentality. The trouble is a lot of people when they buy football clubs leave their brains at the reception desk. You want to deliver. Being a fan of QPR was a disadvantage in that I was very committed to making the club successful and very committed to getting the club back in the Premier League, and all the decisions I took were based on that. I wasn't dispassionate enough, and I wasn't hands-on enough, absolutely.

'I tried to run it like a proper business with a chief executive and a finance director. A football club like that can't be run on that basis. You can't trust anybody ... I mean, football is a very dodgy game. There are a lot of financial shenanigans that go on, as we all know about. You can't leave it to paid employees to run it. It's hard to find good executives in sports management, anyway.'

What would he do differently today? 'The first thing I would do is I wouldn't do it. But if I was going to do it, I'd make sure I had nothing else on in my life of any significance. I would move into the offices myself and I would run it very hands-on.'

With debts totalling about £13 million – £11 million owed to Wright and about £2 million to other creditors – Loftus Road plc applied for administration in April 2001. Queens Park Rangers was at its nadir.

The company appointed to oversee the administration, which formally came into force on 2 April 2001, was BDO Stoy Hayward, a nation-wide audit, accounting and business services firm. It was recommended to the directors of the QPR club board – Blackburn, Ross Jones, chief executive of a specialist market money bank, and chief executive David Davies, whose expertise was in managing entertainment venues and ice hockey in the UK and the USA – by Charles Levison, and represented by business restructuring partners Ray Hocking and Simon Michaels. The events that followed left the supporters' trust, QPR 1st, formed in April 2001 to represent the fans' interests in the administration process, far from happy, and suspecting that the club was about to be short-changed.

Within days of the suspension of shares dealing, Chris Wright made an offer to buy QPR's 24-acre training ground in Twyford Avenue, Acton, for £2.5 million, and the Wasps rugby team for £2.5 million, which was set against the £11 million he had loaned to QPR. Wright claims his motive was to reduce the club's debt level by £5 million to make it more attractive to a buyer. He certainly appeared to be generous in agreeing to pay £2.5 million for QPR's training ground, particularly as he had put up the money for the club to buy the land from British Gas for £1 million just 18 months earlier. At the same time, though, it seemed a very good deal for Wright.

Hocking had publicly stated two days earlier that the combined value of the Loftus Road ground and the Twyford Avenue training ground was well in excess of £15–20 million. With Loftus Road valued at approximately £15 million, Twyford Avenue was therefore potentially worth as much as £10 million. Situated in a prime residential area, its residential development potential was quickly recognised by Sorbon Homes Ltd, of Beaconsfield, Buckinghamshire. It stumped up half of the £2.5 million in return for joint ownership with Wright. But the supporters' trust, QPR 1st, was concerned that the land could rocket in value, without any real benefit to QPR, if planning permission were to be granted by the local Ealing Council.

As a result of pressure from Trust representatives at a stormy extraordinary general meeting in May 2001, Wright, who initially offered to give QPR 10 per cent of any future windfall, agreed to put the proposal of a three-way split – with a third also going to Wasps Rugby Club – to Sorbon Homes Ltd. But Ealing Council dashed any hopes of Wright and Sorbon Homes Ltd cashing in. It designated Twyford Avenue training ground a Community Open Space, killing at a stroke its residential redevelopment potential for the next 15 years. A formal objection against the proposed designation was made by RPS Consultants, a company specialising in planning applications and appeals, on behalf of Wright in March and December 2002, but was rejected.

Sorbon Homes Ltd and Wright decided to cut their losses and sell the training ground to the trustees of Wasps RC for just under £2 million, which was paid out of the money they had received in High Court damages awarded against Lambert Smith Hampton in respect of the sale of the rugby club's former ground at Sudbury. Wasps continue to own an adjoining four acres, comprising derelict tennis courts and a bowling green, which is not part of the training ground. Wright estimates that his little dabble in property development, with loss of interest factored in, left him more than £250,000 out of pocket.

His links with QPR effectively came to an end when, to help the club get out of administration, he agreed two things. The first was to write off £3.5 million of loans now totalling £6.7 million. The second was to hand back all but 14.9 per cent of his majority shareholding to Loftus Road plc to help facilitate a highly controversial deal brokered by Hocking with a Panama City-registered company called the ABC Corporation, which agreed to a loan of £10 million over ten years, secured against QPR's Loftus Road ground, to pay off creditors, not least Wright himself. Wright had been unable to agree terms to sell QPR to any one of several potential buyers, ranging from a fans' consortium to a bid from the boardroom, comprising Blackburn – who, on exit from administration, was to become club chairman of QPR – Davies and Jones.

QPR had also been under considerable pressure from the Football League, which wrote to the club in March 2002 to state that, before it could be allowed to start the 2002–3 season, it would have to prove that it had sufficient money to complete it. At that point the club couldn't. The Bank of

Scotland had come close to agreeing a loan of £10 million at 8 per cent, but pulled out at the credit committee stage, wary of loaning money to a football club. An Irish bank responded similarly.

The situation had become desperate. QPR had survived largely because of the sale of Peter Crouch to Portsmouth in July 2001 for £1.25 million, the £1.25 million from Sorbon Homes Ltd through Wright's purchase of the Twyford Avenue training ground, and a £1-million loan arranged by Hocking through London United Properties Ltd.

The ABC Corporation loan appeared to be the only deal in town. Without it, Blackburn, who, with Davies and Jones, worked with Hocking throughout the period of administration to find investors, believes QPR would have gone under. Such was the club's plight that when Hocking told Blackburn and Davies at the last minute that the interest rate would be 10 per cent instead of 8 per cent, they could do nothing but acquiesce. With the loan from the ABC Corporation in place, Hocking made an application in the High Court for the order of administration to be lifted. It was granted on 27 May 2002.

The £10-million loan went, said Blackburn, in paying Wright the balance of money owed in loans – £3.2 million; the £1-million loan arranged by Hocking; a £1-million fee to Hocking's employers, BDO Stoy Hayward; and about £2 million to creditors, totalling £7.2 million. The rest was banked to give the club a season's working capital.

The man behind the ABC Corporation was Michael Hunt, a convicted fraudster who, as a former managing director of Nissan UK, conspired with his Romanian boss, Octav Botnar, to siphon off £149.2 million from Nissan UK and cheat the Inland Revenue of £53.6 million. The money was laundered through bogus companies and charitable trusts overseas, principally in Panama. He was jailed for eight years in 1993 for his part in the biggest tax fraud ever perpetuated in the UK. Botnar fled to Switzerland, out of reach of the Inland Revenue, where he died in July 1998.

Hunt owns a portfolio of property, including the East Sussex National Golf Club in Uckfield, East Sussex. One of its directors was Philip Englefield, who in May 2002 was appointed by Hunt as his representative on the QPR board, where he remained for two months, until it was discovered that he was a debarred solicitor who, between July 1988 and June 1990, had taken nearly £900,000 from the clients' bank account in 91 separate payments of 'a personal nature'. The discovery forced him to stand down from the board, although for a while he continued as Hunt's representative in the ABC Corporation's dealings with QPR.

Hocking himself also had fallen foul of his professional body, the Institute of Solvency Practitioners, in November 1999, when he was severely reprimanded and fined £37,000, plus six-figure costs, relating to his work as liquidator of four companies. Charges included that he 'drew remuneration without obtaining the appropriate authority to do so' and that he 'drew remuneration in excess of the authority he was given to do so'. He also admitted failing 'to take independent expert advice prior to accepting proof of debt from a major creditor in liquidation'.

While Hocking's work at Loftus Road had come to an end, it seems his relationship with the ABC Corporation continued to an extent that he ended up on the company's payroll. It came to light about two years later when QPR Holdings Ltd, which succeeded Loftus Road plc, fell behind in its monthly payments of £83,333, which, for a club that hadn't shown a profit in more than five years, was proving to be the proverbial millstone. Even though a clause stated that the ABC Corporation could take ownership of the Loftus Road ground if payments fell three months in arrears, the club was still regularly two months in arrears.

In the hope of acquiring a loan elsewhere on more favourable terms, the ABC Corporation was asked how much it would cost to buy out the loan. The information was requested by wealthy businessman Bill Power, appointed chairman of QPR Holdings Ltd following the resignation of Blackburn in July 2004. The operations director of a communications company in which he was a principal shareholder, Power joined the board in July 2003 after acquiring £200,000 worth of shares, followed by a further stake totalling £650,000 when he bought 14.6 per cent of the shares returned to the club by Chris Wright.

The man sent to deliver the ABC Corporation's reply was none other than Hocking, with a request of his own for information. He wanted to see the company books, claiming that there was concern at ABC over the arrears of payment. Power said he was astonished to discover that Hocking now represented the company with whom he had negotiated the loan on behalf of QPR. He said: 'He was the last person I expected to walk through the door. His virtual opening line was: "I'm here to look at your books", to which I responded, "Oh, no, you're not." He said, "Right, I'm going to be appointed a director of the club to watch what you're doing." I said, "You're not, my old friend." It was a very short meeting.'

Power said he was surprised by the size of the loan agreed by Davies, Blackburn and Jones. 'Why they needed £10 million was beyond me. When I came along, it seemed to me that they had no clue about how they were going to stop the losses and turn the club around.' He and his co-directors, he said, found it increasingly difficult to service the £10-million loan, on top of meeting day-to-day operational costs which well exceeded the annual interest on the loan. 'We were getting further and further into the mire,' he said. 'Every penny went into servicing that interest at the expense of creditors, whose goodwill we were dependent upon. Any amount of people could have said, "Look, we want our money." Some of our large debts were to people who had a soft spot for the club, and who, I might add, never, ever put us under pressure.'

Blackburn angrily refutes Power's criticism: '[A loan of £10 million] was the last thing we wanted to do. We knew what we needed to pay off the debt, plus a year's capital. But, technically, it wasn't us who borrowed. It was the administrator. The administrator borrowed what we thought was the right sum and [also to] give us a year's working capital.'

But Power would soon have more to worry about than the club's bills.

20

THE ITALIAN CONNECTION

For some 18 months Blackburn, Davies and Jones tried without success to find an investor with deep pockets and driven by a divine mission to bring a football club on its deathbed back to life. The best to come out of the pack was a charm-oozing, sharp-suited former Italian football agent named Gianni Paladini, who was said to have had a promising career as a footballer until an injury ended his ambition to play for Napoli, the home team of the city where he was born in 1946. He later became an interpreter in transfer deals and went on to manage the careers of Fabrizio Ravanelli, Benito Carbone, and the Brazilians Emerson and Juninho. In the 1960s he moved to the UK and lived in Solihull, near Birmingham, with his wife, Olga, and two children, where he became involved in property development.

In April 2004, through a Leeds-based property company called Moorbound Ltd, of which Olga was the sole director, Paladini paid £650,000 for a 22 per cent stake, later diluted to 14.8 per cent, in QPR, which enabled the club to pay off part of its hefty tax bill. He was described in the media as a multi-millionaire saviour, which was a well over the top: in order to raise the cash he had to remortgage a property.

Paladini was quick to make his presence felt, thanks to what was seen by board members as an aggressive temperament and a zeal to assume responsibilities beyond his authority. His enthusiasm to involve himself in the club's day-to-day operations resulted in Paladini revealing an unorthodox method of doing business that alarmed Nick Blackburn, and which, he said, led to his resignation in July 2004. It came to light in two incidents, said Blackburn, the first during a phone conversation with team manager Ian Holloway over Fulham striker Barry Hayles, whom Holloway rated highly and was keen to sign for QPR.

The player was on a salary of £8,000 a week at Fulham, which, with QPR's top earners on no more than £3,500 a week, was out of the question. The situation had been discussed by Holloway with Paladini, who, said Blackburn, had suggested a solution that might persuade Hayles to sign for QPR. 'Ian Holloway told me that Paladini had suggested that part of the salary offered to Hayles could be paid off-shore to make it more attractive to him because it would be tax-free. It would also help the club to match the salary he was looking for.' This irregular solution, which would have been a clear breach of tax law, and which was also known to a senior official of the club, went no further.

Blackburn also protested at Paladini's actions in holding, without the recollection or authority of the board, separate negotiations with chief executive David Davies about a redundancy pay-off of £95,000 following his departure in July 2004, which, said Blackburn, were being handled formally through the board. 'It was for a bigger figure than the board was negotiating because he was keen to get rid of Davies,' said Blackburn, who raised his concerns at a board meeting in June 2004, and which was attended by Paladini. 'Paladini made no comment,' said Blackburn, who saw these incidents as the final straw in Paladini's confrontational attitude. 'He wanted to get hold of doing the transfers and everything. I then found out about his past reputation as an agent, which was doubtful, to say the least.'

Paladini takes deep umbrage at Blackburn's claims: 'You show me the evidence of that. I never said nothing [sic] to Ian Holloway.' The claim was also denied by Holloway himself. Through his agent, Robert Segal, he said: 'I don't remember this situation at all. The only thing I remember about Hayles and QPR is that Paladini never, ever, wanted to sign him. Paladini also vehemently denies Blackburn's claim that, without authority, he interfered in the daily running of QPR. 'Nick Blackburn tells you I was always trying to get involved? Not true! When he was here, I didn't get involved in anything. In fact, what upset me most, that the moment my money went in – £650,000 – for me that's a lot of money... I wanted to come here and enjoy myself and try to give them some advice on the football side. What annoyed me ... and Bill Power, I can phone him now and he will confirm ... that the day my money went in, I was not allowed to come into the ground any more. I was trying to ask questions to find out what our position was financially. It was

Nick Blackburn and Ross Jones, they were asking questions, phoning Bill Power and saying things.

'The fact that he [Blackburn] says he didn't like my confrontational attitude, I never had any chance to speak with him. He was just running the cub with Chris Wright – y'know, they were Mr Wonderful, but the club was in the shit. They didn't have any money and they were spending money left, right and centre. They wanted to give a half-a-million [pounds] budget to the chief executive when [the club] couldn't pay the wages.'

He adds: 'I was very silly in a way. I just put the money, come to see QPR football club. They only have a £10-million debt, no other problem. I come here to the club and there is 17–18,000 people here ... how can this club go [forward]? I never look... I never had the due diligence. I never had any of that. I just went on the fact that I liked what I saw, and we can put [it] right. The moment I went in to find out, when Bill was telling me, "Y'know, we had to pay this and we had to pay this," I say, "I just put the money in. Where did the money go?"'

Paladini's suspicion that he was being ostracised led to a heated but humorous incident in the club boardroom. Davies and Jones had been working on a three- and a five-year business plan, which, they felt, did not require any input from Paladini. The Italian, who to this point had taken no interest in the plan, nevertheless convinced himself it was clear that evidence was being plotted behind his back. He arrived one evening at Jones's flat in Notting Hill Gate, west London, where the two men were putting the finishing touches to the plan. He unloosed his hair-trigger temper to angrily express his suspicions. Jones told him to cool down and remain, or to leave and make his comments at a board meeting where the plan was to be presented later that week. Paladini decided to leave.

In formally opening the board meeting, Jones began by asking if there were any apologies, an invitation Paladini comically misunderstood. 'You think I fucking apologise to you!' he fumed. The outburst caused Jones to leave the meeting. Several months later, in September 2004, he resigned. 'I had always said that I would leave once we had got new investors, and that had been achieved,' he said. By then, in July, Davies had already departed with a pay-off of £95,000, a decision which infuriated fans, but which Power justified by claiming that protracted legal action to end his contract would have proved more costly.

The supporters' trust had their own reasons for viewing Paladini's arrival with some suspicion. QPR 1st were concerned that if his shareholding was increased to 51 per cent it could lead to a takeover. Just five months earlier, as part of a consortium, he had made a bid for the Second Division side Port Vale, but this had been blocked by a majority of the board after protests by fans who feared that he intended to move the team to another stadium and sell the ground, Vale Park, to a property developer who was a member of the consortium.

But if Paladini wasn't in the millionaire class, he knew people who were, and it was his link to their money that would soon enable him to achieve what had been his ambition all along – control of QPR. His principal contact was fellow Italian Antonio Caliendo, 61, a former door-to-door encyclopaedia salesman who became one of Italy's leading football agents. Caliendo claimed to represent 12 of the 22 players in the 1990 World Cup final between West Germany and Argentina.

The following year he was arrested after a raid on his offices by Italian tax officials. A few days later he agreed a deal with the tax authorities and was given a ten-month suspended sentence after pleading guilty to attempted corruption. A year later, in July 1992, he was arrested and remanded in custody following a lengthy tax investigation into the collapse of Hellas Verona football club, but was released without prosecution.

Paladini's association with Caliendo went back more than 30 years, and both men were skilled in the black arts of football politics and finances. Caliendo agreed to arrange through two New York-registered companies, Barnaby Holdings and Wanlock, representing Monaco-based consortiums, further investments in QPR totalling £1.7 million, most of which, yet again, went to pay off the taxman. In July 2004 Barnaby Holdings paid £675,000 for a 10 per cent shareholding, and three months later Wanlock paid £1.25 million for a 19.9 per cent shareholding.

Representing Wanlock on the board was a 34-year-old Italian named Gualtiero Trucco, a financial expert based in Monte Carlo, and, for Barnaby Holdings, one-time Brazilian international player Carlos Bledorn Verri, better known as Dunga, who was based in Japan. Moorbound Ltd was represented by his wife, Olga. Paladini was now in a powerful position. Bill Power, with a 14.6 per cent shareholding, and his ally Kevin McGrath, who bought a 8.8 per cent stake in December 2002, were outgunned.

Officially Paladini was described as the club's adviser, services for which a monthly cheque of £6,700 was sent to Moorbound Ltd and which, said Power, had been authorised by former chief executive David Davies. But in reality he had become the principal decision-maker. And some of the decisions he was making, particularly concerning payments to agents, alarmed Power and newly-appointed chief executive Mark Devlin, who, after being approached by Power, was hired in July 2004 to replace David Davies.

The Football League's lists of agents' fees showed that, for the six months to 30 June 2004, QPR paid just £12,000, while from 1 July 2004 – three months after Paladini became the major shareholder – to 30 June 2005, the fees paid to agents rocketed to £320,935. Newspaper reports claimed that many of the payments were to Paladini's friends or former associates, and for which, in a libel action against the London *Evening Standard*, he received a qualified apology and £15,000 costs in December 2005. He acknowledges friendships, though, with Mele Eves, a former Wolves defender and England 'B' team player who, after retiring in 1989 through injury, became a licensed FA agent in the mid-1990s, as well as with well-known Midlands agent Brian Hassall, with whom Paladini says he made peace following the conclusion of a successful legal claim by Hassall referred to without detail in a *Guardian* story on 19 October 2005 and which both Hassall and Paladini declined to discuss.

It was Paladini's negotiations with Eves and Hassall that caused particular concern to Power and Devlin, although in one of them Power himself played a role. This particular deal involved the transfer from Chesterfield of 23-year-old defender Ian Evatt in June 2005 for about £200,000. But a problem arose soon after Paladini met Evatt and his agent at The Belfry hotel in Birmingham. It turned out that the agent was not registered with the Football Assocation in accordance with its regulations and therefore unable to represent Evatt.

Evatt flew off to Majorca for a holiday while Paladini contacted Eves with an invitation to join him and Power on a trip to the Spanish holiday island to get Evatt's signature on a contract. In an interview published on QPR's fanzine website in April 2006, Paladini said that 'we needed a FIFA-registered agent to come to Majorca with us and witness the transfer. You need a registered agent to witness the transfer so we took Mel... because you deal with the people you know best.' He said he made it clear to Eves that 'we couldn't pay him very much and agreed £3,000'. The meeting in Majorca was successful, and, with his signature on a contract, Paladini, Power and Eves returned to London.

On their return, the three men went into Devlin's office to go through the transfer paperwork. Power and Paladini then left Devlin to complete it, although Eves remained behind. Devlin proceeded to complete the paperwork, with the figure of £3,000 to be paid to Eves, who both he and Power believed was acting as Evatt's agent. At that point, said Devlin, Eves looked over his shoulder. 'He asked me who had told me that it was £3,000. I told him it was Gianni and Bill. He went out and came back and said, "Oh, that's actually £40,000." I went outside and told Bill and Gianni. Gianni gave me a story, which frankly was difficult to comprehend, and Bill just shrugged his shoulders. It was then that I began to think "this ain't right".'

It made even less sense to Devlin because, he claimed, QPR ended up paying more for Evatt than had been anticipated. A release clause in Evatt's contract with Chesterfield permitted a club to approach him if a bid of not less than £70,000 was made. However, the club, said Devlin, refused to allow QPR to do so. The offer was increased to £100,000 but also refused. QPR finally paid, in Devlin's absence and on the instructions of Paladini, £150,000, recalled Devlin, more than twice the release clause figure. He said: 'I couldn't for the life of me understand for the life of me why we were paying an agent. If he saves us money, then fine, then share a bit with him, but when an agent's involvement hasn't actually worked in your favour, then I certainly couldn't understand what the hell we were paying £40,000 for. Going from three grand to forty grand, there was nothing illegal in it, but it just didn't taste, smell or feel right. I had never come across this before.'

Power said he, Paladini and Eves went to Majorca to get Evatt's signature because they'd heard that one or two other clubs were after him. He said: 'We didn't want to lose out, so why not have a couple of days down there? I paid for my own ticket.' But why was Eves paid £40,000? 'I've absolutely no idea. It was certainly nothing to do with me, I can assure you.'

Evatt had a disappointing time at QPR and after 27 appearances departed for Blackpool in January 2007. When contacted to comment on Evatt's transfer and the £40,000 payment, Eves said he was unable to confirm the fee he was paid by QPR because it would breach his agreement with the club. He also denied that he had acted as Evatt's agent. The player, he said, represented himself. He added that he had been contacted by Paladini in January 2005 'to look after the Ian Evatt situation.' But what did he do to justify the fee? His expertise was needed, he said, 'to get hold of the player.' Given Paladini's expertise as a former agent, why were his services required at all? 'Ask Mr Paladini. I was asked to do a job which I am licensed to do. I've been asked to help... because I know the boy... I've known him since he was a lad at Derby.'

Devlin was no less mystified by the circumstances surrounding the signing of Dean Sturridge, who joined QPR from Wolverhampton Wanderers on a free transfer in March 2005, which also involved Eves. The 28-year-old striker was highly rated three or four years earlier until a run of injuries sidelined him. As with Evatt, Eves was asked by Paladini to 'find out the situation' regarding the player's future at Wolves. He discovered that his contract, due to expire at the end of the 2004–5 season, would not be renewed and that he would be free to find another club. Like Evatt, Sturridge represented himself in talks with Paladini and managed to negotiate an excellent package: £2,500 a week salary, which put himself among the club's top earners, a monthly payment of £2,000 towards his accommodation and living expenses, plus a £1,200 bonus for every goal scored.

Eves, who claimed he did not recommend the player to QPR, said he was acting in a 'consultancy role'. Eves was paid a fee of £10,000, but said he 'received far less than £10,000'. He added that his consultancy included reports on other players as well as Sturridge.

Devlin commented: 'Sturridge was so injury-prone that he was the sort of player you put on a pay-per-game basis. Nobody was happy with this gamble. I was less than happy in authorizing his contract. It all smacked of something that wasn't quite right.' Sturridge's injury problems continued at QPR and he made only eleven appearances without scoring a goal before leaving the club nine months later for Kidderminster Harriers in the Conference League.

Paladini and Eves' friendship and business relationship goes back twenty years. They had worked together on a number of transfer deals, including the £4.3 million transfer of 19-year-old Enzo Maresca from West Bromwich Albion to Juventus in January 2000. Their services were also offered through a Wolverhampton-based financial services company called FSC Investments Ltd where, on the company's website listing its services to professional footballers, they were decribed as 'professional introducers', although Eves claims this was done without their permission or knowledge.

Another signing that left Devlin puzzled was that of little-known Danish striker Marc Nygaard, 29, who joined QPR from Italian club, Brescia, on a free transfer in July 2005. This deal involved Brian Hassall. What alarmed Devlin was not just the structure of the deal but the fee paid to Hassall. He said: 'Nygaard's salary was right up there, with the top two or three earners, yet nobody had ever heard of him. He only attended a couple of training sessions yet Paladini was offering this guy a two-year contract on a very decent salary and with a goal bonus.'

Hassall was paid a fee of £60,000 – the highest single fee paid to an agent during the year to July 2005 when agents' fee rocketed to £320,935. Paladini insists that there was no connection between Hassall's legal claim against him and the payment. Nygaard, who made 72 appearances for the club and scored 19 goals, signed a new one-year contract in July 2007, which was terminated by mutual consent in January 2008.

Yet another signing that perturbed Devlin involved Italian goalkeeper Generoso Rossi, who signed an 18-month contract with QPR in January 2005. But this time it was not the size of the fee to the agent which caused him concern, but the manner in which Paladini agreed to pay the salary of Rossi, who was banned from Italian football for six months for his alleged part in a match-fixing scandal. Valued at £2 million two years earlier, Paladini believed, said Devlin, that, once fit, he could be sold for at least £500,000 in the summer.

However, Rossi wanted £60,000 after tax as a salary. 'I explained to Gianni that that was not the way we paid salaries in the UK. I said if Rossi wanted to be paid £60,000, we'd have to pay him £80-odd thousand.'

Devlin said the issue was resolved after heated discussions between Gianni and some Italians, including Rossi's agent, Marco Sommella. Paladini, said Devlin, told him, 'Well, we're just going to pay him £20,000 salary, and we're going to pay the agent £40,000 and he will sort the money out with the player.' Rossi was at QPR for no more than a few months, playing just twice for the club. Out of contract, he left for an Italian club, Unione Sportiva Triestina, in the summer.

Paladini, who made no comment on his role in the signing of these players, denied that he had been responsible for all the transfer deals between June 2004 and July 2005, or that he had signed the contracts.

'The thing is I never signed any paper,' said Paladini. 'All the papers were signed by the chief executive. I worked together with them [Devlin and Power].' But by now Paladini was effectively in control of the club, and while his signature did not appear on the contracts – he wasn't legally empowered to sign them – it was he who had been responsible for eight of them, including the payments to agents.

Said Power: 'He was the major shareholder in the club. He was an adviser, but, by any other name, he was the top director at the club.' He admits that, as chairman, he signed 'some' of the payments. He said: 'I've seen these figures afterwards [agents' fees]. I was of the opinion, "Don't give him a penny", but invariably there was always [Paladini saying] "...and the next deal I can organise for you"... I certainly signed off some of them, but ... if it had been down to me, not a single new player would have come in, because I just wouldn't have paid them, full stop.' The rest of the payments to agents, he said, were authorised by Devlin.

As chief executive, it was part of Devlin's role to sign off the contracts between the club and players. 'I wasn't happy about various things because it was my name going on the contracts,' he said, 'but only children say they did something because somebody else told them to do so. When you are a man you ought to have bigger balls. If I were at a club again, seeing what people are capable of, and the way they can change from being friendly to all the animosity that went on at QPR, I wouldn't want to get involved in anything like that again.'

He recalls signing at least six contracts, 'maybe eight', in payment of agents' fees. Paladini, he said, was behind 'pretty much every player acquisition that came through. It was Gianni who did most of the networking with agents and the bringing in of players, and certainly dealing with players.'

Paladini established his authority at QPR through the resignations of Blackburn, Davies and Jones, with each of whom he had had an uneasy relationship. Said Devlin: 'He had been behind their departure, and I think Bill [Power] and the rest of the board were happy for Gianni to continue to have

[that] kind of influence, at least in playing matters. Generally, things were going OK and they were willing to put up with Gianni's rough edges.'

But time was running out for Power and McGrath and chief executive Devlin. For Paladini believed, as he had done about Jones and Davies, that Power and Devlin had been plotting behind his back. His misplaced suspicions were caused by a visit to Loftus Road of some Greek businessmen who were keen to invest in an English club, preferably in London. An FA representative had spoken to Devlin, who reported the approach to Power. Power suggested that, although there were no shares for sale, out of courtesy they should be invited to the club and entertained at a pre-season match.

During a 15-minute conversation with the businessmen, Power, said Devlin, confirmed there were at present no shares available but, should there be later, their interest would be kept in mind in. 'Gianni came to the door halfway through the meeting and Bill beckoned him in, but he declined. But the following day Gianni came in screaming and shouting at me, saying that Bill and I had been trying to sell the club from under him, and how could I do that without going back to him, as he was the major shareholder. It was all nonsense, because even if Bill and I had been trying to do some sort of deal, all Bill could have sold were his shares. He couldn't have sold the club.' Devlin is convinced the incident led to Paladini playing his 'trump card' – the removal of Power and McGrath from the board, and his departure as chief executive to strengthen the Italian connection and his control of QPR.

The scene was set at a boardroom meeting on 24 August 2005 attended by the five directors: Power, McGrath, Trucco, Dunga and Paladini, who had recently been appointed a director. Also present were non-board members Devlin, company secretary Chris Pennington and Caliendo. The agenda went smoothly enough until Pennington presented a financial report which forecast a year-end loss of nearly £2 million, a substantial part of it due to payments to agents.

A few moments later Caliendo left the boardroom, to be followed by Devlin. The meeting then got down to the final item on the agenda: 'Examination and modification of the management structure'. Trucco put forward the motion that the board had 'no confidence in the chairman, as both chairman and as a director, and call for his immediate removal'.

With Power as chairman disqualified from voting, it was carried by three votes to one, McGrath being the dissenting voice. A furious row ensued which ended with Power and McGrath storming out of the meeting. They returned 25 minutes later, accompanied by Devlin, to insist that the vote was invalid, citing article 81, sub-section 7 of the club's Articles of Association, which stated that the office of a director shall be vacated if he is absent from board meetings without permission of the board for more than six months. According to Devlin, Dunga had not attended one board meeting. 'He had once flown in for a press conference, but we never saw him again until that day.'

This article invalidated Dunga's vote, who had arrived from Japan to attend the meeting. His response was to claim that he had not been informed of meetings during the preceding six months. Certainly Dunga's vote was crucial to the move to unseat Power. Article 88 stated that any director can be removed by 'extraordinary resolution' before the end of his period in office, providing the resolution is supported by a majority of 75 per cent. Dunga's vote ensured that majority.

McGrath proposed an immediate suspension of the meeting pending clarification of the legal issues, while Power insisted the meeting was closed as he had to visit his father-in-law in hospital. Events turned even more farcical when, in their absence, Trucco proposed another vote of no confidence in Power, which was passed unanimously. Paladini, Trucco and Dunga also approved a motion to make Devlin redundant with immediate effect.

Devlin moved on to become chief executive at Swindon Town, where he was forced to resign in February 2007 due to injuries sustained in a light aircraft crash. Power threatened to take legal action against Paladini and his co-directors, but went no further. In September 2005 Power resigned, followed shortly by McGrath, and sold his 14.5 per cent shareholding to Caliendo for £1.2 million, which took the collective shareholding to 59.3 per cent and put Paladini in total control of QPR. Paladini became chairman of the club, while Caliendo was appointed chairman of QPR Holdings Ltd.

Paladini claims that critical media coverage of Power and McGrath's departure was inaccurate. 'It was … a situation of a group … myself, Caliendo and Dunga on one side, and Bill Power, Mark Devlin, the chief executive who was running the whole thing, and McGrath.

'We decide to take the club forward, OK. We needed to put so much in to pay the bills, otherwise we go bankrupt. At that point, they say, "No, we don't want to pay any money in." There is a choice there: "One, we buy your share … not to throw you out, not to put you out … we buy your share and we take the responsibility to take the club forward, or you buy our share and we go out and you move in." It was very simple, straightforward. That is what happened. The thing is people say we orchestrate a coup to get rid of Bill Power and Devlin. This is not Zimbabwe! Plus the fact that this club, QPR was [registered] at Companies House. This is England, a democratic country, where everything is done properly. You just cannot do things without the directors agree on what is going to happen.

'My other people [in Monte Carlo], they want to pay them off. They say: "Look, we put (in) £500,000 each." I have to remortgage my house and I have to remortgage my other house to keep the club going. Nobody ever say that. What did I gain, other than worried to death about losing everything?'

Devlin said the motion to remove Power had 'come like a bolt out of the blue. They had brought about a situation where Bill could be outgunned, and they seized the opportunity to take control of the club, so it could be run "the Italian way", which was the phrase Paladini used following the changes there.'

At this time Paladini also had another, more public, dispute to worry about. Eleven days earlier, on 13 August, a group of men allegedlly burst into his office during a match against Sheffield United to force him to sign over his stake in the club. It led to shareholders David Morris and John McFarlane appearing with four other men at Blackfriars Crown Court, London, in September 2006, charged with conspiracy to blackmail, false imprisonment and gun possession. On the direction of the judge, Morris and McFarlane were found not guilty, which led to the other men also being found not guilty.

At the time there were rumours that Paladini wanted to move the club away from Loftus Road and sell the ground to property developers, which, along with the team's performance on the pitch, left many fans unsympathetic towards him. Paladini opines that consequently he was seen as the villain of the piece: 'I looked like I am the criminal. I was the person attacked here, and it's a fact ... there is a video of all the people here.' During the months leading up to the trial, Paladini followed the advice of police to wear a bulletproof vest. He retrieved the jacket from a cupboard in his office. 'You feel the bloody weight of that! I more likely to die from that than a bullet.'

The abuse aimed at Paladini spilled over on to the club's message board, mindlessly targeting members of his family. 'I have had so many bad press of everything ... on the message board that my wife was having an affair with a black player, that my daughter was having an affair with one of the players, that my son was a gangster beating people up. Because of that my son don't come here for a long time. Listen, my friend, I don't want to tell you a sob story. But my staff, who have been with me, they know what I gone through.

'I am not denying that I have sleepless nights, that I am crying, waking up in the middle of the night ... I don't know how to tell my wife ... she has breast cancer as well ... a grandson with cerebral palsy ... I lost my mother of a heart attack in the year ... so many things happen. But I kept going. My doctor say, "Mr Paladini, you bend so far it's incredible you don't break." Like I say, I wake up in the middle of the night worrying about how to pay the wages, which I always did, until the very end. I don't know how I managed to get the money.'

Certainly QPR's future looked grim. Contrary to Paladini's breezy claims to the media that the club was on its way to breaking even, it ended the 2005–6 season with total debts of £20.7 million, up from £17.29 million, and with the overall loss for the year up from £2.5 million to £3.34 million. More than £2.6 million was owed in tax and social security. Retail income was down – from £1.46 million to £875,000 – as were average attendances and season-ticket holders – from, respectively, 16,060 to 13,501 and 10,669 to 8,056. The club also took out further loans from the directors, principally Caliendo, totalling £2.57 million.

QPR's financial plight had become so severe that, for the first time, in June 2006, Paladini acknowledged that it had been close to going into administration again, which, with the ground already in hock, would probably have led to its closure. In a statement posted on the QPR website, he blamed media coverage and speculation for 'obscuring' the club's efforts to get back into the Premiership, before adding: 'Without the financial support of the current Board, the club would have gone into administration last season. With the financial resources being made available, the club will not go into administration with the current Board in control.'

The following month Caliendo also went on the offensive against media speculation about QPR's future, optimistically claiming that it was in 'a fantastic position' to end the season in the top half of the Championship (in fact the club finished in 18th position, four places from the relegation zone). Applauding the board's efforts to get QPR back on a sound financial footing, he added: 'Since September, we've put in over £4 million to ensure the club's finances are in a stable position to build for the future.' In reality the club staggered through 2006. As the bills continued to mount, so did negative publicity, including newspaper reports that players had been refused admission to the club's training ground at Imperial College, London, because of non-payment of rent.

Events for Paladini took an even more critical turn at the beginning of 2007, when Caliendo, who, through Barnaby Holdings, had loaned the club almost £7 million, decided that he had stumped up enough cash for the black hole that was QPR. He and non-executive director Franco Zanotti, who represented Wanlock, were ready to sell their shares – respectively, 27.6 per cent and 19.9 per cent – for the price they had paid for them. The club's cashflow crisis became so acute that Paladini, no longer able to approach either Caliendo or the more orthodox channels of financing, was forced in April 2007 to approach wealthy businessman Simon Blitz, the chairman of Oldham Athletic, for a £500,000 personal loan, although he was looking for £1 million. 'They said they can't afford a million,' said Paladini.

Unable to put up QPR's Loftus Road ground as collateral, as it was already in hock to the ABC Corporation for the £10-million loan, Paladini promised it would be paid out of the future sale of left-winger Lee Cook, one of the team's best players, who joined QPR from Watford for a tribunal-fixed fee of £125,000 in August 2004. Blitz agreed. But what Paladini describes as 'a private agreement' went pear-shaped. By now he had received the money but, having spent it and with Cook unsold, was unable to repay the loan. 'They told the Football League, who said it [the agreement] was illegal,' said Paladini. 'Anyway, we got a slap on the hand.' The money was finally paid in mid-July when Cook joined rivals Fulham for £2.5 million.

Paladini was also under pressure from HM Revenue & Customs, which was demanding a long-overdue payment of VAT arrears totalling £800,000. The deadline for payment, 4 July, was just weeks away. This was the final straw for Paladini. On 15 June he announced that he, too, was ready to sell his stake in the club, for the £650,000 it had cost him. But in the meantime, if QPR, which had narrowly escaped relegation the previous season, was to start the 2007–8 season, he had to find some money, and quickly.

Paladini found himself left with one option: he had to return cap in hand to sup with the figures behind the ABC Corporation. The size of the loan was £1.3 million, which he saw as short-term until revenue from season-ticket sales came in. He was also left with £2 million from the timely sale of Cook. This enabled him to repay the loan on time, failure of which would have entitled ABC to claim ownership of the Loftus Road ground. With losses for 2007 predicted at £2.6 million – an actual improvement on the previous year's figures – the additional ABC loan brought Paladini brief respite.

But, at the same time, the ABC Corporation, as it was entitled to do under the terms of its original agreement with QPR Holdings Ltd, took the opportunity to restructure the terms of the £10-million loan and the rate of interest, which was increased from 10 per cent to a fluctuating LIBOR-fixed rate of about 11.5 per cent. And, instead of the final payment falling due in 2012, it was brought forward to 31 July 2008. This meant that if the loan was not settled by that date, ownership of the Loftus Road ground would pass to the ABC Corporation.

The early months of 2007 saw Paladini in a state of high anxiety. He was desperately close to running out of possible sources who could even be vaguely interested in coming to the rescue of a club heavily in debt – even the St John Ambulance Brigade was at one point threatening a winding-up order over an unpaid bill of £18,000 – and facing relegation to League One. 'You won't believe how many people I try. I try everybody,' he said. With just three matches left before the end of the season – against Cardiff City, Wolverhampton Wanderers and Stoke City, teams higher up the table – Paladini was holding his breath.

To be mathematically safe from the drop, QPR had to win the home match against Cardiff City on 21 April. The omens were good. Cardiff's previous two visits to Loftus Road had ended in 1-0 defeats via goals from Marc Nygaard and Danny Shittu. And 20-year-old Dexter Blackstock, bought from Southampton for £500,000 the previous August, ensured that QPR continued the run, by scoring the only goal of the match with a header in the 23rd minute.

Blackstock had been signed by former QPR midfielder Gary Waddock, who had been appointed manager in June 2006 but lasted just three months before being replaced by John Gregory. Ironically, although Waddock, who left the club a month later after a brief spell in a coaching role, faced some criticism for the size of the fee paid for Blackstock – his only signing – it could be said to be the most important signing the club had ever made. For Blackstock's goal led to a fairy-tale reversal of fortunes for QPR, from a lowly, near-bankrupt club barely able to pay its milk bill to one that would come to be billed as the world's richest, with access to an estimated total of £30 billion.

No one knew better than Paladini how disastrous defeat to Cardiff City would have been. He said: 'If we had not won that match and we go down, I think that might have been the end of Queens Park Rangers for sure.' Instead, the win encouraged Paladini to try a long shot and contact a fellow Italian and sports enthusiast by the name of Flavio Briatore. He had met the 54-year-old boss of Renault's Formula One team a couple of times when they appeared together on Italian television. 'I knew Flavio was a football man and I knew he live in London. He support Juventus and I'm friendly with people at Juventus.'

Through a mutual friend, a meeting was arranged at the Billionaire Club, a hang-out near to Harrods in London's Knightsbridge, and owned by Briatore. Paladini said: 'I went to see him and I told him the truth. Y'know, when you are in the shit, you try to tell people it is not that bad. I decided I've got nothing to lose now, so I am going to tell him. I told him we were losing money, we got £10 million debts with the ABC loan, we need another £5 million to pay the creditors. But compared to other clubs, it is not so bad.

'I told him he would get good fun out of it, the club is in central London, the club is five minutes from his home. The moment that the press and everybody else find out he was involved in QPR, he got so much publicity, he couldn't believe it. He get more publicity than in Formula One.' Over the next few months the two men met several times, with Paladini chasing Briatore's hectic schedule. 'I went to meet him all over the place. He was doing all these Grands Prix, and I really needed an answer pretty quick.'

By mid-July 2007 Briatore had discussed Paladini's approach with Bernie Ecclestone, who that month had been linked to a takeover bid for Arsenal following a board upheaval over the departure of vice-chairman David Dein. Ecclestone confirmed his interest in QPR.

However, Paladini had increased his options in case the talks with Briatore went belly up by approaching his old adversary Bill Power two weeks earlier – 'Bill is a nice man, Bill is a good man' – to ask him if he could 'pull a team together' to buy the club. A lifelong QPR fan, who was born in a block of council flats opposite the Loftus Road ground, Power was eager to take control once again of the club's fortunes. With the acrimony of their boardroom bust-up a thing of the past, their next meeting took place in the chairman's suite on 15 July, after a pre-season friendly against Celtic which ended with QPR being hammered 5-1. Power, having consulted certain business associates with the funds to take on the club and its debts, was in a position to sit down with Paladini and talk figures. But this time Paladini was in a chipper mood indeed.

Said Power: 'He told me to put my chequebook away. He said he was confident of being able to do a deal that was going to reverse the fortunes of the club beyond anyone's wildest dreams. He told me to leave it with him.' A few days later Power was taken into Paladini's confidence and was incredulous at what he heard. The people he was talking to, said Paladini, were Briatore and Ecclestone. Power added: 'He said, "Look, be totally discreet, but that's the magnitude of the people I'm talking to." I couldn't believe it. I thought he had gone potty.'

About two weeks later, on the morning of 14 August, Paladini told Caliendo about his talks with Briatore and Ecclestone and how close he was to completing a deal that would resolve the club's long-standing financial problems. During these months of financial crisis Caliendo had also been trying to find a buyer and, said Paladini, claimed to be in promising negotiations. 'He say: "I've got another deal on the table with some Russian or some people for about £50 million." And I say, "Bullshit! I don't believe that, Antonio."'

Paladini claimed that later that day they a signed a legal document stating that whoever failed to conclude an agreement with his party by Friday, 31 August would resign and sell his shares to the other person. 'I sign a piece of paper with Antonio, saying ... if I can get a deal [with Briatore] to get us out of trouble, we don't go bankrupt, we save our face, we lose some money but we get some back, I do it. If you do it, do it. I sign the paper here with my barrister and everything.' The date was important because the club 'had to pay the bill of the taxman, £900,000. So I said: "Antonio, you know our [tax bill] commitment. If you come up [with the money] by Friday [31 August], you can take the club over. I leave the club, you give me my money, you do what you want."'

Later that same day, just hours before QPR lost 2-1 in a home game to Leyton Orient in the first round of the Carling Cup, Caliendo issued a statement through the club's website announcing that Paladini was being dismissed as club chairman, which was followed by another statement asserting that the club was not for sale. Caliendo's actions led to a highly public stand-up row between the two men in the chairman's suite, with directors of both teams looking on, and which was reported the following morning in embarrassing detail on the message board of the Orient fans' website. The animosity between the two men had reached such a pitch that a battle for control of the club was anticipated at a boardroom meeting scheduled for later that month.

But while Paladini's talks with Briatore were continuing on course, Caliendo was having serious problems. And on Thursday, 30 August, 24 hours before the deadline, his deal had gone south. Said Paladini: 'He tell me he can't get these people, that they bullshit him, and they didn't come up with the money. We had a meeting on the Friday with the ABC people and they say: "If you don't do this deal with the one or the other ... I don't care who you do the deal with ... we get the administrator in by Monday."'

After lengthy meetings with Paladini and Briatore's advisers, which continued through to the Friday, Caliendo agreed to stand down as chairman of QPR Holdings Ltd, sell his shares at the price he had paid for them – £276,488 – and waive claim to £4,851,000 he had loaned to the club. A further loan of £2 million, which would be interest free, would be repaid once the £10-million loan to the ABC Corporation had been settled. Zanotti would also have to stand down from the QPR Holdings board and sell Wanlock's shareholding at the price he had paid, £199,000. Paladini, on the other hand, would sell some of his shares, continue in his role as club chairman and have a highly lucrative five-year contract in his pocket.

Paladini believes Caliendo was fortunate. 'He is a lucky man,' he said. 'Like I am. If we didn't have Flavio to come in, we'd have gone bust. Caliendo would have gone bankrupt, I would have gone bankrupt. The club might have gone into administration. What kind of money would he have got back? Yes, he lost £6–7 million. But that's football. Caliendo had a chance to bring in a new investor. It didn't happen.'

The documents accepting the offer from Briatore and Ecclestone were signed by both parties on Saturday, 1 September 2007, shortly before the start of the home match against Southampton, which QPR lost 3-0. Briatore, through his company Sarita Capital Investments Inc, and Ecclestone, as an individual investor, acquired a 69.50 per cent stake in QPR Holdings for £13.70 million. A loan of £5 million was also agreed – £4.25 million from Sarita and £750,000 from Ecclestone – partly to buy new players and the rest to cover outstanding debts. Their joint shareholding was subsequently increased to 95 per cent.

With Paladini continuing as club chairman, Alejandro Agag, a Spanish businessman well connected financially and politically, and a long-standing associate of Briatore and Ecclestone, became chairman of QPR Holdings Ltd, and Bruno Michel, organiser of the Asia GP2 series and a senior figure in Briatore's FBB management company, a director of QPR Holdings Ltd. Ecclestone declined to become a director. He has neither the time nor the interest in football. His main goal is a fat bottom line.

But it was his acquaintance with the Indian steel magnate Lakshmi Mittal which led to the world's sixth richest man investing in QPR. In 2004 Mittal paid £70 million for Ecclestone's 12-bedroomed mansion in Kensington Palace Gardens, at that time described as the most expensive house in London. With a personal fortune of £27.7 billion, Mittal bought a 20 per cent stake in QPR for £200,000, largely at the behest of his son-in-law, Amit Bhatia, a keen soccer fan. Bhatia was subsequently appointed vice-chairman of QPR Holdings, of which, in February 2008, Briatore replaced Agag, now managing director, as chairman.

When the documents were finally signed, Paladini said he was 'so relieved. I say to myself, "If I drop dead now at least I have kept my promise that I would not take the club into administration", which was my only concern. I am very, very proud of what I have done in the circumstances.'

But Paladini claims that the takeover led to a whispering campaign to discredit him. 'So many people phone Flavio and Bernie, saying so many horrible things about me. Everybody say I was going to stay one month or two month, and they boot me out. My position now is stronger than ever. I do my job in an honest way. I am accused of so many things, and no one has come up and say, "Mr Paladini, you are a crook, because you done this, this and this." You find one thing against me.'

Not surprisingly, Paladini boldly shares the confidence of Briatore, who publicly stated shortly after the purchase of the club that he expects QPR to be in the Premier League in four years, that is, by 2011, despite a stadium of limited size in a location which has none of the glamour of Chelsea or even its less illustrious neighbours, Fulham. Nevertheless, Paladini believes Loftus Road compares favourably with Craven Cottage. 'Fulham hasn't got a big stadium,' he said. 'We have more seats than Fulham. They get 15, 16, 17,000. This ground can take 19,000. We have been in the Premier League before with this ground.' True, but not for long. And Fulham's seating capacity is, in fact, 26,500. 'I think it is going to be difficult to rebuild something else [here]. There is nowhere else to go.'

He also claimed, mistakenly, that a quarter of the ground was owned by Hammersmith and Fulham Council, which would prohibit its sale without the council's agreement. 'There is a thing in the deeds that you cannot build ...

one quarter of the ground, it belongs to the council. The council has to agree to sell, so it has to be a joint thing with the council. You just cannot knock it down and build houses. So it's impossible to move from here.' A spokesman for Hammersmith and Fulham Council confirmed it owned no part of the ground. It was not the first time that the council had been put in the embarrassing position of having to deny Paladini's claims. He once informed the press that the club planned to raise the roof of the South Africa Road stand to add a further six to seven thousand seats. He made the claim without any prior consultations with the council, causing a spokesman to deny that permission had been given or was likely to be given.

Paladini also drew encouragement from Fulham's seven-year tenure in the Premier League, which began in 2001 after a four-year meteoric rise from the old Division Three after Harrods boss Mohamed Al Fayed bought the club in 1997. 'They have been there for ten years,' he said, once again in error. 'This year they have done badly because they spend £35–40 million chasing players.' Far from the truth, said a spokesman for the club, which escaped relegation from the Premier League by a whisker after closing the 2007–8 season with a 1-0 win over Portsmouth to end up in 17th position on goal difference. 'What we spent on players is nowhere near those figures,' said the spokesman.

But so far Mohamed Al Fayed is personally out of pocket by about £200 million, which, since 1997, has been spent on players, the purchase of the stadium freehold, general redevelopment and the cost of training ground facilities. He has a genuine interest in Fulham outside of the profit margin. Ecclestone does not have a similar enthusiasm for QPR, which is why he is not on the board. He believes he has better things to do with his time. The moment he gets a whiff of good money being thrown after bad, he will be checking the exit clauses. He is not the kind of businessman who will stump up for the sake of personal passion or face-saving ego. Briatore, too, will not be risking any of his £120 million by going down the Al Fayed road.

The driving force behind the rebirth of QPR, Briatore has declared that the club, which has played its home matches in nearly 20 different stadia, a league record, before permanently settling in Loftus Road in 1917, will become a global brand to rival Manchester United, Chelsea and Arsenal. Briatore has certainly proved himself a successful operator in Formula One in attracting all-important sponsors. In March 2008 the club announced it had signed a five-year deal worth £20 million, reputedly the biggest ever Championship deal of its kind, with Italian firm Lotto Sport Italia as kit manufacturer. He claimed to have three or four similar deals lined up with international companies. Lakshmi Mittal's influential connections in India will also be very important in moving into Asian markets, as will the efforts of his son-in-law Amit Bhatia in developing the links.

In the meantime, Paladini has been given a modest budget to get the renaissance under way on the pitch. He won't say how much because, he claimed, 'the budget change every day, depending on who we are looking for. My job is to try to be clever and not spend silly money, because my job will be on the line. Flavio and the others are not stupid. You have to be very wise, and this board is very wise. They are not going to give me five million, ten million, to go and buy another player. I wouldn't do that. You don't need to spend a fortune to get into the Premier League.'

Paladini summed up the previous 18 months of his life with the emotions of a man who has just heard at the eleventh hour that his execution appeal has been successful. 'You know when you are in trouble and you know there is no escape. That is how I felt for so long. With my wife and family I have to pretend that everything is all right. Before, I used to be as tough as nails but now, over a little thing, I become very emotional. I am not ashamed to say that I did cry many times on my own. I try to do everything I can for this club. I gave my word to the fans that I wouldn't let them down, and I haven't. I never walk out of here and somebody come and smack me and say, "Paladini, you are a bastard". No, I always have the people shake hands with me and say, "We appreciate what you are doing." I have a lot of fans on my side, because they knew what I was trying to do was best for the club.'

The fairy -tale rescue of Queens Park Rangers was concluded in early July – with time to spare before the 31st deadline – when a newly-formed company called Amulya Property Ltd, of which Briatore and Bhatia are directors, made funds available to pay off the ABC loan of £10 million at a reduced interest rate of 8.5 per cent over a two-year period, by when the club optimistically plans to be in the Premier League. As with the ABC loan, if QPR fails to repay the debt, Amulya Property Ltd will become the new owner of Loftus Road Stadium.

Bernie Ecclestone is, of course, perfectly at ease rubbing shoulders with the mega-rich movers and shakers in the world of soccer. They are joined at the hip by the power game, each in the pecking order dictated by their wealth or political pull, which puts Ecclestone way up the grid on both counts. And – who knows? – by the end of his days, with the death-rattle in his throat, he may well have stashed away another few hundred million in the family trust. His equation is simple: the more money he has, the more power he has. When a former business associate and friend of more than 50 years asked him when he was going to retire, he replied: 'What would I do?' Said his friend: 'Money to Bernard is power, nothing else.' He has achieved both infinitely more brilliantly, more shrewdly, more relentlessly and ruthlessly than most, 'yet he must run ever faster simply to stand still, because there is nothing else he can do'.

Whatever the remaining years hold for Ecclestone, who was appointed a vice-president of honour at the FIA's General Assembly in 2001, one can be sure, to abuse Dylan Thomas, that he will not go gently into his good night. He will rage and rage against the dying of the light as his fingers are prised from the arms of his executive chair. It is the supreme and most tragic irony of all, when one considers the truly remarkable life of Bernard Charles Ecclestone – that the man who has fought all his life to be in total control isn't in control after all, and perhaps never really has been. Money has been his lifelong quest, and money has been his master. He is a lonely man, without many close friends and few loved ones. Now, at the end of his years, he has little but the cold, uncaring comfort of his billions. That's Bernie's game.

'What good will it be for a man if he gains the
whole world, yet forfeits his soul?' – Matthew 16:26

NOTES

1: 'SENNA DEAD? NO, HE'S INJURED HIS HEAD'

1. *Life at the Limit*, Professor Sid Watkins, Macmillan.
2. *Autosport*, 12 May 1994.
3. *Sunday Business*, 30 March 1997.
4. Associated Press, 7 November 1997.
5. *Mail on Sunday*, 20 September 1992.
6. Ibid.
7. *Autosport*, 4 August 1994.
8. *Autosport*, 16 July 1977.

2: HOW AUNTIE MAY CHANGED YOUNG BERNARD'S LIFE FOR EVER

1. *The Grand Prix Who's Who*, Steve Small, Guinness.
2. *Autocar*, 4 October 1973.

3: THE RISE TO RICHES OF BRABHAM'S NEW BOSS

1. *Autosport*, 6 August 1987.
2. *Independent*, 9 July 1988.
3. *Guardian*, December 1997.
4. *How Entrepreneurs Get Started*, Rupert Steiner.
5. *Daily Express*, 14 February 1972.

4: THE 'GARAGISTES' TAKE ON THE FIA 'GRANDIS'

1. *Autocar*, 7 June 1973.
2. *Autocar*, 18 January 1973.
3. *Autocar*, 2 August 1975.
4. *Autocar*, 8 October 1977.
5. *Daily Telegraph*, 24 February 1992.
6. *Autocar*, 4 October 1975.
7. *Autocar*, 22 November 1975.
8. *Daily Mail*, 25 November 1976.
9. *Daily Express*, 3 November 1971.
10. *Daily Telegraph*, 11 December 1976.

5: CHAMPIONSHIP TITLE OR POLITICAL POWER? IT'S BERNIE'S DILEMMA

1. *Autocar*, 4 September 1982.
2. *Daily Mail*, 8 September 1979.
3. *Autocar*, 26 January 1980.
4. *Autocar*, 17 June 1978.

6: JEAN-MARIE BALESTRE: LE GRAND FROMAGE

1. *Autocar*, 23 November 1978.
2. *Autocar*, 11 November 1978.
3. *Autocar*, 10 March 1979.
4. *Autocar*, 27 October 1979.
5. *Autocar*, 23 November 1978.
6. *Autocar*, April 1980.
7. *Autocar*, 21 June 1980.

7: THE KEY TO RICHES – TELEVISION RIGHTS

1. *Autosport*, 11 September 1980.
2. *Sunday Times*, 14 December 1980.
3. *Autocar*, 10 January 1981.
4. *The Times*, 18 January 1982.
5. *Autosport*, 18 October 1984.
6. *Autocar*, 23 October 1982.

8: BRABHAM TAKEN FOR A SWISS ROLL

1. *Motor Sport*, January 1998.
2. Ibid.
3. *The Times*, 29 July 1987.

4. *Daily Telegraph* magazine, 4 July 1998.
5. *Autosport*, 31 August 1989.

9: BERNIE GOES WEST – AND MEETS HIS MATCH
1. *A Critique of the Economic Impact Evaluation of the 1996 Transurban Australian Grand Prix*, report of Economist at Large & Associates.
2. *Autosport*, 1 August 1985.
3. Ibid.
4. *Autosport*, 28 June 1990.
5. *Dallas Morning News*, 4 August 1985.

10: HOW CANADA LOST ITS NSA – AND BRANDS HATCH THE BRITISH GRAND PRIX
1. *Autocar*, 28 May 1986.

11: THE BEGINNING OF BERNIE'S TELEVISION RIGHTS STRANGLEHOLD
1. *Autocar*, 30 May 1981.
2. *Daily Mail*, 7 May 1977.
3. *Autosport*, 16 April 1987.
4. *Autosport*, 17 March 1988.
5. *Autosport*, 2 August 1990.
6. *Autosport*, 14 November 1991.
7. *Autosport*, 2 August 1990.
8. *Autosport*, 27 June 1991.
9. *Autosport*, 17 March 1988.
10. *Independent*, 5 February 1988.

12: THE RISE OF PRESIDENT MAX, HOW THE FIA LOST MILLIONS, AND THE SHOWDOWN IN BRUSSELS
1. *Autosport*, 3 October 1991.
2. *Financial Times*, 16 November 1998.
3. Reuters, 13 April 1996.

13: THE SINKING OF BERNIE'S $2.5 BILLION FLOTATION PLANS
1. *Financial Times*, 3 October 1997.
2. *Sunday Times*, 15 March 1997.
3. *Independent on Sunday*, 8 June 1997.
4. *The European*, 10 July 1997.

14: ANNUS HORRIBILIS

1. Reuters, 4 February 1998.

15: BRUSSELS DELIVERS ITS VERDICT – AND BERNIE MAKES ANOTHER BILLION

1. *Sunday Telegraph*, 7 November 1999.

17: THE CASH-FOR-ASH AFFAIR

1. *Sunday Express*, 8 October 2000.
2. Department of Health White Paper 'Smoking Kills', December 1998.

18: MARRIAGE, MONEY AND BLACKMAIL

1. *Sunday Business News Review*, 16 March 1997.
2. *Sunday Telegraph*, 24 June 2001.
3. *Daily Telegraph*, 1997.